COUNTING CIVILIAN CASUALTIES

STUDIES IN STRATEGIC PEACEBUILDING

*Series Editors*
R. Scott Appleby, John Paul Lederach, and Daniel Philpott
The Joan B. Kroc Institute for International Peace Studies
University of Notre Dame

STRATEGIES OF PEACE
Edited by Daniel Philpott and Gerard F. Powers

UNIONISTS, LOYALISTS, AND CONFLICT TRANSFORMATION
IN NORTHERN IRELAND
Lee A. Smithey

JUST AND UNJUST PEACE
*An Ethic of Political Reconciliation*
Daniel Philpott

COUNTING CIVILIAN CASUALTIES
*An Introduction to Recording and Estimating Nonmilitary Deaths in Conflict*
Edited by Taylor B. Seybolt, Jay D. Aronson, and Baruch Fischhoff

# Counting Civilian Casualties

AN INTRODUCTION TO RECORDING AND ESTIMATING
NONMILITARY DEATHS IN CONFLICT

Edited by Taylor B. Seybolt, Jay D. Aronson, and Baruch Fischhoff

OXFORD
UNIVERSITY PRESS

## OXFORD
### UNIVERSITY PRESS

Oxford University Press is a department of the University of Oxford.
It furthers the University's objective of excellence in research,
scholarship, and education by publishing worldwide.

Oxford   New York
Auckland   Cape Town   Dar es Salaam   Hong Kong   Karachi
Kuala Lumpur   Madrid   Melbourne   Mexico City   Nairobi
New Delhi   Shanghai   Taipei   Toronto

With offices in
Argentina   Austria   Brazil   Chile   Czech Republic   France   Greece
Guatemala   Hungary   Italy   Japan   Poland   Portugal   Singapore
South Korea   Switzerland   Thailand   Turkey   Ukraine   Vietnam

Oxford is a registered trade mark of Oxford University Press
in the UK and certain other countries.

Published in the United States of America by
Oxford University Press
198 Madison Avenue, New York, NY 10016

Library of Congress Cataloging-in-Publication Data
Counting civilian casualties : an introduction to recording and estimating nonmilitary deaths
in conflict / edited by Taylor B. Seybolt, Jay D. Aronson, and Baruch Fischhoff.
    pages cm—(Studies in strategic peacebuilding)
Includes bibliographical references and index.
ISBN 978-0-19-997730-7—ISBN 978-0-19-997731-4
1. Civilian war casualties—Statistics. 2. Civilian war casualties—
Case studies. 3. Civilians in war—Case studies. I. Seybolt, Taylor B., editor
II. Aronson, Jay D., 1974–, editor III. Fischhoff, Baruch, 1946–, editor
U21.2.C675   2013
355.4—dc23       2012042272

9  8  7  6  5  4  3  2  1

Printed in the United States of America
on acid-free paper

# Contents

# Preface and Acknowledgments

MILITARY CASUALTIES HAVE been studied for many decades. Most of that work addresses the sensitivity of political leaders (especially in democracies) to the loss of soldiers' lives as a cost of war. However, studies of civilian casualties have only recently begun to appear with regularity. This new literature reflects the increased attention to the plight of civilians in armed conflicts: by policy makers, lawyers, academics, international organizations, and the public, whose awareness is increasingly fed by cellphones, handheld video cameras, and social networking technology. When it comes to *recording and counting* civilian casualties, however, most of the people who are producing the research come from the social, statistical, and health sciences; this is because counting casualties is an inherently technical undertaking. There is a need for better communication between these producers of civilian casualty numbers and the varied groups that consume the data—despite their very different disciplinary backgrounds.

In order to bridge this gap, faculty from Carnegie Mellon University and the University of Pittsburgh invited researchers from a diverse set of disciplines to convene for candid, energetic discussions of how best to record and estimate civilian casualties in times of conflict. That discussion, in October 2009, provided a rare opportunity for experts from various fields to review and discuss one another's approaches, while identifying problems and challenges. It also offered a chance to make the science of casualty recording and estimation more accessible to the practitioners who need it (e.g., human rights organizations, truth and reconciliation commissions, humanitarian relief agencies).

This volume is a record of that conference, designed to serve both of its missions, advancing the science by sharing technical knowledge and advancing the practice by making the work accessible to practitioners in the peacebuilding community, who need clear, authoritative introductions to different methods, including candid assessments of their most appropriate application.

The editors are extremely grateful to the U.S. National Science Foundation (Grant no. 0922638) and the Ford Institute for Human Security at the Graduate School of Public and International Affairs, University of Pittsburgh, for supporting these activities. The opinions, findings, and conclusions or recommendations expressed in this material are those of the editors and authors and do not necessarily reflect the views of the National Science Foundation or the Ford Institute.

The idea to hold a conference on civilian casualty recording and estimation originated in a conversation between Baruch Fischhoff and Donald Burke, dean of the Graduate School of Public Health at the University of Pittsburgh. We thank Don and Joanne Russell for facilitating the planning process that led to the conference. We are indebted to Diane Cohen of the Ford Institute for Human Security and Rosa Stipanovic of the Department of Social and Decision Sciences at Carnegie Mellon University for their work in organizing and managing the logistics of the conference and its follow-on activities. We thank the authors who contributed to this volume, and who continue to devote their time and intellect to the vital enterprise of of recording and estimating civilian casualties. Finally, we are especially grateful to Nigel Quinney, who brought to this project superb editing and manuscript development skills, along with and a keen sense of humor. It has been a pleasure working with him.

# Contributors

**Jay D. Aronson** is an associate professor of science, technology, and society, and director of the Center for Human Rights Science, at Carnegie Mellon University. His research and teaching focus on the interactions of science, technology, law, and human rights in a variety of contexts. He is currently engaged in a long-term study of the ethical, political, and social dimensions of post-conflict and post-disaster identification of the missing and disappeared. He received his PhD in history of science and technology from the University of Minnesota and was both a pre- and postdoctoral fellow at Harvard University's John F. Kennedy School of Government.

**Baruch Fischhoff** is Howard Heinz University Professor, in the Departments of Social and Decision Sciences and of Engineering and Public Policy at Carnegie Mellon University, where he heads the Decision Sciences major. A graduate of the Detroit public schools, he holds a PhD in psychology from the Hebrew University of Jerusalem. He is an elected member of the Institute of Medicine of the National Academies, past president of the Society for Judgment and Decision Making and of the Society for Risk Analysis, and founding chair of the Risk Communication Advisory Committee of the U.S. Food and Drug Administration. His books include: *Risk: A Very Short Introduction* (Oxford University Press, 2011), *Intelligence Analysis: Behavioral and Social Science Foundations* (National Academies Press, 2011), *Risk Communication: The Mental Models Approach* (Cambridge University Press, 2001), and *Acceptable Risk* (Cambridge University Press, 1981).

**Taylor B. Seybolt** is an assistant professor at the Graduate School of Public and International Affairs, University of Pittsburgh. He was a senior program officer at the United

States Institute of Peace in Washington, DC, from 2002 to 2008. During his years in Washington, he was a professorial lecturer at the Johns Hopkins School for Advanced International Studies and an adjunct professor in the Security Studies Program at Georgetown University. From 1999 to 2002, he was leader of the Conflicts and Peace Enforcement Project at the Stockholm International Peace Research Institute (SIPRI) in Sweden. Seybolt is the author of *Humanitarian Military Intervention: The Conditions for Success and Failure* (Oxford University Press, 2007). He was an adviser to the Genocide Prevention Task Force, cochaired by Madeleine Albright and William Cohen. He has received grants and fellowships from the Belfer Center for Science and International Affairs at Harvard University's John F. Kennedy School of Government, the MacArthur Foundation, and the United States Institute of Peace. Seybolt holds a PhD in political science from MIT.

* * *

**Jana Asher** is a statistician who specializes in the collection and analysis of human rights violations data. Among other activities, she has worked on projects for the Truth, Justice and Reconciliation Commission of Kenya, the Zimbabwe Human Rights NGO Forum, the International Criminal Tribunal for the Former Yugoslavia, the Peruvian Truth and Reconciliation Commission, Physicians for Human Rights, Human Rights Watch, the East Timor Truth and Reconciliation Commission, the Sierra Leone Truth and Reconciliation Commission, the American Bar Association, and the U.S. Census Bureau.

**Patrick Ball** is the chief scientist and director of the Human Rights Data Analysis Group (HRDAG) at Benetech. He is a leading innovator in applying scientific measurement to human rights. He has spent more than 20 years designing databases and conducting quantitative analysis for truth commissions, nongovernmental organizations, tribunals, and United Nations missions in El Salvador, Ethiopia, Guatemala, Haiti, South Africa, Kosovo, Sierra Leone, Sri Lanka, and Peru. Patrick is currently involved in HRDAG projects in Sierra Leone, Chad, Sri Lanka, Timor-Leste, Colombia, and elsewhere.

**Hamit Dardagan** is the co-founder of Iraq Body Count and its principal analyst. In 2007 he became consultant on civilian casualties in war for the Oxford Research Group (ORG), a UK-based think tank, and now co-directs ORG's Every Casualty programme. He has written or co-written many analytical articles on the civilian casualties of post-invasion Iraq, including peer-reviewed papers in the *New England Journal of Medicine*, *PLoS Medicine*, and *The Lancet*, as well as comment pieces outlining the case for the recording of all casualties of armed violence in publications as diverse as *The Guardian* and the *British Army Review*. He is a former chair of Kalayaan, a minority rights campaign for overseas domestic workers in the UK that led to significant enhancement in their legal rights.

**Anita Gohdes** is a PhD candidate at the University of Mannheim, and an associated doctoral researcher with the International Peace Research Institute Oslo. She also works as a field consultant for the Benetech Human Rights Data Analysis Group, where she has conducted research on the challenges and biases of convenience samples and provided statistical analysis on human rights violations in Iran. She holds a Master of Science in Human Rights and Research Methods from the University of Essex. In her dissertation, she explores geographic and temporal variations in the use of lethal and non-lethal violence in civil war. Her research interests include the analysis of micro-level dynamics of violence in conflict, as well as questions pertaining to the measurement of violent incidences in general.

**Madelyn Hsiao-Rei Hicks** is an associate professor in the Department of Psychiatry at the University of Massachusetts Medical School, USA. She is also an honorary lecturer with the Department of Health Service and Population Research at the Institute of Psychiatry, King's College London and a nonexecutive director of Iraq Body Count. She is a cross-cultural psychiatrist with a background in medical anthropology whose publications have focused on civilian casualties of war, immigrant and refugee mental health, military mental health, domestic violence, suicidality, and depression. Her research on war combines public health and human rights perspectives.

**Amelia Hoover Green** is an assistant professor in the Department of History and Politics at Drexel University, and a field consultant for the Human Rights Data Analysis Group. Her work with HRDAG includes writings on Kosovo, Colombia and Liberia, among others, as well as an ongoing project to bridge the academy-advocacy divide. Her academic research primarily concerns the effects of armed group institutions on violence against civilians, and the politics of human rights statistics.

**Britta L. Jewell** is a doctoral candidate in infectious disease epidemiology at Imperial College, London. She completed an MSc degree in the history of science, medicine, and technology at Oxford University in 2011. She also holds a BA degree in history, with highest honors, from the University of California, Berkeley. Her interests lie in the intersection of science and medicine with social historical phenomena, with particular emphasis on issues affecting the rights of women and their place in societies.

**Nicholas P. Jewell** is a professor of biostatistics and statistics at the University of California, Berkeley. He has held various academic and administrative positions at Berkeley since his arrival in 1981, most notably serving as vice provost from 1994 to 2000. He has also held academic appointments at Stanford University, Princeton University, the University of Edinburgh, Oxford University, and the University of Kyoto. He is a fellow of the American Statistical Association, the Institute of Mathematical Statistics, and the American Association for the Advancement of Science (AAAS).

**Jeff Klingner** is a computer scientist and consultant for the Human Rights Data Analysis Group at Benetech. Dr. Klingner has collaborated with HRDAG since 2005, analyzing government documents and other data associated with human rights abuses in Chad and India. He has designed and written a machine-learning software package for de-duplicating and merging lists of violent deaths and other human rights violations. HRDAG has applied this technology to many analyses, including its work Colombia, El Salvador, Liberia, Sierra Leone, and Syria.

**Keith Krause** is a professor of international politics at the Graduate Institute of International and Development Studies in Geneva, and director of its Centre on Conflict, Development and Peacebuilding. He is also the founder and programme director of the Small Arms Survey. His research and published work focuses on political violence, arms proliferation and regulation, and multilateral security cooperation. He is a Rhodes scholar.

**Jule Krüger** is a field consultant for the Human Rights Data Analysis Group at Benetech. At HDRAG she has conducted data analysis of human rights violations during the armed conflicts in Liberia and other locations, and has coauthored the HRDAG Report and Annex to the Final Report of the Truth and Reconciliation Commission of Liberia. Her research interests include disaggregate conflict analysis, dynamics of conflict violence and repression, and the effects of violence and human rights reporting on data used in empirical analysis.

**Todd Landman** is a professor of government and director of the Institute for Democracy and Conflict Resolution at the University of Essex. He is author or coauthor of many books, including *Protecting Human Rights* (Georgetown University Press, 2005), *Studying Human Rights* (Routledge, 2006), *Issues and Methods in Comparative Politics* (Routledge, 2000, 2003, 2008), *Assessing the Quality of Democracy* (International IDEA 2008), and *Citizenship Rights and Social Movements* (Oxford University Press, 1997, 2000). He has carried out numerous projects for the United Nations, the European Commission, Minority Rights Group International, Amnesty International, and the governments of the United Kingdom, Denmark, Canada, Sweden, and the Netherlands.

**Meghan Foster Lynch is** an assistant professor of political science at Temple University. Her doctoral dissertation examines the microdynamics of violence during civil war and genocide, with a regional focus on sub-Saharan Africa. She has done extensive fieldwork in Burundi, analyzing the causes of the escalation, de-escalation, and non-escalation of violence at the local level during the civil war. Her research has been funded by a Jacob K. Javits Fellowship, a National Science Foundation Graduate Research Fellowship, a National Science Foundation Doctoral Dissertation Improvement Grant, and research grants from the Yale Institute for Social and Policy Studies and the MacMillan Center for International and Area Studies at Yale, where she received her PhD.

**Daniel Manrique-Vallier** is a statistician at Duke University. Between 2001 and 2003 he was a member of the Peruvian Truth and Reconciliation Commission where he led, designed, and coordinated the development of the human rights violations database, and coauthored a statistical study estimating the number of casualties during the internal armed conflict in Peru. He holds a PhD in statistics from Carnegie Mellon University and has also served as an adviser for human right documentation projects in Sri Lanka and for HURIDOCS, Switzerland.

**Megan E. Price** is a senior statistician with the Human Rights Data Analysis Group (HRDAG) at Benetech, where she works with other HRDAG team members to design strategies and methods for statistical analysis of human rights data. She also leads large-scale statistical analysis projects. She earned her PhD in biostatistics and a certificate in Human Rights from the Rollins School of Public Health at Emory University. Dr. Price also has a MS and BS in statistics from Case Western Reserve University.

**Romesh Silva** is a demographer. He has consulted and led projects for the Human Rights Data Analysis Group at Benetech, the Commission for Reception, Truth and Reconciliation (Timor-Leste), International Center for Transitional Justice, Asia Foundation, Unicef, USAID, Center for Civilians in Conflict, and United Nations Development Programme. He has worked in settings as diverse as India, Sri Lanka, Timor-Leste, Chad, Somalia, Lebanon, Colombia, Sierra Leone, Guatemala, and Bangladesh. His research and practice has focused on the measurement of conflict-related mortality and displacement in armed conflict situations and has resulted in a number of policy-related reports and scholarly publications.

**John Sloboda** is the codirector of the Every Casualty Programme at Oxford Research Group (ORG) and was executive director of ORG from 2004 to 2010. He is a cofounder of the Iraq Body Count project. He is also emeritus professor of psychology at the University of Keele and a fellow of the British Academy. He is coauthor of a number of articles and chapters on casualty recording and is co-author (with Chris Abbott and Paul Rogers) of *Beyond Terror: The Truth About the Real Threats to Our World* (Rider, 2007).

**Michael Spagat** is a professor of economics at Royal Holloway College, University of London. He gained his PhD at Harvard University and has held faculty posts at Brown University and the University of Illinois. His papers on armed conflict have been published in such places as *Nature*, the *New England Journal of Medicine*, the *Journal of Peace Research*, the *Journal of Conflict Resolution* and *PLoS Medicine*. His current research addresses universal patterns in modern war, the Dirty War Index, and civilian casualties in the Iraq conflict.

**Ewa Tabeau** is a senior researcher at Wageningen University's Agricultural Economics Institute. Previously she was the project leader of the Demographic Unit at the Office of the Prosecutor (OTP), International Criminal Tribunal for the former Yugoslavia (ICTY), in The Hague. At the tribunal she studied demographic consequences of the wars in the former Yugoslavia and provided crime statistics to trials and investigations at the OTP, most notably in the cases of Slobodan Milosevic, Radovan Karadzic, and

Vojislav Seslj. She also acted as an expert for the Khmer Rouge Tribunal in Phnom Penh, Cambodia, for which she assessed the existing estimates of casualties of the Khmer Rouge regime of 1975–1979.

**Jan Zwierzchowski** is a researcher at the Institute of Statistics and Demography of the Warsaw School of Economics in Poland. In 2009 and 2010, he worked for the Demographic Unit, Office of the Prosecutor, of the International Criminal Tribunal for the former Yugoslavia.

# Glossary

*Terms in italics have their own entries in this glossary.*

**ACQUIESCENCE BIAS:** Bias that occurs when survey or interview respondents give researchers the answers that the researchers seem to expect. Acquiescence bias may lead to underestimating or overestimating the number of casualties, with the direction of bias determined by respondents' beliefs about the researchers' expectations.

**ADAPTIVE SAMPLING:** A method for selecting a sample that changes (adapts) as data are collected. For example, adaptive designs have been used in clinical trials to modify the assignment of patients to treatments based on observed outcomes to that point in the study.

**BAYES' RULE:** A mathematical rule specifying how a person should change his or her beliefs in response to new evidence. It directs scientists in combining new data with existing knowledge.

**BAYESIAN INFERENCE:** A form of statistical inference that uses Bayes' rule to update the assessed probability of a hypothesis when additional evidence is received. Bayesian inference incorporates prior beliefs about the probability of the hypothesis through formalized *prior distributions*; as a result, two experts using Bayesian inference could make the same observations but reach different population estimates because of their differing prior beliefs. Bayesian inference can also proceed with a "non-informative prior," meaning that prior beliefs do not influence estimates.

**BAYESIAN (SUBJECTIVE) PROBABILITY:** Typically contrasted with *frequentist probability*. The Bayesian approach views probability as a measure of degree of belief.

**BIAS:** Data and estimates are said to be biased when they do not accurately represent the underlying reality. Bias may be random, meaning that errors of measurement fall in a random pattern around the true value, or non-random (systematic), meaning that measurements are generally "wrong in the same way" because they are correlated with some characteristic of the underlying data or some latent variable.

**CAPTURE PROBABILITY:** The probability that an individual will be included in a set of observations (e.g., a list of casualties). The terminology refers to the development of capture-recapture estimation in ecology, which estimates populations based on animals' probability of being caught and tagged, then caught again. Within the population of casualties, individuals' "capture" probabilities may vary over time, across space, and as a function of victim characteristics.

**CAPTURE-RECAPTURE ESTIMATION/ANALYSIS:** Capture-recapture estimation refers to estimating the total size of a population by finding the overlap between two incomplete sets of observations collected from it. "Capture-recapture" is sometimes used to refer to "multiple recapture" estimation (see *multiple systems estimation*), when more than two lists are used for estimation.

**CASUALTY ESTIMATION:** The process of moving from incomplete evidence about a population of casualties (e.g., casualty lists, survey data, indirect evidence) to an inference about the full population (typically, its size).

**CLOSED POPULATION:** A population in which, during the period of measurement, no members may leave and no additional members may enter.

**CLUSTER SAMPLING:** Selection based on groups (clusters) of population members rather than on individuals. For example, a number of villages, schools, or clinics may be sampled as a more cost-effective way to reach individual members of the population.

**CODING:** The process of extracting quantitative data from qualitative information. For example, a newspaper article may mention that three bodies were discovered in a river in Colombia and that all victims appeared to be adults. Coding rules provide consistency in making decisions such as whether to record these as "three adult victims in Colombia" or as "three victims of undetermined ages in Colombia." Such rules are organized into a "code-book" (or "vocabulary"). Intercoder reliability checks ensure the reliability of coding over time as well as across coders.

**COGNITIVE INTERVIEWING:** Asking survey respondents to *think aloud* as they answer questions in order to reveal additional information about their thinking and behavior, beyond literal responses to the questions. This method is common when developing a survey, prior to field use.

**CONFIDENCE INTERVAL:** In Bayesian statistics, a range of values said to contain the true value with some degree of confidence. For example, one might say, "based on these data, we can say with 90 percent confidence that the population size was between 13,000 and 19,000." In *frequentist* statistics, a confidence interval refers to the number of times the true (population) value would fall in the range if the measurement were repeated many times (e.g., "if we conducted a similar survey 100 times, we would expect the calculated interval would include the true [population] value 90 times").

**CONTEXT BIAS:** Bias arising when survey or interview respondents give different answers depending on the context of the question. "Context" might include interviewer identity, question wording, or the location and time of interview.

**CONTINUOUS VARIABLE:** A variable that can, in principle, assume infinitely precise values in contrast to dichotomous ("yes or no"—see *dichotomous data*) and categorical ("1, 2, 3, 4, or 5") variables. For example, the open-ended question "How long have you lived here?" is a continuous variable because it can be answered in years, months, days, hours, minutes, seconds, and so forth. "Have you lived here less than one year?" is a dichotomous variable (based on a continuous one). "Are you a native, refugee, or visitor?" is a categorical variable.

CONVENIENCE SAMPLE/DATA: Convenience samples (or data) are collected based on what is possible or is convenient for the researcher (e.g., ease of access by car, newspaper report, safety, or availability of the subject by telephone). When using convenience samples, researchers cannot guarantee that a sample represents the entire population. In contrast, a probability sample (or random sample) means that each member of the population has an equal probability of being selected.

COVARIATE INFORMATION: Systematically collected information in addition to the main variables. For example, in additional to characterizing individuals by their casualty status, researchers might collect each person's name, gender, and age, as well as details of the event. Covariate information enables researchers to create and evaluate models regarding relationships between violence and other measures.

DATASET: An organized representation of observations, often in a spreadsheet, with each case (e.g., acts of violence) characterized in the same terms (e.g., victim's name, age, gender, location, date).

DEMOGRAPHIC BALANCING EQUATION: A calculation for the change in a population's size. The population $(P)$ at any time equals births minus deaths $(B - D)$, plus in-migration minus out-migration (Mi – Mo). It is expressed as follows: $P = (B - D) + (Mi - Mo)$.

DICHOTOMOUS DATA: Dichotomous variables record the answers to "yes or no" questions (e.g., "Is an individual above age 18?").

ENUMERATOR: Person trained to administer a survey. Enumerators may be residents of the area in which the survey is being conducted.

EVENT-BASED DATA: Records with features of individual events (e.g., violent events in an armed conflict). The features (or codes) might include the date, duration, location, groups involved, human rights abuses against noncombatants, territorial changes, and the type and number of individuals involved.

EXCESS MORTALITY/DEATHS: Deaths in excess of the "normal" (baseline) number that one would expect in a population over a given period of time. In conflict settings, these are often divided into "direct" (violent) deaths and "indirect" (nonviolent) ones, such as those arising from lost access to food, water, shelter, and health care. (See also *nonviolent death*.)

FOUND DATA: Data not originally intended for systematic study, such as newspaper reports, hospital records, and discarded bureaucratic paperwork.

FREQUENTIST PROBABILITY: Defined as the limit of an event's relative frequency in a large number of identical, repeated trials (e.g., 50 percent for tossing a head [or tail] with a fair coin).

HOMOGENEITY ASSUMPTION: That all individuals in a population (e.g., casualties) have an equal probability of being selected into a sample. This is a necessary assumption for two-system *capture-recapture analysis* but not for *multiple systems estimation* with three or more systems.

INCLUSION PATTERN: The overlap in lists used in *multiple systems estimation*. For example, a victim may be on lists compiled by the government and a church group but not that of a local nongovernmental organization.

INDEPENDENCE ASSUMPTION: The assumption that inclusion in one list or dataset (A) does not affect an individual's probability of inclusion in another (B). In probability terms,

$P(B|A) = P(B)$. This is a core assumption of two-system *capture-recapture analysis* but need not be assumed (and may be adjusted for) in *multiple systems estimation*.

**IN-DEPTH INTERVIEWS:** Interviews that seek detailed, contextualized understanding, typically using open-ended questions. Interviewers are usually prompted to follow up on topics raised by individual informants rather than adhering tightly to a script. In-depth interviews are typically used for oral histories.

**INFORMED CONSENT:** The agreement of an individual to participate in an experiment, interview, or survey after a researcher has provided the information (e.g., about potential harms and benefits) necessary to a free, informed choice.

**LOG-LINEAR MODEL:** A family of linear regression models in which the log of the dependent variable is modeled as a linear function of the independent variables.

**MULTIPLE SYSTEMS ESTIMATION (MSE):** A family of statistical methods that uses the overlap between three or more sets of observations to estimate the number of instances not counted by any dataset, thereby allowing calculation of the total number (both observed and unobserved). In addition to its use with casualty estimation, MSE has been extensively used for estimating wildlife populations and "elusive" human populations such as HIV sufferers, homeless persons, and substance abusers.

**NARRATIVE DATA:** Qualitative data that, to avoid sacrificing meaning, are not converted into quantitative form, although such transformation may be done for other purposes (see *coding*). Narrative data may be collected directly (e.g., by in-depth interviews or group discussions) or may be found data (e.g., journals or diaries, stories).

**NON-OBSERVED/UNOBSERVED:** Deaths that have occurred (hence are part of the population of casualties) but have not been recorded in any list or dataset.

**NON-PARAMETRIC:** describing statistical methods that do not assume a specific underlying distribution (e.g., a normal distribution).

**NONVIOLENT DEATH:** In the context of this volume, any death that occurs during a conflict that is not caused directly by the weapons of war. Nonviolent deaths may be unrelated to the conflict (e.g., deaths from untreatable cancer) or indirectly related to the conflict (e.g., starvation as a result of destroyed crops or disrupted supply lines). Indirect deaths may be measured as *excess mortality*.

**ORAL HISTORIES:** Interviews in which respondents describe their recollections of past events that they experienced.

**PETERSEN ESTIMATOR:** Also known as the Lincoln-Petersen estimator, it is the total population estimated by two-system *capture-recapture analysis*.

**POPULATION:** The entire group of individuals, localities, events, or objects that is the focus of study and from which samples are drawn. Also called universe.

**PRIOR DISTRIBUTION:** Background information incorporated into calculations by means of Bayesian inference.

**PROBABILITY MODEL:** A mathematical description of a relationship between variables (e.g., between violent events and their location).

**PROBABILITY SAMPLE:** A method for selecting members of a population with a known probability of selection. Examples include simple random, systematic, stratified, and cluster.

**PROPORTIONAL SAMPLING:** See *stratified sampling*.

**RANDOM SAMPLE:** A synonym for *probability sample*.

**RECALL BIAS:** Bias created when respondents forget or misremember the answer to a question. Recall bias can be affected by the time elapsed since the event, the intensity of the experience, subsequent experiences, and concurrent events, among other factors.

**REGRESSION:** A family of statistical techniques that measure the relationship between a dependent variable (e.g., death) and independent variables (or predictors). Methods exist for evaluating causal relationships among these statistical associations.

**REPEAT INTERVIEWS:** The process of interviewing the same individual multiple times, to verify the consistency of information provided, to build rapport in the hopes of eliciting better or more information, or to obtain more information than can be collected in one interview.

**REPORTING BIAS:** Form of bias that arises when individuals deliberately misreport events (e.g., to avoid the stigma attached to reporting sexual violence).

**REPRESENTATIVE SAMPLE:** A sample from which inferences can be made directly regarding its population.

**RESIDUAL CATEGORY:** Includes items that do not fit into any other categories (e.g., not stated, refused to answer, don't know, outside geographic area).

**RETROSPECTIVE SURVEY:** A survey focused on questions about the past.

**SAMPLING ERROR:** The difference in quantity (e.g., number of casualties) estimated based on a sample and the "true" number in the population.

**SAMPLING FRAME:** The list from which a sample is selected (e.g., a sample of villages may be selected from the sampling frame provided by a census of all villages in a region).

**SAMPLING UNIT:** The "size" of the element selected into a sample (e.g., an individual, household, classroom, or document).

**SELECTION BIAS:** Any deviation from a representative sampling (see *representative sample*).

**SELF-REPORTED DATA:** Information that is provided to a researcher by the subject rather than collected through another form of measurement.

**SENSITIVITY ANALYSIS:** Assessing the sensitivity of analytical results to violations of assumptions by considering the range of plausible values. For example, if the model requires an estimate of pre-conflict mortality rates, but the only available mortality rate is for a neighboring state, the model could be calculated by using different rates reflecting regional variability in mortality.

**SOCIAL DESIRABILITY BIAS:** Bias resulting from subjects' having provided incorrect information in a survey or interview in order to conform to social norms or to avoid being perceived negatively by the researcher (e.g., the reluctance to admit to being racist).

**SPEARMAN RANK CORRELATION:** A measure of the relationship between two variables that uses ranked values rather than actual ones.

**STANDARDIZED QUESTIONNAIRE/SURVEY:** A survey instrument using the same questions and response options for all respondents.

**STOCHASTIC:** A synonym for "random."

**STRATIFIED SAMPLING:** A procedure whereby researchers divide the population into different groups (or strata) and choose a random sample within each. Also called "proportional sampling."

**SURVEILLANCE SURVEY:** A survey conducted repeatedly in order to detect changes.

**THINK-ALOUD:** A form of cognitive interviewing in which respondents are asked to verbalize their thought processes while taking the survey ("concurrent think-aloud") or after it has been completed ("retrospective think-aloud"). Respondents are often asked how they interpret survey questions and formulate responses.

)

# I Who Counts?

# 1 Introduction

Taylor B. Seybolt, Jay D. Aronson, and Baruch Fischhoff

## Civilian Casualties and Strategic Peacebuilding

It is important to know how many people die in violent conflicts. Governments need the information to make political and military decisions. Societies need to know so they can honor the fallen. It can be extraordinarily difficult, however, to gather accurate information about the number and identity of people who are killed and injured. Even in the best of circumstances it is difficult to establish accurate, reliable numbers about complex social phenomena (Alonso and Starr 1987). Violent conflicts often pose conditions that are rife with technical challenges and political controversies between antagonists who want the "facts" to support their political, legal, or social claims (Greenhill 2010). To obtain reliable figures on who died, where, and when, researchers must not only overcome the practical problems of tallying the dead and injured during wars and rebellions, but also circumvent rival parties' attempts to distort those numbers.

An example from Bosnia and Herzegovina (Bosnia) illustrates the tension between these two central themes of this volume: the political incentive to mislead and the growing ability of scientifically sound research to overcome such deception. For years, journalists, diplomats, partisans, and academics accepted the claim of 200,000–250,000 Bosniaks (Bosnian Muslims) killed between 1992 and 1995. Research has found those numbers to overstate the toll—which is nonetheless horrific. Political and military leaders deliberately fabricated the numbers to support their assertions of Serbian nationalists' brutality against Bosniak civilians on a massive scale. In the summer of 1992, Bosnian president, Alija Izetbegovic, its foreign minister Haris Silajdzic, and army commander Sefer Halilovic met to decide how many deaths to publicly blame on Bosnian Serb military and militia units. They were not interested in an accurate reflection of the costs of war. They wanted powerful representation of the suffering of Bosniaks at the hands of Serbs—that suffering was all too real, but the Bosnian leaders felt a need to exaggerate it. President Izetbegovic suggested 150,000 civilians killed; during a press conference after the meeting, however, the foreign minister cited 250,000 dead. By the summer of 1993, one year later, it had become conventional wisdom that Serbian nationalists had killed 200,000–250,000 Bosniaks (Nettelfield 2010, 160–61). Although the conflict continued until December 1995, the casualty "estimate" did not change. The fabricated number persisted, in large part because there was no viable alternative estimate. The claim could not be challenged until investigators found ways to overcome the practical and methodological difficulties created by the war.

Eight years after the 1995 Dayton Peace Agreement brought the war to an end, a study done for the International Criminal Tribunal for Yugoslavia (ICTY), using demographic techniques, estimated the number of people killed as 102,622, of whom 55,261 were civilians (Tabeau and Bijak 2005). That estimate has since been refined to 104,732 (see chapter 11, by Tabeau and Zwierzchowski, in this volume). An independent effort to record every death during the war also arrived at a similar number. The Population Loss Project of the Research and Documentation Centre in Sarajevo published in 2007 the *Bosnian Book of the Dead* that identified 97,207 deaths as a direct result of military activity. Of those, 57,523 were soldiers and 39,684 civilians (Ahmetasevic 2007).

The case of Bosnia is far from unique. Obfuscation and promotion of false information are common and relatively easy when even rudimentary data collection is hard and dangerous. Creating authoritative records and counts requires rigorous attention to detail. Without this safeguard, recording and counting can promote conflict, rather than peace, as the parties fight over perceived injustices. As a result, accurate, accepted records and counts of civilian casualties are fundamental to peacebuilding.

The principal goal of peacebuilding is to prevent "the outbreak, the recurrence or the continuation of armed conflict" using political, development, humanitarian, and human rights programs and methods (Call and Cousens 2008, 6). Peacebuilding is strategic when it intentionally links international, national, and local actors in a holistic effort to address the sources of conflict within a society. As Daniel Philpott wrote in *Strategies of Peace*, the inaugural book in this series on strategic peacebuilding,

> Strategic peacebuilders are like doctors who understand that the body is composed of interconnected systems and then specialize in certain regions of connection with the conviction that these subsystems crucially sustain the entire anatomy. A feature of this medicine is its interest not only in laws, institutions, and policies but in emotions, attitudes, beliefs, legitimacy, and, broadly speaking, the wide range of relationships among citizens. (Philpott 2010a, 9)

Systematic, authoritative treatment of civilian casualties is—or should be—an essential element of strategic peacebuilding that connects varied interests through diverse interactions, from enforcing international law to validating individual emotions. Transparent, accountable treatments of civilian deaths are critical to stitching broken societies together again. Those efforts not only further the healing process but also reduce the conflicts that can arise from stakeholders seeking to manipulate these processes, and thereby threatening to derail the peace process. Unlike many other aspects of peacebuilding, casualty recording and estimation is as much a scientific endeavor as it is a political one. As a result, it is important to clarify the scientific issues, promote adherence to best practices, and candidly recognize their limits—so as to limit political efforts to distort and impeach the work.

Unfortunately, it has been difficult for nonspecialists to understand this science, its controversies, and hence what constitute reliable, valid, and useful data on violence. Most discussions of the science have either been oversimplified in public and political discourse or couched in forbidding jargon and technical detail. For example, most media reports on the violence in Darfur, Sudan, reported vague, unreliable guesstimates of the numbers killed.[1] One newspaper offered a guesstimate in June 2004 of 320,000 people killed in that year alone, then a lower guesstimate of 300,000 total deaths two years later (April 2006), followed by "maybe 400,000," two days later. None of these numbers were accompanied by any discussion of their derivation or reliability (Kristof 2004, 2006a, 2006b). While such oversimplified accounts can reach huge audiences, highly technical, peer-reviewed articles describing the results of careful research and well-documented data collection tend to appear in journals with titles such as *Morbidity and Mortality Weekly Report*. These journals are respected by specialized audiences but are unknown beyond those communities.

This book seeks to make technically sophisticated methods of counting casualties accessible to nonspecialists, as well as to promote open dialogue among scientists. Its chapters present the practices, strengths, and weaknesses of the most commonly used approaches to casualty recording and estimation in understandable, accessible terms. It is aimed at people who encounter casualty records and figures in their work and want to know more about how these materials are generated, how far they can be trusted, and what debates surround the different methodologies. These accounts should enable policy makers, military officials, journalists, human rights activists, judges, lawyers, students, and the broader public to become better informed "consumers" of such accounts.[2]

By concentrating on civilian casualties, this book addresses some of the gaps in the literature left by research that has focused on military losses. The effects of attrition on combat capability are a long-standing research topic, central to forecasting the outcomes of military engagements (see, e.g., Lanchester 1916; Mearscheimer 1988) and, more recently to their effects on public support for continuing conflicts (see, e.g., Gelpi et al 2005/2006; Gartner 2008). Research on civilian casualties has often focused on how they affect counterinsurgency operations (e.g., Condra et al 2010) or when and why belligerents target civilians (Valentino et al 2004; Downes 2008; Slim 2008). There is relatively little, though, on the diversity of methods for recording and estimating civilian casualties (Ghobarah et al 2003).

Much of the actual work of recording and estimation is done by uncoordinated humanitarian groups, human rights organizations, and journalists, typically working under extreme conditions with limited resources and widely varying technical expertise. Recognizing the importance of documenting and sharing that work, several authors have recently drawn portions of it together (see, e.g., Daponte 1993; Landman 2005; Asher 2007; Guha-Sapir and Degomme 2007; Silva and Ball 2007; Brunborg et al. 2010; Höglund and Öberg 2011). Building on their work, the present book offers a range of approaches, allowing the drawing of comparisons among alternatives. This book also benefits from direct exchanges among many of its contributors at a conference dedicated to the topic of counting civilian casualties.

In the past, most such exchanges have been conducted in the context of often bitter controversies over specific events, as with the debate over casualty figures in the war in Iraq. In the case of Iraqi civilian casualties sustained since 2003, when the country was invaded by a coalition led by the United States, research groups using different methodologies have calculated estimates ranging from less than 100,000 (Iraq Body Count 2009) to 151,000 (Iraq Family Health Survey Study Group 2008) to 601,000 (Burnham et al., 2006) to more than 1,000,000 (Opinion Research Business 2007). The ensuing controversies over how these numbers were generated have distracted attention from a human death toll that was high by any estimate (Munro and Cannon 2008).

The thirteen chapters that follow this one provide introductions to approaches that include event-data recording, surveys, ethnography, demography, and multiple systems estimation (MSE). The authors describe the advantages and disadvantages of their methods. They also discuss how their products are used (and sometimes misused) by parties that include governments, rebels, human rights advocates, and war crimes tribunals.

As seen in the Bosnia example, people who have experienced political violence tend to blame those outside their own community, leading to depressing tales of politicians, activists, and survivors obstructing the establishment of more accurate pictures. As seen in the same example, though, sound research can sometimes supplant inaccurate accounts with more accurate ones. This opportunity is created by research like that reported here.

## The Structure and Content of this Volume

Although the chapters in this book attest to the progress in recording and estimating the magnitude and patterns of killing and human rights abuses, they also show the limits to these methods given the harsh conditions under which they must be applied. The differing attributes and limitations of these methods can produce conflict even among researchers who share a deep commitment to a common cause. The editors and contributors to this volume hope to encourage such conflicts to become conversations, and to facilitate the professional exchange needed to make best use of the methods we have, individually and in combination, and improve them all. Candid expositions of each approach's goals, strengths, weaknesses, and assumptions are a step toward those objectives.

The next two chapters in part I of this volume address the political context within which the methods are used. In chapter 2, Taylor Seybolt challenges the common perception that civilian suffering is worse now than in the past, arguing that war has had devastating effects on civilians for millennia. Concern for civilian safety and efforts to reduce civilian casualties are what distinguish the contemporary era from the past. The increased attention to civilian casualties is not a fleeting interest, as some have suggested, but a manifestation of long-term normative and legal changes in international affairs that lead to the recognition of the rights of people as commensurate with the rights of states. In that context, understanding the fate of populations in zones of conflict is crucial for peacebuilding.

In chapter 3, Jay Aronson argues that counting people is an inherently political exercise. "Consumers of casualty statistics," Aronson says, "must understand the political dimensions of the numbers with which they are presented in order to properly analyze and interpret them." Knowing *why* a particular casualty count has been produced is as important as knowing *how* the number was generated. Aronson examines the politics of casualty numbers in the 1991 Gulf War, the 1992–1995 conflict in Bosnia, the Iraq War that began in 2003, and the fighting in Darfur that began in 2003. He concludes that quantification does not remove politics from the picture; to the contrary, it opens the door to more political intervention.

Parts II, III, and IV of this volume consider the science. Broadly speaking, there are two families of methods for keeping track of civilian casualties. "Recording" tracks those deaths that appear in reliable eyewitness accounts, often requiring corroboration by an independent source. Such records, systematically collected from observed events, are known as "event data." "Estimation" uses statistical techniques to infer the numbers and circumstances of civilian casualties. Table 1.1 compares the two approaches' objectives, techniques, limitations, and strengths, all discussed at length in chapters 4 through 13.

The chapters in part II lay out the methods and rationale for key approaches to event recording. In chapter 4, John Sloboda, Hamit Dardagan, Michael Spagat, and Madelyn Hsiao-Rei Hicks describe the work of the Iraq Body Count (IBC), a project that has recorded violent civilian deaths in Iraq since 2003. The project has the short-term goal of "collecting and organizing emergent data as soon as feasible, and making it available for public view," and the long-term goal of producing "a complete and final published list of the dead." The authors build data records using news reports and government agencies' records (e.g., from morgues and hospitals). These reports are cross-checked according to the time, location, and other unique identifiers to avoid duplication and to track the occurrence of violence temporally and geographically. This type of data collection "is premised on the presence of a well-connected and active press, and a reasonably robust information infrastructure" and, therefore, is not feasible in all places. The IBC has been criticized for both undercounting the dead and sensationalizing the violence in Iraq.

TABLE I.I.

Comparison of Recording and Estimation Methods

|  | Recording | Estimation |
|---|---|---|
| **Objective** | Comprehensive account of all instances of civilian casualties | Accurate estimate of the number and patterns of casualties |
| **Method of collecting information** | Creating or gathering reports of individual events | Collecting recorded observation<br>Creating records by surveying a sample of the population |
| **Sources of information** | Media reports<br>Official records | Surveyed members of the population<br>Existing records compiled for other purposes |
| **Techniques** | Cross-checking for assessing accuracy and completeness | Statistical analysis |
| **Results** | Compilation of individual records<br>Descriptive statistics | Estimate of overall numbers in the population<br>Inferential statistics |
| **Main limitations** | Miss casualties without authoritative records<br>Omissions difficult to establish | Difficult to design and implement<br>Limited context for individual deaths |
| **Main strengths** | Verified data<br>Each death put in context | Can reveal patterns<br>Can compute measures of confidence |

In response, IBC has always acknowledged that its insistence on verified accounts guarantees an indeterminate account that draws warranted, and not sensationalized, attention to the level of violence.

In chapter 5, Todd Landman and Anita Gohdes describe an event-based approach to understanding the complex nature of violence that seeks to uncover "the 'grammar' of an event" that distinguishes the perpetrators, the victims, and the acts committed in specific events. Their analysis of casualty data in Peru and Sierra Leone demonstrates both the potential of the approach and the constraints imposed by the sparseness of data on individual events. Meager data, for instance, limits "the ability to provide statistical estimates for particular periods of time or particular areas of each country." Landman and Gohdes conclude by advocating reliance on multiple sources of data to circumvent the data poverty that "limit[s] our ability to carry out more in-depth analyses of the contours of conflict."

The chapters in part III address methods that rely on surveys to infer the number of casualties in a population. In chapter 6, Jana Asher tackles the challenges of securing samples that accurately represent the overall population and crafting surveys that accurately capture the views of respondents. Drawing on her experience in Sierra Leone and Timor-Leste, Asher notes both problems and unique possibilities. In particular, she notes that, "unlike newspaper reports, random sample survey methods are considered unbiased and truly reflective of the opinions and/or experiences of the population." Asher guides readers through the design of questionnaires for casualty estimation in conflict environments. Compared with other methods of data collection, they are "significantly less expensive than censuses, and are particularly useful when demographic records are not maintained or have been discontinued during the conflict period."

Meghan Foster Lynch, writing from an ethnographer's perspective in chapter 7, questions the assumption that people "will answer [survey] questions either truthfully or in a predictably biased way." She argues that anthropology and psychology research have found that people communicate differently from culture to culture. As a result, survey respondents provide information that "deviates from the truth in unpredictable directions," leading to civilian casualty estimates that are "representative, statistically significant, and wrong." Lynch argues that ethnography "is uniquely equipped to deal with issues of culture, trust, and contradiction," hence ethnography-based investigations are better suited than survey methods for obtaining sensitive information, explaining political violence, developing preventive policies, and prosecuting crimes against humanity.

Part IV deals with inferential methods for extrapolating from samples to the entire population. Like parts V and VI, it focuses on the statistical technique known as multiple systems estimation, reflecting the attention that MSE is currently receiving.

In chapter 8, Jeff Klingner and Romesh Silva explain the method, grounded in the observation that the weaknesses of different data types and estimation methods are sometimes complementary. Multiple systems estimation is designed "to improve estimates of conflict mortality by combining multiple data types or estimation methods." Using Timor-Leste, India, and Kosovo as examples, the authors describe how "found data—data created for some purpose other than mortality estimation—can be combined with surveys and other intentionally gathered data to improve estimates of the magnitude and patterns of conflict mortality."

In chapter 9, Daniel Manrique-Vallier, Megan E. Price, and Anita Gohdes introduce the statistical techniques used in MSE in order "to quantify the probability that a death will be missed—that no enumeration effort will record it—and therefore, a way to estimate the undercount." The authors describe limits to MSE, along with the successes demonstrated in their studies of Kosovo and Peru, which "illustrate that in certain situations, [MSE] can considerably improve our knowledge of conflict trajectories." While recognizing that using these statistical models requires specialized expertise, the authors seek to make their assumptions and interpretation clear.

The two chapters in part V advocate matching research methods with the objectives of specific analyses. In chapter 10, Nicholas P. Jewell, Michael Spagat, and Britta L. Jewell ask, "When, and under what conditions, can multiple systems estimation provide accurate and useful counts of the number of conflict casualties?" The authors consider the case of Kosovo, where different researchers used three different techniques to assess the death toll: MSE, a survey, and an attempt to list all victims. Noting the general agreement among findings with the three methods, Jewell, Spagat, and Jewell conclude that all "methods for counting casualties . . . face serious statistical challenges and there is no method that is clearly best for all circumstances. A determination to count casualties pushes us to search for alternatives that seek to both minimize assumptions and data problems and maximize validity, rather than attempting to generate perfect numbers."

In chapter 11, Ewa Tabeau and Jan Zwierzchowski demonstrate demographic approaches by analyzing the 1992–1995 war in Bosnia and the 1975–1979 Khmer Rouge regime in Cambodia. From these experiences, they conclude that recording event data is a reliable method "for low death toll conflicts and countries with a good availability of individual level sources on war deaths, such as in Bosnia," as long as the counting is accompanied by undercount estimation. However, sample surveys are not reliable in such cases "due to massive population movements which prevent [researchers from] correctly identifying the right sample." For "high death toll conflicts and countries with dramatic lack of statistical sources on the population, such as in Cambodia," they propose combining "a qualitative historical approach based on multiple sources, cross-referenced and integrated with each other," with a demographic technique called "cohort component population projection."

Part VI discusses the problems that remain despite improvements in recording and estimation methods. In chapter 12, Jule Krüger, Patrick Ball, Megan E. Price, and Amelia Hoover Green, MSE practitioners, critically assess the usefulness of databases for understanding what violence occurred and informing policy responses. They review multiple databases compiled with event-recording methods that sought to measure the same events but arrived at different outcomes in Colombia, El Salvador, Sierra Leone, and Timor-Leste. The authors argue recording efforts can both document violence and provide evidence essential to humanitarian and peacebuilding measures—without being appropriate for planning or implementing those measures. They note that records are inevitably incomplete and uncertain, hence "cannot provide a rigorous evidentiary basis for peacebuilding policy or impact assessment." They contend that well-designed strategic peacebuilding policies require separating short-term data that is "good enough" to spur action from longer term statistical analysis of patterns that require greater precision.

In chapter 13, Keith Krause welcomes the increased attention to improving evidence-based understanding of armed violence, which he situates in the broader trend of global public policy. He cautions, though, that the "limitations with *what is counted* and *how it is counted* . . . pose serious challenges to the goal of developing adequate public policies."

Krause proposes expanding the set of relevant data with "an integrated approach to counting victims of violence that blurs (or effaces) the boundary between so-called 'conflict' and 'non-conflict' victims of violence." The purpose of a broader perspective is to find new ways of understanding the dilemmas of violence. Once researchers succeed in producing work that is scientifically rigorous, Krause recommends they acquire the skills needed to effectively communicate with policy makers so that the science has policy influence.

Part VII concludes the book with an assessment by the editors (Jay Aronson, Baruch Fischhoff, and Taylor Seybolt) of the progress and challenges in accounting for civilian lives lost in conflict. The chapter notes that the contributing authors' differing backgrounds and goals allow them to provide complementary perspectives to this problem, as well as to bring fresh views to strategic peacebuilding. Together, they show the rich potential of the nascent science of civilian casualty recording and estimation for helping to understand conflicts, rebuild societies, and create healing peace. The authors' work provides the foundation for two proposals that conclude the chapter and volume. The first is to create guidelines for conducting such studies and allowing nonspecialists to evaluate them. The second is to create an international convention on civilian casualty recording that would require signatories to report all casualties and establish a formal protocol for doing so. That convention would apply scientific principles to support the political commitment to protect human rights in conflict.

## REFERENCES

Ahmetasevic, Nidzara. 2007. "Justice Report: Bosnia's Book of Dead." *Balkan Investigative Reporting Network.* At: http://birn.eu.com/en/88/10/3377/ (accessed December 15, 2010).

Alonso, William, and Paul Starr. 1987. *The Politics of Numbers: The Population of the United States in the 1980s.* New York: Russell Sage Foundation.

Asher, Jana, David L. Banks, and Fritz Scheuren. 2007. *Statistical Methods for Human Rights.* New York: Springer.

Ball, Patrick. 1996. *Who Did What to Whom? Planning and Implementing a Large Scale Human Rights Data Project.* Washington, DC: American Association for the Advancement of Science. At: http://shr.aaas.org/www/contents.html.

Brunborg, Helge, Ewa Tabeau, and Henrik Urdal, eds. 2010. *The Demography of Armed Conflict.* New York: Springer.

Burnham, Gilbert, R. Lafta, S. Doocy, and L. Roberts. 2006. "Mortality After the 2003 Invasion of Iraq: A Cross-Sectional Cluster Sample Survey." *The Lancet* 368(9545): 1421–1428.

Call, Charles T., and Elizabeth M. Cousens. 2008. "Ending Wars and Building Peace: International Response to War-Torn Societies." *International Studies Perspective* 9(1): 1–21.

Campaign for Innocent Victims in Conflict (CIVIC). 2011. At: http://www.civicworldwide.org/about-us/our-accomplishments (accessed June 6, 2011).

Commission for Reception, Truth, and Reconciliation Timor-Leste. 2005. *Chega! The Report of the Commission for Reception, Truth, and Reconciliation Timor-Leste.* Timor-Leste. At: http://www.cavr-timorleste.org/.

Condra, Luke N., Joseph H. Felter, Radha K. Iyengar, and Jacob N. Shapiro. 2010. *The Effect of Civilian Casualties in Afghanistan and Iraq*. NBER Working Paper Series, Working Paper 16152. Washington, DC: National Bureau of Economic Research.

Daponte, Beth O. 1993. "A case study in estimating casualties from war and its aftermath: The 1991 Persian Gulf War." *PSR Quarterly* 3(2): 57–66.

Downes, Alexander B. 2008. *Targeting Civilians in War*. Ithaca, NY: Cornell University Press.

Feaver, Peter, and Christopher Gelpi. 2004. *Choosing Your Battles: American Civil-Military Relations and the Use of Force*. Princeton, NJ: Princeton University Press.

Gartner, Scott S. 2008. "The Multiple Effects of Casualties on Public Support for War: An Experimental Approach." *American Political Science Review* 102(1): 95–106.

Gelpi, Christopher, Peter D. Feaver, and Jason Reifler. 2005/2006. "Success Matters: Casualty Sensitivity and the War in Iraq." *International Security* 30(3): 7–46.

Ghobarah, Hazem Adam, Paul Huth, and Bruce Russett. 2003. "Civil Wars Kill and Maim People—Long after the Shooting Stops." *American Political Science Review* 97(2): 189–202.

Guha-Sapir, D., and Olivier Degomme. 2007. *Estimating Mortality in Civil Conflicts: Lessons from Iraq: Triangulating Different Types of Mortality Data in Iraq*. Brussels: Centre for Research on the Epidemiology of Disasters.

Greenhill, Kelly M. 2010. "Counting the Costs: the Politics of Numbers in Armed Conflict." In *Sex, Drugs, and Body Counts: The Politics of Numbers in Global Crime*, edited by Peter Andreas and Kelly M. Greenhill, 127–158. Ithaca, NY: Cornell University Press.

Höglund, Kristine, and Magnus Öberg. 2011. *Understanding Peace Research: Methods and Challenges*. New York: Routledge.

Kristof, Nicholas D. 2004. "Dare We Call It Genocide?" *New York Times*, June 16. Late Edition—Final, Section A, Column 6, Editorial Desk, 21.

———. 2006a. "Osama's Crusade In Darfur," *New York Times*, April 25. Late Edition—Final Section A, Column 1, Editorial Desk, 27.

———. 2006b. "China and Sudan, Blood and Oil," *New York Times*, April 23. Late Edition—Final, Section 4, Column 1, Editorial Desk, 13.

Lanchester, Frederich W. 1916. *Aircraft in Warfare: The Dawn of the Fourth Arm*. London: Constable and Company.

Landman, Todd. 2005. *Protecting Human Rights: A Comparative Study*. Washington, DC: Georgetown University Press.

Lederach, John Paul, and R. Scott Appleby. 2010. "Strategic Peacebuilding: An Overview." In *Strategies of Peace: Transforming Conflict in a Violent World*, edited by Daniel Philpott and Gerard F. Powers, 19–44. New York: Oxford University Press.

Mearscheimer, John J. 1988. "Numbers, Strategy and the European Balance." *International Security* 12(4): 174–185.

Munro, N., and Cannon, C. M. 2008. "Data Bomb." *National Journal* At: http://news.nationaljournal.com/articles/databomb/index.htm (accessed January 15, 2008).

Nettelfield, Lara J. 2010. "Research and Repercussions of Death Tolls: The Case of the Bosnian Book of the Dead." In *Sex, Drugs, and Body Counts: The Politics of Numbers in Global Crime*, edited by Peter Andreas and Kelly M. Greenhill, 159–187. Ithaca, NY: Cornell University Press.

Philpott, Daniel. 2010a. "Introduction: Searching for Strategy in an Age of Peacebuilding." In *Strategies of Peace: Transforming Conflict in a Violent World*, edited by Daniel Philpott and Gerard F. Powers, 3–18. New York: Oxford University Press.

———. 2010b. "Reconciliation: An Ethic for Peacebuilding." In *Strategies of Peace: Transforming Conflict in a Violent World*, edited by Daniel Philpott and Gerard F. Powers, 91–118. New York: Oxford University Press.

Silva, Romesh, and Patrick Ball. 2007. "The Demography of Conflict-Related Mortality in Timor-Leste (1974–1999): Empirical Quantitative Measurement of Civilian Killings, Disappearances and Famine-Related Deaths." In *Statistical Methods for Human Rights*, edited by Jana Asher, D. Banks, and F. J. Scheuren, 117–140. New York: Springer.

Slim, Hugo. 2008. *Killing Civilians: Method, Madness, and Mortality in War*. New York: Columbia University Press.

Tabeau, Ewa, and Jakub Bijak. 2005. "War-Related Deaths in the 1992–1995 Armed Conflicts in Bosnia and Herzegovina: A Critique of Previous Estimates and Recent Results." *European Journal of Population* 21(2–3): 187–215.

Valentino, Benjamin, Paul Huth, and Dylan Balch-Lindsay. 2004. "'Draining the Sea': Mass Killing and Guerrilla Warfare." *International Organization* 58 (Spring): 375–407.

## NOTES

1. A guesstimate is "an estimate based on a mixture of guesswork and calculation." http://oxforddictionaries.com/definition/guesstimate?view=uk

2. Most of the chapters in this volume discuss civilian mortality, but several chapters also discuss outcomes of violence against civilians in addition to killing and wounding, such as human rights violations and forced migration.

# 2 Significant Numbers
## CIVILIAN CASUALTIES AND STRATEGIC PEACEBUILDING
Taylor B. Seybolt

## Introduction

A prominent argument in the late 1990s held that contemporary wars are more brutal on civilians than were past wars. The specific claim was that wars at the beginning of the twentieth century killed one civilian for every eight soldiers, while wars at the end of the century were killing eight civilians for every soldier (Kaldor 1999, 8). The neat reversal of numbers (1:8, 8:1) was widely repeated in academic and policy publications.[1] It fit well with an argument many observers found appealing, that the post–Cold War world holds pockets of Hobbesian brutishness where "new wars" do not follow established rules and civilians are the primary targets (Kaldor 1999). The more the ratios were cited, the more trusted they became.[2] Subsequent research, however, found no evidence that the ratio of civilians to soldiers killed in war had changed dramatically over time (Murray et al. 2002; Greenhill 2010).[3]

Undoubtedly, civilians are victims of violence in contemporary wars, often intentionally so. Targeting civilians, however, is not a new phenomenon (see chapter 10, by Jewell, Spagat, and Jewell in this volume). Thucydides described Athenian soldiers executing the men and enslaving the women and children during the sack of Melos in 416 B.C.; Genghis Khan would slaughter entire towns in his conquest of Eurasia in the thirteenth century; General Sherman pursued a doctrine of "total war" during the American Civil War in the 1860s; and the British military was infamous for its scorched- earth practices during the Boer War in South Africa at the beginning of the twentieth century. War often has been hell for civilians (Downes 2008).

What is new is widespread concern for the protection and well-being of civilians.[4] There are now laws of war to protect civilians from harm; an international network of humanitarian organizations delivers aid to zones of conflict; and civilian casualties have become an important factor in policy makers' decisions about where, when, and how to respond to violent conflicts.[5] The concern for civilians in conflict is so strong that governments occasionally undertake humanitarian military interventions, at great risk and cost, to protect strangers in distant lands (Wheeler 2000; Seybolt 2007; Weiss 2007).

The two purposes of this chapter are to trace the evolution of legal and political concern for the fate of civilians in wartime and to link civilian casualty recording and estimation to strategic peacebuilding. The next section traces the historical development of norms and rules of war as they relate to civilians, beginning with states' original interest in helping combatants and ending with the current idea that protecting civilians from violence is a universal responsibility. This normative shift has had the effect of increasing the influence of civilian casualty numbers on policy choices, making it all the more important to get the numbers right. The section entitled "Strategic Peacebuilding and Civilian Casualty Numbers" identifies strategic peacebuilding as an ambitious attempt to establish both lasting peace *and* a degree of justice, in part by placing civilian casualties at the center of retributive justice proceedings, such as criminal tribunals, and restorative justice processes, such as truth and reconciliation commissions. In these highly politicized environments, the process of revealing information about civilian losses can be as important as its outcome.

## The Changed Attitude toward Civilian Casualties

Early efforts to draw attention to the human costs of war concerned the plight of combatants. Henri Dunant's description of the suffering of wounded soldiers in the 1859 Battle of Solferino—the bloody affair that was the last major military engagement in the war to unify Italy—launched an advocacy campaign that led to founding the International Committee of the Red Cross (ICRC) and the Geneva Convention on Prisoners of War. In 1898, a six-volume study on likely casualty rates of a renewed war in Europe helped inspire the 1899 Hague International Peace Conference (Gregorian 2001, ix).

The Hague Convention codified five basic normative principles of war, the second, third, fourth, and fifth of which revealed a prevailing attitude that civilians did *not* deserve protection. The first principle held that conduct during war was subject to rules and legal conventions. The second declared that all parties to a conflict, whether invading or defending a country, had legal parity and equal rights. The concept of who constituted a party to the conflict, however, was restricted to professional soldiers and did not extend rights to civilians. The third principle called on belligerents to distinguish between lawful and unlawful combatants. The distinction lent some protection to civilians but only if they offered no resistance to occupation. Even nonmilitary resistance was considered unlawful and could be punished severely. The fourth principle held that the population of an occupied territory should be obedient to a "reasonable" occupier. The fifth principle insisted that the code of war strike a balance between military necessity and humanity. These five principles were intended to specify who had a legitimate claim to combatant status and the rights that went with that status. In effect, they excused violence against civilians unless the population remained completely passive (Nabulsi 2001, 12–18).

Modern international humanitarian law, which *is* intended to protect civilians, is set out in several post–World War II conventions and treaties. The United Nations General Assembly adopted the Convention on the Prevention and Punishment of the Crime of Genocide (known as the Genocide Convention) in December 1948, after a concerted lobbying effort by Raphael Lemkin, the originator of the word "genocide" (Power 2002). Each state signatory to the Genocide Convention is obligated to prevent and punish acts intended to destroy ascriptively defined groups of people. The convention is intended to protect people, but it neither addresses the rights of individuals nor distinguishes combatants from civilians.

The 1949 Geneva Convention on the Protection of Civilians (the Fourth Geneva Convention) recognized civilians as a category distinct from combatants and noncombatants (e.g., captured soldiers) with rights that previously had been extended only to states and their agents. The Fourth Geneva Convention explicitly banned many of the practices previously used to punish civilians who resisted occupation, such as deportation, collective punishment, and torture (Johnson 2000; Nabulsi 2001, 18–19). The legal protection afforded to civilians and noncivilians by the Geneva Conventions applied only to international wars.

As wars within states became more common than those between states (a change discernible as early as the 1950s), governments saw the need to amend the legal basis for the protection of civilians. In 1977, Additional Protocols I and II of the Geneva Conventions extended the rules of war to intrastate conflicts. Additional Protocol II made it a war crime to indiscriminately attack civilians and the physical infrastructure that they need to survive. Although it did not replace the principle of balancing military necessity with humanity, Additional Protocol II continued the trend toward greater emphasis on humane treatment of people who have not taken up arms.

The niceties of formal agreements do not, of course, guarantee actual protection for civilians in conflict. Ample evidence can be found in the unimaginably inhumane conflicts in the Democratic Republic of the Congo, 1996–2012, and northern Uganda, 1986–2009, where rebel and government forces killed entire villages, used rape as a weapon, and taught children to kill other children. The limited efficacy of formal agreements to control behavior, especially of non-state actors who are not signatories of the Geneva Conventions or their Additional Protocols, has led to efforts to enforce legal and normative standards of behavior and, on occasion, to physically protect civilians (Holt 2006).

With the end of the bipolar balance of power and threat between the United States and the Soviet Union in 1989, the UN Security Council enforced the new liberal internationalist agenda by authorizing multinational military interventions to help feed and protect civilians in the Kurdish area of Iraq (1991), Somalia (1992), and Bosnia and Herzegovina (Bosnia) (1992).[6] In 1991, the United States, the United Kingdom, and France set a precedent when their military forces provided food, water, shelter, and protection to Kurds stranded along the mountainous border between Iraq and Turkey after fleeing Iraqi government attacks. Operation Provide Comfort (as the Americans called it) promoted the strategic interest of weakening Saddam Hussein and was also a response to public pressure to help desperate people whose plight was broadcast on the evening news. By way of comparison, Shia communities in southern Iraq rebelled and were violently suppressed at roughly the same time. International television cameras did not broadcast their plight and there was no intervention to protect them, even though protecting the Shia could also have weakened Saddam and military assets were already in the region. In 1992, the United States led a multilateral military effort to support humanitarian aid operations in Somalia. The intervening countries justified their action on humanitarian grounds and, indeed, one is hard pressed to find any national security interests at stake.[7] Beginning that same year and lasting until 1995, European countries operating through the United Nations led humanitarian protection efforts in Bosnia (Seybolt 2007).

Skeptical observers argued that humanitarian intervention in the early 1990s was a short-lived manifestation of a "unipolar moment" after the fall of the Soviet Union, when the United States was free to flex its muscle and push its idealism (Krauthammer 1990/1991). That critique appears to have been wrong. Numerous governments, usually with UN authorization, have continued to use military intervention as a policy instrument to protect people from violence and privation.

In 1999, NATO engaged in its first-ever combat operation, designed to drive Serbian military units out of the province of Kosovo, on the grounds that the majority Albanian population was in imminent danger of being attacked by the Serbian government. Australian military intervention stopped Indonesian militia groups from attacking the civilian population in Timor-Leste (known at the time as East Timor) after the people voted for independence from Indonesia in 1999; the European Union conducted "Operation Artemis" in 2003 to protect civilians from rebel and militia groups vying for political and territorial control in the east of the Democratic Republic of the Congo; and the joint United Nations–African Union operation in Darfur, Sudan received a civilian protection mandate from the Security Council in 2007, in response to widespread attacks on civilians.

Twenty years after the end of the Cold War, military intervention for the stated purpose of helping a population under threat looks less like a historical aberration and more like an accepted practice. This shift reflects a sustained and dramatic change in the status of civilians from being legitimate targets of violence to having the right to protection

(Wheeler 2000; Teitel 2001). That right to be protected from widespread, systematic violence, and the corresponding responsibility of governments to provide that protection, is articulated in *The Responsibility to Protect* (R2P) report, published by the multi-country International Commission on Intervention and State Sovereignty (ICISS 2001).

The ICISS report responded to Secretary-General Kofi Annan's challenge to UN member-states that they resolve the tension between the nonintervention principle associated with state sovereignty and the need to protect the basic human rights of people in extreme danger. The report takes the usual concept of sovereignty as imparting rights to the state, especially the right to nonintervention, and turns it around so that the sovereign right to nonintervention is predicated on the state fulfilling its responsibility to protect its population. If a government manifestly fails to do so, then the responsibility to protect devolves to other governments acting with authorization from the UN (ICISS 2001). Although the responsibility to protect is not legally codified, 191 heads of state signed the United Nations World Summit Outcome Document in 2005, part of which specifies governments' responsibility to protect their own people and to offer assistance or impose order, by force if necessary, when another government fails to fulfill its responsibility (United Nations General Assembly 2005).

When the Security Council authorized multilateral military intervention in Libya in 2011 "to protect civilians and civilian populated areas under threat of attack" by the Libyan military (United Nations Security Council 2011), it was "the first time the Council had authorized the use of force for human protection purposes against the wishes of a functioning state" (Bellamy and Williams 2011, 825). It is not possible to know at this point whether a consensus will develop on the use of force for civilian protection purposes, but, as Bellamy and Williams (at 826) note, there is no doubt that "international society is now explicitly focused on civilian protection."

Although international legal and normative standards for the treatment of civilians in war have changed significantly over the past century, there is no consensus about the obligations of warring parties when they do, nonetheless, harm civilians. State signatories to the Geneva Conventions and Additional Protocols are legally bound to minimize that harm. However, international humanitarian law is silent. The military actor that has been responsible for harming civilians can still simply walk away.

There are at least two substantial efforts to push civilian rights beyond current international legal safeguards, each undertaken by a coalition of nongovernmental organizations and recognized by intergovernmental organizations. One argues that governments that adhere to international law must acknowledge the civilians they kill and make monetary amends to the victims' families. UN Secretary-General Ban Ki-moon highlighted the concept in a formal Statement to the Security Council in December 2010. All NATO member-states have agreed to abide by this new standard, and coalition forces in Afghanistan and Iraq have implemented compensation programs (CIVIC, n.d.). The other initiative, called the "Every Casualty Campaign," calls on every government to go beyond established legal obligations and to fully report on all people killed in armed violence, using transparent, agreed-upon recording mechanisms, a call that the editors of this volume support (see the concluding chapter; Every Casualty Campaign 2012).

In summary, over the past century, the status of civilians in war has changed such that people who had no legal standing now possess rights that (in principle) begin to rival those accorded to states. However, although belligerents now have an obligation to avoid causing civilian casualties, the human costs of war have limited political or legal resonance in the absence of reliable data. In the pithy (and somewhat hyperbolic) phrase of Andreas and Greenhill (2010, 1), "if something is not measured it does not exist, if it is not counted it does not count." Now, more than ever, civilian casualties are counted (or estimated) and they do count.

## Strategic Peacebuilding and Civilian Casualty Numbers

The concept of peacebuilding is even younger and less well developed than the idea that civilians have a right to protection from violence during war. Depending on whom one consults, the core purpose of peacebuilding ranges from minimal prevention of renewed violence to expansive efforts addressing the root causes of conflict and promoting justice. UN Secretary-General Boutros Boutros-Ghali's seminal essay, *An Agenda for Peace*, published after the United Nations began its post–Cold War activism, declared that peacebuilding's purpose is "to identify and support structures which will tend to strengthen and solidify peace in order to avoid a relapse into [violent] conflict" (Secretary-General 1992, para. 21). Practitioners soon expanded beyond his emphasis on preventing renewed conflict to include efforts to promote equity, justice, and political and social reforms, on the grounds that such reforms would address the deeper reasons for conflict. This more ambitious "multidimensional peacebuilding" had the benefit of recognizing the many problems that societies face as they emerge from periods of violence within a state; the approach, however, was plagued by an inability to set priorities among overlapping and occasionally contradictory objectives (Call and Cousens 2007).

Seeking to make peacebuilding more effective, concerned parties began to concentrate on "institutional peacebuilding" with a "modicum of participatory politics" (Call and Cousens 2007, 4). The institutional approach emphasizes setting standards to guide resource allocation and to evaluate the success or failure of missions, with observers and practitioners focusing on building states' capacity to control violence, demobilize combatants, reform security forces (Stedman et al. 2002; Paris 2004; Toft 2009), and strengthen the rule of law (Stromseth et al. 2006).

Advocates of strategic peacebuilding criticize the institutional "peace from above" approach for focusing on the actions of intergovernmental institutions, national governments, and warring parties, to the exclusion of local and nongovernmental actors. Strategic peacebuilding seeks to deepen the engagement of indigenous actors whose involvement extends beyond a "modicum of participatory politics." This "holistic" approach requires peacebuilding missions to fit the political, economic, cultural, and religious beliefs and interests of a society emerging from violence, and to link actors operating at international, national, and local levels (Philpott 2010). Fletcher and Weinstein's (2002) "ecological model" explicitly ties post-conflict peace to social reconstruction measures that mend relationships between individuals, communities, and societal groups. In a similar vein, Lederach and Appleby (2011) propose culturally grounded processes of justice and reconciliation as the cornerstones of peacebuilding.

The holism of strategic peacebuilding requires strategic linking measures that connect actors operating at international, national, and local levels (Philpott 2010). Investigating civilian casualties can be such a measure, because accounting for the dead and missing is a central concern to international prosecutors, national governments, and survivors. Civilian casualty recording and estimation can link local and international actors and interests in many ways, with the most prominent being observed when political and military leaders appear in criminal court on charges of war crimes or crimes against humanity (a form of retributive justice) and when a truth and reconciliation commission seeks to establish a commonly accepted narrative of events (a form of restorative justice).

Stakeholders concerned about casualties need not have shared objectives. As several chapters in this volume demonstrate, casualty numbers often are invented for political expediency, making the uncertainties and disagreements inherent in recording and estimating a source of conflict rather than a contribution to peace. To minimize the chance that their work will be used to obstruct peacebuilding, researchers need to make it scientifically sound, transparent, and publicly accountable.

National, international, and hybrid criminal tribunals have become a preferred way to hold individuals accountable for their actions and decisions during conflict. During the 46 years from 1945 to 1990, there were 24 trials for people accused of political injustice; during the 17 years between 1990 and 2006, there were 38 (Vinjamuri cited in Philpott 2012, 209 and 325). Although most trials have been domestic, legal precedents for retributive justice were established after World War II during the trials of Nazi officials. The Nuremburg trials held individuals accountable for actions that had been previously defined solely as state crimes of aggression. Furthermore, the Nuremburg Charter recognized that the crime of aggression could be against "any civilian populations," thus establishing that people are deserving of legal protection independent of their state (Teitel 2011, 76–77). The principle that individuals can be put on trial if their actions and decisions implicate them in crimes against humanity came to the fore again half a century later, with the International Criminal Tribunal for the Former Yugoslavia (ICTY), a United Nations court of law established in 1993. When it created the ICTY, the Security Council explicitly linked peace and retributive justice by making reference to Chapter VII of the United Nations Charter, the only part of the Charter that provides for enforcement (79). By 2012, six ad hoc international and hybrid tribunals had been established; in 2002, the International Criminal Court (ICC) became a standing body.[8]

Criminal trials for atrocity crimes require information about civilian deaths and other egregious human rights violations. In a trial setting, the accuracy of that information can make the difference between accountability and impunity. For example, the separatist conflict that pitted the Serbian government against the majority-Albanian population in the province of Kosovo prompted NATO to intervene with a bombing campaign supporting the separatists. The conflict caused masses of Kosovar Albanians to flee across international borders into Albania and Macedonia, where they stayed as refugees until NATO prevailed upon the Serbian military to allow them to return to Kosovo. During the ICTY trial of Serbian President Slobodan Milosevic for war crimes, crimes against humanity, and ethnic cleansing, the defendant insisted that Kosovars fled because of NATO bombing and not because of actions taken by Serbian military units. The Office of the Chief Prosecutor commissioned a rigorous statistical analysis that disproved Milosevic's claim and showed Serbian actions to be strongly correlated with waves of killing and refugee flows (Ball et al. 2002).

The Milosevic trial also showed that evidence judged to be erroneous or weakly supported can be dismissed or even have the opposite of its intended effect. The chief prosecutor, Carla Del Ponte, accused Milosevic of being responsible for the deaths of thousands of Kosovars, in addition to the forced migration already mentioned. The expectation was that forensic investigation would yield evidence of the deaths of 10,000 or more people, the number commonly accepted in NATO countries during the political campaign for military intervention against the Serbian government. Ultimately, the ICTY declared the number of bodies found in Kosovo to be 2,788, a tragic toll but considerably lower than the 10,000 figure, which proved to be a conjecture based on unsubstantiated reports. Milosevic used that discrepancy to discredit a key prosecution witness, a Kosovar journalist who had reported a massacre, but was later quoted as saying his report "was a supposition, it was not confirmed information" (Greenhill 2010, 154–155).

Trials focus on defendants' responsibility for those deaths for which the prosecutor has the strongest case, which may omit the loved ones of many families. Moreover, for local actors seeking reconciliation, trials may be a secondary concern or even an obstacle, if the adversarial nature of a trial evokes disputatious, partisan framing of the issues. Weinstein and Stover (2004) found that international actors' preoccupation with formal trials of suspected war criminals in Bosnia and Rwanda failed to address the concerns of people who had lived through the violence and faced the challenge of rebuilding their lives alongside their erstwhile enemies.

Truth and reconciliation commissions, which are official bodies but not courts of law, have become a prominent method for seeking society-wide reconciliation. Between 1974 and 2011, 40 truth commissions were convened, 22 of them since the year 2000 (Hayner 2011, xi–xii). Many commissions were deeply flawed, such as the 1974 Commission of Inquiry into the Disappearance of People in Uganda, which whitewashed Idi Amin's dictatorship. Others, though, such as the 1997–1999 Commission for Historical

Clarification in Guatemala, have succeeded in revealing hidden information and holding perpetrators of abuses accountable for their actions. Where they are properly framed and conducted, truth commissions draw on public testimony and scientific investigation of past violations of human rights to reveal and officially acknowledge a comprehensive account of who the victims were; where and when they died, disappeared, or suffered abuse; and who was responsible for the abuses (Hayner 2011).

There is no definitive study on the impact of truth commissions on peacebuilding, and some scholars doubt their efficacy. Mendeloff (2004) questions their core assumptions that truth telling promotes reconciliation, that repressing information makes further conflict more likely, and that a commission's purpose is to reveal the truth. Daly (2008) doubts that "the truth" will reconcile people holding different views in deeply divided societies. If so, then even the best evidence may not help.

People often do not know, or hold misconceptions about, the extent of violence during civil wars; moreover, the human toll of political conflicts is often unknown, given restrictions on news reporting that prevent awareness of events, as well as the silencing of official and unofficial sources. In Peru, for example, the 20-year conflict between the Shining Path guerrilla movement and the national military was believed to have killed over 69,000 people, more than all the country's other wars combined. Nonetheless, the extent of the violence remained unknown to most people in the capital, Lima,[9] until information revealed by the Peruvian Truth and Reconciliation Commission provided evidence of culpability of the government and the rebels (Truth and Reconciliation Commission 2003). Such official recognition might help to sustain peace in the continuing contest for political power and legitimacy, while addressing victims' need for acknowledgment (Hayner 2011).

In cases like Peru, where the objective is restorative justice rather than retribution, the very act of creating records and estimates of those who died can be as important as the accuracy of the final numbers produced. Roht-Arriaza (2010) argues that when such a process includes the local population and accepts imperfect knowledge, it can facilitate reconciliation through shared understanding of recent traumatic events. For communities that experienced the trauma, using the evidence to acknowledge past trauma that had been denied can be more important than pursuit of scientifically rigorous results. The Peruvian commission exhumed only a few of the mass graves in the Ayacucho region; but even those few allowed widows to openly mourn for the first time, while making it harder for the government and the rebels to deny past wrongs (Truth and Reconciliation Commission 2003; York 2007).

In Timor-Leste, conflicting local and national priorities created profound differences in the treatment of casualties. In January 1999, Indonesian President B. J. Habibie announced that he would permit a referendum in East Timor to determine if the former Portuguese colony would remain part of Indonesia or become an independent country. The Indonesian military, an important political player with vested economic interests in East Timor, established, trained, and directed local militia groups in a campaign of intimidation designed to prevent that referendum. When an overwhelming majority of the population voted for independence in June 1999, the violence escalated, leading to a UN-authorized, Australian-led military intervention to protect the East Timorese people. One of the new country's first acts was to set up a truth and reconciliation commission (United Nations 1999;,2000).

The Commission for Reception, Truth, and Reconciliation (known by its Portuguese acronym CAVR) was an internationally supported, culturally sensitive undertaking seeking to establish a unified narrative of the past as a way to heal wounds, hold violent offenders accountable, and lay the foundation for a functioning polity. One of the commission's core aims was seeking the truth about who did what to whom during the period from the end of Portuguese colonial rule in 1974 through the end of the turmoil following the referendum, documenting human rights violations of *all* sides—the Indonesian government forces, pro-Indonesia militia, and separatist rebels. Its work included both recording statements of individuals who volunteered to tell their stories and conducting a retrospective mortality survey, drawing population estimates from a random sample (Commission 2005).

The truth-seeking effort responded to the Timorese desire to recognize their suffering. The CAVR was problematic from the perspective of quantifying what happened during the 25-year period of Indonesian control. As discussed by Krüger, Ball, Price, and Green (chapter 12, this volume), data collected through witness statements differed substantially from inferences drawn from a survey in terms both the number and timing of deaths.[10] Those discrepancies imply different causes and sources of the deaths of thousands of people. Testimony to the Truth Commission indicated that violent and nonviolent (e.g., hunger and disease) causes accounted for roughly equal numbers of deaths, whereas the retrospective mortality survey indicated the more people died from hunger and disease than from violence (Krüger et al, this volume; Commission for Reception, Truth, and Reconciliation Timor-Leste 2005).

Rather than being troubled by the discrepancy, however, stakeholders accepted both sets of information as valid and meaningful. The process of discovery producing the testimony gave local communities—"the most critical constituencies for peacebuilding" (Richmond 2010, 357)—a meaningful role, thereby making possible reconciliation at the local level. Statistical analyses using multiple systems estimation—drawing on the survey and other data—provided complementary information on patterns and causes of mortality over time (see chapter 9 by Manrique-Vallier, Price, and Gohdes in this volume).

In this light, civilian casualty estimates represent more than just technical efforts to get accurate numbers. Rather, they enable individuals to understand the nature and causes of a conflict and the roles that various actors played in it. Accurate numbers, produced in transparent ways, with candid acknowledgments of potential error and limits can reduce the chance of politically determined figures becoming social facts. Accurate, trustworthy casualty records and numbers cannot by themselves avoid renewed violence.

But lack of them, and the story they tell about past abuses, can contribute to future conflict, as biased interpretations keep resentment smoldering (see chapter 11 in this volume by Tabeau and Zwierzchowski). Accountability and truth telling require information that is accurate, available, and accepted as legitimate.

## Conclusion

Discrepant claims about casualties are by no means always due to methodological differences, as they were in the Timor-Leste investigations. Parties to a conflict frequently seek to shape the numbers and beliefs about the causes behind them because they know the results can have serious consequences in the realms of politics, justice, and social reconstruction. They want the "facts" to support their political, legal, or social claims. The more we care about civilian casualties, the greater the incentive for rival parties to hide evidence of massacres and other atrocities.

People usually emerge from conflict with biased interpretations of events that are based on their traumatic experiences and the limited information to which they have access. Those who live through violent conflict often tell stories within the confines of their families and communities about "what they did to us." These stories are crafted to justify the behavior of the narrator and his or her community during wartime and to vilify the actions of the other side. Accurate and transparent accounts of civilian casualties can disrupt the cycle of violence by establishing a less politicized body of information that holds each side accountable for what its members did and recognizes the suffering both sides endured. Getting the data right on who did what to whom makes it possible to engage political interests in a manner that provides a context for sustainable peace, rendering future vengeance less likely.

REFERENCES

Andreas, Peter, and Kelly M. Greenhill, eds. 2010. *Sex, Drugs, and Body Counts: The Politics of Numbers in Global Crime*. Ithaca, NY: Cornell University Press.

Asher, Jana, David L. Banks, and Fritz Scheuren. 2007. *Statistical Methods for Human Rights*. New York: Springer.

Ball, Patrick, et al. 2002. *Killings and Refugee Flow in Kosovo, March–June 1999: A Report to the International Criminal Tribunal for the Former Yugoslavia*. Washington, DC: American Association for the Advancement of Science/American Bar Association Central and East European Law Initiative.

Bellamy, Alex J., and Paul D. Williams. 2011. "The new politics of protection? Côte d'Ivoire, Libya and the responsibility to protect." *International Affairs* 87(4): 825–50.

Call, Charles T., and Elizabeth M. Cousens. 2007. "Ending Wars and Building Peace: International Responses to War-Torn Societies." *International Studies Perspectives* 9 (February): 1–21.

CIVIC (Campaign for Innocent Victims in Conflict). At: http://civiliansinconflict.org/who-we-are/our-impact (accessed December 21, 2012).

Commission for Reception, Truth, and Reconciliation Timor-Leste. 2005. *Chega! The Report of the Commission for Reception, Truth, and Reconciliation Timor-Leste*. Timor-Leste. At: http://www.cavr-timorleste.org/ (accessed July 9, 2012).

Daly, Erin. 2008. "Truth Skepticism: An Inquiry into the Value of Truth in Times of Transition." *International Journal of Transitional Justice* 2: 23–41.

Downes, Alexander B. 2008. *Targeting Civilians in War*. Ithaca, NY: Cornell University Press.

Elliott, Michael A. 2011. "The institutional expansion of human rights, 1863–2003: A comprehensive dataset of international instruments." *Journal of Peace Research* 48 (4): 537–46.

Every Casualty Campaign. At: http://everycasualty.org/about (accessed July 9, 2012).

Fletcher, Laurel E., and Harvey M. Weinstein. 2002. "Violence and Social Repair: Rethinking the Contribution of Justice to Reconciliation." *Human Rights Quarterly* 24: 573–639.

Greenhill, Kelly M. 2010. "Counting the Cost: The Politics of Numbers in Armed Conflicts." In *Sex, Drugs, and Body Counts: The Politics of Numbers in Global Crime and Conflict*, edited by Peter Andreas and Kelly M. Greenhill, 127–158. Ithaca, NY: Cornell University Press.

Gregorian, Vartan, foreword to *Civilians in War*, by Simon Chesterman, pp. ix–xiv. Boulder, CO: Lynne Rienner Publishers, 2001.

Guha-Sapir, Debra, and Olivier Degomme. 2007. *Estimating Mortality in Civil Conflicts: Lessons from Iraq: Triangulating Different Types of Mortality Data in Iraq*. Brussels: Centre for Research on the Epidemiology of Disasters.

Hall, Katharine, and Dale Stahl. 2006. *An Argument for Documenting Casualties: Violence against Iraqi Civilians*. Washington, DC: RAND.

Hayner, Priscilla B. 2011. *Unspeakable Truths: Transitional Justice and the Challenge of Truth Commissions*. New York: Routledge.

Holt, Victoria. 2006. *The Impossible Mandate? Military Preparedness, the Responsibility to Protect and Modern Peace Operations*. Washington. DC: The Henry L. Stimson Center.

Human Security Report Project. 2005. *Human Security Report 2005: War and Peace in the 21st Century*. Vancouver: University of British Columbia, Human Security Centre.

———. 2011. *Human Security Report 2009/2010: The Causes of Peace and the Shrinking Costs of War*. New York: Oxford University Press.

ICISS (International Commission on Intervention and State Sovereignty). 2001. *The Responsibility to Protect Report of the International Commission on Intervention and State Sovereignty*. Ottawa: International Development Research Centre.

Johnson, James Turner. 2000. "Maintaining the Protection of Non-Combatants." *Journal of Peace Research* 37: 421–48.

Kaldor, Mary. 1999. *New and Old Wars: Organized Violence in a Global Era*. Stanford, CA: Stanford University Press.

Krauthammer, Charles. 1990/1991. "The Unipolar Moment." *Foreign Affairs* 70 (1): 23–33.

Lederach, John Paul, and R. Scott Appleby. 2011. "Strategic Peacebuilding: An Overview." In *Strategies of Peace: Transforming Conflict in a Violent World*, edited by Daniel Philpott and Gerard F. Powers, 19–44. New York: Oxford University Press.

Mendeloff, David. 2004. "Truth Seeking, Truth Telling and Postconflict Peacebuilding: Curb the Enthusiasm?" *International Studies Review* 6: 355–380.

Murray, Christopher, et al. 2002. "Armed Conflict as a Public Health Problem." *British Medical Journal* 324: 346–349.

Nabulsi, Karma. 2001. "Evolving Conceptions of Civilians and Belligerents: One Hundred Years After the Hague Peace Conferences." In *Civilians in War*. Edited by Simon Chesterman. Boulder, CO: Lynne Rienner Publishers.

Nettelfield, Lara J. 2010. "Research and Repercussions of Death Tolls: The Case of the Bosnian Book of the Dead." In *Sex, Drugs, and Body Counts: The Politics of Numbers in Global Crime*, edited by Peter Andreas and Kelly M. Greenhill, 159–187. Ithaca, NY: Cornell University Press.

Obermeyer, Ziad, Christopher J. L. Murray, and Emmanuela Gakidou. 2008. "Fifty Years of Violent War Deaths from Vietnam to Bosnia: Analysis of Data from the World Health Organization Survey Programme." *British Medical Journal* 336: 1482–1486.

Paris, Roland. 2004. *After War's End*. New York: Cambridge University Press.

Philpott, Daniel. 2010. "Introduction: Searching for Strategy in an Age of Peacebuilding." In *Strategies of Peace: Transforming Conflict in a Violent World*, edited by Daniel Philpott and Gerard F. Powers, 3–18. New York: Oxford University Press.

———. 2012. *Just and Unjust Peace: An Ethic of Political Reconciliation*. New York: Oxford University Press.

Power, Samantha. 2002. *"A Problem from Hell": America and the Age of Genocide*. New York: Harper Perennial.

Richmond, Gerard F. 2010. "Conclusion: Strategic Peacebuilding beyond the Liberal Process." In *Strategies of Peace: Transforming Conflict in a Violent World*, edited by Daniel Philpott and Gerard F. Powers, 353–368. New York: Oxford University Press.

Roht-Arriaza, Naomi. 2010. "Human Rights and Strategic Peacebuilding: The Roles of Local, National and International Actors." In *Strategies of Peace: Transforming Conflict in a Violent World*, edited by Daniel Philpott and Gerard F. Powers, 231–246. New York: Oxford University Press.

Secretary-General. 1992. "An Agenda for Peace: Preventive Diplomacy, Peacemaking and Peace-keeping." At: http://www.un.org/Docs/SG/agpeace.html (accessed July 9, 2012).

Seybolt, Taylor B. 2007. *Humanitarian Military Intervention: The Conditions for Success and Failure*. Oxford: Oxford University Press.

Stedman, Stephen John, Donald Rothchild, and Elizabeth M. Cousens. 2002. *Ending Civil Wars: The Implementation of Peace Agreements*. Boulder, CO: Lynne Rienner Publishers.

Stromseth, Jane, David Wippman, and Rosa Brooks. 2006. *Can Might Make Rights? Building the Rule of Law after Military Interventions*. New York: Cambridge University Press.

Teitel, Ruti G. 2011. *Humanity's Law*. New York: Oxford University Press.

Toft, Monica Duffy. 2009. *Securing the Peace: The Durable Settlement of Civil Wars*. Princeton, NJ: Princeton University Press.

Truth and Reconciliation Commission (Comisión de la Verdad y Reconciliación, CVR). 2003. *Final Report*. Online at http://www.cverdad.org.pe/ingles/ifinal/index.php. (accessed July 9, 2012).

United Nations. 1999. "Secretary-General Calls for Immediate End to Escalation of Violence by All Sides in East Timor." *United Nations Press Release*, SG/SM/6961. April 19.

———. 2000. *Millennium Report of the Secretary-General of the United Nations*. New York: United Nations Department of Public Information.

United Nations General Assembly. 2005. "Resolution adopted by the General Assembly 60/1 [2005 World Summit Outcome]." A/RES/60/1. October 24.

United Nations Security Council. 2011. Resolution 1973. S/Res/1973. March 17.

Uppsala Conflict Data Program. At: http://www.pcr.uu.se/research/ucdp/program_overview/about_ucdp/ (accessed July 9, 2012).

Weinstein, Harvey M., and Eric Stover. 2004. "Introduction: Conflict, Justice and Reclamation." In *My Neighbor, My Enemy: Justice and Community in the Aftermath of Mass Atrocity*, edited by Eric Stover and Harvey M. Weinstein, 1–26. Cambridge: Cambridge University Press.

Weiss, Thomas. 2007. *Humanitarian Intervention: Ideas in Action*. New York: Polity Press.

Wheeler, Nicholas J. 2000. *Saving Strangers: Humanitarian Intervention in International Society*. New York: Oxford University Press.

York, Steve. 2007. "Confronting the Truth: Truth Commissions and Societies in Transition." Documentary film. 72 minutes. York Zimmerman Inc., July.

NOTES

1. The ratio is sometimes presented as 1:9 and 9:1.

2. People have a psychological tendency to "anchor" their beliefs on the first number they see or hear, especially if the number is sensational. Once anchored, a piece of information becomes a "social fact" that persists even when more reliable, more accurate information is available (Andreas and Greenhill 2010, 17).

3. There is a debate about the trend in the overall deadliness of war that is distinct from the issue of the civilian/combatant mortality ratio. Data collection projects engaged in the deadliness of war debate either do not distinguish between civilians and combatants (Obermeyer et al. 2008) or count only combatants (Uppsala/PRIO, annual).

4. Despite the influence of civilian casualty estimates on important policy decisions, little has been written on the subject (Hall and Stahl 2006; Asher, Banks, and Scheuren 2007; Guha-Sapir and Degomme 2007).

5. Attention to violence against civilians in conflict zones is one aspect of the broader expansion of human rights. Elliott (2011) has documented the institutionalization of human rights from 1863 to 2003 by compiling a dataset of 779 human rights instruments.

6. Three military interventions during the Cold War are cited, in retrospect, as humanitarian in effect although at the time the intervening countries justified their actions on national security grounds. India intervened when East Pakistan broke away to become Bangladesh in 1971; Tanzania overthrew Ugandan president Idi Amin in 1979; and Vietnam defeated the Khmer Rouge regime in Cambodia in 1979 (Wheeler 2000).

7. Some of the countries that contributed troops might have seen a national security advantage in responding positively to the request for assistance of the remaining superpower.

8. The list includes the International Criminal Tribunal for Rwanda, and hybrid national-international courts in Cambodia, East Timor, Kosovo, Lebanon, and Sierra Leone.

9. "The TRC has established that the tragedy suffered by the populations of rural Peru, the Andean and jungle regions, Quechua and Ashaninka Peru, the peasant, poor and poorly educated Peru, was neither felt nor taken on as its own by the rest of the country. This demonstrates, in the TRC's judgment, the veiled racism and scornful attitudes that persist in Peruvian society almost two centuries after its birth as a Republic." *Final Report of the Truth and Reconciliation Commission* (Comisión de la Verdad y Reconciliación, CVR). 2003. Conclusion, paragraph 9, English edition.

10. The retrospective mortality survey was done for CAVR by Patrick Ball and his colleagues at Benetech.

# 3 The Politics of Civilian Casualty Counts
Jay D. Aronson

POLICY MAKERS, MILITARY officials, scientists, statisticians, and human rights activists involved in the debate over civilian casualty recording and estimation in times of conflict seem to be able to agree on only one thing without hesitation: war regrettably kills innocent people. It is difficult if not impossible to achieve consensus on how many noncombatants have died in a given conflict, on whether it is possible to know how many die in the short term or even in the long term, on whether international law mandates an effort to count civilian deaths, and on the possible implications of these deaths for the peacebuilding process. One reason for this situation, as can be seen throughout this volume, is that there are strong differences of opinion about the validity and reliability of methods and techniques used to record and estimate casualties.

Another and equally important reason is that counting people, whether dead or alive, is an inherently political undertaking (Anderson 1988; Kertzer and Arel 2002). Politics play a major role in answering questions about which methods are used, who gets counted, who does the counting, and how the counts will be interpreted and used to distribute resources or apportion blame (see, e.g., Anderson and Fienberg 1977; Kertzer and Arel 2002). Thus, counting not only is relevant to the study of social problems but is also a social problem in and of itself. As sociologists Aryn Martin and Michael Lynch note:

The work of counting involves determination of what counts as a possible object [to be] counted. Such determination often occurs at the very same time that a count is produced, contested, and reproduced. To count something is to make it accountable as a member in a class of relevant objects. In this sense of the word, "counting" is both a calculative operation in which numbers are used, and also a case-by-case determination of what to count and, correlatively, of what counts as something to be counted, (Martin and Lynch 2009, 246)

None of this should be surprising, for the process of quantifying and producing estimates has always been this way. Statistics as we know it today is largely a product of the modern bureaucratic state and is integral to its functioning (Porter 1996; Desroisieres 1998; Scott 1998). Numbers are meant to convince skeptical or adversarial citizens and decision makers that a particular course of action is the best one from an objective point of view (Porter 1996). Thus, those who are able to control the production of numbers control the public discourse and policy debates. But the corollary is also true: policy discussions can be altered when the state refuses to produce numbers, when it does not cooperate with the production of useful numbers by others, or when it contests or casts doubt upon the numbers that have been produced by others to influence policy. This, in essence, is the production of "official ignorance" (Mathews 2005; Proctor and Scheibinger 2008).

Making things even messier, casualty counts have a tendency to take on a life of their own when they are made public (McArdle 2008; Greenhill 2010). Stakeholders such as the media, politicians, military officials, activists, and scientists may choose to downplay or prominently publicize a count, depending on its value to their particular goals and imperatives. They may also choose to overlook or to highlight the complexity, uncertainty, and methodological shortcomings associated with a particular count in order to meet their own objectives, whether these be purely scientific, purely political, or (most likely) both at the same time. Stakeholders and citizens may latch onto the first number they hear and refuse to believe that any other number may be correct. Further, it is often difficult to determine whether support for, or critique of, a particular casualty count is rooted chiefly in politics, science, or simply faith. Yet this is precisely the determination that both policy makers and the public must make when deciding whether to accept contested casualty counts. It also offers clues to why the kind of "closure" that occurs in most technical controversies is rarely reached in the context of civilian casualties in conflict.

This chapter examines the politics of casualty counting in four recent conflicts: the 1991 Gulf War, the 1992–1995 war in Bosnia and Herzegovina (Bosnia), the Iraq War since the U.S.-led invasion of 2003, and the conflict in Darfur that has been under way since 2003. These cases were chosen because in each one, disputes about the number of civilians killed became integral to public discourse, and political decision making, about the conflict. Casualty counts in these four cases have been subjected to the intense scrutiny of politicians, journalists, human rights advocates, political scientists, and the casualty-counting community itself, making it possible to use them to illuminate some of the leading methodological and political concerns that dominate contemporary debate.

Additional research is needed to determine the extent to which casualty counts that do not generate intense public debate differ from the ones described in this chapter.

Each case will highlight the various ways that politics played a role in the production of casualty records and estimates. Sometimes the influence of politics is overt—for example, the decision by the American military, particularly since Vietnam, not to report casualty statistics in war or the refusal of the Bosnian government to accept lower estimates of Bosniak (Bosnian Muslim) mortality after the Balkan Wars of the 1990s. At other times, the influence of politics is more subtle—in a researcher's decision to use one recording or estimation method over other available options, for example, or in the preference of a government agency or media outlet for one casualty count over another when there are many plausible choices, as in the Darfur conflict. It is important to note from the outset that political influence does not automatically lead to inaccuracy or an inherent lack of scientific reliability. It is often the case that political motivations can lead to greater accuracy and more reliability, as in Bosnia.

Ultimately, consumers of casualty statistics, including the media, the military, decision makers, and the public, must understand the political dimensions of the numbers with which they are presented in order to properly analyze and interpret them. It is usually just as important to know why a particular casualty count has been produced (or not) as it is to know how the particular number was generated.

## Case Study 1: Bosnia and the Balkans

The story of casualty counting in the Balkan Wars of the 1990s actually begins in the aftermath of World War II, when Marshal Josip Broz Tito sought to unite the various national groups present in the Balkan region into a single republic, the Socialist Federal Republic of Yugoslavia. In an effort to make integration proceed smoothly, and to ensure that the diverse populace would work together, Tito and his advisers not only created a national historical narrative that made the Socialist Yugoslavia seem natural and inevitable, but also sought to dole out equally to all national groups praise and blame for earlier problems in the region (Banac 1992). Atrocities committed by one group against another in World War I and World War II were downplayed in the official histories of the fledgling country (Verdery 1999), and class antagonism tended to be emphasized over ethnic or religious tensions. And when it came to producing an official body count from World War II, Tito and his advisers submitted the inflated number of 1.7 million to the International Reparations Commission in order to extract significant payment from Germany. They did not, however, elaborate on the number or provide much evidence about how it was calculated. Further, while vague and general monuments were erected to the collective dead, the losses of families, communities, and ethnic/nationalist groups went unrecognized.

According to historians of Yugoslavia, most notably Ivo Banac, this historical fiction and the Yugoslav state held together under the rule of Tito but began to dissolve after his death in March 1980. Nationalist leaders and historians from the federal republics who had been marginalized during Tito's rule began to openly question the dominant Communist accounts of World War II and its aftermath. Serbian nationalists began to wonder out loud how many of their people had been killed by the Croatian Ustaša government during the war.[1] Bosnian Muslims (Bosniaks) asked how many of their people had been killed by Serbian "chetniks."[2] And Croats sought to show that they had been victimized in large numbers by "communists." As Verdery (1999), Ballinger (2003), Denich (1994), and Hayden (1994) all point out, by the late 1980s and early 1990s, nationalist leaders from each group were organizing exhumations and reburials of the remains of their World War II–era victims—not only in an effort to provide proof of their claims of victimhood, but also to establish new collective identities of us and them (as opposed to the collective "we" enforced by Tito) (Verdery 1999). Indeed, in the run-up to the bloody Balkan Wars of the 1990s, remains were paraded through the streets of Yugoslavia by all groups to incite nationalist pride and aggression and to remind ethnically defined brothers and sisters who their enemies were (Denich 1994; Hayden 1994; Ballinger 2003).

It should come as no surprise then, that the bloodshed taking place in the former Yugoslavia, and particularly in Bosnia between 1992 and 1995, would lead to major disputes about how many people had died, how many were civilians and not military personnel, and which national/ethnic group was the biggest victim of the war. Victimhood, of course, provided some measure of moral authority to hold power and to punish those who were determined to be perpetrators. As Lara Nettelfield (2010) has documented, all three sides in the Bosnian conflict, and particularly the Bosnian Serbs and the Bosniaks, sought to portray themselves as having suffered a far greater loss of human life than they had caused, a strategy with a long history in the region (Verdery 1999). In the wake of the war, Bosnian Serbs sought to portray their people as victims, between 1992 and 1995, of a massive, unacknowledged ethnic cleansing and genocide in Sarajevo, depicting their plight as rivaling that of the Bosniaks in Srebrenica during the same period—although the Serbs had little evidence to prove it. Similarly, the Bosniak public, as well as many members of the international community, settled on the view that between 200,000 and 350,000 Muslims had perished during the war—a number that emerged as an educated guess in the midst of the war from Bosniak officials—without strong evidence to back up the claim (Nettelfield 2010). Inherent in these casualty counts were political claims about land, punishment of perpetrators, and authority to govern (see later, Nettelfield 2010).

It was in this context that Mirsad Tokača founded the Research and Documentation Centre (RDC) in Sarajevo in 2004 with funding from the Norwegian government and other international sources. Tokača, who had been the secretary of the Bosnia-Herzegovina State Commission for Gathering Facts about War Crimes, had access to the millions of pages of documentation that had been gathered by this commission. The centerpiece of the RDC's mission from the outset was to produce as complete a database as possible of all Bosnians, regardless of ethnicity or nationality, who had been killed or had gone missing between 1991 and 1995 as a direct result of violence.[3] It is important to note that the project did not document indirect deaths, such as those from infection, malnutrition, and lack of adequate health care. The RDC used a wide variety of sources, including media sources, military records, church documents, official police reports, and ultimately testimony from ordinary citizens and data from gravesites around the country.

By June 2007, it was becoming increasingly clear to the RDC that most of the information that it was receiving pertained to deaths that had already been documented. At this time, the RDC announced that it had documented 97,207 cases of killed or missing persons, 39,684 of whom were civilians. Of these non-military personnel, 83 percent were Bosniak, 10 percent were Serb, 5 percent were Croat, and 2 percent were "other" (primarily Jewish or Roma). Although this figure did not represent the total number of deaths, it was considered by many people to be a legitimate minimum number and a good starting point for a discussion about what happened in the Bosnia between 1992 and 1995.

An independent evaluation of what RDC dubbed the *Bosnian Book of the Dead* (BBD) was undertaken by quantitative sociologist Patrick Ball (who directs the Human Rights Data Analysis Group at Benetech), demographer Ewa Tabeau (who until recently worked for the International Criminal Tribunal for the former Yugoslavia [ICTY]), and statistician Philip Verwimp. These researchers concluded that the database was of high quality and was a generally accurate record of deaths in Bosnia during the war (Ball, Tabeau, and Verwimp 2007).[4] While the group suggested that there were still some deaths and missing person cases left to document, the number of additional entries could not be much more than 10,000. Adding weight to the validity of the BBD is a separate study by Zwierzchowski and Tabeau (2010), based on multiple systems estimation (MSE) and carried out under the auspices of the Office of the Prosecutor of the ICTY, which put the estimated number of casualties at 104,732.[5] (For a full historical review of efforts to estimate the number of deaths in Bosnia, see Tabeau and Zwierzchowski, chapter 11 in this volume.)

One serious issue that has been raised about the BBD is that it overestimates the number of military casualties and underestimates the number of civilian casualties because of the availability of better information about combatant deaths and because many families of civilian victims had registered their dead loved ones as military victims in order to obtain veteran's benefits. This of course does not change the minimum number of casualties, but it does alter on the ratio of combatant to noncombatant deaths.

Although the actual percentage of victims confirmed the belief that Bosniaks were disproportionately the victims of military violence during the Bosnian War, and the sense that ethnic cleansing by Bosnian Serbs against Bosniaks appears to have taken place in Srebrenica and surrounds, many Bosniak politicians and nationalist intellectuals were incensed by the RDC study. As Nettelfield demonstrates, the notion that between 200,000 and 350,000 Bosniaks had died in the conflict had become a part of the nationalist narrative that justified not only fighting back against Bosnian Serb aggressors but also a Bosniak-dominated distribution of political power and land in the newly constituted Bosnia. Victims of both Serb aggression and international indifference, Bosniaks needed to protect themselves from both (Nettelfield 2010). They wanted to see a unified Bosnia rather than one that left room for a semiautonomous Republika Srpska (Serb Republic), and the notion that more than 200,000 Bosniaks had been killed at the hands of the Bosnian Serbs seemed to lend support to this geopolitical configuration. Bosniak academics and politicians repeatedly argued that Tokača's project was a disservice to his people and to a unified Bosnia-Herzegovina.

Aside from noting the overt politics of the situation, Nettelfield argues that the dispute was not just about numbers; it also was about academic pride and a lingering sense that control over history belonged to academicians. The small Bosniak intellectual community of Sarajevo had settled on a narrative of the war that involved 250,000–300,000 deaths, and it was embarrassing when Tokača, an outsider, showed them to have been shown to be so far off in their casualty estimates. Sarajevo-based Bosniak intellectuals derided Tokača's methods as suspect and his results as lacking in scientific foundation. They also took him to task for accepting money from the Norwegian government to conduct this work (Nettelfield 2010). While critics of the RDC were often presented in an unfavorable light in the mainstream media, Nettelfield (2010) notes that they enjoyed significant support among family associations and survivors of Srebrenica and other massacres. Further, it did not help the RDC that international experts who were involved in negotiating an end to the war in Bosnia and bringing stability to the region often commented on the current situation there without having kept up with the latest developments. These experts, such as Richard Holbrooke, who brokered the Dayton Peace Accords (which ended the war in Bosnia) while serving as an assistant secretary of state under President Bill Clinton, continued to state that 250,000–300,000 Bosniaks had died in the war, rather than the more modest figures calculated by RDC and ICTY's Office of the Prosecutor (Nettelfield, 2010).

For Tokača and the RDC, the main goal of the project was not simply to produce a number—it was to honor the lives of the dead and missing as human beings whose lives had been cut short by the violence of war, and to replace the myths that were circulating about the war with verifiable, objective fact. In a 2010 interview, he stated:

I believed we should not repeat such mistakes and that any effort to build a myth surrounding one nation's victims, keeping them in the position that serves political goals, represents in fact the new crime against victims. The process of building the historic memory of one society should lie on fact-based truth. We were in a somehow perverted situation that as the years went on, the number of victims [claimed by Sarajevo] grew, up to 300 or 400 thousand, with no memory about them being cherished. We wanted to keep the memory of them alive, to establish the lists with names, and reconstruct the events if we honestly wanted to face the past. Only when the past is put behind with truth we can look to the future. (Zimonjic 2010)

Yet, it is important to note that such a strategy was not simply apolitical and science based. It was a bid to remove the power to produce truth from the dominant regime of the time and to make knowledge production more scientific and democratic (Nettelfield 2010). The longer term success of Tokača and his colleagues is uncertain. Although the figure of approximately 100,000 total deaths has ultimately been accepted by many people and organizations both domestically and internationally, the large cultural shift that Tokača hopes for has yet to occur.

## Case Study 2: The 1991 Gulf War

The debate over civilian casualties in the Gulf War, in which the United States and allies sought to expel Iraqi invaders from Kuwait, can be understood only within the context of a phenomenon often referred to as the "Vietnam syndrome"—the perception on the part of American political elites that the American public turned against the war in Vietnam as U.S. military body counts began to rise and the mass media transmitted into American homes horrific images of innocent civilians suffering (such as that of young Kim Phuc, running naked from her village after it was attacked with napalm, or the horrific tale of the My Lai massacre).

The United States was essentially engaged in a war of attrition against the North Vietnamese (Gibson 1986). The U.S. government did not want to take over North Vietnam; rather, it wanted to ensure that the South Vietnamese government would survive as a bulwark against the communist north. The general consensus among American military planners was that there were a limited number of potential Viet Cong soldiers and that if the United States just kept at the war long enough, it would eventually eliminate this population of potential enemies (or at least cause those still alive to give up the fight), thus enabling the pro-American government in South Vietnam to survive. Success in Vietnam therefore came to be measured not by territorial gains or the destruction of specific targets but by comparative body counts, which we now know was an inappropriate metric.

Since Vietnam, American politicians and top military brass have come to believe that military victory depends upon the public not demanding an end to intensely violent, but not yet complete, campaigns (Norris 1991; Mueller 2000). Foreshadowing General Tommy Franks' statement in 2003 that "we don't do body counts," General H. Norman Schwarzkopf, in the midst of the 1991 Gulf War, had said essentially the same thing: "I have absolutely no idea what the Iraqi casualties are, and I tell you, if I have anything to say about it, we're never going to get into the body-count business" (Cushman 1991).

Although it is unclear whether the U.S. military was or was not keeping track of the number of civilians who were killed during the Gulf War,[6] the U.S. government fought hard to maintain the unknowability of civilian casualties in the eyes of the American public and the rest of the world. In 1992, U.S. Commerce Department demographer Beth Daponte evaluated prewar and postwar census data, along with reports on battlefield deaths and data from human rights groups about incidents of bombs hitting civilian structures rather than their actual military targets. She estimated that about 13,000 civilians and 40,000 Iraqi military personnel had been killed by U.S. and allied military attacks (and another 70,000 had died as a result of the destruction of such essential components of the civilian infrastructure as hospitals, sanitation, food supply, electrical grid, and water supply) (Daponte 1993). When this figure was leaked to the public by Greenpeace, Daponte was accused by her bosses of disseminating false information and told she would be fired. After a rigorous defense by pro bono lawyers and the American Civil Liberties Union (ACLU), the government backed down and did not fire her. Daponte later left the government for academia (Harbrecht 2003).

Daponte's report was then rewritten in a way that affirmed the impossibility of knowing the exact death toll in the context of the American liberation of Kuwait from Iraqi forces (Harbrecht 2003). Further, initial government estimates of 50,000–100,000 battlefield deaths and an unknown number of civilian casualties were downgraded by most military experts to a range of 10,000–20,000 battlefield deaths and 1,000–2,000 civilian deaths.

But the government did not control public understanding of the human cost of the Gulf War solely through manipulation of numbers. As Phillip Knightley details in *The First Casualty: The War Correspondent as Hero and Myth Maker from Crimea to Iraq* (2004), in lieu of details about the human cost of war, the military used media pools to feed the American public technical and visual information about the precision of new weapons systems and fighting machines as well as inventories of specific physical targets hit (e.g., command centers, airfields, enemy artillery, and communications links). Unlike the situation in Vietnam, the destruction of these targets, rather than body counts, became synonymous with progress in the war.

The U.S. government also sought to control the language being used to describe Iraqi deaths, pushing the notion of "collateral damage" rather than "civilian casualties" or "dead Iraqis" (Norris 1991). According to Norris, "Central to that campaign was the control of necrology . . . with a corresponding practice of exhibitionism—of weaponry, hardware, machines, and technology—that effected a predictable series of displacements with crucial ideological effects: human agency in killing replaced by weapons, soft targets concealed by hard targets, sentience and feeling suppressed by logic and expedience" (Norris 1991, 230–231). In reality, though, the kind of laser-guided "smart bombs," which were often outfitted with TV-friendly cameras, represented just 7 percent of all bombs dropped in the conflict. Further, their chance of hitting their target was roughly 50-50. The accuracy of standard munitions was even worse: nearly 70 percent of the 88,500 tons of bombs dropped in the conflict missed their targets entirely (Knightley 2004, 495).

The 100-hour ground war that began on February 23, 1991, was similarly messy. According to people on the front lines, outgunned and outmanned Iraqi soldiers were simply massacred and bulldozed—some dead and some alive—into mass graves; others were burnt beyond recognition by fissile weapons. When journalists did manage to capture the carnage in words or images, most American media outlets refused to cover the story (Knightley 2004).

Media silence on civilian casualties during the American-led Gulf War can be contrasted to the widespread domestic and international coverage of the bloodbath that Saddam Hussein inflicted upon Shia and Kurdish populations in the wake of the U.S. military's withdrawal from the region upon achieving its immediate objective (Knightley 2004). It is impossible to evaluate in this chapter whether the media had been deceived by the government or had actively participated in an effort to keep the American public in the dark. Moreover, it is difficult to determine whether improved access to information about civilian casualties would have had an effect on public opinion of the war. What we can say, though, is that undercounting, whether deliberate or involuntary, potentially made Americans less likely to take notice of and express concern about civilian deaths in Iraq.

## Case Study 3: The Iraq War

As discussed in the preceding section, since Vietnam, the U.S. military has stated that it does not officially take note of the civilian casualties that it causes. Almost all other nations make the same statement. Thanks to the release of the U.S military's Iraq War Logs by WikiLeaks on October 22, 2010, however, the public now knows that this claim is misleading. The U.S. military was indeed keeping records of civilian casualties in Iraq, but officials were not making the information public. It was known that the U.S. military was making at least some effort to understand the level civilian casualties in the Iraq War because the Pentagon reported summaries of this data on a regular basis to the U.S. Congress and occasionally released their figures to the public (Tavernise 2005). Because of the lack of transparency in these reports, however, little was known about the sources used to gather the underlying data, the amount of information available on particular incidents, and the extent to which the reports contained deaths that were not already known through other sources such as media reports or morgue records. The only clear conclusion that could be reached about the data before the WikiLeaks release was that the total casualty counts produced by the U.S. military were lower than almost all other available estimates.

Dissatisfied by the lack of a requirement for states and non-state forces to transparently monitor the civilian casualties they cause in conflict, a host of organizations and institutions have recently emerged to fill the gap. Yet, because they lack large-scale presence on the ground, they are forced to use a variety of imperfect methodologies to record and estimate deaths that result from violent conflict. This represents an interesting case of the state actively producing ignorance (see, Proctor and Schiebinger 2008) while civil society and the scientific community attempt to produce politically sensitive knowledge under very difficult circumstances.

On October 29, 2004, the British medical journal *The Lancet* published a peer-reviewed article by researchers at Johns Hopkins University and al-Mustansiriya University in Baghdad arguing that the invasion and occupation of Iraq had caused an estimated 98,000 excess civilian deaths in its first 17.8 months (95 percent confidence interval [CI], 8,000–194,000) (Roberts et al. 2004). The researchers used a method called "cluster survey sampling" to arrive at this figure. The basic idea behind this methodology is that it is usually impossible to conduct a complete survey of most large populations because of time and resource constraints, but it is possible to sample a small but well-chosen subset of the population. To ensure that the subsample is representative of the larger population, clusters that represent a section of the population are chosen.[7] In the case of the 2004 *Lancet* mortality study, the goal was to measure mortality rates in different geographic regions around the country before and after the invasion and occupation of Iraq; accordingly, 33 clusters were chosen to represent the Iraqi population as a whole. Once these clusters had been chosen, 30 households were visited, and interviewers asked residents a comprehensive set of questions about deaths in their homes before and after the invasion. To ensure that there was no particular bias within these clusters (e.g., to guard against the possibility that interviewers would visit houses known to have had a high rate or low rate of deaths in the pre- or post-invasion period), the households were to have been selected at random; however, the extent to which this condition was met is not generally agreed upon. Once the interviews had been completed, the researchers calculated baseline mortality rates for the pre- and post-invasion periods, with the difference between post- and pre- becoming a measure of excess mortality as a result of the war.

The estimate provoked a strong denunciation by British secretary of state for foreign and commonwealth affairs Jack Straw (2004) and produced a brief flurry of media attention but soon faded from public view. Neither the scientific community nor the mainstream media on either side of the Atlantic displayed any sustained interest in this number. Although violence was escalating and the body counts were clearly rising in many parts of Iraq, the British press did not spend much time informing the public of the existence of a potential controversy. In the United States, the same general pattern was seen but with even less attention paid to the potential controversy over the methods used by the research team. The American government did not publicly comment on the study.

This relative disinterest would change in October 2006 when *The Lancet* published a follow-up study to the 2004 article, which concluded that there had been an astonishing 654,965 excess deaths as a result of the war from March 2003 to July 2006 (95 percent

CI, 392,979 to 942,636), 601,027 of which were caused directly by violence (95 percent CI, 426,369 to 793,663) (Burnham et al. 2006). Although the methodology was roughly equivalent, this time the research team selected 50 clusters and planned to interview 40 households in each one, hoping to increase the robustness of the final results and reduce the CI. Scientists and medical researchers paid more attention to the second *Lancet* study than to the first, probably because the shortcomings of the Coalition's initial strategy were quite apparent by this point and public opinion had become much less favorable toward the war in Iraq (Keeter 2007). In letters to the editor of *The Lancet*, and subsequent commentaries and peer-reviewed articles, scientists, statisticians, public health advocates, and medical researchers voiced concern about a range of technical and ethical issues, from the methods for choosing the households to be surveyed to the practices used by interviewers to gather information from individuals. There were also concerns about the pre-war mortality rates chosen to compare with the post-invasion rates, as well as a host of other issues.

The reaction in the mainstream media was also remarkably more active than it had been at the time of the 2004 study. According to a count by journalists Neil Munro and Carl M. Cannon, within a week, the 2006 study had been featured on 25 American news shows and discussed in 188 newspaper articles in major American publications (Munro and Cannon 2008). Newspaper editorials cited the study as further evidence of the futility of the war, and the Internet was abuzz with discussion of the *Lancet* study's claims. Given the extent to which the American public was questioning the likelihood of success in Iraq, President George W. Bush, at the behest of his advisers, swiftly, unequivocally, and publicly denounced the credibility of the second *Lancet* study during an October 12, 2006, press conference (Bush 2006).

Among the most ardent critics of the 2006 *Lancet* survey were members of the Iraq Body Count team and their collaborators. The Iraq Body Count (IBC) is a not-for-profit organization based in the United Kingdom. Like the *Lancet* survey, the IBC's principal aim is to document the loss of life in Iraq that can be directly attributed to the Coalition-led invasion and occupation, including deaths caused by the Coalition military, insurgents, and criminal elements (Iraq Body Count 2010 and chapter 4 in this volume). The major difference between the *Lancet* study and IBC's methodology is that IBC does not attempt to estimate violent deaths by actively surveying the conditions on the ground. Rather, it extracts data about specific events and victims for input into its database from reputable commercial English-language and credibly translated news reports, the documents of reputable nongovernmental organizations (NGOs), and a variety of official sources of information (e.g., hospital and morgue admissions lists). The IBC approach assumes that commercial news outlets accurately and nearly completely report on wartime casualties in a very dangerous situation without biases for or against certain types of killings.

As of January 2, 2013, the IBC estimates that the death toll in Iraq since the invasion stands between 110,937–121,227. (For the period covered by the second *Lancet* study, the

IBC's total was approximately 50,000 [Dardagan et al. 2006a].) This number, however, is often misinterpreted: it is not an estimate of the total mortality from the war, but rather a count of violent deaths recorded in IBC's source list. As such, it will always undercount the true total mortality to some degree (Dardagan et al. 2006b). Despite the care the organization takes to point out that its totals will always be underestimates, the IBC has been criticized by many scientists, advocates, and journalists for this limitation of its methods (Medialens 2006a; 2006b; 2006c; 2007; Hoover Green 2008). According to the IBC's own preliminary analysis, the Iraq War Logs made public by WikiLeaks suggest that IBC's methodology missed approximately 15,000 civilian deaths from January 2004 to December 2009. Most of these casualties were the result of small incidents involving one or two people, a trend predicted by many people who were skeptical of the ability of press accounts to produce a reasonably accurate account of civilian casualties even in a widely reported war like the one in Iraq. Despite this shortfall of 15,000 deaths, however, the IBC database contains approximately 27,000 civilian deaths not recorded by the U.S. military (IBC 2010).[8]

After a brief window of coverage in which some media outlets unquestioningly accepted the *Lancet* number and others rejected it based on the large discrepancy with the IBC count, the story was largely ignored in the United States and Great Britain. At this point there seemed to be no way of knowing for sure which number was a more accurate representation of the true civilian casualty figure. According to an analysis by the Center for Media and Democracy's Diane Farsetta (who was sympathetic to the *Lancet* study), "most news reports presented the study as 'controversial' (Associated Press, *Los Angeles Times*, *San Francisco Chronicle*, and *Christian Science Monitor*, among others), 'discredited' (*Boston Herald*), 'politically motivated' (*Baltimore Sun*), or even an 'October surprise' (*Washington Post*) designed to hurt Republicans in the November 2006 midterm elections." In contrast, editorial coverage (letters to the editor and the vast majority of editorial columns) did accept the conclusions of the *Lancet* study. The analyst notes that in March 2007, when news outlets were assessing the first four years of the war, they tended to use the lower estimates rather than report the range of available estimates (Farsetta 2008).

Controversy reemerged on January 9, 2008, when the *New England Journal of Medicine* published the results of another survey that measured post-invasion mortality in Iraq: the Iraq Family Health Survey (IFHS), which was conducted by the Iraqi Ministry of Health, in partnership with the country's Ministry of Planning and Development Cooperation, the Central Organization for Statistics and Information Technology (COSIT), and the World Health Organization's Iraq office (WHO/Iraq) (Alkhuzai et al. 2008). The survey was launched in September 2006 and focused first on the central and southern regions; it ended in March 2007, after examining Kurdistan. The IFHS survey provided an estimate of violence-related mortality from March 2003 until June 2006 based on visits to 9,345 households in 971 clusters and a variety of corrections for underreporting of deaths and difficulties in reaching clusters in certain areas where violence had been very high. The IFHS calculated that the unadjusted mortality rate/thousand persons/year was

6.01 (95 percent CI, 5.49–6.60), with a violence-related mortality rate of 1.09 (95 percent CI, 0.81–1.50). After making various corrections, described shortly, the IFHS calculated an adjusted violence-related death of 1.67 (95 percent CI, 1.24–2.30). This rate translated into an estimated number of violent deaths of 151,000 (95 percent CI, 104,000–223,000) from March 2003 through June 2006—a result somewhat larger than IBC's self-described undercount but much lower than the estimate published in *The Lancet*. That said, like the second *Lancet* study, the IFHS found that violence was the main cause of death in Iraq for men between the ages of 15 and 59.

Although it has received very little attention in the mainstream media, a third estimate of violent deaths in Iraq was made public on January 28, 2008: a London-based international market research firm Opinion Research Business (ORB), which conducted a telephone sample of 2,414 predominantly urban adults over the age of 18 (response rate: 2,163), and then an additional "booster" survey of 600 rural Iraqi residents in August and September 2007, concluded that the total number of casualties was 1,033,000 (95 percent CI, 946,000–1,120,000) (Opinion Research Business 2008). Because this was a number that few people could take seriously (given the incredible magnitude of violence that would have had to take place daily for such a number to be even remotely possible), the ORB study has largely been ignored.

Once again, the discrepancy between the lower estimates and the second *Lancet* study estimate provided an interesting news story for the media. The 2008 story by Neil Munro and Carl Cannon, mentioned earlier, castigated the *Lancet* team for political bias, bad methodology, and unethical behavior (Munro and Cannon 2008). Among the most noteworthy allegations were that the study was bankrolled by major Democratic Party funder George Soros, that the lead authors were against the war in Iraq and felt that it was ethical to use fabricated and manipulated data to make a case against it, and that the research team refused to hand over raw data from their surveys in order to cover up incompetence or malfeasance.[9]

The article by Munro and Cannon, which appeared in the *National Journal*, had an immediate impact on the way the *Lancet* study was discussed in the mass media. While most stories thus far had tended to describe it as contentious or controversial, few had come out and denounced it as a political fiction. Yet, on January 8, 2008, a *Wall Street Journal* editorial proclaimed: "We know that number was wildly exaggerated. The news is that now we know why. It turns out the *Lancet* study was funded by anti-Bush partisans and conducted by antiwar activists posing as objective researchers" (*Wall Street Journal* 2008). An editorial by Jeff Jacoby with exactly the same message appeared in the January 13, 2008, edition of the *Boston Globe* and in other papers, including the *New York Times* two days later (Jacoby 2008). The *National Journal* allegations were also discussed in the editorial sections of British newspapers, including the *Sunday Times* and the *Spectator* (Medialens 2008). The result left the authors of the 2006 study and their supporters scrambling to defend the *Lancet* team both personally and professionally (Lambert 2008; Mills and Burkle 2009).

In addition to being the subject of debates about which number is the more accurate, the IBC count and the IFHS estimate (i.e., in the range of 100,000 to 150,000 civilian casualties between March 2003 and mid-2006) have been used by scientists, politicians, and journalists to dismiss the larger estimate of 601,000 violent deaths that appeared in the 2006 *Lancet* study. While the U.S. and Iraqi governments have not publicly accepted the IBC or IFHS estimates, preferring to adhere to the very low counts from "official" Iraqi Ministry of Health records, the IBC and IFHS estimates allow them to publicly ignore the *Lancet* findings. Indeed, in an interview with NPR in 2008, Sarah Sewall, director of the Carr Center for Human Rights at Harvard, stated that the IBC count had come to be the "floor in the civilian casualty counting business. I remember very well a couple of different conferences with military officials where everyone was questioning the method and the motive of the IBC's approach. And it wasn't until the first *Lancet* survey came out that everyone said, oh, well, goodness. The Iraq Body Count is so much more reliable" (National Public Radio 2008). In this state of confusion and disagreement, it is hard to appropriately acknowledge the lives of those who have died or to hold the perpetrators (whether they be the U.S. military or an insurgent group) accountable for their deaths.


## Case Study 4: Darfur

Darfur has been called the "ambiguous genocide" by Gerard Prunier (2005). He notes that despite the tragic deaths of a very large number of "African" civilians at the hands of the "Arab" Janjaweed, it is unclear whether the patterns of killing amount to a concerted effort by the Arab-dominated government to systematically exterminate the African population (which would meet the legal definition of genocide) or simply an attempt to prevent further rebel attacks on the government by guerrilla groups from this population (ibid.). In Prunier's view, though, such a distinction simply does not matter. Genocide or not, he argues that the international community had to get involved to help broker a real solution to the crisis in Darfur and prevent continued bloodshed in the region (ibid.). But another kind of ambiguity was being used by the international community, especially the United States, to avoid getting directly involved in the conflict: dispute about the number of African civilians being killed by the Janjaweed.

John Hagan (2008) argues that the U.S. State Department and the U.S. Government Accountability Office have been key sources of uncertainty in the discussion over whether the Darfur situation should be classified as a genocide. In his view, the U.S. government purposefully sought to sow confusion and cast doubt on the casualty statistics by challenging the highest estimates on technical grounds, but not the lowest ones, and by privileging methods borrowed from complex emergency epidemiology. Hagan points out that the medical approaches to statistics focus on immediate public health needs of populations still living, rather than adopting a more forensic approach, which would have paid much closer attention to people who had already died and to the identification of the forces responsible for their deaths (Hagan 2008). The decision to examine the data epidemiologically instead of forensically would lead, Hagan believes, to lower overall estimates of mortality during the crisis, and would make the American public less likely to demand official action against the government of Sudan. He argues that the U.S. government was willing to endorse the lower estimates because it was courting the favor of the Sudanese government, which Washington had come to believe might be a valuable player in the fight against terror, particularly by providing valuable intelligence about Osama bin Laden, who had had operated out of the country in the 1990s (Hagan 2008).

While it is, of course, difficult to provide definitive evidence to prove Hagan's assertions, a great deal of circumstantial evidence supports accusations regarding the influence of politics in the U.S. government's position on civilian deaths in Darfur. In late 2004, for example, President Bush called the crisis in Darfur a genocide; but he had backed off this claim by early 2005. Further, under Secretary of State Colin Powell, the U.S. State Department's Bureau of Democracy, Human Rights and Labor and Bureau of Intelligence and Research had conducted a mortality survey that affirmed that large numbers of people (180,000–400,000) were dying as a result of the Darfur conflict. Once Condoleezza Rice replaced Powell as secretary of state, the department quickly distanced itself from these claims and offered a much less grim picture. By 2005, the death toll had been revised down (to 63,000–146,000 excess deaths) and the original survey results were completely ignored. This new number was based on work done by the Centre for Research on the Epidemiology of Disease (CRED), which is based in Belgium, at the Catholic University of Louvain. The CRED researchers relied heavily on World Health Organization studies conducted in refugee camps in Central African Republic and in Chad. As several commentators have noted, these surveys tended to undercount violent deaths because the researchers were focused on deaths in the refugee camps rather than the violent deaths that actually precipitated the mass exodus of persecuted people from Sudan (U.S. GAO 2006). In addition to the State Department estimates, other workers have suggested that the violent death toll for Sudan could be as high as 400,000, perhaps more (Lacey 2005).

In this situation of uncertainty, and with no standards or guidelines to apply, the U.S. Government Accountability Office convened experts who had experience with conflict mortality studies and asked the panel to provide American policy makers with advice on how to evaluate the divergent estimates. Ultimately, although the GAO panel did not wholeheartedly endorse any of the estimates, it said that it found the CRED results to be the most trustworthy and that, in general, the studies that reported the highest mortality levels were the most methodologically flawed (U.S. GAO 2006, 3). Ultimately, the GAO report called for better standards and greater openness with data on the part of all stakeholders, noting in particular that the State Department had refused to cooperate with the accountability agency's inquiry about the reliability of State's estimate.

Citing as evidence the State Department's refusal to provide information on how its number was reached, Hagan concluded that the goal of the GAO inquiry was simply to call into question his own estimates, which were much higher than that of State. Hagan also noted that the GAO committee had failed to evaluate an estimate he had published in *Science* with coauthor Albert Palloni for the stated reason that it came out too late; yet the article (Hagan and Palloni 2006), which was included in the bibliography of the government document and had been available for review during the committee's deliberations. This 2006 article concluded that the death toll in Darfur for the same period covered by the CRED study could be placed between 170,000 and 255,000 and was likely to be even greater. Accordingly, the authors explicitly argued that the State Department and journalists should stop using the language of "tens of thousands" of deaths and start using "hundreds of thousands" to describe the humanitarian crisis in Darfur (Hagan and Palloni 2006). Hagan also argued that mortality studies ought to be done specifically for the purpose of determining criminal responsibility rather than relying on public health studies that are more focused on keeping people alive than counting those who have already died and trying to figure out what or who caused their deaths.

The debate over the death count in Darfur has not ended. The most widely cited estimate is now that published by Degomme and Sapir from CRED in a January 2010 *Lancet* article, in which they conclude that the excess number of deaths was around 300,000 from early 2004 to the end of 2008 (95 percent CI, 178,258–461,520) (Degomme and Sapir 2010). Some activists continue to argue that the death toll is much higher.

## Discussion

In the cases examined in this chapter, politics and casualty counts are intertwined in several ways. During and immediately after the war in Bosnia and Herzegovina, the factions involved sought to *continue the conflict* by nonmilitary means. The Bosnian government in particular sought to maximize the number of Muslim victims of the war in order to cement their status as true victims of aggression and deserving of political power in order to avoid falling under the rule of Serb perpetrators. In opposition to this situation, Mirsad Tokača (a Bosnian Muslim) and his colleagues at the RDC sought to *promote resolution of the conflict* by simultaneously honoring the lives lost during the fighting and putting an end to strongly nationalist narratives that he believed were poisoning the reconciliation effort. The RDC's incident-based count is slowly coming to be accepted by the many stakeholders in the region. An independent effort to estimate casualties by the ICTY using demographic methods has produced an estimate that is similar to total number of deaths documented by the RDC. This has provided additional confirmation of the RDC's record of the dead in Bosnia for those who are open to being convinced.

In the case of the U.S. government's actions in the Gulf War and then the Iraq War, we see efforts to *produce official ignorance*—that is, the refusal of a warring party to count casualties, or deliberate efforts to diminish the credibility of existing estimates or counts. When a government employee attempted to produce an estimate of civilian deaths in the Gulf War, her efforts were actively squelched by her superiors, being made public only through of the work of NGOs such as Greenpeace and the ACLU. In the absence of official information about casualties in the Iraq War, a diverse group of researchers, who shared a desire to see the United States, Great Britain, and their allies accept responsibility for the deaths of innocent civilians, stepped in to *correct this ignorance*. Because of a lack of accepted standards for casualty recording and estimation and because there is no agreement about which techniques are most appropriate for particular situations, the counts differ dramatically. It is still too early to determine whether a strong consensus is emerging on the number of civilian casualties in Iraq. Evidence suggests, however, that the IBC's numbers, particularly when analyzed in light of new information revealed by WikiLeaks, are definitely an undercount that nevertheless tells us something meaningful about the magnitude of casualties in the country. This view has been strengthened by slightly higher, but not dramatically different, results from the comprehensive WHO-sponsored Iraq Family Health Survey.

In Darfur, multiple factors led to the production of widely divergent, and not particularly scientifically robust, estimates of civilian casualties: the difficulty of obtaining good data to analyze, the involvement of many different governmental organizations and NGOs with a variety of political commitments and methodological stances, and ever-shifting U.S. government interests in the region. To date, no single estimate has been widely accepted, although a middle-of-the-road estimate endorsed by the U.S. Government Accountability Office is now the one most widely cited. Because of lingering concerns that this estimate achieved credibility at least in part through political maneuvering, and because no two estimates are very similar, it is too soon to tell which number will, in the future, be seen as the most accurate.

## Conclusion

One conclusion that emerges from this analysis is that it is difficult but not impossible to count the civilian casualties of war—but counting cannot proceed at all unless information about these deaths is available to researchers. As we have seen, this is an area where politics is often involved in the most pernicious way. The case studies described in this chapter suggest many reasons that might lead warring parties to deem it advantageous to disguise the true human cost of war, and disadvantageous to keep good records of civilian casualties. Therefore, one important mechanism for resolving this problem would be the emergence, promotion, and institutionalization of an international norm for recording civilian casualties in times of conflict and making the data available to independent researchers. The editors of this volume develop this proposal further in the concluding chapter.

A second conclusion is that many different methods should be employed to analyze civilian casualty data. Although this may lead to confusion in the short term, as we have seen in the cases of Bosnia and Iraq, efforts to replicate results in two or more methodologically distinct casualty counts can highlight strengths and limitations of each. On the other hand, similarity of results of multiple efforts can support claims to the accuracy of these counts and insulate them from overt political meddling. Similarity of results could, of course, arise through error, chance, or systematically biased data, but the use of many different methods should increase the likelihood that these problems are identified.

Perhaps the most important conclusion from this chapter is that *quantification is rarely an escape from politicization in civilian casualty counting; rather, it is an invitation for further political intervention.* Institutions and individuals do not produce (or prevent the production of) casualty estimates unless they have strong political, ethical, or tactical motivations for doing so. Thus it is naïve to try to completely remove politics from casualty counting—not even the most rigorous methods and practices will make this possible. But as we have seen, it is possible to produce robust, socially and scientifically valid casualty counts and estimates that, while still problematic, can provide a stronger basis to apportion blame, distribute political power in the aftermath of conflict, and create a foundation for the beginnings of lasting peace. In the long term, few people benefit from a complete lack of clarity about the human cost of war—the families, friends, and communities of the dead least of all.

## REFERENCES

Alkhuzai, A. H., I. J. Ahmad, M. J. Hweel, T. W. Ismail, H. H. Hasan, A. R. Younis, O. Shawani. 2008. "Violence-Related Mortality in Iraq from 2002 to 2006." *New England Journal of Medicine* 358, no. 5: 484–93.

Anderson, Margo J. 1988. *The American Census: A Social History.* New Haven, CT: Yale University Press.

Anderson, Margo, and Stephen E. Fienberg. 1977. "Who Counts? The Politics of Census Taking." *Society* 34, no. 3: 19–26.

Arce, Dwyer. 2010. "ICC Charges Al-Bashir with Genocide." At: http://jurist.org/paperchase/2010/07/icc-charges-al—bashir-with-genocide.php (accessed August 5, 2010).

Ball, Patrick, Ewa Tabeau, and Philip Verwimp. 2007. *The Bosnian Book of Dead: Assessment of the Database.* Sussex, U.K.: Households in Conflict Network.

Ballinger, Pamela. 2003. *History in Exile: Memory and Identity at the Borders of the Balkans.* Princeton, NJ: Princeton University Press.

Banac, Ivo. 1992. "Historiography of the Countries of Eastern Europe: Yugoslavia." *American Historical Review* 97, no. 4: 1084–1104.

Burnham, G., R. Lafta, S. Doocy, and L. Roberts. 2006. "Mortality after the 2003 Invasion of Iraq: A Cross-Sectional Cluster Sample Survey." *The Lancet* 368: 1421–1428.

Bush, George W. 2006. "Transcript: Bush's News Conference." At: http://www.cnn.com/2006/POLITICS/10/11/bush.transcript/ (accessed August 3, 2010).

Checci, Francesco, and Les Roberts. 2008. "Documenting Mortality in Crisis: What Keeps Us From Doing Better?" *PLoS Med* 5, no. 7: e146.

Cushman, John H. 1991. "War in the Gulf: The Casualties; Pentagon Seems Vague on the Iraqis' Death Toll." *New York Times*, February 3. http://www.nytimes.com/1991/02/03/world/war-in-the-gulf-the-casualties-pentagon-seems-vague-on-the-iraqis-death-toll.html.

Daponte, Beth Osborne. 1993. "A Case Study in Estimating Casualties From War and Its Aftermath: The 1991 Persian Gulf War." *The PSR Quarterly* 3, no. 2: 57–66.

Dardagan, Hamit, John Sloboda, and Josh Dougherty. 2006a. "Reality Checks: Some Responses to the Latest *Lancet* Estimates," Press Release 14. London: Iraq Body Count.

John Sloboda, and Josh Dougherty. 2006b. "Speculation Is No Substitute: A Defence of Iraq Body Count." London: Iraq Body Count.

Degomme, Oliver, and Deborati Guha Sapir. 2010. "Patterns of Mortality Rates in Darfur Conflict." *The Lancet* 375: 294–300.

Denich, Bette. 1994. "Dismembering Yugoslavia: Nationalist Ideologies and the Symbolic Revival of Genocide." *American Ethnologist* 21, no. 2: 367–390.

Desrosieres, Alain. 1998. *The Politics of Large Numbers: A History of Statistical Reasoning* (translation). Cambridge, MA: Harvard University Press.

Farsetta, Diane. 2008. "Jousting with the Lancet: More Data, More Debate over Iraqi Deaths." *PR Watch*, February 26. At: http://www.prwatch.org/node/7034 (accessed April 5, 2010).

Gibson, James William. 1986. *The Perfect War: Technowar in Vietnam*. New York: Atlantic Monthly Press.

Greenhill, Kelly M. 2010. "Counting the Cost: The Politics of Numbers in Armed Conflicts." In *Sex, Drugs, and Body Counts: The Politics of Numbers in Global Crime and Conflict*, edited by Peter Andreas and Kelly M. Greenhill, 127–158. Ithaca, NY: Cornell University Press.

Hagan, John. 2008. "The Unaccountable Genocide: A Case Study of the Roles of the U.S. State Department and U.S. Government Accountability Office in Calculating the Darfur Death Toll." In *Supranational Criminology: Towards a Criminology of International Crimes*, edited by R. Haveman and A. Smeulers. Antwerp: Intersentia.

Hagan, John, and Alberto Palloni. 2006. "Social Science: Death in Darfur," *Science* 313: 1578–1579.

Harbrecht, Douglas. 2003. "Toting the Casualties of War (an Interview with Beth Daponte)." *Businessweek*, February 6,

Hayden, Robert M. 1994. "Recounting the Dead: The Discovery and Redefinition of Wartime Massacres in Late-and Post-Communist Yugoslavia." In *Memory, History, and Opposition Under State Socialism*, edited by Rubie S. Watson, 167–184. Santa Fe, NM: School of American Research Press.

Hoover Green, Amelia. 2008. *Commentary on the Oxford Research Group Discussion Document*. Palo Alto, CA: Benetech Human Rights Data Analysis Group.

IBC (Iraq Body Count). 2010. "Iraq War Logs: What the Numbers Reveal." At: http://www.iraqbodycount.org/analysis/numbers/warlogs (accessed January 25, 2011).

Jacoby, Jeff. 2008. "The Lancet's Outlandish Exaggeration." *Boston Globe*, January 13.

Keeter, Scott. 2007. "Trends in Public Opinion about the War in Iraq, 2003–2007." At: http://pewresearch.org/pubs/431/trends-in-public-opinion-about-the-war-in-iraq-2003-2007 (accessed June 7, 2011).

Kertzer, David I., and Dominique Arel, eds. 2002. *Census and Identity: The Politics of Race, Ethnicity and Language in National Censuses*. Cambridge: Cambridge University Press.

Knightley, Philip. 2004. *The First Casualty: The War Correspondent as Hero and Myth-Maker From the Crimea to Iraq.* Baltimore, MD: Johns Hopkins University Press.

Lacey, Marc. 2005. "Tallying Darfur Terror: Guesswork with a Cause." *New York Times*, May 11.

Lambert, Tim. 2008. "Flypaper for Innumerates: National Journal Edition." At: http://science-blogs.com/deltoid/2008/01/flypaper_for_innumerates_natio.php (accessed April 27, 2010).

Martin, Aryn, and Michael Lynch. 2009. "Counting Things and People: The Practices and Politics of Counting." *Social Problems* 56, no. 2: 243–266.

Mathews, Andrew S. 2005. "Power/Knowledge, Power/Ignorance: Forest Fires and the State in Mexico." *Human Ecology* 33, no. 6: 795–820.

McArdle, Megan. 2008. "Body Counting." *The Atlantic*, April. At: http://www.theatlantic.com/magazine/archive/2008/04/body-counting/306698/.

Medialens. 2006a. "Paved With Good Intentions—Iraq Body Count—Part 1." At: http://www.medialens.org/alerts/06/060125_paved_with_good.php (accessed May 3, 2010).

———. 2006b. "Paved With Good Intentions—Iraq Body Count—Part 2." At: http://www.medialens.org/alerts/06/060126_paved_with_good_part2.php (accessed May 3, 2010).

———. 2006c. "Iraq Body Count Refuses to Respond." At: http://www.medialens.org/alerts/06/060314_iraq_body_count.php (accessed May 3, 2010).

———. 2007. "Iraq Body Count: 'A Very Misleading Exercise.'" At: http://www.medialens.org/alerts/07/071003_iraq_body_count.php (accessed May 3, 2010).

———. 2008. "All Smoke, No Fire—the National Journal Smears the Lancet." At: http://www.medialens.org/alerts/08/080122_all_smoke_no.php (accessed April 6, 2010).

Mills, Edward J., and Frederick M. Burkle. 2009. "Interference, Intimidation, and Measuring Mortality in War." *The Lancet* 373, no. 9672: 1320–1322.

Mills, E. J., F. Checchi, J. J. Orbinski, M. J. Schull, F. M. Burkle, C. Beyrer, C. Cooper, C. Hardy, S. Singh, R. Garfield, B. A. Woodruff, and G. H. Guyatt. 2008. "Users' Guides to the Medical Literature: How to Use an Article about Mortality in a Humanitarian Emergency." *Conflict and Health* 2: 1–9.

Mueller, Karl P. 2000. "Politics, Death, and Morality in US Foreign Policy." *Aerospace Power Journal* 14, no. 2: 12–16.

Munro, Neil, and Carl M. Cannon. 2008. "Data Bomb." *National Journal*, January 4.

National Public Radio. 2008. "Iraqi Casualties Estimated At 151,000" (*Talk of the Nation* transcript). At: http://www.npr.org/templates/transcript/transcript.php?storyId=17993630 (accessed August 3, 2010).

Nettelfield, Lara J. 2010. "Research and Repercussions: The Case of the Bosnian Book of the Dead." In In *Sex, Drugs, and Body Counts: The Politics of Numbers in Global Crime and Conflict*, edited by Peter Andreas and Kelly M. Greenhill, 159–187. Ithaca, NY: Cornell University Press.

Norris, Margot. 1991. "Military Censorship and the Body Count in the Persian Gulf War." *Cultural Critique* 19: 223–245.

Opinion Research Business. 2008. "New Analysis 'Confirms' 1 Million+ Iraq Casualties." At: http://www.opinion.co.uk/Newsroom_details.aspx?NewsId=120 (accessed May 29, 2010).

Porter, Theodore. 1996. *Trust in Numbers: The Pursuit of Objectivity in Science and Public Life.* Princeton, NJ: Princeton University Press.

Proctor, Robert N., and Londa Schiebinger, eds. 2008. *Agnotology: The Making and Unmaking of Ignorance.* Stanford, CA: Stanford University Press.

Prunier, Gerard. 2005. *Darfur: The Ambiguous Genocide*. Ithaca, NY: Cornell University Press.

Roberts, I., R. Lafta, R. Garfield, J. Khudhairi, and G. Burnham. 2004. "Mortality Before and After the 2003 Invasion of Iraq: Cluster Sample Survey." *The Lancet* 364, no. 9448: 1857–1864.

Scott, James C. 1998. *Seeing Like a State: How Certain Schemes to Improve the Human Condition Have Failed*. New Haven, CT: Yale University Press.

Soldz, Stephen. 2006. "When Promoting Truth Obscures the Truth." At: http://www.zcommunications.org/when-promoting-truth-obscures-the-truth-by-stephen-ssoldz (accessed April 7, 2010).

Straw MP, Right Honorable Jack. 2004. "UK Government Response to First Lancet Mortality Survey." At: http://www.parliament.the-stationery-office.co.uk/pa/cm200304/cmhansrd/vo041117/wmstext/41117mo2.htm (accessed April 7, 2010).

Tabeau, Ewa, and Jakub Bijak. 2005. "War-Related Deaths in the 1992–1995 Armed Conflicts in Bosnia and Herzegovina: A Critique of Previous Estimates and Recent Results." *European Journal of Population* 21, no. 2–3: 187–215.

Tavernise, Sabrina. 2005. "U.S. Quietly Issues Estimate of Iraqi Civilian Casualties." *New York Times*, October 20, 1.

U.S. GAO (United States Government Accountability Office). 2006. *Darfur Crisis: Death Estimates Demonstrate Severity of Crisis, But Their Accuracy and Credibility Could Be Enhanced*. Washington, DC: Government Accountability Office.

Verdery, Katherine. 1999. *The Political Lives of Dead Bodies: Reburial and Post-Socialist Change*. New York: Columbia University Press.

*Wall Street Journal*. 2008. "The Lancet's Political Hit." *Wall Street Journal*.

Working Group for Mortality Estimation in Emergencies. 2007. "Wanted: Studies on Mortality Estimation Methods for Humanitarian Emergencies, Suggestions for Future Research." *Emerging Themes in Epidemiology* 4: 1–9.

Zimonjic, Vesna Peric. 2010. "Laying to Rest the Ghosts of the Past—With Truth" (an interview with Mirsad Tokača). At: http://ipsnews.net/print.asp?idnews=51809 (accessed August 5, 2010).

Zwierzchowski, Jan, and Ewa Tabeau. 2010. "The 1992-95 War in Bosnia and Herzegovina: Census-Based Multiple Systems Estimation of Casualties' Undercount." Conference paper for the International Research Workshop on "The Global Costs of Conflict," February.

NOTES

1. The Ustaša government was an ultranationalist, fascist organization installed into power by the occupying Nazis in 1941. They advocated for a "pure" Croatia, cleansed of all other ethnic groups, and freed from what they believed was an illegitimate Yugoslavian kingdom.

2. The "chetniks" were a Serbian nationalist movement that collaborated with the Ustaša government and Nazis in World War II. Their goal was to create a pure Serb homeland through the defeat of the communists and an ethnic cleansing of Muslims, Jews, Roma, and other groups. In the 1980s, after a period of dormancy, Serb nationalists began to refer to themselves as chetniks, while Bosnian Muslims began to use the term in a much more negative way around the same time to symbolize a return of nationalist Serbian aggression.

3. The database includes some individuals who died in Slovenia and Croatia in 1991, but the vast majority of casualties are from the 1992–1995 war in Bosnia and Herzegovina.

4. Their analysis consisted of evaluating the BBD database for missing or incomplete data, duplicate records, and obvious data errors (e.g., dates of birth outside the range of possibility). They also made numerous suggestions on how to improve the overall quality of the database.

5. MSE involves the statistical comparison of event reports in many different data sources. See chapters 8–10 of this volume for a full review of this method.

6. The release in 2010 by WikiLeaks of the U.S. military's data on civilian casualties in the war in Iraq (see Case Study, this chapter) belies the claim that the U.S. government does not do body counts.

7. For a more detailed discussion of the estimation of civilian casualties using surveys, see chapters 6 and 7 in this volume.

8. In addition to identifying previously unknown cases, the Iraq War Logs have allowed IBC to fill in details about individual victims and also to disaggregate deaths reported in a single article that in fact had occurred in different violent events.

9. The *Lancet* study authors stated that they were being very careful with the raw data because they did not want to put survey respondents in danger (Burnham et al. 2007).

# II Recording Violence
INCIDENT-BASED DATA

# 4 Iraq Body Count

## A CASE STUDY IN THE USES OF INCIDENT-BASED CONFLICT CASUALTY DATA

John Sloboda, Hamit Dardagan, Michael Spagat,
and Madelyn Hsiao-Rei Hicks

## Introduction

Iraq Body Count (IBC) is a nonprofit nongovernmental organization (NGO) that has systematically collated media reports of Iraqi civilian deaths from incidents of armed violence since the beginning of the Iraq War on March 20, 2003 (Dardagan et al. 2005; Iraq Body Count 2011). The IBC method integrates data extracted from media reports on civilian deaths with data on deaths reported by hospitals, morgues, NGOs, and official figures, using systematic cross-checks to eliminate double-counting, with the aim of providing as complete a record as possible of individual Iraqi civilians killed by armed violence since the beginning of the war. In this chapter, we discuss the uses, merits, and limitations of incident-based casualty data, using the IBC database as our example.

We begin by describing the origins and aims of the Iraq Body Count project; the characteristics, methods, and sources of IBC's data; and examples of how IBC's incident-based data have been used in efforts to improve understanding of the effects of armed conflict on civilians, to commemorate individual deaths, and to advocate for civilian protection. We then discuss how IBC's database on Iraqi civilian deaths compares against other sources of information on violent deaths in Iraq, and we discuss the strengths and limitations of using media-based data and of using incident-based data. We end by describing our view on what improvements could be made in the incident-based recording of civilian casualties in order to support the increased protection of civilians from the violence of armed conflict.

Although we will not focus in this chapter on how specific uses of IBC's incident-based casualty data contribute to the aims and methods of strategic peacebuilding (Schirch 2008; Philpott 2010), some connections can be made here that can be kept in mind during the chapter. In keeping with the holistic, long-term goals of strategic peace-building, IBC's specific, immediate aim has always been ending the violence of the Iraq War. In the longer term, IBC seeks to use the data it collects to further the goal of bringing the civilian impact of war into the forefront in considerations of current and future wars, with the hope of ending, or at least minimizing, direct violence toward noncombatants. We describe how IBC's data have been used in an effort to increase awareness of the impact of the war on civilians, women, and children. We believe that increased awareness has the potential to shift attitudes and priorities of a spectrum of communities, policy makers, and actors in war toward a more civilian-protective focus, especially when data are communicated in emotionally and culturally relevant quantita-tive terms. Further, we believe that the main contributions of incident-based civilian casualty data to strategic peacebuilding may be in the potential to provide data-based evidence for advocacy, the ability to highlight the importance of making civilian protec-tion an explicit priority, and the potential to change the social and moral acceptability of tactics used by actors in war by revealing the toll of various tactics on civilians.

## The Origins and Aims of Iraq Body Count

The IBC project was founded by two of the authors of this chapter, John Sloboda and Hamit Dardagan, when an invasion of Iraq by a coalition of forces led by the United States appeared to be imminent. The founding principles of IBC are that there can be no justification for insulating ourselves from knowledge of war's effects, and it is a matter of simple humanity to record the dead. This means that, at a minimum, the basic facts about who was killed, where they were killed, and when they were killed should be established, recorded, and preserved as a matter of historical record. Whatever the practical barriers, there can be no moral justification for refusing to record war deaths by every available means, except where doing so risks further loss of life. An immediate responsibility is to preserve knowledge of those deaths already verified but lost from view because the ac-counts of these incidents were published piecemeal and have become highly dispersed.

The project was based on one overarching premise: as in previous conflicts involving Western nations, civilian deaths would be reported by the international media, but each day's events would soon be forgotten as they were overtaken by the next day's news. But with new Web-based technologies for accessing, collecting, collating, and publishing data, a suitably designed project, which might not prevent this loss of lives, could never-theless prevent their becoming lost from the historical record.

Three primary factors underlie IBC's decision to focus on civilians. First, legal and moral considerations make noncombatant deaths particularly unacceptable; these considerations are embodied, for example, in international humanitarian laws and customary standards, including the Geneva Conventions of 1949 (International Committee of the Red Cross 2011). Despite this codification of noncombatant protection, civilians are all too often given scant attention, if any, in official recording of casualties from armed conflict. Second, with respect to the war in Iraq, Coalition military and contractor deaths are relatively well recorded by other sources, such as military and government institutions. Third, being a small, volunteer-run NGO with limited human and material resources, the IBC project team has had to focus its efforts on the systematic recording of casualties of one delineated group.

An incident-based approach to recording civilian deaths was taken for the following reasons: immediate deaths and injuries caused by violence happen at a specific time and place, and such factual circumstances have the potential to be fully documented and verifiable. These facts provide the basis of a documentary record of the most unambiguous civilian impact of war. In the short to medium term, the only way to get consistent information about the civilian or noncivilian status of victims is early incident-based reporting, derived from direct witnesses who have been in physical and temporal proximity to the victim either before or immediately after death. Similarly, reports emanating close in time and space to a given incident are more likely than reports from distant respondents to supply reliable information regarding the aggressor and the weapons used.

The overriding purpose of the methods employed by IBC is to provide an account that is as full and as detailed as possible, one that describes actual violent fatalities of individual Iraqi civilians and the circumstances of the fatal violent incidents. This approach does not aim to provide an estimated figure for total deaths, in the sense of the term "estimate" as used by those aiming to calculate total deaths in a population by extrapolating from a sample or other inferential means. IBC ultimately seeks to compile a list of all the victims that is as complete and detailed as possible; the list should be open to public scrutiny, and it should be possible to update it. There are now dozens of other organizations around the world whose work exemplifies this approach, many of which are listed at everycasualty.org. *The Bosnian Book of the Dead*, first published by the Research and Documentation Centre of Sarajevo in 2007 (Ball, Tabeau, and Verwimp 2007; Nettelfield 2010), is one of the most recent IT-based projects that embodies this ideal (Nettelfield 2010). Another is the incident-based documentation of individual fatalities caused by Israeli and Palestinian armed forces, with civilians distinguished from combatants, and minors distinguished from adults (B'Tselem 2011). The approach taken by IBC lies within a tradition of quantitative documentary and archival historical research in which the central activity is collecting and organizing all relevant records, whose data can then be analyzed by using descriptive statistics (Tilly 1969; Tilly and Schweitzer 1980; Grimes and Schulz 2002). IBC's priority was to provide a robust baseline of verifiably recorded civilian deaths, together with the available information about the victims and the incidents that killed them, that could be examined from any point in time from the beginning of the war. By contrast, aggregate data that cannot be broken down into its constituent parts cannot be challenged or improved because it is impossible to know which victims or incidents are, or are not, included in the underlying data.

Another guiding principle for IBC is that all information about war-related deaths belongs in the public domain. People can make informed decisions about the use of military force only when they are fully aware of its consequences; awareness, in turn presupposes access to high-quality, detailed information. There is no more serious consequence of war than the killing of civilians, and the public deserves and needs to know all it can about the matter. Making a large store of information accessible on the Internet is currently the most cost-effective way of providing global public access to such data. Resources permitting, all of IBC's output is intended for open, and timely, access. Continuous publication of cross-checked civilian casualty data as close as possible to the time of the incident causing violent death brings the further benefit of allowing trends and patterns to be tracked in real time.

This public access allows citizens to inspect the particulars of IBC's data and to submit corrections or missing information, a capacity that is being increased with an expansion program in progress to provide IBC's entire website in Arabic. At the time of writing, public access to the IBC archive of each incident and of each Iraqi civilian who could be identified (identities of most of the civilian dead have not yet been reported) is at this page of the IBC website: http://www.iraqbodycount.org/database/. To facilitate the ability of public viewers to analyze the IBC database directly, IBC also provides continually updated, interactive graphing systems at its website, where public users can pull up and view summary data trends on violent deaths or violent incidents in the country, or in Baghdad, plotted over time (http://www.iraqbodycount.org/analysis/numbers/2010/). For example, users can select data according to variables including date range, weapon (any, explosive, gunfire, suicide attack), perpetrator (any, Coalition and Iraqi state forces, anti-occupation forces, unknown), number of deaths caused (1 or more killed, 5 or more killed, 20 or more killed), and can graph comparisons between deaths, or incidents, associated with different variables.

## The Characteristics and Sources of IBC Data

### CHARACTERISTICS

IBC's database has five key characteristics:

1. It lists documented deaths of individuals.
2. It does not provide estimates of total deaths in Iraq.
3. It includes only violent deaths (no deaths from nonviolent causes such as disease).
4. It includes only civilian (i.e., noncombatant) deaths.
5. It is constantly updated and revised as new data come in.

A civilian "casualty" of armed violence is defined as a civilian who has been either killed or wounded. IBC data on civilian casualties include only those civilians who were reported killed by armed violence and those civilians who were reported injured in incidents that also killed at least one civilian. Thus, any incidents that resulted in civilian injuries but not in civilian deaths are absent from the IBC dataset.

If an incident occurs in which civilians are killed, media reports of the event will almost invariably contain a specific number of deaths, the date (often with time of day), and the place, regardless of whatever other information may or may not be present. Depending on the level of additional detail that can be extracted from reports, IBC systematically records data relating to some 20 or more variables for each lethal incident. At a bare minimum, IBC records the date of the incident (which includes incidents in which bodies were found), the location, and the number of civilian dead. Further variables recorded by IBC for incidents include time, target, minimum deaths, maximum deaths, minimum injuries, maximum injuries, weapons used, perpetrators, media sources, and primary witnesses. Variables recorded by IBC relating directly to individuals include name, age, sex, marital status, parental status, and occupation.

IBC defines Iraqi "civilians" to include all noncombatants, all children, most women, and police in normal, civil, nonparamilitary roles (e.g., local and traffic police). While police are a Coalition-associated target for insurgent forces in Iraq, this is not incompatible with their civilian status, in the same way that a government administrator or fireman killed in an attack on the Iraqi government (i.e., Coalition-associated) infrastructure retains civilian status. A child is anyone under the age of 18, based on the Convention on the Rights of the Child (United Nations Office of the High Commissioner for Human Rights 1989) and Iraqi law that stipulates that 18 is the voting age and age of consent (Dardagan et al. 2005). Age is determined based on reported age in years, or reported age category as "child" or "adult," or adult occupation.

When entering details in the IBC database, IBC staff draw some logical deductions from the information provided in reports. For example, if the victim is described as a "policeman," the process can assign the victim to the category "adult" and the category "male" even though the victim's age and gender are not explicitly stated in the report. When accounts from independent sources differ, variables are extracted from reports with the most detail or best-placed primary sources (e.g., medical personnel attending to victims). Most frequent sources for reported violent deaths are morgue attendants and hospital medics, police and other Iraqi official sources, eyewitnesses, and relatives. When equally credible reports differ, minimum and maximum civilian deaths are recorded for the incident. Similarly, media reports may disagree, or be uncertain, about whether some among the dead were combatants or noncombatants. This is another situation in which IBC publishes a range covering both possibilities. A final form of uncertainty revolves around the integration of media-reported, incident-level data with aggregate data (e.g., from monthly morgue or hospital reports); where the two kinds of data do not coincide, IBC gives a range. Entries are independently reviewed and systematically error-checked by three IBC members before data are published on IBC's open website. Data are updated as newly reported information emerges, which may add detail to described variables about victims or incidents, or add deaths as additional bodies are discovered (e.g., as building rubble is removed after a bomb blast) or as victims die from injuries.

## SOURCES

Press and media organizations are the most consistent gatherers of (relatively) detailed casualty data worldwide. Their data are not limited to their own investigations. The media also publish information provided by governments, official agencies, and NGOs. Media sources taken as a whole, and integrated with data from other sources in the manner developed by IBC, can thus be used as an "aggregator" for all public-domain information on known casualties. The Iraq War has attracted persistent, continuous effort by international and local media organizations to capture stories about violence, which has resulted in detailed reports on tens of thousands of incidents that caused civilian death in Iraq's armed conflict.

Every day, IBC systematically identifies reports of armed violence in Iraq directly resulting in civilian death by using search engines and subscription-based press and media collation services (e.g., LexisNexis) to scan reports from over 200 separate press and media outlets meeting IBC's criteria of producing original material under professional editorial control. Sources include Arabic-language news media that report conflict-related violent incidents in English (e.g., Voices of Iraq, National Iraqi News Agency, and Al Jazeera English) and the output of translation services such as the BBC Monitoring Unit. Coverage of non-English-language reports is currently limited to those that are available from proficient translators.

Figure 4.1 shows the results of an IBC analysis of the per-source coverage of all incidents and deaths in the IBC database from January 2006 to September 2008, a period of about a thousand days, for the top 12 contributing media among the more than 200 independent media sources tracked by IBC. No single media source covered more than 43 percent of the incidents and 60 percent of the civilian deaths of the combined output of the media collated by IBC. Most contributed only a small fraction of the total.

IBC assumes that any agency that has attained a respected international status runs its own veracity checks before publishing stories (including from eyewitness and confidential sources). To avoid reliance on any single agency for its data collection, however, IBC casts a wide net and is therefore largely unaffected by vagaries in reporting by any one organization. IBC operates across commercial boundaries, meaning that no primary data source is considered proprietary by IBC or given preference over others. Media outlets, being competitive and proactive, rely on their ability to increase their access and reach in covering a conflict. In Iraq, most Western agencies have Iraqi stringers, informants, and correspondents across the country. As described by a Reuters bureau chief, "We have people in 19 or 20 cities—ideally a cameraman, photographer and reporter—although in some places one or two people will cover more than one specialisation"

Media sources and their contribution
*Jan 2006–Sep 2008*

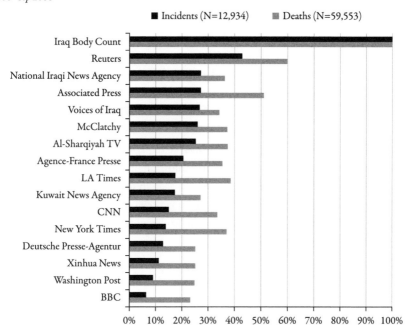

FIGURE 4.1  Per-Source Coverage of Incidents and Deaths in the IBC database, January 2006–September 2008

(Reuters Foundation 2006). Journalists intensively monitor each others' outputs. IBC has rarely found medium-sized incidents (i.e., involving four or more deaths) in the Iraqi press (whether in Arabic or English) that are not also reported by one or more of the Western media agencies present in Iraq. The linkage that IBC retains in its database between the data and their media sources provides the potential to assess media coverage by different agencies over time and space.

IBC's systematic data collection makes it possible to obtain far more data than would be apparent to most news consumers, who access only a few major news sources. Coverage in these major sources is dominated by occasional stories of large incidents in which numerous Iraqis died. Rarely do they report the death of a single, anonymous Iraqi, or even two or three. IBC gives equal prominence to, and archives, every incident it finds, including those relegated to newswires and back pages or buried deep within other articles. Nearly half (45 percent) of IBC's incident records involve the death of a single individual, and 75 percent involve an incident in which three or fewer civilians were killed (Iraq Body Count 2007b).

The integration of aggregate data from morgues (primarily the Baghdad morgue), hospitals (from the Iraqi Ministry of Health), other official sources, and NGOs supplements the casualty data extracted from incident-based reporting. For deaths recorded from aggregate data (e.g., reports of bodies of the executed delivered to morgues upon discovery), the incident causing death may or may not have been reported, and sometimes may not be knowable with certainty. Data from aggregate reports are included only if sufficient detail on time and location allows cross-checking of casualties against casualties already recorded in the IBC database, to avoid double-counting.

Additional sources of detailed, incident-based data have been obtained by a series of Freedom of Information Act requests to the U.S. and British governments, and by analyzing a probability sample of incidents from the Iraq War Logs released by WikiLeaks (Iraq Body Count 2010a, 2010b, 2010c, 2010d, and later in this chapter). Since 2007, data obtained by Freedom of Information Act requests to the U.S. military have disclosed nearly 400 incidents, resulting in the addition of nearly 500 civilian deaths to the IBC dataset (Iraq Body Count 2010e). In 2010, analysis by IBC of the data released by WikiLeaks suggested that an additional 15,000 previously unidentified civilian deaths may be present in these logs, hence available to be added to the IBC database (see the discussion later in this chapter).

## Putting IBC Data to Use

On most days, there are thousands of individual visitors to the IBC website. This is our primary indicator of the level of continuing public concern about Iraqi deaths. The detailed, incident-based and victim-centric data produced by IBC have both "essential value," for capturing the social and cultural meaning of individual casualties, as well as "instrumental value," for relating patterns of casualties to possible causes, trends, and effects (Fischhoff, Atran, and Fischhoff 2007). So far, IBC data have mainly been used for two primarily instrumental purposes: to inform analysis, commentary, and advocacy in relation to the conflict in Iraq, and to contribute to discussions about the ethical, legal, and methodological aspects of monitoring casualties of all conflicts, not just the conflict in Iraq. The essential value of IBC data (e.g., to memorialize and identify the dead) may significantly rise as the Arabic translation of IBC's website increases access to the data by Iraqis who have been affected directly by the Iraq War.

Some features of the IBC dataset facilitate uses of certain types, such as the identification of trends and patterns. These include trends over time, the geographical distribution of violence, the age and sex of those killed, the comparative lethality of different weapons and of different categories of perpetrators, and the efficacy (or lack of it) of changes in military tactics designed (or at least purported) to protect civilians. Additionally, credible information empowers people to act. When reliable information is organized and put into the public domain, it becomes possible for individuals and organizations to put it to multiple uses, whether educational, political, or humanitarian. IBC invites and, where feasible, assists any not-for-profit use of its data, particularly when the purpose is to benefit war's casualties, whether actual or potential.

IBC's research has been explicitly referenced in informed assessments of civil security by leading institutions concerned with Iraq, including the UN Office for the Coordination of Humanitarian Affairs (OCHA), ReliefWeb, the UN High Commissioner for Refugees (UNHCR), the World Health Organization, the International Monetary Fund, the World Bank, the International Criminal Court, the Brookings Institution, the U.S. Council on Foreign Relations, and the U.S. Congressional Research Service (see Iraq Body Count 2007a for a fuller list). Some research groups have also commissioned specific analyses from IBC; one such entity is the Empirical Studies of Conflict Group, involving the universities of Princeton, Stanford, and California (Condra et al. 2010).

Numerous academic and scholarly analyses have drawn on IBC data. For example, Alvarez-Ramirez et al. (2010) used IBC's time-specific data to study the dynamics of civilian fatalities over different periods of the Iraq war marked by major military and political events. Their goal was to examine mathematical methods that could provide insights into ways to design better policies and strategies to reduce the adverse effects of violence on civilians. Boyle (2009) used IBC geographic and time variables to study the localization of violence in Iraq as a product of interactions between perpetrators of violence in Iraq involving bargaining, fear, and denial. Bohorquez et al. (2009) used an innovative analysis of IBC's data, along with other data from a wide range of high-quality datasets for modern wars, to develop the first unified model of insurgency, explaining the ecology of modern wars and predicting general patterns of insurgent groups and of large- and small-sized incidents of insurgent violence over time and space. Mubareka et al. (2005) used IBC's media-reported temporal, geographic, and fatality data from violent incidents to identify levels of violence and "security events" to create dynamic maps depicting the working situation on the ground in crisis-affected regions for donors and humanitarian aid agencies that plan to deploy personnel.

## Direct Uses of IBC in the Medical Literature

One use of IBC's incident-based data with which the authors of this chapter have been directly involved is research designed to improve understanding of the impact of violence on Iraqi public health in general and on vulnerable demographic subgroups, and to support efforts to develop civilian-protective, preventive policies for future conflicts. This work has consisted so far of two analyses: one of the impact on Iraqi civilians of different weapon types (Hicks et al. 2009), and one of the main perpetrators of violence in Iraq's armed conflict (Hicks et al. 2011).

Our 2009 study analyzed 14,196 violent incidents contained within the IBC database detailing 60,481 civilian deaths that occurred in the first five years following the invasion of Iraq. These incidents were specifically chosen for analysis because they were confined to a single time and place and only one type of weapon was used. This design provided a uniquely comprehensive overview of the relative harm that different weapons—from low- to high-tech—brought to Iraq's civilian population. The average number killed per incident (for incidents in which a civilian was killed) was 4, but the average number killed per incident involving air-launched bombs or combined air and ground attacks was 17, and the average number killed by suicide bombers traveling on foot was 16.

We also analyzed the demographic characteristics of noncombatants killed by different forms of violence. Execution after abduction or capture was the single most common form of death overall, with 95 percent of execution victims being male. For Iraqi females, and children, incidents involving air attacks and mortar fire were the most dangerous. In air attacks causing civilian deaths, 46 percent of victims of known sex were female, and 39 percent of victims of known age were children. Mortar attacks caused similarly high proportions of female and child victims (44 percent and 42 percent, respectively). We considered this compelling evidence that because such weapons and such attacks kill civilians indiscriminately, they should not be directed at populated areas. Such weapon-specific findings have implications for a wide range of conflicts, because the patterns found in this study are likely to be replicated for these weapons whenever they are used.

Our 2011 study analyzed civilian deaths caused by weapons of different types as used by the main perpetrators of violence in Iraq. Of the 92,614 Iraqi civilians reported killed by armed violence during the five-year period of the study, 74 percent were killed by unidentified (i.e., un-uniformed) perpetrators who were directly targeting civilians in the absence of any military or Coalition-associated target; 11 percent were killed by anti-Coalition forces during attacks on Coalition-associated targets; and 12 percent were killed by Coalition forces. Incident-based analysis showed that the highest average number of civilians killed per event in which a civilian died were from unidentified-perpetrator suicide bombings targeting civilians (19 per lethal event) and from Coalition aerial bombings (17 per lethal event).

Because IBC's incident-based database interlinks specific violent events with their perpetrators, civilian deaths can be examined not only as an important public health outcome, but also as an indicator of combatants' compliance with international humanitarian laws and customary standards (e.g., the Geneva Conventions) protecting civilians (Hicks and Spagat 2008; International Committee of the Red Cross 2011). We therefore measured proportional rates at which perpetrators in Iraq killed women and children by using a Woman and Child "Dirty War Index" (DWI) (Hicks and Spagat 2008) to indicate indiscriminate harm. We found that compared with anti-Coalition forces, Coalition forces caused a higher total Woman and Child DWI for 2003–2008, with no evidence of a significant decrease over time. We also examined small-arms deaths caused by Coalition and anti-Coalition forces; we found that relatively indiscriminate effects from Coalition gunfire persisted over five years post-invasion, with the clear implication that to assess and strengthen civilian protection, Coalition efforts to minimize civilian casualties must be coupled with systematic quantitative monitoring of these casualties.

A temporal analysis of Coalition weapon-effects showed that numbers of woman and child deaths, and numbers of civilian deaths from air attacks, peaked between March 20, 2003, and May 1, 2003, when Coalition forces led by the United States used heavy air power in the invasion of Iraq. These findings, combined with findings of high Woman and Child DWI outcomes from air attacks, suggested that heavy reliance on air power during the invasion may have been particularly costly for Iraqi civilians—and especially for women and children—in terms of deaths and injuries. Our findings on temporal and victim demographic patterns from Coalition air attacks supported the position taken by Landmine Action (2009), the United Nations Security Council (2009), and the United Nations Institute for Disarmament Research (2010): namely, that indiscriminate lethal effects of explosive aerial weapons on civilians should be addressed through changed practice and policy on the use of air power in armed conflict, with air attacks on populated areas prohibited or systematically monitored to demonstrate civilian protection.

Overall, our 2009 and 2011 findings using IBC incident-based data illustrate the feasibility as well as the public health and humanitarian potential of detailed tracking of war's effects on a civilian population, To assess and strengthen civilian protection, it is necessary that military efforts to minimize civilian casualties be coupled with systematic monitoring of casualties, of which IBC's work is an example.


## How Do IBC Data Compare with Other Sources of Data?

One way to test the validity of IBC's trends and overall numbers of civilian violent deaths is to look at alternative sources that are not journalistically based (and thus unlikely to be affected by reporting restrictions), and see if they follow the same trends.

Figures 4.2 and 4.3 compare trends in IBC's data on civilian violent deaths against those of the Iraqi Ministry of Health and of the U.S. Department of Defense over extended periods of the conflict. IBC's figures on civilian deaths have historically been higher than from these official sources; over time, however, closely matching trends are seen.

In the second half of 2010, a unique opportunity to compare media-reported data with government-collected data became possible through the public release by the WikiLeaks organization of what they and others describe as the Iraq War Logs (see, e.g., www.iraqwarlogs.com). These logs, which are a near-complete run from the U.S. Department of Defense (DoD) SIGACTS (Significant Activities) database for 2004–2009 (missing only two months, May 2004 and March 2009), contain more than 54,000 reports of incidents in which violent deaths occurred. This constitutes by far the largest database of individual conflict-related incidents ever released for a single conflict. It appears that these logs are the primary source of the composite figures publicly released by DoD from time to time.

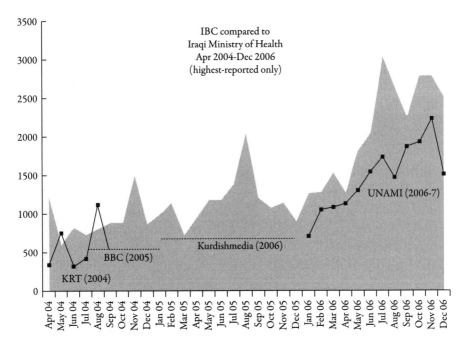

FIGURE 4.2 IBC Trends against Figures from the Iraqi Ministry of Health, April 2004–December 2006

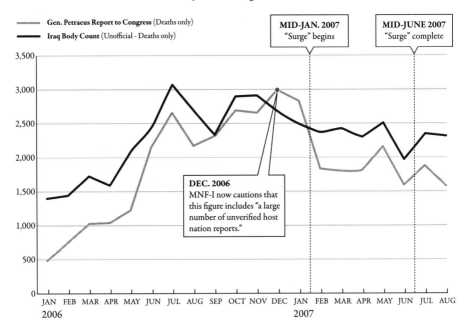

**Notes:** Iraq Body Count numbers from May - August 2007 are estimates.

FIGURE 4.3 IBC Trends against Figures from the U.S. Department of Defense, January 2006–August 2007
*Source:* IBC/DoD chart credit: *Washington Post*, Dobbs (2007).

Use of a preliminary sampling and detailed cross-checking method undertaken between August and October 2010 (Iraq Body Count 2010a, 2010d) allowed us to determine that there is significant but not complete overlap between IBC and the Iraq War Logs. We estimated that 64,000 deaths are recorded in both IBC and the logs, 15,000 are unique to the logs (i.e., not in IBC), and 27,000 are unique to IBC (i.e., not in the logs).

As of this writing, further analysis is being conducted, but preliminary findings clearly indicate two of the chief reasons for the differences between the Iraq War Logs and the IBC. First, deaths uniquely reported in the Iraq War Logs arise predominantly from incidents in which one or two individuals were killed. These are precisely the types of incident known to receive less extensive coverage by commercial media (http://www.iraqbodycount.org/analysis/beyond/put-to-work/4). Second, deaths uniquely reported in IBC include some for which on-the-ground sources identify civilian casualties, whereas DoD sources code the casualties as predominantly combatant. This is particularly noticeable in major air-led military actions (Iraq Body Count 2010a). Despite these differences, however, the overall trends (in terms of violence over time and by governorate) revealed by the two datasets closely match.

IBC data correlate closely, too, with the results produced by two surveys of samples of the Iraqi population. The Iraq Family Health Survey shows similar trends and distribution of violent deaths by region (Iraq Family Health Survey Group 2008). The Iraq Living Conditions Survey data (Government of Iraq 2005a, 2005b) for war-related deaths by governorate (Guerrero Serdán 2009) likewise correlate closely with IBC findings. In both cases, some differences do exist, but these are at least partly attributable to the failure of the surveys to distinguish adult male victims according to combatant or civilian status.

The validity of IBC data on civilian violent deaths in Iraq can also be assessed by comparing demographic patterns in IBC data against demographic patterns in civilian violent death data issued by the Government of Iraq. Demographic data released by the Government of Iraq for 2009 (the only full year for which the government has released demographic data) shows that 4,068 civilian violent deaths occurred in 2009, of which 80 percent were men, 11 percent were women, and 9 percent were children (United Nations Assistance Mission for Iraq 2010). IBC's database documents 4,691 civilian violent deaths for 2009, and of those that are demographically identifiable, 77 percent were men, 11 percent were women, and 12 percent were children.

## Strengths and Limitations of IBC's Methodology

All methods of counting casualties have their advantages and disadvantages. In this section, we describe the strengths and limitations of using incident- and media-based casualty data (with IBC as the example), and of using survey-based data. We also discuss how conflict circumstances may make one method more feasible or valid than another.

In many cases, including the Iraq conflict, data derived from different methods can be mutually complementary and can produce a more comprehensive picture of the civilian impact of war.

Media coverage of casualty information and the ability to quickly integrate that information have been significantly enhanced by recent technological developments. The IBC project exploits these developments and points to what may be possible as the techniques and equipment evolve. Press and media reports are too rich and valuable a source of information on violence to be disregarded. The IBC method for compiling a database of civilian deaths from reported incidents of armed violence is premised not only on the existence of active press coverage of armed violence and media access to reliable information on violent incidents, but also on reasonably robust information networks across the country that support the rapid dissemination of reports. In Iraq, details of incidents in remote regions of the country almost always reach the newswire services within 24 hours. The rapid production of media reports, as opposed to the publication of monthly or yearly aggregate reports from official sources, allows IBC to continually update its database by incorporating new reports of violent deaths as soon as they emerge.

In contrast, a survey is based on retrospectively gathered data and cannot be updated once the survey has ended. Therefore, although surveys have the advantage of providing an estimate of the total number of deaths (whereas the methods employed by IBC tally only recorded deaths), a survey's estimate is limited by the fact that it is static. Surveys cannot be used to track trends unless similar surveys are repeated at multiple points over time. Periodic surveys of conflict-associated violent deaths are difficult to implement because of the logistical difficulties, high cost, and danger involved in carrying out surveys in conflict settings (Thoms and Ron 2007). Epidemiological surveys in armed conflicts can be affected by recall bias, reporting bias, survival bias, sampling bias, and difficulties in implementation (Murray et al. 2002; Daponte 2007; Thoms and Ron 2007; Johnson et al. 2008). IBC's methodology minimizes recall bias—99 percent of events being investigated are reported within 24 hours (Iraq Body Count 2007b)—and permits surveillance over time of traceable events. These characteristics have been described as valuable attributes for monitoring and analyzing conflict mortality trends (Murray et al. 2002; Daponte 2007; Geneva Declaration Secretariat 2008; Iraq Family Health Survey Study Group 2008).

The kind of reporting environment that exists in Iraq is not found everywhere, but elements of it are appearing in more and more conflict zones. Examples include the Ushahidi system (http://www.ushahidi.com/), which maps international crises in real time, and initiatives such as OCHOA's Libya Crisis Map (http://libyacrisismap.net/), a collation of reports on the unfolding crisis in Libya in 2011. There is evidence that robust modern information infrastructures can be quickly established. The Internet is the prime example; but cellular telephone networks are also important, since they afford nonprofessional individuals greater access and mobility than the Internet for documenting and reporting violent casualties from the midst of armed conflict. Barriers to reporting conflict casualties that existed ten or even just five years ago are disappearing.

In addition, the professional media companies are themselves resourceful, adaptive organizations that can be agents in developing informational and technical infrastructure. In Iraq, Western news agencies have given training and substantial support to some new Iraqi media. Aswat al-Iraq (Voices of Iraq), for instance, was set up with the support of the Reuters Foundation (Reuters Foundation 2006). Because of the importance of media interest to its methodology, the IBC approach in its current form is particularly well suited for conflicts in which major powers with multiple, independent commercial media agencies are engaged intensively and over the long term. These circumstances ensure a high level of interest and involvement in reporting the conflict by the best-resourced and most technologically advanced media.

There is widespread agreement that media reports can provide systematic, meaningful data on conflict casualties (Taback and Coupland 2005; Coupland 2007; Daponte 2007; Geneva Declaration Secretariat 2008; Harbom and Sundberg 2008; Urlacher 2009). However, in some conflicts, the frequency, coverage, and quality of media-reported data may be degraded by difficulties of data gathering, by censorship, or by other limitations imposed on the media's monitoring effort. The net effect may be that little or no casualty data can be obtained. The considerations specific to each conflict require examination to assess the advantages and disadvantages of using media-reported data on that conflict. The media-based approach is ill suited for describing casualties that occur during periods of conflict in which major military powers impose "lockdowns" or information blackouts on a particular town or region. In Iraq, the U.S. military has imposed some effective temporary, localized lockdowns but has not been able to sustain them. As a consequence, U.S. forces have prevented the reporting of many individual incidents but not, ultimately, the reporting of overall resulting casualty totals, which are relayed to the media by local hospitals and medics. These casualty totals, however, remain relatively uncertain in comparison to incident-based records and lack many of the factual details that typically accompany incident-based data (Iraq Body Count 2004a, 2004b). The enforcement of such lockdowns—which have included attempts to muzzle medics—has itself been an immediate and unflattering source of media attention; given that the purpose of lockdowns is to control negative publicity, media criticism of them may act as a check on the practice (Dominick 2004).

Carefully designed quantitative and qualitative studies are needed to determine what biases may affect media reporting on casualties of armed conflict, in Iraq and elsewhere. In the case of IBC, we have speculated that media reports may identify women and children more readily than adult male civilians among the dead, perhaps for human interest or from a normative assumption that a victim of armed violence is a man unless stated otherwise (Hicks et al. 2011). If such a bias existed, it could affect proportional findings of women and children among civilian deaths of men, women, and children. We have also considered the possibility that the media may underreport injuries relative to deaths. IBC records casualties only from events that caused at least one civilian death. This automatically leads to an underdetection of civilians injured by armed violence in the conflict.

In addition, the media generally reports deaths more consistently than injuries in nearly all reporting on armed violence (Coupland and Meddings 1999). This is a second factor lowering the detection of injuries by IBC's media-reported data (and one reason that IBC uses its injuries data only rarely). For these reasons, IBC injury data may be considered to be a minimum that can be useful for analyzing trends (e.g., over time) and for performing comparisons (e.g., between different weapon-effects), but should not be considered an accounting of total injuries. Determining the degree to which the media underreport injuries relative to deaths would allow statistical adjustment for a more accurate picture of the impact of armed violence on civilians. The establishment of standards for reporting victim information could improve the contribution of media reports to understanding violence.

A general limitation of using media reports to study armed conflict is that journalists collect and report information for purposes other than systematic inquiry. IBC has found that all media, and especially most of the Western media, are significantly more likely to report larger incidents (more than five deaths) than incidents that killed one or two Iraqi civilians. Above ten deaths, there tends to be blanket coverage by a wide range of media, both Iraqi and Western. If most of the deaths in Iraq were of this sort, then one would not need to monitor more than a few of these sources. For fewer than three deaths, however, the coverage begins to become patchier, even within the local press, which is why IBC has had to monitor all relevant media and to supplement it with aggregate data to piece together the most comprehensive picture possible. These efforts result in nearly half (45 percent) of the incidents in the IBC database having involved the killing of a single individual.

As shown in figure 4.4, incidents that kill a greater number of individuals attract a greater number of media reports. One implication of this correlation is that incidents that kill few individuals are more likely to be missed by IBC than incidents that kill many individuals. Another implication is that above a certain casualty threshold for an incident, it becomes highly unlikely the incident will go completely unreported. The smaller incidents coded by IBC (e.g., those that caused a single death) are the most likely to be missed in direct reporting by any one media source; however, they appear to some extent in aggregate form in the IBC database in reported morgue and hospital figures (Iraq Body Count 2007b).

A strength of IBC's incident-based approach is its capacity to provide verifiable data on a very high number of actual civilian deaths from armed violence, with data on over 110,000 individual deaths as of May 2011 (Iraq Body Count 2011). Surveys extrapolate from relatively few actual violent deaths (e.g., the Iraq Family Health Survey of 9,345 households recorded 164 violent deaths [Iraq Family Health Survey Group 2008]), and numbers of violent deaths at this scale preclude the meaningful extrapolation of a survey's even smaller raw numbers of different demographic groups killed by different weapons.

Governments and other significant official and unofficial sources announce aggregate casualty totals and trends from time to time. The availability of detailed incident-level data such as that provided by IBC offers an opportunity to evaluate such announcements.

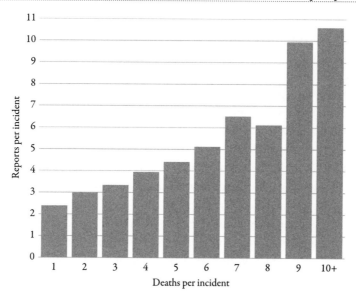

FIGURE 4.4 The Relationship between Deaths per Incident and Reports per Incident

For instance, according to figures from Iraq's ministries of Interior, Health, and Defense published on December 31, 2007,there were 16,232 civilian deaths and 1,300 police deaths in 2007. Despite their lack of detail, these figures were considerably lower than the IBC totals for the comparable period (as they had been in earlier years). IBC's documented civilian death toll for 2007 lies in the range of 22,586–24,159, and each of these deaths is associated with a published report tying that death to a specific date and location. Therefore, the onus is on those who have provided lower aggregate figures to explain which of the specific IBC-recorded incidents are not included in their 2007 civilian death toll and why not (Iraq Body Count 2008).

The IBC database directly links data on a violent incident (e.g., time, location, perpetrator, and weapon used) with data on the specific individuals killed or injured by the incident (e.g., occupation or age). This linkage between incident and victim data allows for analysis of direct causes of individual Iraqi casualties. The analyses we described earlier of civilian deaths from perpetrators and their weapons during five years of the Iraq war illustrate the feasibility, as well as the public health and humanitarian potential, of detailed tracking of war's effects on a civilian population based on incident data. Survey data and clinical data on casualties are generally untraceable to the specific weapon or event that caused an individual casualty. Further, IBC specifically identifies civilian deaths, whereas surveys mix combatant and civilian deaths (Spiegel and Salama 2000; Burnham et al. 2006; Thoms and Ron 2007), thereby limiting direct comparisons of violent death data from IBC and from surveys.

A general limitation of reported incident-based data, such as IBC's, is the tendency to provide a less than total count of conflict deaths; this is because not every violent death and incident is reported or officially recorded, even in relatively developed and bureaucratic societies such as Iraq. It is therefore important for efforts like IBC's not to claim otherwise, and indeed to draw attention to this limitation. However, such caveats are sometimes ignored by audiences less interested in the factual accuracy of casualty data than in the political capital to be made from them.

The methods used by IBC are inappropriate for documenting indirect deaths from conflict, such as deaths from conflict-associated diseases or starvation. Indirect deaths are not reported consistently in the media or, for many conflict-affected nations, in official reports. IBC's method tracks only direct deaths from armed violence. Data derived in this way are also generally ill suited for allocating a precise place or date for secret executions or other violent incidents that have no third-party witnesses or are not recorded in publicly released, primary documentation. In the case of secret executions, which accounted for one-third of Iraqi civilian violent deaths in 2003–2008 (Hicks et al. 2009), victims' bodies were typically discovered later, commingled in mass graves, floating down rivers, or dumped by roadsides. Bodies discovered after the event are delivered to morgues, hospitals, and police stations, where cumulative records are kept. Victim data from these official sources, predominantly morgues, are typically available in aggregate, monthly reports. Data from these reports can be integrated into the IBC database, provided location can be determined to the governorate level and time frame to the monthly level, even if the exact place and time of death cannot be determined.

Another limitation of using incident-reported data from media and aggregate sources is that the coverage of data for different variables varies widely. As shown in figure 4.5, nearly all incidents have data on variables such as location by nearest town, target, and weapons used. However, only a quarter of perpetrators were identifiable, a phenomenon

**Incident details present for extraction in % of 12,934 DB entries**
*Jan 2006–Sep 2008*

| | |
|---|---|
| Number Killed | 100.0% |
| Location (by nearest-town) | 99.9% |
| Targeted or hit | 96.8% |
| Exact Date | 94.8% |
| Weapon | 94% |
| Primary sources | 86.1% |
| Location (within-town) | 82.2% |
| Number Injured | 80.9% |
| Time of day | 76% |
| Perpetrator | 23.2% |

FIGURE 4.5 Coverage of Key Reported Variables of Incidents Deadly to Civilians

that is due in part to the characteristics of the asymmetrical, irregular warfare being carried out in Iraq. Coalition forces were identifiable by uniforms or weapons (e.g., only Coalition forces used air attacks). Anti-Coalition forces did not wear uniforms but were identifiable because their target was a Coalition or Coalition-associated target. The third group, the largest, consisted of "unknown" perpetrators: un-uniformed combatants and criminals who attacked purely civilian targets in the absence of any military or Coalition-associated target. IBC's media-reported, incident-based victim variables were also subject to coverage limitations, with age and sex determined for only one-third of victims. Occupation was determined for only 13 percent of victims (Iraq Body Count 2007b).

## How to Improve Incident-Based Casualty Recording?

Active, daily monitoring of media reports, as IBC has shown to be feasible under the conditions of the Iraq War, has the clear potential to provide timely information that can be used both to identify trends or tactics that endanger civilians and to devise measures and alternative tactics to protect civilians. To realize this potential fully, however, researchers need access to various kinds of data: the commercial data streams available to major news media; the data held by governments and militaries, which tend not to release data on civilians until decades after a conflict, if at all; and data held by NGOs, which are often released in aggregate form but with raw data withheld from the public. In all cases, raw data can and should be appropriately anonymized as part of the data processing if the release of victim or incident data might place individuals at risk.

The systematic compilation and integration of incident-based casualty data, which must be accompanied by cross-checking to avoid double-counting if it is to be useful, is highly labor intensive. It depends on the methodical scrutiny of tens of thousands of documents for data extraction and codification, and a series of quality control checks before publication of results, on a continuing basis. If data are to be produced and disseminated on a timely basis, this process requires a sizable workforce of highly trained, and ideally multilingual, readers. Advanced technology is also essential, in particular computerized platforms designed specifically to deal with very large, relatively unordered, and rapidly moving data streams. These platforms should be customizable for different projects but able to embody common frameworks for data entry, data management, data security, and data presentation.

Because communication, innovation, and sharing of ideas, experiences, and methods are critical to moving the field of civilian casualty recording forward, a properly resourced meeting ground is needed on which casualty recording practitioners from different conflict environments can interact and learn from one another's methods. In fact, one such venue for interaction now exists: everycasualty.org is a network created recently by 20 member organizations that take incident-based approaches to casualty recording. Financial support from the United States Institute of Peace, the Federal Division of Foreign Affairs of the Swiss Government, and the "zivik" program of the Institute for Foreign Cultural Relations funded by the German Federal Foreign Office has allowed everycasualty.org to launch an initial program of networking and development activities (see http://www.oxfordresearchgroup.org.uk/projects/recording_casualties_armed_conflict). Our hope is that this effort will spur the development of the nascent professional field of conflict casualty recording, able to discuss and develop best practices and context-aware practice, support the training and development of individuals, and legitimately represent the field to governments and the public.

In the case not only of Iraq but of armed conflicts generally, no official public mechanism exists to count individual civilian victims, let alone identify them, in an ongoing and comprehensive manner. The IBC project is one among a number of unofficial contributions toward filling that gap. However, governments and intergovernmental agencies should as a matter of principle facilitate and support comprehensive and long-term casualty recording, not only of their soldiers but of the civilians killed in their wars. Whatever level of official support and engagement may eventually be forthcoming, the establishment of an independent and politically neutral monitoring agency would help foster trust and engagement in the mission to record individual civilian casualties. This agency could serve either as a central organization for civilian casualty monitoring or as a looser umbrella organization promoting good practice among multiple, conflict-specific monitoring groups.

There will always be a role for autonomous groups and individuals, such as those involved in IBC and many similar NGOs, to participate on a grassroots level in data collection, monitoring, advocacy, innovation, and holding governments to account. Citizen involvement also ensures that projects reflect local priorities. However, to rely entirely on the volunteers who staff these poorly funded groups to carry out the prolonged, extensive, and labor-intensive work of monitoring civilian casualties of war is to deny and to defer the responsibility of parties to war, the societies that support them, and the international community to assess the direct impact of war on civilians by using the best systematic methods available.

REFERENCES

Alvarez-Ramirez, J., Rodriguez, E., Tyrtania, L., and Urrea-Garcia, G. R. 2010. "Regime-Transitions in the 2003–2010 Iraq War: An Approach Based on Correlations of Daily Fatalities." *Peace Economics, Peace Science and Public Policy*, 16(1): Art. 11. At: http://www.bepress.com/peps/vol16/iss1/11 Accessed June 10, 2011.

Ball, P., Tabeau, E., and Verwimp, P. 2007. "The Bosnian Book of Dead: Assessment of the Database (Full Report)." *Houses in Conflict Network Research Design Working Paper 5*. Brighton, East Sussex, U.K.: HiCN.

Bohorquez, J. C., Gourley, S., Dixon, A. R., Spagat, M., and Johnson, N. F. 2009. "Common Ecology Quantifies Human Insurgency." *Nature* 462: 911–914.

Boyle, M. J. 2009. "Bargaining, Fear, and Denial: Explaining Violence Against Civilians in Iraq 2004–2007." *Terrorism and Political Violence* 21: 261–287.

B'Tselem. 2011. At: http://www.btselem.org/. Accessed June 11, 2011.

Burnham, G., Lafta, R., Doocy, S., and Roberts, L. 2006. "Mortality After the 2003 Invasion of Iraq: a Cross-Sectional Cluster Sample Survey." *The Lancet* 368: 1421–1428.

Condra, L. N., Felter, J. H., Iyengar, R. K., and Shapiro J. N. 2010. "The Effect of Civilian Casualties in Afghanistan and Iraq." *Working Paper 16152, National Bureau of Economic Research Working Paper Series.* Cambridge, MA: NBER.

Coupland, R. 2007. "Security, Insecurity and Health." *Bulletin of the World Health Organization* 85: 181–184.

Coupland, R. M., and Meddings, D. R. 1999. "Mortality Associated with Use of Weapons in Armed Conflicts, Wartime Atrocities, and Civilian Mass Shootings: Literature Review." *British Medical Journal* 319: 407–410.

Daponte, B. O. 2007. "Wartime Estimates of Iraqi Civilian Casualties." *International Review of the Red Cross* 89: 943–957.

Dardagan, H., Sloboda, J., Williams, K., and Bagnall, P. 2005. "Iraq Body Count: A Dossier of Civilian Casualties 2003–2005." Oxford: Oxford Research Group. At: http://www.iraqbodycount.org/analysis/reference/press-releases/12/ Accessed March 19, 2011.

Fischhoff, B., Atran, S., and Fischhoff, N. 2007. "Counting Casualties: A Framework for Respectful, Useful Records." *Journal of Risk and Uncertainty* 34: 1–19.

Dominick, B. 2004. "In Fallujah, U.S. Declares War on Hospitals, Ambulances." *The New Standard*, November 9. At: http://newstandardnews.net/content/index.cfm/items/1208. Accessed June 10, 2011.

Geneva Declaration Secretariat. 2008. *Global Burden of Armed Violence.* Geneva, Switzerland: Geneva Declaration Secretariat.

Government of Iraq. 2005a. "Iraq Living Conditions Survey 2004." *Volume I: Tabulation Report.* Baghdad: Ministry of Planning and Development Cooperation. At: http://cosit.gov.iq/english/pdf/english_tabulation.pdf. Accessed May 18, 2011.

———. 2005b. "Iraq Living Conditions Survey 2004." *Volume II: Analytical Report.* Baghdad: Ministry of Planning and Development Cooperation. At: http://www.fafo.no/ais/middeast/iraq/imira/Tabulation%20reports/eng%20analytical%20report.pdf. Accessed May 18, 2011.

Grimes, D. A., and Schulz, K. F. 2002. "Descriptive Studies: What They Can and Cannot Do." *The Lancet* 359: 145–149.

Guerrero Serdán, G. 2009. "The Effects of the War in Iraq on Nutrition and Health: An Analysis Using Anthropometric Outcomes of Children." *Households in Conflict Network Working Paper 55.* Brighton, East Sussex, U.K.: HiCN. At: http://www.hicn.org/papers/wp55.pdf. Accessed May 18, 2011.

Harbom, L., and Sundberg, R., eds. 2008. *States in Armed Conflict 2007.* Uppsala: Uppsala University Press.

Hicks, M. H., and Spagat, M. 2008. "The Dirty War Index: A Public Health and Human Rights Tool for Examining and Monitoring Armed Conflict Outcomes." *PLoS Medicine* 5(12): e243.

Hicks, M. H., Dardagan, H., Guerrero Serdán, G., Bagnall, P. M., Sloboda, J. A., and Spagat, M. 2009. "The Weapons That Kill Civilians—Deaths of Children and Noncombatants in Iraq, 2003–2008." *New England Journal of Medicine* 360: 1585–1588.

———. 2011. "Violent deaths of Iraqi civilians, 2003–2008: Analysis by Perpetrator, Weapon, Time, and Location." *PLoS Medicine* 8(2): e1000415.

International Committee of the Red Cross. 2011. "War and International Humanitarian Law." At: http://www.icrc.org/eng/ihl Accessed June 12, 2011.

Iraq Body Count. 2004a. "No Longer Unknowable: Fallujah's April Civilian Toll is 600." At: http://www.iraqbodycount.org/analysis/reference/press-releases/9/ (Published October 26)

———. 2004b. "581–670 in Nine Neighborhoods of Falluja." At: http://www.iraqbodycount.org/database/incidents/x453 (Published December)

———. 2007a. "How Has IBC Been Used by Others?" At: http://www.iraqbodycount.org/analysis/qa/used-how/ (Published September 3)

———. 2007b. "How Can the Utility of Press Reports be Assessed? Some Preliminary Approaches to Testing Media Completeness and Reliability in Reporting Civilian Casualties." At: http://www.iraqbodycount.org/analysis/qa/assessment/21 and http://www.iraqbodycount.org/analysis/qa/assessment/22. Accessed June 11, 2011.

———. 2008. "Civilian deaths from Violence in 2007." At: http://www.iraqbodycount.org/analysis/numbers/2007/) (Published January 1)

———. 2010a. "Iraq War Logs: What the Numbers Reveal." At: http://www.iraqbodycount.org/analysis/numbers/warlogs/ (Published October 23)

———. 2010b. "Iraq War Logs: The Truth is in the Detail." At: http://www.iraqbodycount.org/analysis/beyond/warlogs/ (Published October 23)

———. 2010c. "Iraq War Logs: Context." At: http://www.iraqbodycount.org/analysis/qa/warlogs/ (Published October 23)

———. 2010d. "Iraq War Logs: Technical Appendix to IBC Analysis." At: http://www.iraqbodycount.org/analysis/numbers/warlogs-appendix/ (Published October 26)

———. 2010e. "For the Public Record, in the Public Interest." At: http://www.iraqbodycount.org/analysis/qa/aclu-ibc/ Accessed June 11, 2011.

———. 2011. "Iraq Body Count." At: http://www.iraqbodycount.org/.

Iraq Family Health Survey Study Group: Alkhuzai, A. H., Ahmad, I. J., Hweel, M. J., Ismail, T. W., Hasan, H. H., Younis. A. R., Shawani, O., Al-Jaf, V. M., Al-Alak, M. M., Rasheed, L. H., Hamid, S. M., Al-Gasseer, N., Majeed, F. A., Al-Awqati, N. A., Ali, M. M., Boerma, J. T., and Mathers, C. 2008. "Violence-Related Mortality in Iraq from 2002–2006." *New England Journal of Medicine* 358(5): 484–493.

Johnson N. F., Spagat, M., Gourley, S., Onnela, J., and Reinert, G. 2008. "Bias in Epidemiological Studies of Conflict Mortality." *Journal of Peace Research* 45: 653–663.

Landmine Action. 2009. *Explosive Violence: The Problem of Explosive Weapons.* Landmine Action: London. At: http://www.landmineaction.org/resources/Explosive%20violence.pdf. Accessed June 11, 2011.

Mubareka, S., Al Khudhairy, D., Bonn, F., and Aoun, S. 2005. "Standardising and Mapping Open-Source Information for Crisis Regions: The Case of Post-Conflict Iraq." *Disasters* 29: 287–254.

Murray, C. J. L., King, G., Lopez, A. D., Tomijima, N., and Krug, E. G. 2002. "Armed Conflict as a Public Health Problem." *British Medical Journal* 324: 246–349.

Nettelfield, L. J. 2010. "Research and Repercussions of Death Tolls: The Case of the Bosnian Book of the Dead." In *Sex, Drugs, and Body Counts: The Politics of Numbers in Global Crime*, edited by Peter Andreas and Kelly M. Greenhill. Ithaca, NY: Cornell University Press.

Philpott, S. 2010. "Introduction: Searching for Strategy in an Age of Peacebuilding." In *Strategies of Peace*, edited by D. Philpott, and G. Powers. New York: Oxford University Press, 3–18.

Reuters Foundation. 2006. *Reuters Foundation Reporters Handbook*. Reuters Ltd: London. At: http://www.trust.org/trustmedia/resources/handbooks/reportershandbook.pdf. Accessed June 6, 2011.

Schirch, L. 2008. "Strategic Peacebuilding—State of the Field." *Peace Prints: South Asian Journal of Peacebuilding* 1(1): Spring 2008. At: http://www.wiscomp.org/peaceprints.htm. Accessed June 11, 2011.

Spiegel, P. B., and Salama, P. 2000. "War and Mortality in Kosovo, 1998–99: An Epidemiological Testimony." *The Lancet* 355: 2204–2209.

Taback, N., and Coupland, R. 2005. "Towards Collation and Modeling of the Global Cost of Armed Violence on Civilians." *Medicine, Conflict, and Survival* 21: 19–27.

Thoms, O. N. T., and Ron, J. 2007. "Public Health, Conflict and Human Rights: Toward a Collaborative Research Agenda." *Conflict and Health* 1: 11.

Tilly, C. 1969. "Methods for the Study of Collective Violence." In *Problems in Research on Community Violence*, edited by R. Conant and M. A. Levin. New York: Praeger Publishers.

Tilly, C., and Schweitzer, R. A. 1980. "Enumerating and Coding Contentious Gatherings in Nineteenth-Century Britain." *Center for Research in Social Organizations Working Paper 210*. CRSO: University of Michigan.

Urlacher, B. R. 2009. "Wolfowitz Conjecture: A Research Note on Civil War and News Coverage." *International Studies Perspectives* 10: 186–197.

United Nations Assistance Mission for Iraq. 2010. "UNAMI Human Rights Report, July 1–December 31, 2009." At: http://www.uniraq.org/documents/UNAMI_Human_Rights_Report16_EN.pdf. Accessed June 12, 2011.

United Nations Institute for Disarmament Research. 2010. "Explosive Weapons: Framing the Problem." *Background Paper 1 of the Discourse on Explosive Weapons (DEW) Project, April 2010*. At: http://explosiveweapons.info/category/unidir/. Accessed October 16, 2010.

United Nations Office of the High Commissioner for Human Rights. 1989. Convention on the Rights of the Child. Geneva: UN Office of the High Commissioner for Human Rights. At: http://www2.ohchr.org/english/law/crc.htm. Accessed March 19, 2011.

United Nations Security Council. 2009. "Report of the Secretary-General on the Protection of Civilians in Armed Conflict. S/2009/277. 27 p. At: http://www.un.org/Docs/sc/sgrep09.htm. Accessed June 12, 2011.

# 5 A Matter of Convenience

CHALLENGES OF NON-RANDOM DATA IN ANALYZING
HUMAN RIGHTS VIOLATIONS DURING CONFLICTS IN PERU
AND SIERRA LEONE

Todd Landman and Anita Gohdes

ANALYZING EVENTS IN the field of human rights and violent conflict involves over-coming a number of challenges related to the nature of the event, the unit of analysis, the complexity of the event itself, the type of source material available, and the ability to overcome inherent biases in the source material. At a basic level, events share a number of characteristic features. They have start dates, end dates, duration, dimensions such as magnitude and size, including the number of actors involved (e.g., individuals, groups, regions, countries, organizations), the types of things that actors do, and the types of things that happen to them (e.g., violence, liberation, suppression). Work on political violence in conflict situations tends to focus on individual deaths and disappearances, where often the perpetrator, context, and other defining features of the death remain obscure. For analysis that is of use in the domains of policy and advocacy, it is precisely this obscure information that needs to be uncovered in ways that provide deeper explanation and understanding of what happened and why it happened in a particular context. Using the cases of Peru and Sierra Leone, this chapter shows how variation in reporting across different sources inhibits the ability to make statistical estimations that are disaggregated over time and space. In both countries, multiple sources of data have been obtained and in one case, Peru, have been used to make statistical estimates of the total number of dead and disappeared during the respective period of conflict. Our analysis shows that biases in reporting from separate sources limit the ability to provide statistical estimates for particular periods of time or particular areas of each country. The key lessons are that multiple sources are preferred as they allow for more accurate estimates of killings and disappearances than projects that rely on single sources, but that significant differences between these sources will limit our ability to carry out more in-depth analyses of the contours of conflict.

In events-based analysis, the basic unit of analysis can be the event itself (attack, massacre, mass detention, etc.), individual people involved in the event (perpetrator, victim, etc.), or the violations that have been committed during the event (detention, torture, execution, disappearance, etc.). It is to this latter unit of analysis that the most recent advances in events-based data analysis have turned, since the structure of a violent event is often highly complex. The metaphor used is one of the "grammar" of an event, where it is essential to break down the perpetrator (and his or her associated features), the victim (and his or her associated features), the act (or acts) committed, and the defining features of the event, such as the time and the context. The model developed to unpack this event grammar is presented in figure 5.1, and is best known as the "Who did what to whom model?" pioneered by Herbert Spirer and Patrick Ball at the American Association for the Advancement of Science (see, Ball 1996).

Events-based data rely on three particular types of source material: (1) "found" data, (2) narrative data, and (3) official statements. Found data include such data as archival records (e.g., Chad, as discussed by Silva et al. 2010), border data on refugees (e.g., Kosovo, per Ball et al. 2002), morgue records (e.g., Haiti), exhumations (e.g., Kosovo) and even gravestones, which often contain names, dates, and cause of death (e.g., East Timor, per Silva and Ball 2008). Narrative accounts are those stories of abuse and events reported to and witnessed by nongovernmental agencies, activists, and newspaper reporters. Official

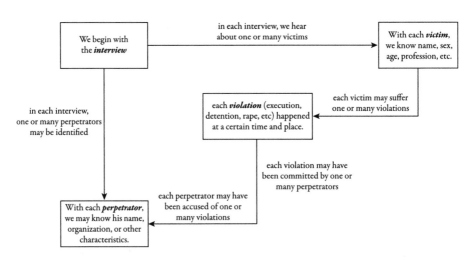

FIGURE 5.1 The "Who Did What to Whom" Model for Analyzing Incidence-Based Data on Human Rights Violations
Source: http://shr.aaas.org/hrdag/idea/datamodel/index.html.

statements are those narrative accounts formally collected through the use of statement forms by truth commissions or equivalent bodies in which individual deponents are given the opportunity to provide a detailed account of single or multiple events. In each case, the raw source material is given quantitative expression through event coding, which then allows for descriptive and statistical analysis to identify patterns, trends, and tendencies in the data from which larger inferences about the situation of violence can be drawn.

Source materials such as those just mentioned are typically "non-random": that is, individual victims, witnesses, or relatives of victims come forward voluntarily and offer information about a violent event; their particular story is then coded into quantitative information. The same holds true for found data, since it can represent only events that have been recorded; it is not a random sample of a population of all events. In the case of voluntary statements, an individual will or will not come forward to bear witness to an event for any number of reasons. To call the source material "non-random" is to acknowledge that human rights violations and other violent events are sometimes misreported: that is, an event may be reported more than once, leading to overreporting, or reported partly or not at all, resulting in underreporting. Because of the over- and underreporting of violent events, the overall "database" of information includes some events more than once and others not at all, making it is difficult to draw secure inferences about the general state of abuse in a particular context. The term "secure inferences" implies that the inferences drawn regarding the magnitude and patterns of violence are representative of the entire population affected. Because non-random samples are not representative of the population, they alone cannot provide secure inferences.

A solution to overcoming the inherent biases in using single non-random samples has been to employ multiple systems estimation (MSE) in which multiple samples of information are used, compared, and analyzed for the degree to which information about particular victims appears in different sources.[1] The ratio of probabilities of those individual victims appearing in different sources can yield statistical estimations (with associated confidence intervals) of the total number of people who were killed or disappeared during the period under investigation. Despite the robustness of MSE in providing estimates for the total number of deaths and disappearances during well-defined periods of time, researchers' ability to provide estimates for specific years or locations is limited by the degree of overlap in the victims reported in each source. In other words, different sources of data about the same context of violence and abuse can give completely different pictures of what actually happened, making reliance on any one source highly problematic when seeking accounts for any episode of violence. Where multiple data sources are available, statistical analysis can significantly increase the accuracy of statements regarding who did what to whom in an armed conflict.

To develop our argument, the chapter discusses the challenges associated with events-based sources, how MSE corrects for the inherent biases in such convenience samples, explains the problems encountered in analyzing data from Peru and Sierra Leone, and summarizes why analysts must address the limitations of convenience samples in future events-based data projects.

## The Challenges of Events-Based Sources

Measuring the scope and structure of violence in a conflict or post-conflict setting is challenging and sometimes seems virtually impossible. Researchers are usually confined to using source materials that were not originally or directly intended for statistical purposes, but still contain enough information to allow analysis with frameworks such as the "who did what to whom" model (Ball 1996). Events-based source materials have many different forms. For example, records of police units, prisons, hospitals, mortuaries, and even graveyards are existing sources that can be mined to collect information on past incidences of violence. In contrast, official statements need to be collected by a truth commission or an NGO before any individual acts of violence can be extracted and coded quantitatively. Similarly, narrative accounts of killings and other forms of violence, as often delivered to journalists and reported in newspapers, have been analyzed and used as the basis for such events-based data projects as the Iraq Body Count project (see chapter 4 in this volume), the Brookings Afghanistan Index, and the recent reports of violence in the Mexican war on drugs released by the Mexican government (Landman and Carvalho 2010).[2]

All these disparate sources have one main feature in common: they record available and observable information. They are known as "convenience" samples, since they are generated without the help of a random selection process. This does not necessarily imply that they are the result of "convenient" data collection efforts; neither does it presuppose an unsystematic collection or recording effort. But even well-planned projects that collect information on violations in a systematic way generally end up with data unrepresentative of the patterns they are attempting to uncover. As the cases of Sierra Leone and Peru in this chapter show, there are many reasons for the central problem with non-random samples, together producing a biased view on the structure, dimensions, and variation of violations that occurred in any given conflict.

Why are data from non-random samples unrepresentative? Some of the main sources of bias are factors relating to time, resource, and space, as well as issues of security and victim visibility. Changing circumstances can have an impact on the collection of data at many different levels. To begin with, organizations collecting information on incidences of violence are susceptible to changes in staffing, reputation, and resources. These changes influence their ability to record violence in a constant way, as well as the relationship between the organization and individuals who face the decision of whether to step forward and report an incidence of violence. Variations within these factors lead to fluctuations in the level of recorded violations that cannot be distinguished from the actual changes in violence. For example, during the data collection phase of the Peruvian

Truth and Reconciliation Commission, the number of statements far exceeded expectations and prolonged the collection phase. Moreover, while additional funds were sought to continue the work, staff on the data team worked without pay for a period, to keep the statement-taking process moving forward. There was an additional "political" problem of divisions between the data collection team and other elements of the truth commission. Absence of "fast" results from the data team and allocation of limited funds to the data team led to tensions and friction that ultimately were resolved.

Beyond such organizational factors, the dynamics of a conflict itself can influence the level of reporting over time. Problems of personal and organizational security can influence levels of recording and reporting, and changes in public attitudes and perceptions can alter field workers' ability to collect data. For example, statistical analysis conducted in Guatemala revealed an inverse relationship between violence in the civil war reported by the newspapers and violence recorded by local NGOs (Davenport and Ball 2002). At precisely the time when the worst atrocities were being committed by the state, news agencies failed to make them public or had even failed to record the events themselves (Ball et al. 1999). Violence that is too dangerous to investigate and report is violence that remains unreported.

A problem of particular concern in long-lasting conflicts is that general attitudes toward the importance of keeping track of violence can change and thereby alter reporting behavior. Thus, fluctuations in recorded violence may not reflect actual changes in the severity of conflict; rather, decreased levels of reported violence can indicate a lower priority on collecting and reporting data, rather than an actual reduction in experienced violence. Moreover, projects that rely on multiple sources of data often have sources that were collected during the period of investigation and are then used alongside data sources (e.g., projects run by truth commissions) compiled after the period of investigation. The probability of reporting victims and events to these different sources will naturally vary according to the time of data collection.

Just as violent acts are not uniformly collected and reported across time, various spatial factors can bias data collection efforts. In the case of the Peruvian Truth and Reconciliation Commission, analysis revealed that killings and disappearances occurred at a significantly higher level in the mountainous and rural regions of the country than in the urban area of the capital, Lima (Ball et al. 2003). Indeed, nearly 40 percent of reported killings occurred in the region of Ayacucho alone, with the analysis showing that peasants and indigenous people constituted the majority of victims killed throughout the 20-year conflict.

These examples address two significant points relating to the challenges of data sources. First, data projects that focus on specific geographic areas are likely to misrepresent the overall situation within conflict zones because they are likely to either over- or underestimate the actual numbers, depending on the region where the work is being done. When the only sources available deal with incidences that occurred or were reported in the major population centers of a country, rural incidences of violence will likely to be portrayed in biased fashion. Second, violence is exercised differently not only across geographic spaces, but also across different social sectors. Organizations that record—willingly or unwillingly—data about a specific ethnicity, class, gender, or religion fail to capture the distinctive forms and patterns of violence that differ within these strata. The perceived political orientation or ideological predisposition of different organizations (e.g., a human rights NGO, the Catholic Church) can influence the type of people who report violations and the persons identified as perpetrators of the violations reported.

The last factor addressed here, victim visibility, relates to the relative probability that an event will be reported, given its overall visibility when it occurred. Since the victims of killings cannot report their own loss of life, data collection projects necessarily rely on other individuals or institutions to report the killings. The "visibility" of the violation is thus crucial in determining whether an incident will be reported. Obviously, an execution committed in broad daylight in front of a village under siege has a much higher probability of being reported by one or even more people than a disappearance, which was effected covertly.[3] Related to these challenges are those of victim visibility in remote locations that are relatively isolated geographically, due to altitude or terrain.

It is clear from this brief discussion that the list of factors potentially affecting the reporting and recording of violence and human rights violations is very long. In most cases, multiple factors interact across time and space, making it impossible to uncover biases when only a single source is available. Seven truth commissions to date have adopted the "Who did what to whom?" data model for collecting events-based data on large-scale human rights violations: El Salvador, Haiti, South Africa, Sierra Leone, Guatemala, Peru, and Timor-Leste (the former East Timor). Four of them (El Salvador, Haiti, South Africa, and Sierra Leone) either relied on a single source of data or did not combine their data sources in order to strengthen their inferences about the patterns of violence they uncovered (Landman 2006). The next section examines the opportunities and challenges of working with multiple data sources.

## Correcting for Bias with Multiple Systems Estimation

The discussion of inherent biases in single, non-random samples presents a grim picture regarding the usefulness of individual databases that record violence. However, in many cases there exist multiple sources, which offer a key solution to correcting for some of the problems of bias described in the preceding section. Specifically, the statistical method known as multiple systems estimation, which uses multiple lists of data from different sources, can provide estimates for the unreported cases (Bishop et al. 1975; Zwane and van der Heijden 2005). In addition to the Peruvian story, which is presented in this chapter and is also discussed in chapter 9 in this volume, MSE has been used for estimating large-scale human rights violations in Guatemala, East Timor, and Colombia (Ball et al. 1999;

Silva and Ball 2008; Guberak et al. 2010). MSE is based on recognition that each incidence of violence[4] has the possibility of being recorded in one, two, or more data sources. For example, if three data sources, A, B, and C, are available, a given case may have been reported only to source A, with neither being mentioned in sources B and C nor having been captured by A and C, but not B, and so on. If all the available information is divided up into these different groups, the question that remains is, How many violations were not recorded by *any* source? MSE is a statistical method for using known information to estimate something that is not known—here, the number of violations unrecorded by any source—by looking at the overlap between different sources of information.

The MSE approach takes advantage of multiple data sources to estimate the number of unknown events in the story of violence that a conflict has to tell. However, like any other statistical technique, the method comes with strict assumptions that must be fulfilled if the estimations are to be reliable. We address the four main assumptions only briefly here, as they are discussed in much more detail in chapter 9 (Manrique-Vallier, Price, and Gohdes) in this volume. The first assumption demands that all samples refer to the same closed system of observations. This is usually met, since the conflict period under investigation lies in the past and individuals cannot retrospectively "disappear." The second assumption is that the observations reported in more than one source must be perfectly matched. If, as was the case in Peru, incidents in different sources are matched with a high level of accuracy, the second assumption can also be treated as fulfilled. The last two assumptions are more challenging (as discussed in chapter 9, as well),. The third assumption demands that every observation in one list (in this case, every individual) has the same probability of being recorded as any other. The fourth assumption requires that the sources documenting the observations be independent in their recording efforts (Guberak et al. 2010, 29).

Meeting these four key assumptions introduces the challenge posed by the fact, noted earlier, that individual deaths and disappearances differ in their probability of being reported. A way to deal with this problem is to divide the data into groups for which the probability of individuals being reported is more equal. For example, if we assume that individuals who died in a certain year had a similar probability of being captured and that the geographical position of a person's death largely determines whether that individual is included in a database, we can separate the data into subgroups for different locations at different times in the conflict. Controlling for the effects of time and space can thus present a means to account for certain assumptions made in conjunction with MSE.

## MSE and Source Biases: The Case of Peru

The MSE approach can overcome source biases of the kinds discussed here, and the cases of Peru and Sierra Leone provide concrete examples of the many challenges associated with multiple sources of data and the ability for MSE to overcome them. In Peru, MSE was used to estimate that between 61,007 and 77,552 people died or disappeared in the armed conflict that ravaged the country between 1980 and 2000, as described by Ball et al. (2003).[5] The Peruvian Truth and Reconciliation Commission (Comisión de Verdad y Reconciliación, CVR) identified the main perpetrators of killings and disappearances during the 20-year conflict as the Peruvian government (police and military) and the Sendero Luminoso (Shining Path) revolutionary movement.[6] The CVR further distinguished five periods of conflict: (1) 1980–1982, when the armed violence began in earnest with Sendero Luminoso's first armed action; (2) 1983–1986, which featured increased militarization in the area of Ayacucho and killings in prisons in Lima and Callao; (3) 1986–1989, when the violence spread nationally; (4) 1989–1992, an acute crisis that culminated in the capture of Sendero leader Abimael Guzmán; and (5) 1992–2000, the period of authoritarian rule under President Alberto Fujimori.

The CVR relied on numerous sources of data collected during its mandate, as well as sources that other organizations had collected throughout the conflict. These were the National Coalition of Human Rights (CNDDHH), the Agricultural Development Center (CEDAP), the Human Rights Commission (COMISEDH), the Defender of the People (DP), and the International Committee of the Red Cross (CICR).[7] Our estimation process treated cases collected by CNDDHH, CEDAP, COMISEDH, CICR and cases that the DP received from NGOs as a single list.[8]

The final report published by the CVR revealed unexpected findings regarding the magnitude of the violence, its spatial and racial differentiation, and the political actors primarily responsible for it. The report's statistical analyses estimate the total number of people who died or disappeared as nearly three times greater than the number assumed earlier by human rights NGOs and newspapers. Media reporting had created the impression that the conflict was less severe than was in fact the case, and Peruvians became aware of its extent only after Sendero Luminoso brought its campaign of violence to Lima. The report's estimates also show that the conflict claimed most lives in the rural and highland areas. Further, Peruvians had long thought that government forces were the main perpetrators of the violence; the CVR estimates suggested, however, that Sendero Luminoso was responsible for between 41 percent and 48 percent of the total number of people killed or disappeared (for the full report, see Ball et al. 2003).

The report presented significant differences in the number of casualties across Peru's regions. However, the estimates did not reveal how many Peruvians died in each year of the conflict or the patterns within areas. Doing so requires dividing up the data by perpetrator, for each region in Peru, in each year of the conflict:(e.g., SLU in Lima in 1980, EST in Lima in 1980, etc.; SLU in Ayacucho in 1980, 1981, etc.). Unfortunately, despite the wealth of data collected, its distribution across time and geographical location made it impossible to estimate those numbers at this level of disaggregation. The data were thus adequate for the estimation of total deaths and disappearances but insufficiently dense for any analysis looking at specific temporal *and* spatial patterns at the same time.

Figure 5.2 shows the time-series trends in reported deaths and disappearances of all combined sources for the entire period from 1980 and 2000 distinguishing between the two main perpetrators: The state (EST in figures 5.2 and 5.3) and the Sendero Luminoso (SLU). These are data in which each victim was reported and captured by at least one of the three sources. Some of the victims appeared in more than one source and others appeared in all three, while the total number of dead or disappeared remains a reported number and not a statistical estimate. The figure shows that the number of reported deaths and disappearances at the hand of both the state and Sendero Luminoso peaked in 1984, while state-committed deaths and disappearances rose again in the late 1980s and then declined from 1992, and Sendero committed deaths and disappearances peaked a second time in 1989 and then declined from 1993, one year after the capture of its leader, Abimael Guzmán.

The timeline of recorded data shows a visible difference in the use of violence throughout the conflict. But did the state really kill roughly a third more people than did Sendero between 1983 and 1986? Do the reversed positions of the two main perpetrators after 1986 to 1990 indicate that people were more willing to report killings and disappearances committed by the state before the mid-1980s? Or, did the level of state-sponsored killings remain constant, with the reporting of Sendero violence increasing after the conflict had spread across the entire country in the late 1980s? What happened after 1993, when the overall level of reported violations rapidly decreased? Did reported violations drop precipitously as a result of the capture of Guzmán in 1992, leaving Sendero a "headless" movement with no overarching structure? Or was it because of Fujimori's authoritarian approach that reporting such violations became more difficult? Is it possible that either the state or one of the rebel groups was so "successful" at killing its opponents that there was no one left behind to give testimony about the atrocities committed? In their present form, the data leave any one of these stories as plausible as

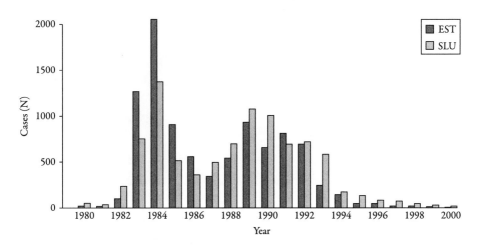

FIGURE 5.2 Reported Deaths and Disappearances by Perpetrator in Peru, 1980–2000

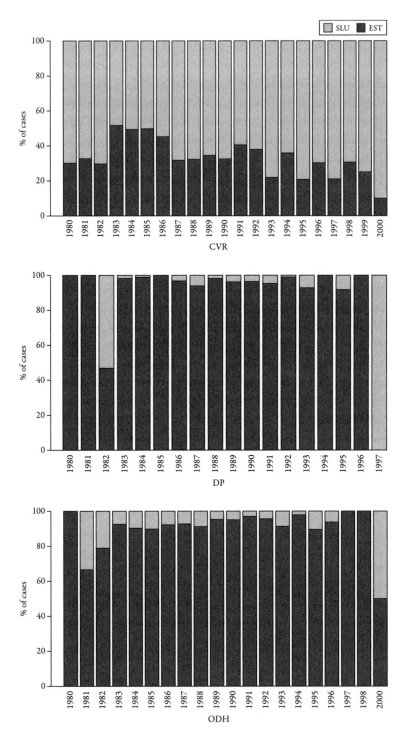

FIGURE 5.3 By Source: Percentage of Reported Cases Attributed to Three Main Perpetrators in Peru, 1980–2000

any other, and the sparse distribution of the data means that the statistical evidence is inadequate to allow verification of any story.

To gain further insight into the data and its potential for telling stories about the temporal dynamics of the conflict, the different lists can be examined, as they were compiled prior the multiple systems estimation. Figure 5.3 presents timelines for the lists, respectively, of the Truth and Reconciliation Commission (CVR), the Public Defense (DP)[9] and the four remaining combined sources (ODH), which depicts what percentage of yearly reported cases is attributed to each of the three main perpetrators.

The most striking feature is that the data collected by the CVR account for almost all the cases attributed to Sendero. Only for the year of 1982 do the Public Defense data record half the cases as having been committed by Sendero. For the remaining years, Sendero-violence is reported to be less than 5 percent, with an increase to just under 10 percent for the years of 1993 and 1995. The ODH list reports that Sendero committed roughly a third of all cases of violence recorded for 1981 and just over a fifth for 1982. From 1983 the percentage declines, with slight increase in 1993 and 1995. Both the DP and ODH lists have surprising peaks: DP records 100 percent Sendero-cases for 1997 and ODH reports that in 2000 allegedly half of all cases were attributed to Sendero.

Two important points can be made here. First, seeing the three time series in a single graph puts these proportions in perspective and quickly leads to the conclusion that the vast differences between the reported perpetrators must be a product of the sources themselves. Evidently, the three versions of what happened throughout the conflict are contradictory and cannot stand side by side. It is important to keep in mind that this perspective would not have been possible with information from a single source. Second, and most crucially, analyzing the differences between these sources reveals their bias; it does not, however, reveal the true story. Since the stratification needed to solve this puzzle with the help of MSE could not be achieved, questions of the temporal dynamics of the conflict in Peru and of the level of responsibility of the different perpetrators remain unanswered.

## Source Biases in the Case of Sierra Leone

Like Peru, the case of Sierra Leone provides an opportunity to compare the "stories" that different data tell about the same conflict.[10] It is a particularly interesting case, since the different sources are exemplary projects for systematic and thorough data collection. This allows us to compare the differences (and similarities) of the samples with respect to different violation categories and time periods. Such a comparison calls for the determination of the six most frequently reported violation types, which are present in all three sources. For each dataset, these six violations are then ranked, as a way of comparing the relative frequency with which each type of violence was reported to the different collecting organizations. Rank correlation allows for an analysis of the differences between the sources that does not require the estimation or determination of a "ground truth," an impossible undertaking. Another advantage is that structural differences can be accounted for without having to control for the very different sizes and dimensions of the databases. This method thus offers a scale-invariant, non-parametric and dimensionless comparison. Most important, the results reveal that even for this simple measure of similarity, the differences found between the sources are significant and substantial across all databases and relevant strata.

Information on violations that occurred during the Sierra Leone civil war was collected in three data sources.[11] The first dataset was built on the basis of the statements recorded by the Truth and Reconciliation Commission (TRC) between 2002 and March 2003.[12] The testimonies given to the Truth Commission entail information on 40,242 individual violations.[13] The second database was collected by the nongovernmental organization Campaign for Good Governance (CGG). Statements collected by the CGG between 2002 and 2004 mention a total of 25,477 violations. Both the Truth Commission and the CGG data follow human rights database design standards.[14] The third source of data does not, strictly speaking, fall into the convenience sample category; it consists of the raw violation counts of the ABA/Benetech Sierra Leone War Crimes Documentation Survey (SLWCD). However, the weighted household survey data do not include estimations for killings, one of the most frequently reported violations. Since this dataset is not comparable to the other sources, we are confined to using the raw counts, entailing 65,719 total records.

To apply our method, we order the six most reported violations across all datasets with respect to their frequency. After this has been done for each dataset, we compare these rankings with Spearman's rank correlation, which is calculated between each pair of data sources (SLWCD and TRC, SLWCD and CGG, TRC and CGG), producing three correlation coefficients.

Spearman's rank correlation coefficient (corr) measures whether a pair of datasets has the same ranking of violations (corr = 1), an inverse ranking (corr = −1), or something in between (−1 < corr < 1). In an ideal, unbiased world of collecting data, all three sources would reflect the actual number of violations as they occurred and thus the frequency with which the different types of violence were committed would be ranked in the same way for all sources. In such a situation, Spearman's correlation coefficient between the pairs of sources should approach corr = 1. To visualize this measure of association, consider figure 5.4, in which the correlation coefficients are presented as an equilateral triangle that spans a radar graph in the ideal case of corr = 1.

The radar graph in figure 5.5 visualizes the three rank correlation coefficients for each pair of data sources. The smaller size and uneven shape of the triangle in the graph represents the extent to which the rankings of the datasets match or do not match. For example, in figure 5.4, the corner of the triangle that represents the correlation of SLWCD and CGG spreads all the way to the circle labeled with 0.8, which means that the Spearman rank correlation of these two datasets is about corr = 0.8. In comparison, the overall rank correlation between the Truth Commission and CGG is much smaller

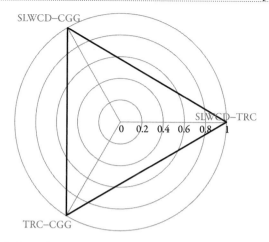

FIGURE 5.4 Example for Perfect Rank Correlations

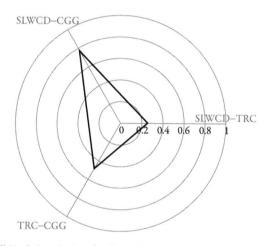

FIGURE 5.5 Overall Rank Correlations for Sierra Leone

(corr < 0.5). Last, the corner representing the relationship between the household survey data and the Truth Commission is the smallest, with a correlation of less than corr = 0.3.

According to the report published by the Truth Commission, the conflict can roughly be divided into three main phases. Correspondingly, in all three databases there are peaks of violence visible in 1991, 1994/1995, and 1998/1999. We therefore rank the six most reported violations separately for each of the three time periods and by dataset. Figure 5.6 displays how the similarity in rankings increases over time. For the time period between 1991 and 1993, the correlation of the relative reported violation frequencies is relatively low, especially when we compare the household survey data with the other two sources. The correlation coefficient for the period from 1993 to 1996 almost triples for the survey and the NGO data, as do the other two coefficients. For the final, peak conflict period, the three data sources reveal similar pictures for the relative frequency of reported violations.

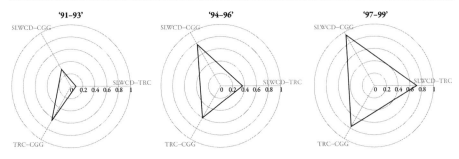

FIGURE 5.6 Correlations across Sources in Sierra Leone, by Time Periods

What does this discrepancy between reporting patterns for the three data sources at the beginning of the conflict tell us about the reliability of these sources? There are several possible explanations. One is that people's memories of the conflict were more variable for the earlier period, leading to less agreement, reflecting a potential recall bias that in turn would reduce the validity of evidence gathered retrospectively. Alternatively, the differences across time might indicate that the three data sources captured different sectors of Sierra Leone society at the beginning of the conflict but had access to similar sectors for the later years. In either case, these findings cast doubt on using these data sources to compare patterns of violations across the periods of the conflict, with the earlier data seeming to be the least reliable.

These comparisons across important conflict periods confirm previous analyses that have cautioned against relying on individual sources to inquire retrospectively about violence (Hoover et al. 2009). Similar analyses across other strata such as region, age, ethnicity, and gender reveal similar levels of disagreement among the sources (Gohdes 2010), indicating that the potential reasons for bias demands increased attention from the research community.

## Summary and Implications

We have argued throughout this chapter that the empirical records of human rights violations and violence are often biased, incomplete, and prone to significant error. The two fundamental errors are the underreporting of rights violations that have occurred and the overreporting of violations that have not. Any measurement effort thus needs to find ways to contend with the causes of error, which include the selection of sources, the number of sources, the development of a coding scheme, the use of the coding scheme, the reliability of the coding scheme, and the use of appropriate statistical methods for analyzing the measures once they have been produced.

It is clear that work in the field of events-based measures of the kinds covered in this volume has advanced tremendously since the early days of newspaper coding (see, e.g., Sloboda, Dardagan, Spagat, and Hicks, chapter 4 in this volume). Multiple systems estimation has allowed for the generation of highly valid and reliable event counting for particular periods of history in particular cultural contexts. This work has in many ways approached a "normal science" (see Kuhn 1962) of human rights events-coding and statistical analysis. Practitioners using the method have now devised a set of standards for coding, database design, matching, and analysis in ways that have evolved since the early days of development at the American Association for the Advancement of Science. Learning and exchange between experts has taken place across different truth commissions and other documentation projects. In deconstructing the grammar of human rights events, the "Who did what to whom?" model has provided fine-grained measures of human rights events, where the violation itself is the basic unit of analysis.

But as we have shown here, MSE is only as good as the original sources of data that underpin it. High degrees of overlap between different sources allow for more accurate statistical estimations with smaller margins of error. In the case of Peru, MSE produced valuable total estimates of the numbers of dead and disappeared in different contexts. The data in these cases also allowed for analysis that showed the disproportionate number of violations against particular groups and the identity of the groups that committed those violations. Nevertheless, this chapter's examples of Peru and Sierra Leone show that any attempt to carry out analysis at more disaggregated levels runs into trouble owing to significant differences in reporting across sources. The data from the Peruvian CVR, which show reporting of violations significantly different from either of the other two data sources, consequently paint a different picture of who the main perpetrators were and where most of the victims were located. The data from Sierra Leone also show significant differences between sources, with widely varying rank order correlations as shown in the radar charts. Further work in this difficult field of analysis should recognize both the value and the significant limitations to the use of multiple sources of information on violence and human rights abuse.

REFERENCES

Ball, Patrick. 1996. *Who Did What to Whom? Planning and Implementing A Large-Scale Human Rights Data Project.* Washington, DC: American Association for the Advancement of Science.

Ball, Patrick, Paul Kobrak, and Herb F. Spirer. 1999. *State Violence in Guatemala, 1960–1996: A Quantitative Reflection.* Washington, DC: American Association for the Advancement of Science.

Ball, Patrick, Wendy Betts, Fritz Scheuren, Jana Dudukovich, and Jana Asher. 2002. *Killings and Refugee Flow in Kosovo March–June 1999.* Washington, DC: American Association for the Advancement of Science.

Ball, Patrick, Jana Asher, David Sulmont, and Daniel Manrique. 2003. *How Many Peruvians Have Died? An Estimate of the Total Number of Victims Killed or Disappeared in the Armed Internal Conflict between 1980 and 2000.* Washington, DC: American Association for the Advancement of Science.

Bishop, Yvonne M., Stephen E. Fienberg, and Paul H. Holland 1975. *Discrete Multivariate Analysis: Theory and Practice*, Cambridge, MA: MIT Press.

CVR (Comisión de la Verdad y Reconciliación de Perú). 2003. *Informe Final*. Lima: Comisión de la Verdad y Reconciliación de Perú.

Davenport, Christian, and Patrick Ball. 2002. "Views to a Kill: Exploring the Implications of Source Selection in the Case of Guatemalan State Terror, 1977–1996." *Journal of Conflict Resolution* 46(3): 427–50.

Gohdes, Anita. 2010. *Different Convenience Samples, Different Stories: The Case of Sierra Leone*. Palo Alto, CA: Benetech. At: http://www.hrdag.org/resources/publications/Gohdes_Convenience%20Samples.pdf. accessed September 18, 2010.

Guberek, Tamy, Daniel Guzmán, Romesh Silva, Kristen Cibelli, Jana Asher, Scott Weikart, Patrick Ball, and Wendy M. Grossman. 2006. "Truth and Myth in Sierra Leone: An Empirical Analysis of the Conflict, 1991–2000." A Report by the Benetech Human Rights Data Analysis Group and the American Bar Association. Palo Alto, CA: Benetech.

Guberek, Tamy, Daniel Guzmán, Megan Price, Kristian Lum, and Patrick Ball. 2010. *To Count the Uncounted: An Estimation of Lethal Violence in Casanare*. Palo Alto, CA: Benetech. At: http://www.hrdag.org/resources/publications/results-paper.pdf. accessed September 18, 2010.

Hoover Green, Amelia, Romesh Silva, Tamy Guberek, and Daniel Guzmán. 2009. "The 'Dirty War Index' and the Real World of Armed Conflict." (working paper by the Benetech Human Rights Data Analysis Group). Palo Alto, CA: Benetech.

Kuhn, Thomas. 1962. *The Structure of Scientific Revolutions*. Chicago: University of Chicago Press.

Landman, Todd. 2006. *Studying Human Rights*. London and New York: Routledge.

Landman, Todd, and Edzia Carvalho. 2010. *Measuring Human Rights*. London and New York: Routledge.

Lum, Kristian, Megan Price, and Patrick Ball. 2010. "Measuring Elusive Populations with Bayesian Model Averaging for Multiple Systems Estimation: A Case Study on Lethal Violations in Casanare, 1998–2007" *Statistics, Politics and Policy* 1(1). At: http://www.bepress.com/spp/vol1/iss1/2. accessed October 1, 2010.

Silva, Romesh, and Patrick Ball. 2008. "The Demography of Conflict-Related Mortality in Timor-Leste (1974–1999): Reflections on Empirical Quantitative Measurement of Civilian Killings, Disappearances, and Famine-Related Deaths." In *Statistical Methods for Human Rights, edited by* J. Asher, D. Banks, and F. Scheuren. New York: Springer, 117–140.

Silva, Romesh, Jeff Klingner, and Scott Weikart. 2010. *State Coordinated Violence in Chad under Hissène Habré*. A Report by Benetech's Human Rights Data Analysis Group to Human Rights Watch and the Chadian Association of Victims of Political Repression and Crimes. Palo Alto, CA: Benetech.

Zwane, Eugene, and Harold van der Heijden. 2005. "Population Estimation Using them multiple System Estimator in the Presence of Continuous Covariates." *Statistical Modelling* 5: 39–52.

NOTES

1. While other units of analysis are possible, to date MSE has been applied to estimating the number of people killed during a particular period of conflict, occupation, and/or authoritarian rule. For a detailed mathematical description and discussion on MSE, see Manrique-Vallier, Price, and Gohdes, chapter 9, in this volume. For recent developments in the field, see Lum et al. (2010).

2. On the Mexican drug war data, see http://www.guardian.co.uk/news/datablog/2011/jan/14/mexico-drug-war-murders-map. Accessed February 5, 2011.

3. The issue of victim visibility becomes even more important when one is analyzing specific violation types that frequently bring with them social stigma, such as rape and other forms of sexual violence.

4. To date, MSE has been used to estimate uncounted populations of people killed or disappeared in conflicts. The method can be transferred to any case that meets the basic assumptions of MSE, which are addressed in more detail in the text.

5. Ball et al. 2003. *Peru.* The point estimate was 69,280 with a 95 percent confidence interval that covered the range from 61,007 to 77,552; see Ball et al. (2003).

6. The most comprehensive summary and periodization of the conflict in Peru is published in the final report of the Peruvian Truth and Reconciliation Commission (CVR 2003).

7. Ball et al. 2003. *Peru*, pp. 13–14. The multiple sources of data were then compared and the names from each were matched with a high level of accuracy across the sources to build a final database of all reported deaths and disappearances. The resulting data file used in the analysis presented here has a separate row for each person killed or disappeared and then columns for other identifying features, such as year of the death or disappearance, age, level of education, occupation, and geographical region. There are also columns for those sources to which the person was reported, including the Truth and Reconciliation Commission and the other organizations outlined earlier in the text. These columns appear as dummy variables coded 1 for "reported" and 0 for "not reported." See Ball et al. (2003, 13–14).

8. The reports of the major sources were collated on approximately 24,000 people who were either dead or disappeared, and of these, 18,397 were identified by their complete names. See Ball et al. (2003, 3).

9. Note that the data collected by the Public Defense covers only the time period from 1980 to 1997.

10. This section builds on Gohdes (2010).

11. The information regarding the databases is taken from Guberek et al. (2006).

12. The data collected by the TRC is available at: http://hrdag.org/resources/SL-TRC_data.html.

13. All testimonies were given voluntarily; of the 149 chiefdoms, 141 were represented. Refugee statements were taken in the Gambia, Guinea, and Nigeria, as well.

14. A "case" is defined as the information given by a single deponent concerning violations that happened at a particular time and place. "Violations" are instances of violence, including killings disappearances, torture, acts of displacement and acts of property destruction. "Victims" are people who suffer violations. A human rights "case" may be very simple (with one victim who suffered one violation,) or it may be very complex (with many victims each of whom suffered many different violations) see Guberek et al. (2006, 5).

# III Estimating Violence

SURVEYS

# 6 Using Surveys to Estimate Casualties Post-Conflict
## DEVELOPMENTS FOR THE DEVELOPING WORLD
### Jana Asher

THE USE OF random sample surveys[1] for casualty estimation is a particularly valuable tool when that estimation occurs post-conflict. Some of the conditions that might make use of a random sample survey problematic during conflict—the danger to the interviewers being perhaps the most compelling—are more easily avoided during the post-conflict phase. Random sample surveys, significantly less expensive than censuses, are particularly useful when demographic records are not maintained or have been discontinued during the conflict period. Unlike newspaper reports, random sample survey methods are considered to be *unbiased* and truly reflective of the opinions and/or experiences of the population.[2]

However, the use of random sample surveys is not without controversy. The use of 30 × 30 cluster surveys for casualty estimation was called into question after publication in *The Lancet* of studies on Iraqi mortality (Roberts et al. 2004; Burnham et al. 2006; see Aronson, chapter 3 of this volume, for an in-depth discussion of that situation). Critics of those studies have brought virtually every aspect of the survey-based research into question. The benefit of that controversy has been that researchers have started to question their assumptions about the validity of accepted survey techniques for casualty estimation. In truth, although random sample survey methods have been accepted and used since the 1950s, few of the techniques developed over the past 60 years have been adequately tested in the post-conflict setting and/or for the measure of casualties.

This chapter will not delve into issues surrounding the sample design for such surveys; other researchers have previously done so (Johnson et al. 2008; Marker 2008). Instead, this chapter will focus on an underdeveloped and equality deserving topic: the design of questionnaires for casualty estimation. Although this topic has been somewhat neglected, it is essentially important if good estimates are to be created. Indeed survey methods researchers have understood the importance of appropriate questionnaire design for decades.[3] However, to the author's knowledge, the first attempt at a detailed study of questionnaire design in the post-conflict casualty estimation context—which represents an intersection of survey methods for developing countries, survey methods in multicultural, multilingual environments, survey methods for sensitive/traumatic topics, and survey methods for morbidity and mortality estimation—was by the author in the context of two random sample surveys: a retrospective mortality survey in Timor-Leste (formerly East Timor) in 2003–2004 and a random sample survey taken in 2004 on human rights abuses experienced during the 1991–2002 armed internal conflict in Sierra Leone.

This chapter first summarizes the available literature related to casualty estimation and questionnaire design. It then outlines the research completed in Timor-Leste and Sierra Leone as a case study of current best practices for questionnaire design in the post-conflict casualty estimation context.

## Data Collection in Developing Countries

Methodological and practical challenges regarding data collection in the developing world are apparent throughout the survey methods literature.[4] They include high birth and mortality rates and high mobility, resulting in the rapid obsolescence of data; lack of distinct addresses or postal infrastructure; lack of sampling frames;[5] sampling frames containing significant error (e.g., missing units, duplications, and data inaccuracies); lack of survey infrastructure (i.e., field workers, data processing facilities, and survey methodologists); inadequately trained/educated survey personnel; difficulties traveling to and finding households; lack of pretesting or formal questionnaire structure; lack of quality control; multiethnic, multilingual populations that were surveyed even though questionnaire design techniques intended for such populations were lacking; illiterate populations; lack of respondent privacy; underreporting of infant/child deaths; social desirability bias; and delays in processing and analyzing data.

Fortunately, there are also some advantages: if appropriate steps are taken to gain permission of traditional authorities to interview members of their villages, response can be extremely high. If the available sampling frame lacks information on households, but contains a reasonably accurate list of villages, then villages serve as a natural sampling unit. Enumerating housing units in a randomly sampled village is typically not difficult and, once field personnel have arrived, this approach yields an excellent household survey. And respondents in developing countries—especially in rural areas—are more patient with longer interviews than respondents in wealthier countries. Although this list of advantages is short, there are potential solutions to most, if not all, problems encountered during random sample surveys in the developing world.

The survey methods literature is rich with suggestions. A central warning is that indiscriminate transfer of survey methods (e.g., random sampling techniques) from the developed to developing world is almost guaranteed to be problematic. Sample designs should be kept as simple as possible; modifications to standard random sample designs used in developing countries include the World Health Organization's Expanded Program of Immunization (EPI) method and the use of satellite imagery as a sampling frame. Multiuse surveys, meaning surveys that are designed to measure concepts of two different types, are discouraged, as are "verbatim" questionnaire design techniques in which the interviewer must read exactly what is on the questionnaire to every person. Strong pretesting of questionnaires is encouraged. Adequate training of local personnel is essential, but care must be taken to train those committed to their countries rather than those seeking higher wages as expatriates. If a trainer does not speak the language of the survey staff, excellent translation is required and written materials must be available in all relevant languages. Training also might be needed to persuade staff to use techniques such as random sampling at all.

Examples of random sample surveys for casualty estimation in the developing country context are limited. Although some surveys have been performed by government organizations and United Nations programs, nongovernmental organizations and private research groups (e.g., Women's Rights International, Physicians for Human Rights, Benetech) have implemented random sample surveys, as well. The academic community also has contributed to this field, most famously through the *Lancet* studies regarding mortality in Iraq, mentioned at the beginning of the chapter.

Ethical issues related to collection of casualty data are particularly thorny. Special care must be taken to ensure that the benefits of the survey to the target population are not outweighed by the potential harm. Casualty surveys typically involve reporting traumatic information, therefore retraumatizing the respondent during an interview is a significant risk. Appropriate precautions include use of questionnaire design methods for eliciting sensitive information, proper training of interview personnel, and use of counselors during fieldwork. Another ethical issue is the potential harm to respondents if their participation in the survey is revealed to the wrong individuals. In some cases, the mere presence of an interviewer at a respondent's house increases the likelihood of harm. In other cases, if proper methods for ensuring confidentiality are not used, data might become available to those with malicious intentions.

## Questionnaire Design

Questionnaire design for casualty estimation is best understood within the context of general questionnaire design. Questionnaire design practices mitigate error through careful development and pretesting of questionnaires. The mitigated error can be classified as either measurement error (misunderstood questions, memory issues, misstating of answers, refusals, and coding errors) or intention error (occurring when the questionnaire does not measure what the researcher intended). Examination of measurement and intention errors began in earnest in the late 1940s, with efforts to improve the quality of opinion research. At that time, researchers discovered that the highest contributor to survey error was interviewers who unintentionally elicited responses that conformed to their own opinions. The concept of the "standardized" survey arose—a pretested questionnaire read by the interviewer exactly as given. Interviewers who encounter respondent confusion are permitted to do no more than reread the question without offering a personal interpretation. Survey standardization intends to create more *reliable* estimates: that is, if the same question is asked of two respondents and it yields identical answers, those answers are equivalent in meaning. Proponents argue that survey standardization is the only way that thousands of interviews can be meaningfully "distilled" into quantifiable code and analytically compared. In the past 50 years, the standardized interview has become the method of choice for government statistical agencies and research organizations.

The literature, however, offers several arguments against this approach. The most noteworthy is that the assumption of increased reliability might not be true. Additionally, standardized interviewing can be frustrating to respondents who are asked to recast information in the format required by the survey instead of the format natural to their memory processes. The standardized interview approach allows little leeway for the interviewer to assist a respondent who is obviously confused, and respondent misunderstanding can lead to measurement error greater than the associated reduction in interviewer bias. Through assisting the respondent in understanding the survey instrument, suggesting strategies for recall, and allowing more free-form reporting, the interviewer might be able to help respondents more accurately provide information. Proponents of survey standardization respond that reducing respondent confusion calls for improved questionnaire pretesting and understanding of respondent cognition, not ad hoc interpretation by interviewers.

QUESTIONNAIRE TESTING METHODS

The movement to do just that—improve questionnaire design through better understanding of cognitive processes of respondents—began in the late 1970s in the United Kingdom and the United States. Improvements in questionnaire pretesting have been made steadily since. A particular questionnaire testing technique that has become popular is *cognitive interviewing*, or the administration of a survey while the interviewer is collecting additional information about the thinking and behavior of the respondent. The information is then evaluated to determine whether the survey questions were interpreted correctly. In a cognitive interview, two main methods are used: *think-aloud* and *probing*. Think-aloud requires respondents to verbalize their thought processes while taking the survey (*concurrent think-aloud*) and/or after the survey is complete (*retrospective think-aloud*).

Probing involves asking respondents questions about how they interpret survey questions and formulate responses. The probes can be either determined beforehand or spontaneous, depending on the creativity and expertise of the cognitive interviewer.

A second methodology developed for questionnaire testing is *behavior coding*. During a field test of the survey instrument, an observer records codes that correspond to behaviors of the respondent and/or interviewer, such as deviations from question wording or facial expressions. After several replications, each survey question is rated on how often it caused problematic behavior. Behavior coding can be remarkably objective; however, it does not provide direct insight into why particular questions are problematic.

A third option for pretesting, given in Jansen and Hak (2005), is the three-step test interview (TSTI). First, the respondent is asked to "think aloud" while completing the survey (as in cognitive interviewing) and the interviewer simultaneously takes notes on verbal and nonverbal behaviors (as in behavior coding). During the second step, the interviewer reviews the survey from the beginning, asking the respondent for explanations of observed behaviors and responses during the first step (much like the probing in cognitive interviewing). The final step is a respondent debriefing during which the person is asked why he or she found particular questions difficult to understand or answer.

Finally, note that long-established methods for questionnaire pretesting, including expert review and field tests, are still considered to be invaluable for enhancing survey quality. Field tests—during which a small number of interviews are performed so that statistics can be formed to see whether the data fall within expected ranges and interviewers can practice the survey and report issues they encounter—can also be modified to include behavior coding and other cognitive activities.

Although extensive pretesting does much to alleviate issues associated with the standardized questionnaire approach, in a world where surveys across cultural groups and countries are increasingly prevalent, the assumption that pretesting will sufficiently reveal all possible interpretations of a question is less and less valid. The important question is whether nonstandardized interviews can establish "relevance, clarification of meaning, detection and repair of misunderstanding . . . without the introduction of interviewer bias" (Suchman and Jordan 1990, 233). The case study explores this issue thoroughly.

## GENERAL QUESTIONNAIRE DESIGN ISSUES

Several common questionnaire design pitfalls are discussed widely in the literature: "double-barreled" questions that confound two questions or concepts (e.g., "Is Coca-Cola tasty and refreshing?"); double negatives; words that are easily mispronounced to sound like words of opposite meaning (e.g., "allowing" and "outlawing"); words with multiple meanings; overly complex questions; and ambiguities due to sentence structures that produce multiple interpretations. The response format for a question also has repercussions on data quality. An open-ended question better allows the respondent to answer as the individual desires. A closed-ended question provides several categories, from which one or more are selected; this format may elicit more accurate responses because options are presented that might not be recalled otherwise. Although the literature does not consider one type of question to be "better" than the other, it does recognize that differing question formats elicit different distributions of answers to the same question.

An issue specific to attitude surveys is "context bias," which may be found when question order affects the responses. Context bias can affect either the distribution of answers to a question or the correlation between two questions. Context bias related to response categories for closed-ended questions includes primacy and recency effects (where response categories listed first or last are chosen more often). Closed-ended questions with unordered categories might also produce a "satisficing" effect—that is, respondents choosing the first category that seems satisfactory instead of waiting for all options before picking the best one.

Another issue that affects survey quality is "acquiescence bias," or the tendency of respondents to answer the way they think the interviewer wants them to answer. Acquiescence bias, which is more likely among respondents with lower education levels, can be mitigated somewhat by good interviewer training.

## RECALL AND QUESTIONNAIRE DESIGN

Sometimes a survey is designed to elucidate patterns of behavior or events over time. Surveys of two types are used for that purpose: panel surveys, which involve multiple interviews at different time points, and retrospective surveys, which collect retrospective data at one time point. Although panel surveys are generally more reliable, they have their own unique issues, such as respondent attrition and changing definitions and questionnaires.

Retrospective surveys are appropriate when the events of interest occurred only in the past or when financial constraints prohibit the use of panel surveys, but they introduce higher recall error for many reasons. Memories can be altered over time, causing misrepresentation of events. An event might be completely forgotten and, if so, its frequency might then be underreported. Even unique, important events in a respondent's life can be forgotten in the survey setting in as little as 9 to 12 months. Factors that increase recall ability include event rareness and event emotionality as measured by the intensity of the emotions associated with the memory. Some authors report a tendency toward better recall of positive memories; others report that highly negative events can be recalled in detail even decades after they occur.

Good questionnaire design can better enable respondents to access their memories of events; for example, probes can be incorporated into the survey process to elicit more accurate response. Several authors suggest the use of a written time line or event history calendar (EHC) to aid recall. The distinction between time lines and EHCs is somewhat arbitrary; the written time line is a simplified form of the EHC. In either case, the time line/calendar is first populated with memorable personal experiences of the respondent (called "landmarks" or "anchors") through a series of probe questions for different domains (e.g., births of children, marriages). The main survey questions then are asked, and the respondent uses the time line/calendar for reference while answering. When the survey goal is to collect information about sporadic events that occurred over a lifetime, the literature suggests a version of the EHC called the life history calendar (LHC).

Overall, research has shown that time lines, EHCs, and LHCs can reduce recall error, but the method is highly visual. If a retrospective survey is administered to a population that is not only illiterate but also unfamiliar with visual representation of information, an EHC or LHC has little value as a tool for guiding recall. However, landmark usage does not need to be constrained to a visual format. Use of verbal prompts containing landmarks is discussed later, in the section entitled Case Study.

### SENSITIVE QUESTIONS

Often respondents decline to answer sensitive questions or deliberately answer them incorrectly. The literature suggests that socially desirable behaviors such as voting and charitable contributions are overreported, but socially undesirable/private behaviors such as drug usage and sexual practices are underreported. Sensitive question bias might be mitigated by providing privacy to the respondent, matching gender of the interviewer and respondent, using open-ended questions, including supportive wording before the sensitive question, asking sensitive questions toward the end of the survey (to allow development of rapport between interviewer and respondent), and using methods of questionnaire administration perceived to be more private (e.g., self-administered questionnaires). Use of "proxies" is also effective: for example, asking about a friend's behavior instead of the respondent's.

### MULTICULTURAL SURVEY ISSUES

Multicultural survey research is complicated and prone to measurement error. When questionnaires are translated for the purpose of multicultural surveys, or created by a researcher from one cultural group for use with respondents from a different group, careful planning is necessary to ensure that the survey instrument measures both what the researcher wishes to measure and also a quantity relevant to the population being surveyed. Several issues can arise in this process, and "research imperialism"—that is, individuals from one culture performing research on a different culture without regard to that culture's interests—should be avoided at all costs, for both ethical and methodological reasons.[6] The processes surrounding the multicultural survey might require different approaches in different cultures, such as matching interviewer and respondent as to gender in Muslim countries. Similarly, differing institutions or family structures might affect the format or administration of a survey. There is also variation by culture with respect to the topics that are in fact sensitive.[7]

## QUESTIONNAIRE TRANSLATION ISSUES

Questionnaires are translated for three purposes: research across countries, research within a country where different languages are spoken by different groups, and research in one country implemented by researchers from another country. Surveys administered to respondents that speak multiple different languages present unique challenges. An ineffective technique is to simply hire multilingual interviewers and have them translate verbally in the field; field translation causes significantly more interviewer error than the use of pretranslated surveys.

The most common method for developing a multilanguage questionnaire is sequential: the questionnaire is first developed in a source language and then translated to one or more target languages. The most common process for checking on the accuracy and validity of translations is *forward and back translation*: that is, the pretested questionnaire is translated into the target language, translated back into the source language, and then compared to the original version. This approach can be problematic, however, because *semantic* equivalence of language may not equate to *functional* equivalence, especially if biases are associated with certain words. An alternative approach is forward and back translation followed by pretesting in each of the target languages. The World Health Organization advocates a version of this method in which forward translation is followed by back translation by an expert panel, then followed by separate pretesting and cognitive interviewing in each target language. Each version of the survey is subsequently finalized in the target language, with all pretesting designed to bring the survey versions into functional equivalence with the source language questionnaire (World Health Organization 2007.

Although pretesting in multiple languages is an invaluable step, alone it may not be sufficient to ensure functional equivalence across multiple language translations. For example, if semantic and/or functional equivalence is impossible with respect to certain concepts or phrases, the source questionnaire will have to be adjusted. For that reason, a potentially better questionnaire development procedure is *decentering* (Harkness, Van de Vijver, and Mohler 2002). During decentering, the source language questionnaire is developed first but left open for revision during the translation process. If conceptual issues arise, the initial survey can be modified to allow functional equivalence across translations. A similar process, called *harmonization* (Harkness, Pennell, and Schoua-Glusberg 2004), involves testing a single language survey in multiple countries in which slight variations in meaning could occur and producing a single questionnaire that is appropriate for all the countries to be surveyed. A final option is *simultaneous development* (Harkness, Van de Vijver, and Mohler 2002), during which surveys for each language are developed by separate teams working "side by side," and several decentering steps bring the questionnaire versions into alignment. This option holds great promise for reducing error, as all steps in the questionnaire development process are exploited for each language.

There is a small but growing literature related to cognitive issues in questionnaire design for multilanguage surveys. The literature confirms that significant response error can be introduced into multiple-language surveys by favoring semantic equivalence over functional equivalence.[8] Additionally, the value of cognitive interviewing as a method for determining translation difficulties is shown. The case study presented next confirms these results and also confirms the inadequacy of the forward and back translation approach in the case of multiple target languages.

## Case Study

In 2004, the author was involved in the American Bar Association (ABA) War Crimes Documentation Survey in Sierra Leone (the SL Survey). For the purpose of informing the newly formed Sierra Leone Special Court, the U.S. Department of State had contracted with the ABA to determine the scope of human rights abuses during the preceding period of armed conflict. With a view to establishing perpetrator culpability, additional goals were set; these included the capture of place and time of abuses, perpetrator affiliation and ethnicity, and victim age and ethnicity. The author, as a contractor recommended by the Human Rights Data Analysis Group of The Benetech Initiative, was tasked with almost all phases of the survey, including sample design, questionnaire design, oversight of fieldwork, and final analysis of the data. An additional contractor, Richard Conibere, was hired to oversee the data entry process.

### SAMPLE DESIGN

Sierra Leone is composed of 4 regions, split into 13 districts, further split into approximately 150 chiefdoms. The Central Statistics Office (CSO) of Sierra Leone shared with us a sampling frame of 2,522 maps developed for the 1985 population and housing census. Taken together, the maps covered the country of Sierra Leone, without overlap. We based our sample on those maps, but incorporated corrective measures for changes since 1985. First, the maps were subdivided into "rural" or "urban" categories, based on the density of the population in these areas in 1985. The "rural" maps were further subdivided by chiefdom, and the "urban" maps were further subdivided by region and current population size according to CSO population projections for 2004. Six hundred maps were chosen across the subgroups proportionally to population size, resulting in the selection of 407 rural and 193 urban maps.

Within each area given on a rural map, the survey team first consulted with a local expert to update the map, and then randomly selected a village within the area. When the field staff arrived at the village, the number of households in the village was determined in consultation with the village chief. Six households were then selected through a randomization device.[9] If there were fewer than six households in the village, all households were interviewed. Male and female interviewers were assigned randomly to the households picked, and interviewers were instructed to interview the household head of their gender whenever possible.

For urban maps, the procedure for selecting households was quite different. The urban maps contained visual layouts of the housing units and streets. First, the housing units on the map, including any dubious (potentially commercial) units, were numbered. In some cases, lots without housing units were numbered as well, to account for houses that had been built on those lots since 1985. The numbers were then randomly ordered, split in half, and recorded on the map as two separate lists. The first list was assigned to a male interviewer, the second to a female interviewer. Each interviewer visited the housing units in the random order given by the lists until three successful interviews had been completed.

QUESTIONNAIRE DEVELOPMENT

The preliminary questionnaire was modeled in part on the 2003 survey used by Physicians for Human Rights in Iraq and the 2003 survey developed for the East Timor Retrospective Mortality Survey.[10] The questionnaire had three sections: a household register in which all living household members were assigned a unique code, seven violation registers on which violations of particular types were recorded, and a single page with questions about the greatest needs of the respondent's community and what the respondent believes caused the war. The unique code for household members was used to identify victims in the abuse registers; in this way, the household and violations registers were interlinked.

The translation languages for the survey were chosen based on their geographic distribution within Sierra Leone. Written translations into six languages—Krio, Temne, Mende, Kono, Koranko, and Limba—would allow approximately 98 percent coverage of individuals in each of the 13 districts of Sierra Leone; because of financial constraints, additional indigenous languages would be translated in the field. After an expert review of the questionnaire by subject and cultural experts, a start-up team performed forward and back translations for the six target languages. The back translations were then reviewed for conceptual issues.

A cognitive interviewing step followed. The cognitive interviewing was performed in all target languages, and feedback from the interviews in each language informed editing for all. After the start-up team had been trained in cognitive interviewing techniques, the members worked in pairs—one would administer the survey, while the other observed and recorded answers, body language of both interviewer and respondent, and the respondent's emotional reactions.[11] At least four interviews were performed in each of the six languages of the survey.[12] Additionally, the cognitive interviews were performed in four "waves," with editing of the survey occurring after each wave to allow further testing in the next.

We quickly determined that in this setting, a "standardized" method of interviewing would not work for obtaining date information. As a solution, a list of scripted probes, based on major events during the internal conflict, was made available to the interviewers for use in determining ages and dates. This was a "middle ground" between the completely controlled script of a standardized interview and a completely open conversation format, with the goal of increasing respondent understanding without increasing interviewer-induced biases.

To determine the violation codes to be used to record responses, we started with the categories of violations determined by the Sierra Leone Truth and Reconciliation Commission (SLTRC). It seemed, however, that some categories were sufficiently ambiguous to require modifications. We therefore created new categories that were not motivation based; for example, instead of separate torture and physical assault categories, we used a single physical assault category. We also discovered that the SLTRC had missed an important category of violation: although the SLTRC did record instances of cannibalism in its database, other instances of forced consumption, such as consumption of feces, were not captured.

After the categories of violations of interest had been determined, we developed a question for each category and a series of very specific codes for each type of violation within the category in order to remove as much ambiguity as possible from the coding. Our goal was to improve the "inter-rater reliability" of the interviewers, who were making judgments in the field as to how to code violations. Our final categories were Physical Violations (including Amputations and Physical Assaults), Property Violations, Movement Violations (including Forced Displacement and Arrest and Detention), Drugging, Labor Violations (including Forced Recruitment, Sexual Slavery, and Forced Labor), Sexual Violence, and Forced Consumption.

A final, difficult questionnaire design step was the "decentering" of the language translations. During the cognitive interviewing, each of the six target languages was being updated individually based on group decisions. The decentering step was undertaken to ensure that conceptual equivalence was being maintained across the translations. This process took three days and was eye-opening. We discovered that multiple word choices in English did not translate uniformly across languages, an issue we had not noticed during the forward and back translation step. Some minor modifications to the English allowed us to bring the translations into conceptual equivalence. For example, we discovered that some languages do not have separate concepts for "detainment" and "imprisonment." The initial English was "imprisonment (detainment)," which was translated to sometimes include both concepts and sometimes only one. We switched the English to "imprisonment or detainment" and updated the translations for all languages to make sure both concepts were represented.

## INTERVIEWER TRAINING AND FIELD LOGISTICS

Our interview team was chosen so that each target language was spoken by at least four interviewers and as many districts as possible were represented. The goal of the interviewer training was to motivate and empower the interviewers to collect high-quality data. Thus one goal of the training was to teach the interviewers their role in the entire data collection and analysis process. The first 1.5 days of training were therefore devoted to statistical methods. Training on "counseling" techniques completed the second day, providing interviewers with mechanisms to support respondents during recall of traumatic events. Four days of training on interviewing techniques followed, including training on persuasion techniques, body language and voice control, sensitive question techniques, and safety protocols.[13]

Several themes were stressed in the training. The first was the sensitive and traumatic nature of the information we were collecting; we did not want to leave respondents worse off than we found them. At the suggestion of the interviewers, we determined which of them had counseling experience and designated those interviewers as team "counselors." They assisted the other interviewers when respondents or the interviewers themselves became emotionally overwhelmed. The second theme was practice with and understanding of the survey instrument, including probing techniques and coding; one day was spent eliciting feedback and making modifications to the codes to bring the group into agreement on the coding scheme. Then, multiple practice sessions with the surveys were scheduled. The third theme was empowerment—interviewers were encouraged to participate in decisions about field logistics such as equipment required, food carried in the vehicles, and length of missions.

After the end of the formal training period, staff practiced in enumeration areas within Freetown that were not part of the final sample. During that phase, start-up team members were paired with two or three interviewers. The start-up team members and interviewers took turns administering interviews, allowing each field worker who participated to be observed and provided with direct feedback. Any final comments about the questionnaire were accepted until the end of the second day of the field test; the finalized questionnaires were distributed on the third day of the field test.

To ensure that everyone understood the urban enumeration area sampling scheme, all interviewers were located in Freetown during the first official week of the survey. Frequently occurring issues from one day were discussed at the beginning of the next day. Also, since several interviewers had incorrectly selected housing units on the urban enumeration area maps, the maps were studied closely and interviewers who had not used the randomized lists to select households were required to return to the same enumeration area and redo the interviews.

A few problems related to staff management arose during that first week. By the end of the second day of fieldwork it became obvious that interviewers were cranky and unmotivated in the late afternoon. Consultation with team leaders revealed that interviewers were skipping lunch to save money for their families; a "must eat lunch" policy, utilizing funding that was controlled by the team leader, was therefore implemented. In addition, upon discovering the prohibitive cost of health care in Sierra Leone and noting that the interviewers were not covered by health insurance, the author committed to providing health care not only for interviewers who became ill in the field but also for family members who became ill in an interviewer's absence. A policy of providing emergency evacuation of interviewers in the case of extreme illness in the field was also communicated to the staff. This was a "make or break" point for the project's success; improved communication about and attitude over problems encountered in the field was noted after that point.

When interviewing moved to the areas outside Freetown, we engaged in a set of "public relations" missions, which had been advised by the start-up team. As Sierra Leonean society is quite hierarchical, the buy-in of chiefs at all levels of the society—districts, chiefdoms, and local villages—was needed to assure a good response rate. In addition, because many data collection projects had already taken place, the start-up team believed that unless a positive publicity campaign preceded the effort, many urban respondents would refuse to participate. To address those issues, we created an advance team for each district, using staff members who knew the paramount chief. The advance team traveled ahead of the interviewers and asked permission of each district-level and chiefdom-level chief to interview in his or her territory to determine the scope of human rights abuses during the preceding period of armed conflict. To reassure villagers that they would not be subpoenaed if they reported casualties, the advance team stressed that this project was to determine the scope of human rights abuses during that earlier conflict period. In each district, the advance team also attempted to speak on the local radio channel to advertise the survey in urban areas. In Freetown, we developed both a TV show and a radio interview to inform local residents about our survey; even so, we needed an additional radio interview to assure people in the Western Area of Freetown—who had not experienced many abuses—that we needed to talk to them regardless of whether they had any abuses to report. The result of our efforts was a remarkably high response rate, given the local animosity toward more interviewing projects in general and toward the Special Court specifically.

The quality of the SL Survey depended on the interviewers' ability to reach and effectively interview the randomly sampled respondents. Several aspects of the fieldwork made this goal particularly challenging. First, the road system in Sierra Leone was one of the most primitive in the world at that time. The only vehicles available in the country that were sturdy enough to use on those roads were Land Rovers, and even they were prone to many difficulties. Second, some areas of Sierra Leone were simply not directly accessible by car, and the interviewers needed to find other methods of transportation, including bikes, boats, and just plain walking. Third, malaria and typhoid were constant worries for field staff, and despite primitive hospitals in each of the district capitals, four emergency medical evacuations to Freetown were required during the course of the fieldwork.

To encourage the interviewers to go to the correct randomly sampled village even if doing so was extremely difficult, we issued E-Trex global positioning systems to each team leader for all fieldwork outside of the Western Area.[14] The team leader was responsible for obtaining GPS readings for each of the households interviewed. Each team leader was additionally issued a satellite phone, allowing regular contact and consultation with management in Freetown. A specific quality control process for individual surveys was also implemented: another member of the team checked every survey at the end of the day. Each team leader was responsible for the quality of his or her surveys, was required to sign the cover sheet after reviewing the survey, and was responsible for oversight (by observing the work of the interviewers in the field).

## ANALYSIS OF SURVEY INNOVATIONS AND EXPERIMENTS

The questionnaire design procedure for the SL Survey was informed by the extensive literature review summarized in this chapter as well as the author's previous field experience.[15] That procedure incorporated several innovations and included experiments designed to improve data quality specifically for a multicultural, multilanguage survey on civilian casualties in a developing country. The results of those experiments and innovations are described here.

*The use of household follow-up questions to refine the household composition register.* The concept of household is difficult to pinpoint; however, correct enumeration of households is essential for accurate survey estimates. Definitional issues include tenure in the household before being accepted as a member, children away at school and other institutionalized individuals, very small/young children and elderly people, and live-in servants. To address this issue, we used a simple household definition in the main question and then refined the household definition by asking a series of follow-up questions as given in figure 6.1.[16] Of the 3,553 respondents that answered the five questions, 2,380 (67.0 percent) answered "no" to all five, leaving 33 percent of the surveys requiring use of at least one of these questions as a household-refinement tool. Focusing on the first two questions, which have to do with household members that might be "forgotten" (older people, infants, hired help, etc.), there were 3,568 respondents: 920 (25.8 percent) answered yes to at least one of questions 1.9 and 1.10. A reasonable conclusion is that follow-up questions regarding "easy to forget" members of a household make a significant difference in the household composition accuracy.[17]

*The use of scripted probes to elicit better time information in a time-illiterate population.* Interviewers were provided with a set of scripted probes to assist them in determining the year and month of an event, and in each case where an age or date was needed, they were instructed to use the probes and then record which probes were used. Interviewers engaged in probing at five points in the survey—to determine ages of household members, victim age during a violation, the start date of the violation, the duration of the violation, and the time between the violation and a death caused by the violation. Figure 6.2 gives the usage for each type of probe code. The violation start date was the variable that required the most probing—over 79 percent of the violation start dates required at least one probe. The resident age variable required the next highest level of probes—but required probes in only 11 percent of cases. The duration variables—violation duration and death duration—required probing for only 3.5 percent of cases.

| **Question from Sierra Leone Survey** | **Instructions for Question** |
|---|---|
| 1.9 *Are there any other persons in your household such as small children, infants, elderly persons that we have not listed?* | IF YES, GO TO PREVIOUS SHEETS OR CONTINUATION SHEET AND LIST THESE PEOPLE, THEN GO TO NEXT QUESTION. |
| 1.10 *Are there any other people who may not be members of your family, like servants, friends, lodgers, but who usually live here?* | IF YES, GO TO PREVIOUS SHEETS OR CONTINUATION SHEET AND LIST THESE PEOPLE, THEN GO TO NEXT QUESTION. |
| 1.11 *Are there any other guests or visitors who have been temporarily staying with you for the last four weeks or more?* | IF YES, GO TO PREVIOUS SHEETS OR CONTINUATION SHEET AND LIST THESE PEOPLE, THEN GO TO NEXT QUESTION. |
| 1.12 *Are there any persons who usually live here who have been away for less than four weeks?* | IF YES, GO TO PREVIOUS SHEETS OR CONTINUATION SHEET AND LIST THESE PEOPLE, THEN GO TO NEXT QUESTION. |
| 1.13 *Are there any persons who we have listed who have been away for four weeks or more?* | IF YES, GO TO PREVIOUS SHEETS OR CONTINUATION SHEET AND CROSS OUT THESE PEOPLE. |

FIGURE 6.1 Follow-up Questions for the Household Register on the SL Survey (the American Bar Association War Crimes Documentation Survey in Sierra Leone)

*The use of violation-specific questions, rather than a single general question, to elicit greater reporting of human rights abuses.* As stated earlier, the survey asked for information about specific categories of violations rather than one general "tell us what you experienced" question. If this tactic is successful, we expect that each respondent will report more violations than he or she would have otherwise. One way to measure this "increase" in violations reporting is to compare the results for the SL Survey with the results of the SLTRC statement taking. In fact, the mean number of violations per statement for the

| Probe Type | Victim age during Violation | Violation Start Date | Violation Duration | Death Duration | Resident Age |
|---|---|---|---|---|---|
| **Year-based Probes** | | | | | |
| A-H (before or after landmark) | 54 | 38,578 | 263 | 46 | 1 |
| AO-HO (day of landmark) | 5 | 1,119 | 5 | 1 | 14 |
| J (years before/after landmark) | 1 | 17 | 9 | 0 | 4 |
| K (other year-based probe) | 11 | 7,358 | 8 | 0 | 0 |
| *Total year-based probes* | *71* | *47,072* | *285* | *47* | *19* |
| **Season-based Probes** | | | | | |
| L (rainy/dry season) | 33 | 19,926 | 16 | 0 | 0 |
| M-O (before/after Christmas, Ramadan, Easter) | 37 | 1,969 | 79 | 6 | 4 |
| P (school term probe) | 6 | 189 | 134 | 2 | 0 |
| R (other season-based probe) | 0 | 15 | 1 | 0 | 0 |
| *Total season-based probes* | *76* | *22,099* | *230* | *8* | *4* |
| **Age-based Probes** | | | | | |
| S (age of victim at time of event) | 10,312[i] | 67 | 33 | 5 | 140 |
| T (how long ago/how old now) | 3,338 | 1,172 | 1,706 | 318 | 812 |
| U (other age-related probe) | 2,786 | 135 | 19 | 2 | 3,337 |
| *Total age-based probes* | *16,436* | *1,374* | *1,758* | *325* | *4,289* |
| ***Total probes*** | ***6,271*** | ***70,454*** | ***2,273*** | ***380*** | ***4,312*** |

FIGURE 6.2 Probes Used during the SL Survey

| | Victim age during Violation | Violation Start Date | Violation Duration | Death Duration | Resident Age |
|---|---|---|---|---|---|
| **Probe Type** | | | | | |
| **No probe** | | | | | |
| W (exact age/date known) | 44,934 | 11,211 | 57,573 | 10,038 | 32,714 |
| missing | 3,228 | 2,107 | 4,899 | 370 | 1,825 |
| ***Total cases with no probe*** | *58,474* | *13,318* | *62,472* | *10,408* | *34,539* |
| | *(90.4%)* | *(20.6%)* | *(96.5%)* | *(96.5%)* | *(88.9%)* |
| ***Total cases with probes*** | *6,243* | *51,399* | *2,245* | *380* | *4,311* |
| | *(9.6%)* | *(79.4%)* | *(3.5%)* | *(3.5%)* | *(11.1%)* |

[i] Given that the probe is for the variable itself, these cases will be counted as "no probe" cases.

FIGURE 6.2 (*continued*)

SL Survey was 18 and the median was 15; for the SLTRC statements, a mean of 8.5 violations and a median of 7 violations were collected for each statement/interview.

There are other possible explanations for a difference in the number of violations reported, including differences in interviewer gender and training and interview environment. Female interviewers appear to elicit greater response (see next subsection), and the SLTRC statements were given in central city locations, while the SL Survey was completed in the respondent's home or another comfortable environment. However, even taking those possible reasons for the difference in the number of violations reported into account, the difference between the two data collection efforts is remarkable.

*The pairing of interviewer and respondent by gender in order to elicit greater response to the question on sexual violations.* Figure 6.3 gives the violations per interview, by violation category, for each interview/respondent gender pair. In almost all violation categories, the pairing that yields the most violations per interview is a female interviewer with a male respondent. The next "best" pairing is either a female interviewer with a male respondent or a male interviewer with a male respondent. Interestingly, the pairing of female interviewer with male respondents failed to yield the highest level of violations per interview only in the case of forced recruitment, a mostly (but not completely) male-specific violation.

Based on these results, it appears that, overall, male respondents report more violations than female respondents, and female interviewers elicit more responses than male interviewers. This follows even in the case of sexual violations, where female interviewers elicited more responses from male and female respondents. Perhaps female interviewers

| Violation | Interviewer | | | |
|---|---|---|---|---|
| | female | | male | |
| | Respondent | | Respondent | |
| | female | male | female | male |
| | $n = 629$ | $n = 1,195$ | $n = 411$ | $n = 1,350$ |
| **Residence Violations** | | | | |
| Forced displacement | 4.14 | 5.23 | 4.08 | 4.86 |
| All Residence Violations | 4.14 | 5.23 | 4.08 | 4.86 |
| **Property Violations** | | | | |
| Destruction of property | 3.03 | 4.49 | 1.88 | 2.77 |
| Property theft | 0.86 | 0.97 | 1.34 | 1.17 |
| All Property Violations | 3.90 | 5.46 | 3.22 | 3.94 |
| **Physical Assault Violations** | | | | |
| Assault and beating | 3.58 | 4.20 | 2.87 | 3.36 |
| Amputation | 0.22 | 0.23 | 0.16 | 0.13 |
| Physical torture | 0.02 | 0.05 | 0.00 | 0.01 |
| All Physical Assault Violations | 3.82 | 4.48 | 3.03 | 3.50 |
| **Internment Violations** | | | | |
| Arbitrary detention | 1.78 | 2.29 | 1.45 | 1.81 |
| Disappearance and abduction | 0.22 | 0.27 | 0.18 | 0.17 |
| All Internment Violations | 2.00 | 2.55 | 1.64 | 1.98 |
| **War Labor Violations** | | | | |
| Forced recruitment | 0.48 | 0.69 | 0.47 | 0.71 |
| Drugging | 0.19 | 0.31 | 0.18 | 0.25 |
| Forced labor | 0.63 | 1.06 | 0.65 | 0.94 |
| Total | 1.30 | 2.06 | 1.30 | 1.90 |
| **Sexual Violations** | | | | |

FIGURE 6.3 Mean Violations by Violation Type Reported per Interview, by Gender of Interviewer and Respondent, from the SL Survey

| | Interviewer | | | |
| --- | --- | --- | --- | --- |
| | female | | male | |
| | Respondent | | Respondent | |
| | female | male | female | male |
| Violation | *n* = 629 | *n* = 1,195 | *n* = 411 | *n* = 1,350 |
| Rape | 0.87 | 0.96 | 0.65 | 0.88 |
| Sexual slavery | 0.40 | 0.41 | 0.25 | 0.29 |
| Sexual abuse | 0.09 | 0.13 | 0.04 | 0.06 |
| Total | 1.36 | 1.51 | 0.94 | 1.23 |
| Consumption Violations | | | | |
| Forced consumption | 0.16 | 0.28 | 0.14 | 0.20 |
| Total | 0.16 | 0.28 | 0.14 | 0.20 |
| Overall Total | 16.39 | 21.17 | 13.98 | 17.14 |

FIGURE 6.3  (*continued*)

seem more sympathetic, or perhaps these male respondents did not feel threatened by female interviewers because females hold relatively less social power than males in Sierra Leonean society.

*Advance missions to local Sierra Leone districts to explain the survey and achieve local buy-in in rural areas.* As described earlier, an "advance team" was sent to each district to obtain the permission of the traditional leaders of the district to conduct the survey and to arrange for advertising over the radio and in the urban areas. If possible, the advance team included a staff member who knew the paramount chief for the district in question.[18] Whenever possible, the advance team would travel to a district the week before the beginning of the survey in that district; in each district an attempt was made to visit every chiefdom.

The advance team represented a large expense. We decided on this budget allocation in response to the political and social climate in Sierra Leone in the first half of 2004. Both the Truth and Reconciliation Commission and the Campaign for Good Governance had conducted countrywide statement-taking exercises before us, and potential respondents might have felt that they had already talked to enough people about their tragedies, with no direct benefit to their communities. Also of concern was the imminent commencement of operations of the Special Court, for both urban and rural people were afraid of being called in to testify before the new tribunal. To allay those fears, the advance team would educate the local communities about our mission. We also made sure to be honest about the limitations of what we could offer in terms of assistance to local communities.

The question of interest is whether this effort and expense did make a difference in the response rate. Nonresponse occurs when an interview for a sample unit is not achieved for any reason: refusal to participate, nobody home, and so on. The response rate for the rural areas was extremely high: there were 2,434 completed interviews out of 2,443 attempted interviews in the rural areas, yielding a response rate of 99.6 percent. The evidence that the response rate was due to the advance team's work is anecdotal: obviously, we cannot know what would have happened had the advance team not existed. We do know that the climate in the country toward the Special Court was so negative that the tribunal, toward the end of our survey, mounted a dedicated positive publicity and public education program.[19] We also know that a second phase of the Campaign for Good Governance statement-taking project occurred simultaneously with our survey and that statement takers for that project reported difficulties in finding people who were willing to be interviewed.[20]

*Radio and TV advertising to increase response for the Sierra Leone survey in the urban areas.* The buy-in of the local traditional leaders was most likely to have an impact in the rural areas of the country, where villages were led by lower level chiefs who reported to the chiefdom chiefs. In the urban areas, the traditional authority structure was not as strong. In these areas, we used a positive publicity campaign consisting of local radio interviews and a TV program that could be aired locally.[21] The response rate for Freetown is estimated to be 85.8 percent, versus an estimated response rate of 96 percent for all other urban enumeration areas combined.[22] The difference between those rates could be due to several factors. First, although there is no traditional leader inside the Western Area, each district of Sierra Leone has a district paramount chief who presides over villages and urban areas alike. Therefore, the urban areas are more likely to have been affected by the work of the advance team. Second, the urban areas outside Freetown are significantly smaller than Freetown, and therefore residents behave more like the villagers in the rural areas than residents of Freetown do—the coming of the interviewers would therefore be a more significant event in these urban areas, and residents would be more likely to respond to social pressure to participate.

The difference in nonresponse rates in Freetown and outside the capital can serve as a proxy measure for the effect of the advance team in the districts. Although all urban areas received the "radio/TV" treatment, the urban areas outside Freetown received the "traditional leader" treatment as well. A coarse measurement of just this aspect of the advance team's work, then, is a 70 percent reduction in the nonresponse rate.

*Staff-friendly management style and staff empowerment through training, to motivate staff in difficult field conditions.* From the first interactions with the start-up team to the final project party, the SL Survey management invested heavily in staff. In review, the start-up team was encouraged to consider themselves equal partners in developing the questionnaire, and they contributed substantial ideas to the survey implementation. Staff were trained not only in interviewing techniques, but also in basic descriptive statistics so that they would understand the entire data collection process and their role in it: during the training, staff were given the opportunity to work with management on refining and finalizing the coding system for the survey; staff were provided with money for lunch and reimbursement for medical expenses for themselves and their families; and severely ill staff were emergency-evacuated from the field. None of these policies were standard practice in Sierra Leone at the time of the survey. The extra care given to the staff of the survey most likely yielded higher levels of dedication and honesty, but measuring the effect of these policies is difficult.

There are, however, some ways in which the efficacy and honesty of the staff can be examined. First, the readings taken through the global positioning systems in the field can be compared to a map of Sierra Leone. If the staff had been attempting to avoid long walks and boat trips, they might have self-selected villages close to main roads instead of the villages picked through the random sample process. If so, the GPS readings would be clustered along the main roads of Sierra Leone, or many GPS readings would be missing. Figure 6.4 shows that GPS readings are spread throughout the country, along main roads and also in more remote areas, suggesting that the sampling plan was followed honestly. Note that the cluster of readings in Port Loko is associated with two chiefdoms for which the Sierra Leone Central Statistics Office projected 2004 population was especially high.

A second (albeit) imperfect way of measuring the effect of the training and empowerment techniques for the staff is to examine the item nonresponse rates for the items that required a great deal of interviewer attention and input. For several variables (Tribe of Victim, Languages Spoken by Victim, Gender of Victim, Perpetrator Identity, and Perpetrator Ethnicity), response rates are higher than 99.9 percent. Other variables yielded response rates between 97 and 99 percent. Thus item nonresponse was extremely low.

## Conclusion

The efficacy of random sample survey methods for casualty estimation is mixed. Although most sample surveys used for casualty estimation have defined sampling processes clearly, assumptions underlying random sampling, including a complete, accurate sampling frame and high-to-perfect response, are almost always violated in active-conflict settings and strained in post-conflict settings. In the author's experience, random sample surveys are better suited to refugee camps and other post-conflict settings than to areas of active warfare. Even in post-conflict areas, however, care must be taken not to overstate the applicability of the results if the random sampling is compromised. In addition, many

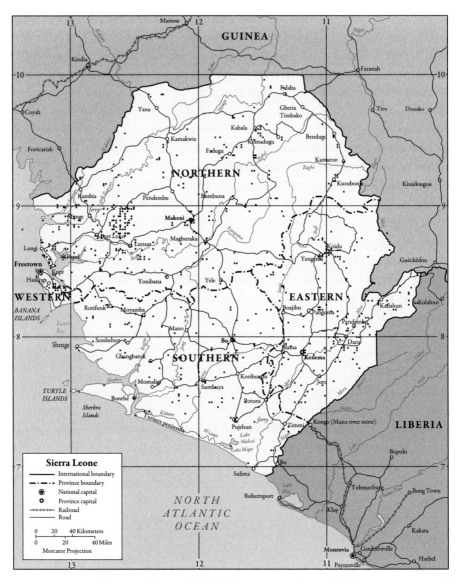

FIGURE 6.4 Map of the Sampled Households of the SL Survey. The small black squares correspond to latitude and longitude measurements acquired from a global positioning system used by the team leaders to mark the locations of the sample housing units. Note that the sample is not confined to the main roads (indicated by the lines on the map).

*Source for Base Map:* U.S. Central Intelligence Agency.

surveys used for casualty estimation are not adequately pretested. This must change if casualty estimation through random sample surveys is to be scientifically defensible. The level of care with which the Sierra Leone War Crimes Documentation Survey was tested and fielded is extremely unusual in practice and, in fact, may be the only example of its kind.

When random sample survey results are used to inform casualty estimates, understanding the limitations of the sampling scheme, as well as the full process used to design the questionnaire, is essential for determining whether the data are of sufficient quality to merit trust. If the estimates are of great political interest or are to be used in legal proceedings, even small issues in the methodology, regardless of whether they significantly affect the results, could be exaggerated by those who wish to discredit the data. As a result, the simplest, most defensible methods should be employed and employed well, with direct oversight of all parts of the survey, including the data collection.

Although many difficulties are encountered when random sample surveys are used for casualty estimation, new techniques for mitigating those difficulties show great promise. But much remains to be done: research on the effects of new types of sampling frame (e.g., satellite imagery), new technology (GPS, laptops), and new questionnaire design techniques (probing, universal landmarks) are needed. The case study in this chapter is one example of what creative, directed approaches to casualty estimation can accomplish.

REFERENCES

Asher, J. 2011. "Methodological Innovations in the Collection and Analysis of Human Rights Violations Data." Unpublished dissertation.

Behling, O., and Law, K. S. 2000. *Translating Questionnaires and Other Research Instruments.* London: Sage.

Blair, J., Conrad, F., Ackermann, A., and Claxton, G. 2006. "The Effect of Sample Size on Cognitive Interview Findings." Paper presented at the American Association for Public Opinion Research Conference, Montreal, Quebec, Canada.

Burnham, G., Lafta, R., Shannon, D., and Roberts, L. 2006. "Mortality after the 2003 Invasion of Iraq: A Cross-Sectional Cluster Sample Survey." *The Lancet* 368: 1421–1428.

Carrasco, L. 2003. "The American Community Survey (ACS) en Español: Using Cognitive Interviews to Test the Functional Equivalence of Questionnaire Translations." At: www.census.gov/srd/papers/pdf/ssm2003-17.pdf. Accessed February 25, 2005.

Cochran, W. G. 1977. *Sampling Techniques*, 3rd ed. New York: John Wiley & Sons.

De Leeuw, E. D., Hox, J. J., and Dillman, D. A. 2008. *International Handbook of Survey Methodology.* New York: Lawrence Erlbaum Associates.

DeMaio, T. J., and Landreth, A. 2004. "Do Different Cognitive Interviewing Techniques Produce Different Results?" In *Methods for Testing and Evaluating Survey Questionnaires*, edited by S. Presser, J. M. Rothgeb, M. P. Couper, J. T. Lessler, E. Martin, J. Martin, and E. Singer. Hoboken, NJ: Wiley-Interscience.

Devereux. S., and Hoddinott, J. 1993. *Fieldwork in Developing Countries*. Boulder, CO: Lynne Rienner Publishers.

Grosh, M., and Glewwe, P., eds. 2000. *Designing Household Survey Questionnaires for Developing Countries: Lessons from 15 Years of the Living Standards Measurement Study*, Vol. 1. Washington, DC: World Bank.

Groves, R. M., Fowler, F. J., Couper, M. P., Jepkowski, J. M., Singer, E., and Tourangeau, R. 2004. *Survey Methodology*. Hoboken, NJ: Wiley-Interscience.

Harkness, J. A., Pennell, B.-E., and Schoua-Glusberg, A. 2004. "Survey Questionnaire Translation and Assessment," In *Methods for Testing and Evaluating Survey Questionnaires*, edited by S. Presser, J. M. Rothgeb, M. P. Couper, J. T. Lessler, E. Martin, J. Martin, and E. Singer. Hoboken, NJ: Wiley-Interscience.

Harkness, J. A., Van de Vijver, F. J. R., and Mohler, P. P. 2002. *Cross-Cultural Survey Methods*. Hoboken, NJ: Wiley-Interscience.

Jansen, H., and Hak, T. 2005. "The Productivity of the Three-Step Test-Interview (TSTI) Compared to an Expert Review of a Self-Administered Questionnaire on Alcohol Consumption." *Journal of Official Statistics* 21: 103–120.

Johnson, N., Spagat, M., Gourley, S., Onnela, J.-P., and Reinert, G. 2008. "Bias in Epidemiological Studies of Conflict Mortality." *Journal of Peace Research* 45(5): 653–664.

Kish, L. 1965. *Survey Sampling*. New York: John Wiley & Sons.

Marker, D. 2008. "Review: Methodological Review of 'Mortality After the 2003 Invasion of Iraq: A Cross-Sectional Cluster Sample Survey.'" *Public Opinion Quarterly* 72(2): 345–363.

Potaka, L., and Cochrane, S. 2004. "Developing Bilingual Questionnaires: Experiences from New Zealand in the Development of the 2001 Māori Language Survey." *Journal of Official Statistics* 20(2): 289–300.

Roberts, L., Lafta, R., Garfield, R., Khudhairi, J., and Burnham, G. 2004. "Mortality Before and After the 2003 Invasion of Iraq: Cluster Sample Survey." *The Lancet* 364(9448): 1857–1428.

Suchman, L., and Jordan, B. 1990. "Interactional Troubles in Face-to-Face Survey Interviews." *Journal of the American Statistical Association* 85(409): 232–241.

Willis, G., Lawrence, D., Thompson, F., Kudela, M., Levin, K., and Miller, K. 2005. "The Use of Cognitive Interviewing to Evaluate Translated Survey Questions: Lessons Learned." Paper presented at the 2005 Conference of the Federal Committee on Statistical Methodology, Arlington, VA, November 14–16.

World Health Organization. 2007. "Process of Translation and Adaptation of Instruments." At: www.who.int/substance_abuse/research_tools/translation/en/. Accessed March 5, 2008.

NOTES

1. Basic texts outlining survey methods are readily available: two that are especially current are the *International Handbook of Survey Methodology* (De Leeuw, Hox, and Dillman 2008) and *Survey Methodology* (Groves et al. 2004).

2. This is true only when the random sample survey techniques are not hampered by conditions such as flaws in the sampling frame, refusals to respond and other types of nonresponse, or badly designed questionnaires. As this chapter shows, "correctly" implementing a random sample survey is a difficult undertaking. In practice, we are often forced to accept some minor flaws in the survey process.

3. The sources given in note 1 contain information on proper questionnaire design techniques, and questionnaire design is a frequent topic explored in survey methods journals such as *Public Opinion Quarterly* and *Survey Methodology*.

4. This section and the following section are based on a more detailed literature review, including citations, given in Asher (2011).

5. A sample frame is a list of the units to be sampled. For example, a list of housing unit addresses might comprise a sample frame, as might a list of students at a particular school if school students are the population of interest.

6. See Devereux and Hoddinott (1993) for discussions on proper field ethics in developing countries.

7. For a more detailed resource on cross-cultural survey methods, see Harkness, Van de Vijver, and Mohler (2002).

8. See Behling and Law (2000), Grosh and Glewwe (2000), Carrasco (2003), Harkness Harkness, Van de Vijver, and Mohler (2002), Potaka and Cochrane (2004), and World Health Organization (2007).

9. For basic information on simple and complex random samples, see Cochran (1977) or Kish (1965).

10. The author was a reviewer for the Iraq survey and a developer/field tester for the survey of casualties in East Timor.

11. DeMaio and Landreth (2004), while discussing different cognitive interviewing techniques, suggest that "properly trained field staff, working in conjunction with experienced survey methodologists, can identify equal numbers of questionnaire problems as professional survey researchers."

12. At the time, we were following the advice of Gordon Willis et al. (2005), who advocated for a minimum of four cognitive interviews for any pretesting study. Since then, Blair, Ackermann, and Claxton (2006) have studied the impact of differing numbers of cognitive interviews on the number of questionnaire problems uncovered; their results suggest that more interviews are needed—and that about 15 interviews are needed before the net gain of each additional interview begins to "taper off."

13. The lectures and practice sessions during these four days of training mirrored the training manual used in Timor-Leste; in fact, the instructor used the Timor-Leste training manual as her lecture notes; students took notes during this training rather than receiving handouts.

14. Fieldwork in Freetown and in the adjacent areas relied on detailed housing unit maps; since all sampled households were marked on those maps, GPS readings were not needed to verify the location of the sample.

15. A description of that work appears in Asher (2011).

16. In Sierra Leone, the main household question was as follows: "Please give me the names of all persons who usually share your cooking pot, starting with the head of household (and including yourself). For each person, please list all of the names that they have used since the Lomé Accord was signed, including society names, nicknames, religious names, and popular names, as well as any other names."

17. A comparison of household size between the 2004 Sierra Leone census and this survey is given in Asher (2011).

18. Owing to the high unemployment rate in Sierra Leone, we were able to hire highly qualified personnel. Our staff was very well educated, with many staff members possessing college degrees

in the social sciences; many staff members came from the more prominent families of their districts. As a result, many of our staff members had connections to the local paramount chiefs—in fact, one staff member was the son of the paramount chief of Bo.

19. Two of our interviewers were hired by the Special Court to create and complete this campaign.

20. This information was provided to the author by Richard Conibere, who was working in the Campaign for Good Governance building at the time of the survey.

21. The TV show was created in Freetown; the author was one of the individuals interviewed in the 30-minute segment, but the majority of the interviews were with the survey team leaders.

22. For more details, see Asher (2011).

# 7 Collecting Data on Civilian Casualties
## SCIENTIFIC CHALLENGES AND ETHNOGRAPHIC SOLUTIONS
Meghan Foster Lynch

## Introduction

Difficult-to-observe phenomena, such as the struggles of the powerless—whether crack dealers in Harlem (Bourgeois 2002), peasants in Malaysia (Scott 1985), or El Salvador (Wood 2003), or miners in Appalachia (Gaventa 1980)—have long been the domain of ethnographers, whose vivid portraits enrich our understanding of conflict. Counting civilian fatalities during war, on the other hand, clearly should not be tasked to ethnographers, who choose depth of understanding over breadth and representativeness. Nonetheless, ethnographers have something to offer to debates about methods for counting casualties. Quantitative researchers can get lost amid discussions of sampling frames, survey designs, and estimation procedures, while neglecting to examine one of their most fundamental assumptions: that most people will answer questions either truthfully or in a predictably biased way.[1] This assumption, particularly when the topic under investigation is as sensitive as conflict-related death counts, ignores important lessons from anthropology and psychology about the complex ways in which people relate their stories and the ways that this storytelling varies from culture to culture. If this key assumption does not hold—if respondents provide information that systematically deviates from the truth in unpredictable directions—our civilian casualty counts will end up representative, statistically significant, and wrong.

Intuitively, as well as from a large body of prior research, we know that it is hard to obtain good data on sensitive information by asking respondents directly (Tourangeau and Smith 1996; Ong and Weiss 2000).[2] The challenges, and possible ways to overcome them, have been studied most systematically for a subset of sensitive information about instances of stigmatized behavior or attitudes. Take prejudiced behavior as an example. In the late 1970s, survey researchers observed that self-reported indicators of racist behavior were decreasing (Quillian 2006). Exciting news: Was the United States entering a post-racial society? External evidence of racism, in the form of job discrimination and persistent income inequality, suggested otherwise. Researchers realized that something important *had* indeed changed: it was no longer socially acceptable (in most circles) to admit to acting in a prejudicial manner. A step forward for society, a step backward for research on prejudice. Researchers had to figure out alternative ways to measure a phenomenon that people were not willing to discuss openly.

It is now widely accepted that directly asking respondents about racist behavior does not provide an accurate measure.[3] Indeed, not only do we expect many people to lie, but we also have come to believe that people cannot necessarily gauge the extent of their own prejudice very well (Greenwald and Banaji 1995). That is, people's reports of their prejudice can deviate from the truth unintentionally as well as intentionally. Researchers think that the conscious or unconscious desire to avoid the perception of racism is so powerful that it can even affect responses to questions not explicitly related to prejudice. For example, during the polling before the presidential election of 2008, researchers worried that people might tell interviewers that they were planning to vote for Barack Obama to avoid being perceived as racist. In the past, this so-called social desirability bias had been put forth as the reason that certain African Americans running for office seemed to be ahead by a large and significant margin in pre-election polls, but when they were victorious, tallies indicated that they had won by a very narrow margin (Traugott and Price 1992).

At this point, the reader may object that measuring prejudiced behavior proves so challenging simply because people are ashamed to admit the truth. Why would people lie if asked who in their family or among their circle of acquaintances was killed? In the rest of this chapter, drawing on lessons from anthropological, psychological, and clinical research, as well as my own fieldwork, I discuss why we should neither assume that respondents will tell the truth when asked about mortality counts nor assume that we can predict the direction of the bias. I will argue that we should consider mortality counts[4] in conflict and post-conflict settings as sensitive information subject to the same measurement problems as stigmatized behavior and other sensitive areas. I expect many of my conclusions to be applicable also to research on stigmatized attitudes or sensitive opinions; however, techniques for the measurement of attitudes and opinions differ from techniques for the measurement of behavior and facts and thus fall outside the scope of this chapter. I am similarly unable to address the ways in which the conclusions may be relevant to researchers who use surveys for nonstigmatized behavior and nonsensitive facts. Even so, researchers may find that many of the conclusions here also apply to what they do, especially when they work in unfamiliar cultural contexts.

This chapter proceeds in three sections. In the first section, using evidence from my 18 months of fieldwork in rural Burundi, I provide examples of how respondents answer questions about sensitive topics in unexpected ways. In the second section, I suggest a three-part classification of reasons respondents may have for modifying the responses they provide: intentional modifications to protect self or others, intentional modifications to promote self or others, and unintentional modifications. I then give some examples of how these modifications might work and how they might systematically bias our results on mortality surveys. Throughout this chapter, I use the terms "modification" or "truth-modification" to describe an inaccurate recounting of facts. I favor these terms because, unlike the terms "lies" and "deception," they do not imply intention on the part of the actor, nor do they carry a similarly negative value judgment. "Truth" is itself a contested term. I readily acknowledge that people construct narratives of reality and that these narratives provide valuable information—indeed, these narratives form an important part of my overall research. I nonetheless believe that an objective truth about many facts—mortality counts among them—exists, and when I refer to "truth," it is this truth that I mean.

In the final section, I start by briefly reviewing current best practices for obtaining sensitive information in survey research. I argue, however, that there are strong reasons to believe that even these best practices may be missing systematic lies that ethnographic methods can often detect. Furthermore, I point out that the best practices are often not practicable (or at least are rarely practiced) in the settings in which we work. I recommend that researchers who want to obtain good count data on civilian fatalities conduct experiments in each culture in which they measure how different methods affect the accuracy of reporting in different cultures. I then discuss the advantages and disadvantages of ethnography as a way to understand violent conflict. It cannot provide good mortality data for a large area, but, I argue, usually neither can our other methods. I make the case that to obtain accurate information about sensitive issues, ethnography does better, because it is uniquely equipped to deal with issues of culture, trust, and contradiction. I conclude by suggesting that focusing so much energy on good count data on civilian casualties during war may be a misguided approach. If the goal is to explain political violence, develop policy prescriptions to prevent and resolve conflict, or prosecute war crimes and crimes against humanity, rigorous ethnography arguably does a better job than surveys at all three.[5]

## Uncovering Contradictions and Complexities: Evidence from Burundi

I spent a year and a half (in 2008–2010) interviewing civilians, former rebels, former and current soldiers, and former and current government officials in Burundi, primarily in rural areas. A small country wedged between Rwanda, Tanzania, and the Democratic Republic of the Congo, Burundi has a postcolonial history marked by coups, dictators, and episodic violence. The most recent civil war began in 1993 with the assassination of Melchior Ndadaye, a Hutu who had been democratically elected president a mere three months before. The last rebel group demobilized only in 2009.

Before I arrived in Burundi, several NGO and academic acquaintances warned me that Burundians were suspicious of outsiders, that they did not like to talk about themselves, and that they would lie to me. I was troubled by the stereotyping and by the idea of a monolithic Burundian culture that would hinder my discussions. However, even before choosing to work in Burundi, I started my project with the belief that people of any culture would be unlikely to tell me the sensitive information I sought about violence within their communities unless they trusted me. I thus had decided to conduct in-depth interviews, often interviewing the same person more than once, in a relatively unstructured format. I asked my interviewees to tell me the history of their community. For some interviewees, that question sufficed to launch them into a long narrative. Others were less sure of how to react, so I started by asking them to describe what life was like when they were children: Were the harvests good? What were the schools like? How were relations among neighbors? Though it was obvious to most of my interviewees that a researcher asking about the history of their community would be interested in the conflict, I never directly engaged interviewees on that topic until they felt comfortable bringing it up on their own.

My choice of method preceded my colleagues' warnings. But through my interviews, I grew to understand why my acquaintances had formed those opinions they held—getting good information took something that the vast majority of those who had cautioned me did not have: time and a demonstrable interest in listening to people tell their stories, even when those stories were not directly relevant to my research topic. With that time and that interest, I found that the vast majority of my interlocutors shared their experiences openly and that they helped me explore apparent contradictions in their stories in ways that led me to new avenues of research.[6] I discuss the advantages of ethnography in greater detail in the final section, focusing first on illustrating how ethnography on sensitive topics reveals complexities and contradictions that would not be accessible from a more superficial discussion. I do not conclude the chapter by giving examples specifically about counting civilian casualties; such was not the purpose of my fieldwork. The examples are nonetheless relevant for researchers trying to measure conflict deaths, because they show the difficulty of obtaining accurate information on violence in conflict and post-conflict settings.

*EXAMPLE 1: INTERVIEW WITH AN ELDERLY MAN IN VYANDA COMMUNE, BURURI PROVINCE*

I am interviewing an elderly Hutu man in the south of Burundi. Dates are not a common marker of time in Burundi, so I begin this interview as I often do, by asking about the timing of some significant events in the life of my interviewee and then situating my questions in relation to these events.

*"How old are you?"*[7]
"Sixty-five."
*"Are you married?"*

"Yes."

*"How old were you when you got married?"*

"Thirty-five."

In my mind I quickly calculate: so he was born around 1944 and married around 1979. I want to know about what happened in his environs during the civil conflicts in 1972 and 1993, but I will start with a calmer time period, to ease into the conversation, and then move forward or backward in relation to that period.

*"Can you describe life here when you were a newlywed?"*

"Ndadaye was killed, and then things went downhill."

A first red flag. The old man's days as a newlywed should have been over a decade before the assassination of President Ndadaye in October 1993. As the interview continues, although I know little about what happened in the interviewee's immediate vicinity, I note several inconsistencies, and I can tell by the way he is connecting local events to national events that the chronology he offers is wildly inaccurate. I decide to rephrase my questions, to try to find out why.

*"When did you get married?"*

"1992."

That fits with what he said about Ndadaye, but it would have made him 48 years old when he got married, rather than 35, as he had told me in the beginning of the interview. "Senility, maybe," I think to myself, "or he's hiding something." I scribble "unreliable" next to my interview notes.

Afterward, I ask my interpreter if she thinks the responses merely indicate confusion or were deliberately misleading and, if the latter, why. She turns discreetly to the man's niece, who is nearby, and asks, "How many children does your uncle have?"

"Oh," the woman replies, "he never married."

My interpreter turns back to me: "He didn't want you to know that he wasn't married."

*EXAMPLE 2: INTERVIEW WITH A LOCAL GOVERNMENT OFFICIAL, RUGOMBO COMMUNE, CIBITOKE PROVINCE*

*"Can you describe the atmosphere after the presidential election [of Ndadaye]?"*

"People were bursting with joy. There were lots of festivities. People paraded throughout the night and were very proud."

*"Who participated in this celebration?"*

"Everyone."

*"Even the members of the opposing party?"*

"No, they stayed home."

*"How were the relationships between the members of the winning party and the members of the opposing party in the days after the election?"*

"They were good. There were no tensions."

*"Were there threats against members of the losing party?"*

"No, there were no threats, not in my zone."

*"In your commune?"*

"No, not in my zone or my commune."

*"In some areas, there were problems between members of the different parties after the election. But here there were no problems?*

"No."

*"No violence?"*

"No. . . . I guess there were some mild threats. People of the winning party sometimes beat up people of the losing party."

*"They beat them up? What would they do exactly?"*

"They would gather around someone from the opposite side and hit him or beat him. They would steal his things."

In this case, I felt certain that my interviewee had not been attempting to deceive me, but rather was so caught up in telling his story that he was immediately saying whatever was most salient to him. When I asked him who participated in the celebration, he remembered a great party, a victory celebration, a time of hope. The absence of the opposition did not affect the atmosphere and did not seem important until I asked about it specifically. Similarly, my interviewee stated several times that there was no violence before eventually recounting that the winning party physically attacked the opposition.

Why did I keep asking him the same question? I knew from multiple other interviews that there had been violence, and my interviewee did not appear uncomfortable with the topic. Under these circumstances, his role as an authority figure allowed me to push him a bit harder than I would have pushed someone who was not in government. Why did he not tell me outright? I suspect again that the beatings were not salient in his memory because beatings are a form of normalized violence in Burundi. They are not necessarily extraordinary or threatening; they occur frequently in a wide variety of settings. But once my question sunk in, the interviewee was very open and gave me detailed descriptions of the different sorts of intimidation.

*EXAMPLE 3: INTERVIEW WITH 70-YEAR-OLD MAN, MUSIGATI COMMUNE, BUBANZA PROVINCE*

*"How were relationships between [the rebel group] and the civilian population?"*

"During the war, our relationships were good. Very good."

*"Many people tell me the rebels hurt the population."*

"No! The rebels did not hurt the population. If a rebel came to pillage the belongings of the population, he was punished by his leader."

*"So how did the rebels feed themselves?"*

"The population fed them. . . . Someone who is armed, he's not going to wait until you give him some beans, he will just take them."

*"Isn't that a way of mistreating the population?"*

"They asked you first. If you refused, they took it by force."

This conversation serves as a reminder of the complexities of collecting data from human subjects. Why did the man deny at first that the rebels had caused any problems? Perhaps he agreed with the rebels ideologically and did not want to tarnish their reputation, or did not believe that his responses would be confidential and was worried about trouble from former rebels. But then why would he eventually tell me that the rebels had forcibly taken food? Perhaps the rebels had won control of the dominant narrative in his neighborhood, and so he started with the community narrative, only moving away from it when he felt more comfortable, or when he realized that he would not be the first to tell me about bad rebel behavior (some people in interviews would not mention the conflict until I made it clear that I already knew it had happened). It is impossible to know why this particular individual started with a modified narrative and moved to an unmodified or less modified one. However, it is one of a multitude of examples during my 18 months of field research in Burundi that made me realize the importance of ethnography. Taking the time to develop an understanding of local history and culture and having the flexibility to explore inconsistencies that arise during interviews produce information that cannot easily be obtained through other means.

## Modified Narratives

The types of questions that may elicit systematically biased responses will vary by location, time, and context, as will the reasons people have for modifying their stories. The goal here is to understand how these modifications affect our research, not to judge the behavior of people who sometimes construct what they say. There are many good reasons to modify one's account of what happened, and not necessarily many obvious ones to try to make one's account as accurate as possible. We often assume that, unless a person has something to hide, the default response will be a direct and truthful recounting of events. But why should this be so? If a person believes that there is even the slightest chance that she could be better off by modifying her story, and she places no value on a book being written by someone she does not know, the better option is always to modify her story. Some people do place value on the writing of a book about their experiences because they want to testify about what happened (Wood 2003; Rubin and Rubin 2005; Fujii 2009). But even their stories may be unintentionally modified by factors we should strive to understand.

In this section, I offer a typology of truth-modifications that distinguishes among three categories of modifications researchers may encounter when seeking information about sensitive topics: (1) intentional modifications to protect self or others, (2) intentional modifications to promote self or others, and (3) unintentional modifications. This classification suggests a way for researchers to reflect on the different sorts of modifications they may encounter, depending on the topic they research and the culture in which they work. In tables 7.1–7.3, I give general examples of each type of modification, as well as more specific examples of the sorts of reasoning that can exist behind each one. The examples are meant to be illustrative, not to form an exhaustive list. Most have been discussed at length elsewhere and are mentioned only briefly here. For the purposes of this chapter, the important point is that the potential reasons for truth-modifications vary enormously and do not allow us to predict the direction of the bias we might obtain in our responses.

In table 7.1, we see some reasons interviewees might have for intentionally modifying their responses to protect themselves or others. One of these reasons, embarrassment, was illustrated in Example 1 of the chapter, in which my interviewee did not wish to tell me that he was unmarried. In other cases, even though the topic itself may be too private

TABLE 7.1.

Possible Reasons for Intentional Modifications to Protect Self or Others

| Reasons | Example of Possible Concerns |
| --- | --- |
| 1. Belief that the interviewer is not who she claims to be | The interviewer might be collecting information to prosecute guilty people. |
| 2. Belief that responses will not be confidential | If my neighbors or the rebels find out that I told the interviewer what they did, they will seek revenge. |
| 3. Embarrassment or guilt | I don't want people to know that I couldn't save my family. |
| | I don't want people to know that I participated in violence. |
| | I don't want people to know that I can't remember what happened. |
| 4. General fear | I don't know what the consequences might be if I talk about what happened, but it's better not to take any chances. |
| 5. Avoidance of emotional stress or retraumatization | Thinking about the past will make me remember things I would rather forget. |

or sensitive for a person to wish to share her experience, cultural norms might dictate complying with a request for an interview out of politeness or deference. Here researchers are putting interviewees in a situation in which lying is the only way out (Bleek 1987)—there is no other way to protect the information that the interviewee does not want to share without breaching norms. Researchers usually try very hard to avoid this bind by seeking informed consent, but it can be difficult or impossible to know whether people actually feel comfortable refusing. Other possible reasons range from not believing the researcher's description of who she is or her assurances of confidentiality to emotions like fear or guilt to the desire to avoid the emotions that might resurface in the course of recounting sensitive experiences. The direction of the bias is not predictable without understanding why people modify their stories, and in certain cases even if we did understand their reasons, the direction of the predicted bias would be unclear.

Table 7.2 lists reasons interviewees might have for intentionally modifying their responses to promote themselves or others. For example, interviewees may modify their descriptions of events to shape how the interviewer perceives the interviewee or for other reasons: if they think they might receive something by editing their remarks; if they do not believe the interviewer's assurances of confidentiality and want anything she repeats to help them; if they want their country or area to be perceived positively by those who

TABLE 7.2.

Possible Reasons for Intentional Modifications to Promote Self or Others

| Reasons | Examples of Possible Concerns |
| --- | --- |
| 1. Belief that something can be obtained | If I say the right thing, maybe the interviewer will provide support for me. |
| 2. Belief that responses will not be confidential | If my neighbors find out that I said nice things about them, they will be appreciative. |
| 3. Desire to be seen in a positive light in front of outsider | I want the interviewer to know that I am important in my community, so I should show that I know what was going on.<br>I do not want the interviewer to know that I am unmarried. |
| 4. Desire to have Burundi or one's locality look good to outsiders | I don't want the people who read the book that is being written to think that people on my hill are bad people. |
| 5. Belief that the interviewer is looking for certain responses | Violence happened on my hill, but the outsiders usually want to hear how both ethnicities get along. |

TABLE 7.3.

Possible Reasons for Unintentional Modifications

| Reasons | Examples |
| --- | --- |
| 1. Details that are being asked about are not salient in interviewee's memory | An interviewee, when asked who attended a celebration, remembers the big crowd that attended, not the fact that the opposition did not attend. |
| 2. Confusion because of multiple periods of violence | An interviewee has had many similar experiences and cannot situate local incidents in relation to dates or national incidents. |
| 3. Collective memory takes over individual memory | An interviewee thinks she remembers something, but the story she is telling is actually the community story, which has been talked about until it erased her own memory. |
| 4. Default response is the story that the interviewee has told in the past | Stories are repeated frequently in small communities, and if the default story is a modification of what actually happened, regardless of intentions, it may be the first story at hand. |
| 5. Difficulty constructing a narrative | Interviewee is not used to telling chronological narratives and so moves forward and backward in time without any indication that is what she is doing. |
| 6. Bias against minor incidents | Interviewee focuses on recounting the worst events, neglecting smaller events. |

will read the interviews; or if they think they know what the interviewer wants them to say and want to say what is expected of them. I believe that I have on different occasions heard stories that were modified as a result of the influence of each of these reasons.

Particularly important in Burundi during my fieldwork seemed to be the desire for oneself and one's area to be perceived positively—what I grew to think of as the "not-on-my-hill" phenomenon. When interviewees recounted past conflict, they would frequently talk about all of the problems on the surrounding hills, while maintaining that their hill had remained peaceful. Once on the neighboring hill, I would hear the same story: yes, there was conflict, but not on my hill. While we rarely know with certainty the reasons an individual interviewee has for intentionally modifying her stories, it is useful to try to understand the range of reasons that might be influencing how a person responds and especially, even if we do not know *why* a person is modifying her response, to identify *that* she is modifying her response, so we can improve our interpretation of her account. Identifying the sorts of questions likely to lead to truth-modification requires both cultural and contextual knowledge.

Finally, people might modify their stories about sensitive topics unintentionally for a number of reasons (Fenton et al. 2001) (see table 7.3). Note first the distinction between a true memory and the historical truth (Ricoeur 2004)—what people remember is not always what occurred. Extensive research on eyewitness testimony has shown the extent to which even well-intentioned witnesses may give false statements. My Example 2 highlights another reason for unintentional modification: an interviewer asks about events that are not salient in an interviewee's memory, or an interviewee focuses on narrating major events at the expense of minor ones. Alternatively, what a person recounts may lack details essential to accurate interpretation. A common obstacle that I encountered was that many of my interviewees were not used to recounting narratives and had difficulty with sequence and chronology. They would sometimes switch back and forth between decades without any indication that they were doing so. Similarly, if I asked about what happened on an interviewee's hill, she might begin by responding to my question and then seamlessly move into a description of what happened on a neighboring hill. I learned, therefore, to pepper my interviews with, "And where/when exactly was that?"

Other reasons for unintentional modifications include confusion about what happened that results from having lived through multiple periods of violence, collective memories that overtake individual memories, or the tendency to default to whatever story an interviewee has previously recounted within her community. For example, a survivor of the Rwandan genocide explains, "'As time passes, I can feel my mind sorting out which memories to save, of its own accord. . . .' Some events are recounted frequently, so they grow, because of all the additions that each person contributes. Those events remain clearly remembered, as if they had happened yesterday or only just last year. Other events are abandoned, and they fade, like a dream" (Munyaneza n.d., 57).

Truth-modifications occur frequently. But are they actually problematic for drawing conclusions, given a large enough sample? Yes, if everyone responds to certain questions in a systematically biased way, or if people in certain subgroups or certain places respond in a systematically biased way, and we do not know the direction of the bias. Taking mortality counts as our subject of investigation, imagine the most extreme case: no one who has had a family member killed reports the death in a household survey. Now imagine a slightly more plausible scenario: people of a high socioeconomic class report family deaths, while people of a low socioeconomic class do not. Multiple systems estimation, a statistical estimation procedure described in other chapters in this volume, can correct for systematic biases when these biases differ across sources (Lynch and Hoover Green 2008; Davenport and Ball 2002), but this correction works *if and only if the bias is not replicated in all the available sources*. Several studies have demonstrated, however, that unintentional truth-modifications about sensitive topics sometimes vary systematically by respondent characteristics, which can result in analyses that produce conclusions that are the opposite from the truth (Fenton et al. 2001; Manesh et al. 2008). In one case, researchers found that, in Iran, mothers who were more educated or better off economically were reporting higher levels of serious child illness and lower levels of child mortality than uneducated mothers. This finding was confusing: we expect higher levels of serious illness to correlate with higher levels of mortality, and we expect higher levels of education to correspond with lower levels of both serious illness and mortality, particularly in countries where education is a good proxy for wealth and the poor do not have access to such essentials as clean drinking water. The researchers argued that less educated mothers systematically underreported child illness because of "socially patterned differential recall and reporting" (Manesh et al. 2008, 199). Further complicating the story, this pattern is not consistent across cultures, as Alireza Olyaee Manesh and her colleagues found: "no obvious socio-economic, regional, religious, or cultural factors can explain the counter-intuitive results appearing in some countries rather than in others, and it appears to be an intrinsic danger of the survey method" (Ibid.,197).

## Discerning the Truth and Learning from Lies: Why Ethnography Succeeds Where Surveys Fail

Once researchers realized that they were unlikely to obtain the answers they sought about prejudice, illicit drug use, or other stigmatized behavior simply by asking, they developed innovative ways to measure this behavior, including both improvements to methods of self-reporting and ways to avoid the need to rely on self-reporting. Improvements in the first category, which are based primarily on the idea that increased anonymity will induce more truthful self-reporting (Ong and Weiss 2000), include measures such as computer-assisted self-interviewing, self-administered questionnaires, and interviews conducted behind screens. But studies attempting to ascertain whether some methods are better than others at eliciting information about sensitive topics have yielded mixed results (Potdar and Koenig 2005). Improvements in the second category include finding ways to measure the stigmatized behavior without people realizing it— for example, by using methods such as implicit attitude tests (Dovidio et al. 1997), name experiments (Bertrand and Mullainathan 2004), or audit studies (Quillian 2006). These methods are often very successful, but they must be conducted contemporaneously; they cannot be used to measure past sensitive behavior. Although they are currently rarely used in conflict setting,[8] these ways to increase the number of people who admit to stigmatized behavior may prove useful in counting civilian casualties. However, despite their potential, these methods, too, have a shortcoming: they have been developed primarily to counter the human impulse to lie about things that embarrass people. As we saw in the preceding section, embarrassment, guilt, and shame are far from the only reasons people have for modifying the stories that they recount when asked about sensitive information. Other commonly used good practices to reduce unintentionally modified responses that we might trigger in an unfamiliar culture include hiring a cultural adviser to review the survey questions and conducting a pilot study to see which questions are misunderstood (see the discussion by Asher in chapter 6 of this volume). However,

I argue that these measures are insufficient: *without a baseline against which to make a comparison, there is no way to tell which questions elicit systematically biased responses.*

## ETHNOGRAPHY VERSUS SURVEYS

Ethnographic methods have not been systematically tested against survey methods. However, the evidence that does exist from comparisons of the two methods suggests that there is reason to believe that ethnography may perform better than surveys in the collection of sensitive information. One anthropologist, whose survey unintentionally overlapped with his ethnographic study of six women, found that the women who had revealed to him during his ethnographic work sensitive information (e.g., about induced abortions) recounted completely different, sanitized stories to survey enumerators (Bleek 1987). One respondent told an enumerator, for example, that she was 24 years old, lived with her husband, and had never used birth control nor had an abortion; she had told the anthropologist that she was 31, did not live with a husband, had used many sorts of birth control, and had had at least three abortions.

Another study tested five different methods to collect data about adolescent sexual behavior (Plummer et al. 2004). This study had several considerable design problems that make it impossible to draw strong conclusions from certain parts of its data, but it had one significant advantage: it used biological data to determine respondents' STD status. Therefore, for those who tested positive for a sexually transmitted disease, there was a baseline against which to compare self-reported data in different treatment conditions. An important finding dealt with the six women who had tested positive; they all participated in one survey condition and in the in-depth interview condition (which included an explicit attempt to develop rapport by informal interactions). In the survey condition, only one of the six reported having had sexual intercourse, whereas five of the six reported having had intercourse in the in-depth interview condition. The vast majority of the respondents in the two survey conditions, which included more than 15,000 youth, did not test positive for STDs, so the researchers did not have a baseline for comparison. However, because many respondents (4,739) participated in more than one condition, the researchers were able to determine whether individuals had given consistent responses across treatments. Out of those who reported sexual experience, only 62 percent of males and 41 percent of females reported that experience in both survey treatments.

Much of the evidence suggesting that ethnography yields better information about sensitive topics than surveys is anecdotal. Particularly suggestive are the reports by researchers of information they received in subsequent interviews that had not been disclosed to them earlier. However, researchers rarely directly test survey methods against ethnographic ones. One reason is that ethnographic methods do not obviously lend themselves to standardization; the success of ethnography relies in large part on allowing unstandardized interactions and on the presumably unstandardizable skills of the ethnographer herself. However, there are ways to standardize some of the elements that we believe make ethnography successful, such as frequent presence in a community, repeat interactions with the same person, and the spending of time to develop trust through conversation about nonsensitive topics.

Although ethnography on some difficult-to-measure topics undoubtedly requires a talented researcher, it is unlikely that collecting sensitive factual information requires significant training. If empathy matters most, it is true that all researchers are not going to be equally good; but it is equally true that advanced training is not required. Instead, time and patience are key, and while true empathy may remain an elusive and unstandardizable characteristic, basic empathetic listening skills can be taught and learned quickly. The second study discussed in this section used both graduate researchers and high school graduates; the ethnographic data collected by the two sets of interviewers were comparable.

We need many more carefully designed field experiments, conducted systematically, to test survey methods against ethnographic ones for the collection of sensitive information. The use of a known baseline against which to compare the results of different treatments is an important criterion. These experiments should ideally be conducted for any culture or subgroup of interest before researchers choose to use surveys rather than in-depth interviews; they are the best way to determine which method will produce the most accurate results.

Ethnography brings its own set of concerns, from researcher subjectivity to unrepresentative samples. But it also provides a different way to grapple with the challenges posed by sensitive information. The advantages of ethnography come from the ways in which both interviewer and interviewee change their perceptions over time. On the side of the interviewee, as trust grows, so too does a willingness to share sensitive information. On the side of the interviewer, as understanding grows, so too does the ability to interpret information correctly. As interactions multiply, so too do opportunities for the interviewer to identify contradiction and opportunities for the interviewee to explain contradiction. These changing perceptions yield the three primary benefits of ethnographic methods over survey methods: increased detection of truth-modification, decreased incidence of truth-modification, and the ability to elicit sensitive information.

### DETECTING AND REDUCING TRUTH-MODIFICATION

Ethnography increases the ability to detect and reduce truth-modification. Two major advantages of ethnographic methods in detecting truth-modification are as follows: they allow the interviewer to learn from what she sees, as well as what she hears, and they allow the interviewer to learn from all of what she hears, rather than from only part. In the first category, ethnographers can observe and record body language to detect the possibility of truth-modification. Such indications not only alert the ethnographer to the possibility of incorrect information, they also suggest that perhaps the interviewee has consented to the interview unwillingly. The ethnographer who suspects that consent has not been entirely voluntary then has a chance either to stop the interview or to review the consent procedure with the interviewee, verifying that true consent is present.

In the second category, verbal confusion can help the ethnographer detect the possibility of truth-modification. It is very difficult to maintain consistent lies over a long interview or over the course of several interviews.[9] Montaigne, back in 1580, noted that when people "disguise or modify [the truth], if we ask them to recount the same story often, it is difficult for them not to betray their lie, because the true story was lodged in their memory first and imprinted on it, . . . and so it springs to mind and chases away the false version, that certainly cannot be as firmly installed. And the circumstances of the original version, always coming back to mind, make them forget the memory of the parts of the story that are added on, false, or twisted" (Montaigne 1580 [author's translation]).

Such contradictions need not be lies, however. Psychological studies have shown us that the retrieval of memory is a process: interviewees add details, correct themselves, or return multiple times to the same subject. Surveys force interviewees to respond on the spot and rarely allow opportunities for people to correct mistakes. Redundant questions can be inserted into surveys to try to detect inconsistencies; but when inconsistencies are detected, the data are generally thrown out of the sample. In ethnographic work, inconsistencies are an opportunity to explore a topic in greater detail and to investigate further (Nachman 1984; Fujii 2010). It may be found that an interviewee is correcting a previous statement or is lying; or perhaps the ethnographer has misunderstood an earlier response. In addition to contradictions, ethnographers can learn from silences and evasive responses; all three often allow the ethnographer to identify new, productive lines of questions by revealing the importance of some topic that the ethnographer had not yet considered (Barnes 1994; Fujii 2009, 2010).

Ethnographic methods also provide the interviewer with techniques to decrease the incidence of intentional truth-modification. One such technique, which involves demonstrating expert knowledge, works because interviewees tend to be less likely to lie if they believe that the interviewer can identify the deception (Robben 1995; Rubin and Rubin 2005; Wood 2007). Ethnographic methods reduce the chances of unintentional truth-modifications by allowing respondents sufficient time to collect their thoughts and respond thoroughly. Finally, ethnography allows interviewers to check specific facts. If an interviewee recounts an important event, the ethnographer can seek out other participants to obtain multiple accounts.

## OBTAINING SENSITIVE INFORMATION

Several features of ethnography make it a useful approach for obtaining sensitive information. The primary features identified by ethnographers, and their interviewees, are the rapport that can develop from ethnographic methods and the trust that can develop over time. In some sense, all of us who interview or survey respondents are "using" them for our own ends. These ends are often justifiable: the information sought can improve medical care or distribution of humanitarian aid. More abstractly, researchers can try to develop an understanding of societal problems as a step toward resolving them, or they can serve as a vehicle through which the "voiceless" can tell their stories. Ethical guidelines dictate that the more likely an interview is to harm a participant, the more direct and obvious the benefit for that participant must be. But the ways in which researchers or internal review boards weigh these risks usually impose the researcher's interpretation of costs and benefits on the participants. Many ethnographers have noted the extent to which some interviewees value telling their story to someone who cares (Wood 2006a; Rubin and Rubin 2005), even if there is no chance of a direct material benefit, either because they enjoy the interaction itself or because they believe that the telling of their story will serve a purpose.

Ethnographic methods respect the interviewee's participation in the research project in unique ways. First, by listening empathetically and demonstrating a (hopefully genuine) interest in the interviewee, researchers show respect for what the interviewee has to say. Second, allowing time for discussion of nonsensitive topics gives interviewees a chance to tell stories at their own speed and avoids boxing them into a corner in which lying seems to be the only way to maintain dignity (Bleek 1987; Fujii 2009). Third, rather than choosing the information a respondent can provide and the ways in which she can provide it, the use of ethnographic methods allows the respondent to express what she thinks is important[10] and to add the nuance that she thinks is necessary. These aspects of ethnography, which show respect for the respondent, build rapport. Allowing the respondent to participate in guiding the conversation also often yields better information, as the respondent may well be better placed than the interviewer to know what information is important. I always ended my interviews by asking whether the interviewee had anything else she wanted to tell me, or whether there were any questions I should have asked but did not. Although most of my questions were open ended ("What was life like here when you were a child?"), and I invited this sort of response throughout the interview, interviewees sometimes took the question seeking to elicit memories of childhood as a chance to provide a general overview, to add details to stories that they had already told, or to tell new stories that had not seemed relevant before.

Ethnographers have often found that repeat interviews increase the quality of data they obtain, both because some stories are too complicated to be understood over the course of one interview and because interviewees seem increasingly willing to reveal sensitive information over time (Fujii 2009; Wood 2006a; Bleek 1987). Trust is also a key to revealing sensitive information (Bourgeois 2002; Wood 2003; Rubin and Rubin 2005; Fujii 2009; Pachirat 2009). If the ethnographer can establish rapport, trust can develop over multiple interviews or even over the course of one interview. Occasionally, before answering a sensitive question, my interviewees would take measures to verify that I would keep their identity confidential, as when I asked a former soldier which rebel group had been the most violent. I took the questions aimed at verification as evidence that the questioners believed my assurance of confidentiality and trusted me.

Another important feature of ethnography is that the interviewer can decide, based on the conversation, how much of her prior knowledge to reveal (Rubin and Rubin 2005; Wood 2007). Interviewees tell different stories based on their assumptions of how much the interviewer already knows. In my interviews, I preferred to start by requesting a detailed account of the local history without revealing any prior knowledge, to allow the interviewee to recount the story as he or she saw fit. However, sometimes it became clear that that technique would not yield a productive interview because the interviewee, assuming I knew nothing, was passing along only generalities. In the interview recounted in my Example 2, after my introductory remarks, the local politician started with a very basic statement: "In Burundi, there are two different groups. In the past, these groups did not like each other." He continued in that vein until it was clear that his narrative, while interesting for the way he portrayed Burundian history, was not providing the microlevel, factual information I sought. Simply mentioning that I was aware that there were Hutus and Tutsis in Burundi, dropping a few dates and details about history at the national level, and reiterating my request for his *local* expertise sufficed to change the interview into an extremely productive one, as shown in the excerpt provided earlier.

Even if one were to concede that ethnography produces more accurate results, one might object that it does not always allow us to accomplish what we seek to accomplish. And indeed, for certain goals, such as figuring out which areas most need specific services or reparations, or constructing descriptions of patterns of violence over a large space, ethnography simply cannot do the job. However, it is not clear that surveys succeed, either. It is common to acknowledge the possible problems with truth-telling in surveys, but then to argue that even if surveys do not produce fully accurate results, the bias will only strengthen or weaken our conclusions, and therefore the surveys still provide valuable information.

Without supporting experimental evidence, we should not accept the foregoing argument. Simply put, systematic bias can yield conclusions opposite from the truth. In the earlier example about reported child illness and mortality in Iran, the policy result could have been improving services for well-off families while reducing services for the worst-off people. If surveys produce results that are systematically biased in unpredictable ways, and these biases are replicated across all available sources, we are in dangerous waters.[11] Using surveys in these cases can ultimately result in more harm than good. Furthermore, although ethnography has limitations, it allows us to accomplish many of the objectives we care about, such as the prosecution of war crimes,[12] the achievement of a causal understanding of certain aspects of violent conflict (Fujii 2009; Wood 2006b; Hinton 2005), and the development of evidence-based policy prescriptions (Autesserre 2010; Ingelaere 2009).

Getting the science of quantitative measurements of mortality counts right cannot eliminate biases that may result from responses that are untrue in systematic and unpredictable ways. Until experimental evidence shows what method works best to obtain information about a certain sensitive topic in a certain culture, we cannot know for sure whether ethnography or surveys produce more truthful answers, or whether surveys provide information that is at least "truthful enough" to be useful. In the meantime, both survey researchers and ethnographers must acknowledge that "truth" is not necessarily the default response, always interpreting data with appropriate caution to ensure that our research at least does no harm.

REFERENCES

Autesserre, Séverine. 2010. *The Trouble with the Congo: Local Violence and the Failure of International Peacekeeping.* New York: Cambridge University Press.

Barnes, J. A. 1994. *A Pack of Lies: Towards a Sociology of Lying.* New York: Cambridge University Press.

Bertrand, Marianne, and Sendhil Mullainathan. 2004. "Are Emily and Greg More Employable than Lakisha and Jamal? A Field Experiment on Labor Market Discrimination." *American Economic Review* 94: 991–1013.

Blee, Kathleen M. 1993. "Evidence, Empathy, and Ethics: Lessons from Oral Histories of the Klan." *Journal of American History* 80(2): 596–606.

Bleek, Wolf. 1987. "Lying Informants: A Fieldwork Experience from Ghana." *Population and Development Review* 13(2): 314–322.

Bourgeois, Philippe. 2002. *In Search of Respect: Selling Crack in El Barrio.* New York: Cambridge University Press.

Davenport, Christian, and Patrick Ball. 2002. "Views to a Kill: Exploring the Implications of Source Selection in the Case of Guatemalan State Terror, 1977–1997." *Journal of Conflict Resolution* 46(3): 427–50.

Dovidio, J. F., K. Kawakami, C. Johnson, B. Johnson, and A. Howard. 1997. "On the Nature of Prejudice: Automatic and Controlled Responses." *Journal of Experimental Social Psychology* 33(5): 510–540.

Fenton, Kevin A., Anne M. Johnson, Sally McManus, and Bob Erans. 2001. "Measuring Sexual Behavior: Methodological Challenges in Survey Research." *Sexually Transmitted Infections* 77: 84–92.

Fujii, Lee Ann. 2009. *Killing Neighbors: Webs of Violence in Rwanda.* Ithaca, NY: Cornell University Press.

———. 2010. "Shades of Truth and Lies: Interpreting Testimonies of War and Violence." *Journal of Peace Research* 47(2): 231–241.

Gaventa, John. 1980. *Power and Powerlessness: Quiescence and Rebellion in an Appalachian Valley,* Chicago: University of Illinois Press.

Greenwald, Anthony G., and Mahzarin Banaji. 1995. "Implicit Social Cognition: Attitudes, Self-Esteem, and Stereotypes." *Psychological Review* 102(1): 4–27.

Hinton, Alexander Laban. 2005. *Why Did They Kill: Cambodia in the Shadow of Genocide.* Berkeley: University of California Press.

Hoover Green, Amelia. 2010. "Learning the Hard Way at the ICTY: Statistical Evidence of Human Rights Violations in an Adversarial Information Environment." In *Collective Violence and International Criminal Justice: An Interdisciplinary Approach,* edited by Alette Smeulers. Antwerp: Intersentia.

Ingelaere, Bert. 2009. "Living Together Again: The Expectation of Transitional Justice in Burundi—A View from Below" (working paper, Institute of Development Policy and Management, University of Antwerp).

Lynch, Meghan Foster, and Amelia Hoover Green. 2008. "Counting the Uncounted: Multiple Data Systems and the Analysis of Count Data." Paper presented at the Annual Meeting of the American Political Science Association, Boston.

Manesh, Alireza Olyaee, Trevor A. Sheldon, Kate E. Pickett, and Roy Carr-Hill. 2008. "Accuracy of Child Morbidity Data in Demographic and Health Surveys." *International Journal of Epidemiology* 37: 194–200.

Mensch, Barbara S., Paul S. Hewett, Richard Gregory, and Stephane Helleringer. 2008. "Sexual Behavior and STI/HIV Status Among Adolescents in Rural Malawi: An Evaluation of the Effect of Interview Mode on Reporting." *Studies in Family Planning* 39(4): 321–334.

Montaigne, M 1580. *Essais Livre 1*, "Des menteurs" [On Liars].

Munyaneza, Janvier. n.d. Cited in Jean Hatzfeld, *Dans le nu de la vie: Récits des marais Rwandais*. Paris: Seuil, 2000, 57.

Nachman, Steven R. 1984. "Lies My Informants Told Me." *Journal of Anthropological Research* 40(4): 536–55.

Ong, Anthony D., and David J. Weiss. 2000. "The Impact of Anonymity on Responses to Sensitive Questions." *Journal of Applied Social Psychology* 30(8): 1691–1708.

Pachirat, Timothy. 2009. "The Political in Political Ethnography: Dispatches from the Kill Floor." In *Political Ethnography: What Immersion Contributes to the Study of Power*, edited by Edward Schatz. Chicago: University of Chicago Press.

Plummer, M. L., D. A. Ross, D. Wight, J. Changalucha, G. Mshana, J. Wamoyi, J. Todd, A. Anemona, F. F. Mosha, A. I. N. Obasi, and R. J. Hayes. 2004. "'A Bit More Truthful': The Validity of Adolescent Sexual Behavior Data Collected in Rural Northern Tanzania Using Five Methods." *Sexually Transmitted Infections* 80(2): 49–56.

Potdar, Rukmini, and Michael A. Koenig. 2005. "Does Audio-CASI Improve Reports of Risky Behavior? Evidence from a Randomized Field Trial Among Young Urban Men in India." *Studies in Family Planning* 36(2): 107–116.

Quillian, Lincoln. 2006. "New Approaches to Understanding Racial Prejudice and Discrimination." *Annual Review of Sociology* 32: 299–328.

Ricoeur, Paul. 2004. *Memory, History, Forgetting.* Chicago: University of Chicago Press.

Robben, Antonius C. G. M. 1995. "Seduction and Persuasion: The Politics of Truth and Emotion among Victims and Perpetrators of Violence." In *Fieldwork Under Fire: Contemporary Studies of Violence and Survival*, edited by Carolyn Nordstrom and Antonius C. G. M. Robben. Berkeley: University of California Press.

Rubin, Herbert J., and Irene S. Rubin. 2005. *Qualitative Interviewing: The Art of Hearing Data*, 2nd ed. London: Sage.

Scacco, Alexandra. 2009. "Who Riots? Explaining Individual Participation in Ethnic Violence." PhD dissertation, Columbia University.

Scott, James C. 1985. *Weapons of the Weak: Everyday Forms of Peasant Resistance*. New Haven, CT: Yale University Press.

Tourangeau, Roger, and Tom W. Smith. 1996. "Asking Sensitive Questions: The Impact of Data Collection Mode, Question Format, and Question Context." *Public Opinion Quarterly* 60(2): 275–304.

Traugott, Michael W., and Vincent Price. 1992. "The Polls—A Review. Exit Polls in the 1989 Virginia Gubernatorial Race: Where Did They Go Wrong?" *Public Opinion Quarterly* 56(2): 245–253.

Wood, Elisabeth Jean. 2003. *Insurgent Collective Action and Civil War in El Salvador*. New York: Cambridge University Press.

———. 2006a. "The Ethical Challenges of Field Research in Conflict Zones." *Qualitative Sociology* 29: 373–386.

———. 2006b. "Variation in Sexual Violence during War." *Politics and Society* 34(3): 307–341.

———. 2007. "Field Research." In *The Oxford Handbook of Comparative Politics*, edited by Carles Boix and Susan Stokes. New York: Oxford University Press.

## NOTES

For helpful comments and discussions, I thank Jay Aronson, Séverine Autesserre, Patrick Ball, Michael Goodheart, Adria Lawrence, Sam Foster Lynch, Nigel Quinney, Elisabeth Wood, and the participants in the Counting Civilian Casualties Workshop at Carnegie Mellon University and the University of Pittsburgh. An earlier version of this chapter was presented at the 2009 Annual Meeting of the American Political Science Association. For research assistance, I thank Audifax Bigirimana, David Lynch, Bernard Ndayishimiye, and Révocate Nzikibazanye. This chapter is based on research that was funded under a National Science Foundation Graduate Research Fellowship, a National Science Foundation doctoral dissertation improvement grant, an Enders Fellowship, and research grants from the Yale Institution for Social and Policy Studies, the MacMillan Center for International and Area Studies, and the Leitner Program in International and Comparative Political Economy. The opinions expressed are not those of the funding organizations.

1. In this chapter, I address only methods that rely in some way on people *reporting* deaths. I do not discuss methods of counting deaths that rely on physical evidence.

2. I do not discuss here challenges general to all surveys, or general to those all surveys relying on respondent self-reports, such as question order, interviewer identity, misunderstood questions, and nonresponse bias. See Asher, chapter 6 in this volume, for a review.

3. In addition to prejudice, stigmatized behaviors whose measurement has been studied in great depth are stigmatized sexual behavior and illicit drug use. See, for example: Mensch, et al. (2008).

4. The argument applies not just to mortality counts but to all sensitive information. In conflict and post-conflict settings, many qualitative and quantitative objects of study will be sensitive.

5. If the goal, however, is to figure out which areas most need specific services or reparations, or to construct an overall narrative of the history of a conflict, ethnography falls short. Yet it is not clear that surveys succeed, either (see Asher, chapter 6 in this volume).

6. A similar experience is described in Fujii (2009) and Wood (2006a).

7. In excerpts from my interviews, words spoken by me (via my interpreter) are italicized. All quotes are approximate, having been spoken in Kirundi, translated into French by my interpreter, and then translated into English by me.

8. An exception is Alexandra Scacco (2009).

9. Blee (1993) notes that in her oral histories with members of the Ku Klux Klan, when interviewees were attempting to explain their participation (clearly a sensitive topic), they often changed stories or contradicted themselves. See also Rubin and Rubin (2005).

10. Thanks to Adria Lawrence for this point.

11. Indeed, even when we *can* statistically correct for source biases, the complicated methods required can hinder our ability to achieve our goals. When we are unable to explain our methods convincingly to laypeople, our efforts to improve policy or aid prosecution can be for naught (Hoover Green 2010).

12. Successful prosecution of crimes against humanity requires proof of one act against a background of other widespread and systematic acts, which means that ethnographic work, if conducted to meet criminal legal standards of proof, can suffice.

# IV Estimating Violence

## MULTIPLE SYSTEMS ESTIMATION

Combining Found Data and Surveys to
Measure Conflict Mortality
Jeff Klingner and Romesh Silva

MANY DIFFERENT TYPES of data and statistical estimation methods are used to estimate casualties. Each of these data types and estimation methods has weaknesses, but
the weaknesses are sometimes complementary, so it can be possible to improve estimates
of conflict mortality by combining multiple data types or estimation methods. This
chapter explores one particular data integration strategy in depth: how found data—
data created for some purpose other than mortality estimation—can be combined with
surveys and other intentionally gathered data to improve estimates of the magnitude
and patterns of conflict mortality.

We begin by defining and outlining the strengths and weakness of found data and
surveys, and give several examples of each. We then present three case studies—of
research conducted in Timor-Leste, India, and Kosovo—illustrating how these two
types of data have been fruitfully combined to improve casualty estimates. We conclude
by drawing general principles about this type of data integration from themes common
to all the case studies.

## Found Data

The term *found data* is used informally and refers roughly to any data originally created
or gathered for a purpose other than counting casualties. This is a rather broad definition
that includes media reports, most official administrative records, and many other
sources. Some examples of found data used in mortality analyses are:

- Media reports of deaths, especially newspaper articles and wire reports (see chapter 4 by Sloboda, Dardagan, Spagat, and Hicks in this volume)
- Obituaries (Boak et al. 2008)
- Coroners' reports (Lum et al. 2010)
- Gravestones (Silva and Ball 2006)
- Public cremation ground records (Silva, Marwaha, and Klingner 2009)
- Voter registration lists (Brunborg, Lyngstad, and Urdal 2003)
- Administrative records of security forces (Price et al. 2009)
- Administrative records of prisons (Silva, Klingner, and Wiekart 2009)
- Military personnel records (Howland 2008, 728)
- Border records of refugee crossings (Ball 2000)

We exclude reports gathered by NGOs or truth commissions established to document deaths and other human rights abuses, though such data have much in common with found data. Most found data reflect only a fraction of the universe of mortality, often indirectly, and almost never with the guarantee of representativeness that comes with random sampling. Nevertheless, there are many good reasons for including found data in analyses of conflict casualties and human rights violations, including the lack of intentional bias, additional information related to mortality, contemporaneous recording, and simple availability.

## LACK OF INTENTIONAL BIAS

One reason that found data are useful arises directly from the fact that they are created without the intent of counting casualties. Mortality estimates are often subject to the criticism that the data they are based on is influenced by the goals of the organizations creating or gathering it. Testimonies gathered by victims' advocates are doubted because these groups may be motivated to report on events of particular types or on events that affect particular subpopulations. Many official records are doubted because these military and government groups, for example, have political incentives to avoid recording civilian deaths or to classify ambiguous cases as combatants rather than civilians. Data gathered by truth commissions are shaped by the commissions' official mandates, which usually arise through political negotiations among combatants, governments, and victim groups. Varying participation in and satisfaction with these negotiations on the part of victims' representatives leads to differences in trust in the commission that affect the willingness of the groups to participate.

Of course, all data—including found data—are affected by the purposes, capabilities, and incentives of the people who did the gathering. But the diversity of purposes underlying found data can increase its complementarity with intentionally gathered data, and found data can help us gain new insight into the biases of intentionally gathered data sources.

ADDITIONAL INFORMATION RELATED TO MORTALITY

Because found data are gathered for purposes besides casualty counts, they often reflect deaths indirectly and therefore contain details on events related to the deaths. These details can deepen our understanding of conflict mortality by shedding light on deaths' causes and consequences.

For example, records of police detentions during 1960–1996, a period of intense political violence in Guatemala, found recently in the country's National Police Archive contain information about who ordered the detentions and why (Price et al. 2009). Administrative medical records found in a jail used by former Chadian president Hissène Habré to imprison his political opponents from 1982 to 1990 show us how many people died there; the records also provide data on the causes of death and on prison crowding that clarify whether such mortality was condoned or even encouraged by the government (Cruz, Cibelli, and Dudukovic 2003; Silva, Klingner, and Weikart 2009). Grave markers can tell us about the religions of the deceased as well as the geographic and temporal distribution of deaths—or more precisely, the distribution of burials (Silva and Ball 2008). Obituaries can tell us, among other things, about the impact of deaths on survivors.

CONTEMPORANEOUS RECORDING

When investigators use retrospective data sources such as post-conflict surveys, interview projects, or truth commission testimonies, long delays between deaths and data recording lead to inaccurate recall, which imposes substantial uncertainty on estimates based on the data. Such errors usually take the form of the "transfer" of deaths between time periods (e.g., an approximated year like "1975" instead of an exact date of "October 12, 1973"). In contrast, many types of found data are recorded soon after the date of death.

AVAILABILITY

Finally, and most important, found data are used because they are sometimes the only data available. When estimating casualties, researchers seek to use any data available that add information about conflict deaths and improve our understanding of what happened.

Even given these advantages, the nonrepresentativeness of found data can be a huge obstacle to using this material to gain understanding of conflict mortality or human rights abuses. Single sources of data often provide distorted pictures of conflict mortality. This primary weakness of found data can be mitigated by surveys, which by design provide data that are representative of their reference populations. Although a survey's reference population can differ from the true population of interest, surveys do bring us closer to mortality estimates that encompass entire conflicts or populations.

## Surveys

Through random sampling, surveys can ensure that the selected cases are representative of the broader population, and sampling errors can be quantified. Survey methods are discussed in detail by Asher in chapter 6 of this volume. Here we describe two example surveys to illustrate their typical features.

One of the most carefully implemented surveys in a post-conflict setting was the work to measure mortality among Kosovar Albanians during the 1998–1999 war in Kosovo, conducted by a collaboration of the International Rescue Committee, the Kosovo Institute of Public Health, the World Health Organization, and the Centers for Disease Control and Prevention (Spiegel and Salama 2000). This setting was favorable for a successful survey in many ways. The existence of a recent census of Kosovo, which could be adjusted for the effects of the war using data collected by the UN and humanitarian relief organizations, provided an accurate sampling frame. The end of fighting, good roads, and the trust of the population enabled efficient random sampling of households within clusters and a remarkable 100 percent participation rate. Because the survey was conducted less than a year after the war, recall bias was minimized; all direct-relative deaths were reported with exact dates.

A contrasting example of a post-conflict survey, conducted in Liberia, highlights the difficulties normally faced in post-conflict settings and the survey methods used to cope with them. Women's Rights International and the Women's Health Development Program surveyed women and girls in several locations in and near Monrovia following the end of the country's civil war, primarily to determine the nature and extent of sexual violence the victims had experienced (Swiss et al. 1998). The survey team, which consisted mostly of Liberian women, went to great lengths to adapt the survey instruments and the procedure used to local conditions (Jennings and Swiss 2001). They conducted pilot exercises to discover local euphemisms for rape and to refine interview procedures until they were effective and culturally sensitive. Sampling plans were devised on the fly to adapt to the conditions and layout of the schools, markets, and displaced persons camps that were selected. To avoid pre-exposure to the survey content in the face of the fast spreading of rumors, the team restricted sampling to areas far from pilot test sites and surveyed the entire sample from each selected site in a single day. Household population data for displaced persons camps outside Monrovia were based on food aid censuses compiled by aid organizations. Sampling had to be done at the level of heads of household, however, because household sizes in such censuses are usually inflated. Safety of participants was paramount. A follow-up survey was conducted in refugee camps in neighboring Côte d'Ivoire, but owing to concerns for the security of participants, detailed results of this survey have not yet been published (Swiss and Jennings 1999).

The Kosovo and Liberia surveys were conducted in rather different settings and used different procedures, but they share some characteristics common to all survey methods. The primary advantage of these methods is the use of random sampling, which leads to data that represent the survey's reference population with limited and quantifiable uncertainty.

Unfortunately, most post-conflict settings more closely resemble Liberia than Kosovo. Both during and after an armed conflict, the population may be unsettled, and infrastructure and administrative structures may be damaged. Lists of households are nonexistent and the residential layout is chaotic, so many standard sampling techniques that rely on street grid systems or the stability of addresses cannot be applied, which in turn makes simple or systematic random sampling difficult (Checchi and Roberts 2008). As a result, survey researchers often resort to multistage cluster sampling, in which a few large areas like full villages, for which a good sampling frame is available, are first sampled. This practice allows survey resources to be concentrated within these units, to implement a full enumeration or other method not dependent on a local sampling frame. Results from selected areas are then extrapolated to the full survey area. Although easier to implement, cluster sampling is vulnerable to large imprecision and high design effects; this method yields large confidence intervals, however, which hampers the interpretation of estimates (Spagat and Guerrero Serdán 2009).

Further, the reference population of surveys usually differs from the population of interest in important ways: in addition to the need to indirectly sample the deceased through their surviving kin (Lavallée 2007), populations available for sampling (e.g., people in refugee camps) may not include important segments of the full population (consisting, in the case of refugee camps, of all displaced people). Finally, only phenomena that affect a great enough fraction of the reference population to merit inclusion in the sample can be reliably measured. Rare phenomena, which affect a small fraction of the population, or experiences that are particularly stigmatized or otherwise subject to recall, response, or survivorship bias, are difficult to measure with surveys (Silva and Ball 2008; see also chapter 7 in this volume, by Lynch). Further, even small errors in the classification of deaths as conflict related can lead to large errors in survey estimates of these deaths when their incidence is rare (Spagat 2009).

## ADAPTIVE SAMPLING

One possible solution to the difficulty of measuring rare phenomena or vulnerable populations with random sampling could come from recent advances in adaptive sampling designs and respondent-driven survey methods (e.g., Frank and Snijders 1994; Heckathorn 1997; McKenzie and Mistiaen 2009). These methods bring with them stronger assumptions and more complicated field implementations, but they have been used in a few cases to improve surveys' coverage of casualties. Checchi, Roberts, and Morgen (2009) have incorporated referral-based sampling in their new sampling method used in refugee camps. We describe the use of hybrid cluster and referral-driven sampling design to measure conflict-related mortality in Punjab, India, in a later section. Using referral-driven sampling while maintaining the ability to calculate unbiased estimates requires modeling the social networks within which referrals are embedded, and this modeling requires supplemental survey questions and strict adherence to a sampling procedure that is difficult to achieve in practice (e.g., Frank and Snijders 1994; Thompson and Frank 2000). Nevertheless, such methods are under active development and provide a new alternative to existing approaches to measuring civilian conflict mortality.

## Combining Found Data and Surveys

The three example studies described in this section will demonstrate various ways in which found data have been combined with surveys, including the imputation of missing information and the guidance of survey design. Before describing the studies, it is necessary to introduce in more detail one particular method of combining these two data sources.

### MULTIPLE SYSTEMS ESTIMATION

Multiple systems estimation (MSE) is a mathematical manifestation of the general principle that one can combine many sources of information to gain the strengths and avoid the weaknesses of each.

MSE (also known as capture-recapture estimation) exploits the fact that some casualties end up reported in more than one dataset. Based on the size of the overlapping portions of different datasets, one can model the probability that any single record was recorded in one or some combination of datasets, and this model can then be used to estimate the number of casualties that were recorded by no datasets (Sekar and Deming 1949; Bishop, Fienberg, and Holland 1975; Chao 1987; Madigan and York 1997).

The chief advantage of MSE is that it can, at least in theory, provide unbiased estimates of the number and nature of casualties given only the convenience samples that usually comprise the available data in post-conflict settings. The chief disadvantage of MSE is that its theoretical validity depends on several strong assumptions that are usually not met by conflict data, and the consequences of violating these assumptions are not well understood. Data attributes that can lead to biased estimates include variable reporting probabilities within individual datasets and uncertain identification of victims.

This means that in practice, MSE must be applied cautiously and conservatively. Reporting variability should be minimized through stratification; records of casualties must be carefully matched between datasets; and modeling assumptions should be tested wherever possible.

Chapters 5 (Landman and Gohdes), 9 (Manrique-Vallier, Price, and Gohdes), and 10 (Jewell, Spagat, and Jewell) of this volume cover the casualty-estimating applications and limitations of MSE in detail. Here, we recount three case studies that provide diverse illustrations of how found data have been combined with other datasets, both within and without the context of MSE.

## TIMOR-LESTE

East Timor, now Timor-Leste, was invaded by the Indonesian military in 1975. During the 24-year occupation that followed, in which Timorese independence groups fought against the Indonesian army and pro-annexation Timorese groups, widespread instances of killings, disappearances, and torture were documented. During this period, the country also experienced a five-year famine, which fell particularly hard on people displaced by the fighting and led to many more deaths. The total casualties of the conflict were unknown but were believed to lie somewhere between 50,000 and 250,000 (Silva and Ball 2008, 119; Martinkus 2001, XV), an enormous range of uncertainty given the post-conflict population estimate of 850,000. Did the war kill 6 percent or 29 percent of the Timorese people?

To answer this question, the Commission for Reception, Truth, and Reconciliation (CAVR) recorded about 7,800 narratives given by people who approached the commission to testify about their experiences. These testimonies were typical of data gathered by truth commissions: rich in detail and compelling, but unrepresentative of the population because of self-selection of respondents and variable knowledge of and access to the commission. They were thus insufficient to fulfill the commission's mandate to determine the "nature, causes and extent of human rights abuses," and whether such abuses followed a "systematic pattern" (UNTAET 2001, sec. 13).

To obtain richer data on how people died, and because qualitative and ethnographic evidence suggested that indirect mortality was a substantial factor, the commission supplemented its testimony data with two additional sources: one found and one survey.

The found data the commission used were grave markers. Because of the influence of the Catholic Church during the Portuguese colonial period, most of the dead were buried in publicly accessible, marked graves. A research team enumerated about 282,000 graves in 2,600 public and church cemeteries, recording the location, the decedent's religion, and the plot size of every grave, plus names, dates of birth, and dates of death when these were legible on the grave marker (Silva and Ball 2006, 123). Although conducted as a complete census of grave markers, the data were still subject to selection bias relative to all deaths. The data overrepresent people who were buried in public graveyards and people whose gravestones survived, a circumstance that likely resulted in the exclusion of poor people buried with dirt or wooden grave markers and people buried in private burial plots. Grave marker data also underrepresent people who died during periods of severe famine, when more Timorese were displaced and fewer were buried in public cemeteries.

Additionally, researchers working with the commission conducted a nationwide randomized household survey. The survey used a two-stage cluster design and sampled

1,400 households, with a response rate of 97 percent. The survey questionnaire was designed carefully to accommodate recall difficulties, to support integration with the other two datasets, and to enable investigation of migration as well as mortality (Silva and Ball 2006, 120).

The grave marker data lacked information about the cause of death. To fill in this missing information, needed for an analysis of cause-specific mortality, survey data and truth commission interviews were linked to the grave data whenever legible names on grave markers made it possible to identify the graves in which deceased people reported in the survey were buried (Silva and Ball 2008, 133). Such filling in of the cause of death was possible for 7 percent of grave markers. The rest of the graves were assigned causes of death based on the relative frequency of different causes of deaths for each year as measured by the survey.

The three data sources used in Timor-Leste comprised a notable diversity of data types, each with weaknesses but mutually complementary. The commission's interviews included many reports of killings; but the survey, because of its representative but random coverage, captured only a small number of reported killings and missed particular large events, such as the Santa Cruz massacre (Silva and Ball 2008, 127). On the other hand, the survey did capture many famine deaths, which were not often reported directly to the truth commission. In addition, structured interviewing methods within the household survey allowed for customized interview probes to explore the association between conflict-related mortality and conflict-related migration. The inclusion of the found data on grave markers helped give the analysis nationwide scope, an important consideration because of the urban focus of testimonies gathered by the CAVR.

This variety of data enabled the use both survey-based and MSE mortality estimates. The survey estimates are subject to recall and survivorship bias, and the coverage limitations in these data and uncertainty in the imputation process used to fill in cause of death for grave markers give substantial imprecision to MSE results, but the fact that both methods estimated about 100,000 deaths increases our confidence in both.

Without this synthesis of data sources and estimation methods, our understanding of conflict-related mortality in Timor-Leste would have been incomplete. Alone, the truth commission interviews would have provided a selective historical understanding of conflict-related mortality, largely driven by *direct* conflict deaths, which in fact accounted for only about 18 percent of estimated conflict deaths during the Indonesian occupation. By adding the found data from cemeteries and the survey, researchers were able to gain new insight into famine-related deaths and the association of conflict-related mortality with migration during the conflict.

PUNJAB, INDIA

From 1984 to 1996, the northern India state of Punjab experienced a violent separatist Sikh insurgency and resultant police crackdown. Domestic and international human rights organizations that monitored the conflict concluded that state security forces committed widespread violations of human rights, including extrajudicial executions, forced disappearances, torture, and illegal cremations. Security forces denied these charges, calling the conflict "the most humane counterinsurgency operation in the annals of history" (Parrish 2002).

Unlike many other cases of large-scale enforced disappearances, in Punjab the perpetrators did not build mass graves to dispose of the bodies of the deceased. Instead, they dumped some bodies in canals (Kaur and Dhami 2007, 15), returned some to the victims' families, and delivered others to the municipal cremation grounds. Evidence of the large number of disappearances first emerged in early 1995 when human rights activists Jaswant Singh Khalra and Jaspal Singh Dhillon obtained proof of these "illegal cremations" after interviewing cremation ground workers. Khalra recounted the discovery in a 1995 speech (Khalra 1995):

> [W]e went where our brothers had gone. We went to the cremation grounds . . . When we said we need an account [of bodies delivered by the police for cremation], they told us we could get the account from one place: 'The police gave us the dead bodies, and the municipal committee gave us the firewood.' Because the municipal committee's policy is if they receive an unclaimed body within the city, then the city's municipality will cremate it on its own expense . . . we went and we saw the full account of our disappeared brothers written. What we saw when we reached there were the records of how much firewood was issued daily. It was written how many dead bodies were left by which police officers. And when we went beyond that, it was also recorded which Head Officer brought how many dead bodies there.

The exposure of this set of found data led to the torture and murder of Khalra by police, further investigations, and a case before the National Human Rights Commission of India (Silva, Marwaha, and Klingner 2009).

One of the groups advocating for accountability for disappearances in Punjab is Ensaaf, which has also gathered press reports of state-perpetrated violence during the conflict and obituaries published in the region's English- and Punjabi-language newspapers. In addition, Ensaaf conducted a randomized survey of residents of Punjab's capital district.

From a measurement perspective, Ensaaf's survey is notable for two reasons. First, several questions and follow-up probes in the survey instrument were designed to link the survey results to found data. To link the survey data to the cremation ground firewood records, respondents were asked whether the body of a familial victim was returned to them, whether it was cremated, and so on. To link the survey data to newspaper reports, respondents were asked whether they learned of the death through a newspaper, and if so, the date and name of the paper. They were also asked whether they published an obituary for the victim. These connections to the found data have yet to be analyzed, but it is hoped that they can fill in details missing from the found data and provide an estimate of their coverage rate and biases.

The second notable feature of this survey was a novel hybrid sampling plan, designed in collaboration with Benetech's Human Rights Data Analysis Group. This sampling plan combined a probability-based cluster sample with a referral-based adaptive sample within clusters (Silva, Klingner, and Weikart 2010). In each sampled village, interviewers located at least two persons identified as primary referral points; these could be local village political leaders, civil officials, or elders. The primary referral points were asked for referrals to families who had experienced an enforced disappearance or extrajudicial execution during the conflict. The survey team then attempted to interview all such families still resident in the village, documenting the details of any incidents of lethal violence each family had experienced, and asking each family for further referrals to families resident in the sampled village who had experienced acts of lethal violence. All referrals from both primary referral points and families were followed exhaustively.

Preliminary analysis of the survey data confirmed some victims' claims, including unexpectedly large numbers of overtly religious young Sikh men; the finding that no particularly high level of violence had occurred along the Pakistani border, however, served to refute other claims.

Unfortunately, the referral process used by this survey did not meet all the assumptions required for referral-network-based estimates. Interviewers believe that respondents withheld referrals for a variety of reasons, and it was impossible to record the number of referrals each family *could* have made (i.e., the size of a family's local social network). For these reasons, survey estimates had to be based on the conservative assumption that the referral process reached all victims in each cluster; in addition, it was necessary to use classical Horvitz-Thompson survey estimators.

Referral-driven survey designs like this one aim to address surveys' weakness in measuring rare or elusive phenomena. In Amritsar, the referral-driven procedure did not enable network-based estimates, but it was successful in efficiently finding previously unobserved members of the affected population: about half of survey respondents said that they had not reported their family members' death to any of the organizations tracking casualties from the conflict. This survey, having integrated random sampling at the village level and adaptive sampling methods within villages, revealed notable undercoverage of existing found data.

KOSOVO

From March to May 1999, Serbian forces expelled hundreds of thousands of ethnic Albanians from Kosovo. The effects of this action on its victims have been studied by using several surveys and other interview projects (Physicians for Human Rights 1999; Spiegel and Salama 2000), and MSE was applied to three of these data sources to estimate the total number killed (ABA/CEELI 2000). Of interest here is how the surveys were used, together with found data, to measure another effect of the conflict: forced displacement. The found data in this case come from records of border crossings registered by Albanian border guards at Morina as expelled Kosovars crossed into Albania.

These border crossing registries are remarkably complete. Nearly all of the refugee flow from Kosovo into Albania went through this one small border post, and Albanian officials there attempted to document each crossing. In particular, the border guards recorded where in Kosovo each household came from. By using estimates of transit time within Kosovo from each of these places to the border, together with the date of crossing, it was possible to back-project border crossings into displacements and then map the geographic distribution of displacements through time. Such estimates could be compared to the temporal and geographic distributions of killings, bombings, property destruction, and other events in Kosovo to test hypotheses regarding the causes of the displacements (Hagan et al. 2006). The full details of this analysis are presented in Ball (2000).

Survey data integration aided this analysis by supplying two different types of information missing from the found border registries: the geographic origins of refugees for which this datum was not recorded and transit times within Kosovo.

*Filling in Missing Data on Refugee Origins.* Information about the place of origin was known for about half of the estimated number of people crossing the border. To determine the origin locations for the rest of the refugees, researchers used data from two surveys conducted in Albanian refugee camps by Physicians for Human Rights and by IPLS/AAAS (Institute of Professional Legal Studies/American Association for the Advancement of Science). The reference population for both surveys was households that had crossed the border at Morina. By combining the two samples, removing duplicates, and eliminating any households found on the border crossing registries, a random sample of unregistered crossers for each day was constructed. Though the data were subject to sampling error, the people in this sample served as a much more representative proxy for unregistered refugees than registered refugees in the other half of the border dataset, who probably differed from unregistered refugees in important and unpredictable ways.

*Determining Transit Times.* Data from both surveys were used in a similar way to determine the average transit time within Kosovo for refugees. In this use, interviews from the two refugee camp surveys were used as a representative sample of refugees and were reanalyzed to determine the distribution of transit time for refugees from various regions and crossing the border at various times.

*Sensitivity Analysis.* The data integration used in this migration analysis was complicated. Conclusions about forced displacement depended on a long chain of inference and imputation, so sampling error or bias in the surveys could affect the conclusions in unpredictable ways. Researchers used several approaches to test the sensitivity of their results to various data problems (Ball 2000; Ball et al. 2002):

- To check the impact of the surveys' sampling error on the variance in the final estimates of displacement, they ran a "jackknife analysis"—that is, they determined how much those estimates changed when random subsets of survey responses were omitted.
- To check whether the data imputation (i.e., the making of educated guesses about missing data based on other available information) could be the prime cause of the inferred patterns, overwhelming the influence of data from refugees with known origins, they replaced the data imputation step with a random assignment of origins to refugees and re-ran the calculations.
- To check the influence of transit times used to back-project border crossings to displacements, they altered the distribution of transit times observed in the survey in several ways and re-ran the calculations.

The first check showed an estimated variance that was small relative to the patterns of displacement over time and space that were the study's main findings. The second two checks showed that this pattern was not substantially disrupted by the transformations to the data used to imputed refugee origins and transit times.

In summary, researchers selected data from randomized surveys in refugee camps, useful primarily because the data were representative, together with found border crossing records, useful primarily because they were extensive. The result was an understanding of displacement within an active war zone that would have been impossible to achieve by using either type of data alone.

## Conclusions

The case studies recounted here show that the benefits of combining found data with surveys are attributable to two distinct types of complementarity: complementarity of case coverage and complementarity of case details. Furthermore, the examples show that such combinations enable the exploration of questions beyond simple casualty counts, that adding a survey can provide many benefits to an analysis even when the survey is small, that found data are subject to overflow, and that conclusions drawn from combining these types of data should be evaluated by means of sensitivity analysis or simulation.

### COMPLEMENTARITY OF CASE COVERAGE

Conflict-related mortality can be divided into direct deaths, which result from acts of violence such as killings, and indirect deaths, which result from the deterioration in health services and food access plus increased risk of disease attributable to the violence. Deaths of these two types are rarely distributed in similar ways. Direct-violence deaths tend to be elusive, and targeted at particular subpopulations, whereas indirect-violence deaths tend to occur at higher frequencies and throughout a population.

In their study of Timor-Leste, Silva and Ball (2008) found that classically designed sample surveys are appropriate for estimating population-based phenomena (famine deaths) but are subject to considerable uncertainty for highly targeted and elusive phenomena (direct political killings).

Found data (and intentionally gathered mortality data like truth commission testimonies) often provide good coverage of such elusive phenomena precisely because they were gathered non-randomly. Many more cases can be found by using data that are generated directly or indirectly by the deaths themselves than by sampling an entire population.

## COMPLEMENTARITY OF CASE DETAILS

Surveys that are conducted after found data are in hand can be designed for effective integration by the inclusion of specific survey questions. If it is desired to link specific cases in found data to survey cases, questions can be added that refer to found data details: for example, the questions about press coverage and body disposal added to the survey in Punjab. If it is desired to impute missing details to all found data cases, questions can be added to gather that detail, as with causes of death in East Timor or points of origin and transit times for Kosovar refugees. The representative samples of surveys usually make better sources for such imputed detail than the subset of found data cases for which detail is known.

## DATA INTEGRATION ANSWERS DEEPER QUESTIONS

In all three examples described here, integrating surveys with found data led not only to increased precision in the estimation of mortality (or displacement), but also the ability to answer deeper research questions. As just noted, researchers were able to go beyond total mortality estimates and break down mortality by cause (direct vs. indirect) in East Timor. In Punjab, counting casualties through cremation records also provided insight into police practices and the relative frequencies of disappearances and executions. In Kosovo, it enabled the testing of alternative explanations for why people fled their homes.

## EVEN A SMALL SURVEY HELPS A LOT

In settings where only convenience samples are available, the addition of even a small survey can aid an analysis enormously. Even if a small sample size gives the survey low power, its representativeness still provides a strong check for bias and distortion in other data. Surveys can also provide a valuable source of representative information for filling in missing values from found data. Finally, surveys tend to work well in MSE analyses, even when small, because their random samples have uniform inclusion probability and usually exhibit the partial overlap with other datasets needed for a well-conditioned model. Additionally, even the low-precision estimates calculated from small surveys provide a useful sanity check for MSE estimates. This independent check added confidence to MSE estimates calculated in both Kosovo and Timor-Leste.

## FOUND DATA ARE SUBJECT TO OVERFLOW

The coverage of the border crossing data in Kosovo broke down when tens of thousands of refugees crossed in a single day and border guards could not count or record origin information about all of them. The grave marker data used in Timor-Leste underrepresented people who died during the high-mortality famine years of the late 1970s, when families were displaced from their homes and burial in public cemeteries was not an option. Similar "overflow" problems, in which a data recording process breaks down under high volume, can affect other sources of found data, including morgue records, police records, and press reports. In the case studies described here, this problem was mitigated by linking the found data to other data sources that could help estimate the size of the found data's coverage gap or impute the details of missing cases.

## CHECKING DATA INTEGRATION THROUGH SENSITIVITY ANALYSIS

Chapter 10 of this volume (Jewell, Spagat, and Jewell) points out the need to use sensitivity testing and simulation methods to better understand the robustness of inferential methods such as MSE and survey estimation in conflict-related settings. When survey data are used to fill in details missing from found data, standard statistical methods for calculating margins of error for the results no longer apply, and similar robustness checks are essential. In the Kosovo displacement study, sensitivity analyses were used to check the conclusions against a variety of possible distortions due to data bias and sampling error. The Timor-Leste researchers have recommended that their analysis be extended and checked to assess the error introduced by the use of the survey to impute cause of death for those people with grave markers. They suggest modeling the recall and survivorship bias of the retrospective survey, together with a breakdown of vital information missing from grave markers and undercoverage of the grave marker data.

Measuring conflict mortality is challenging. Successful projects integrate multiple data sources and multiple inferential methods. When independent data sources and methods subject to different types of bias and error agree, they increase our confidence in the basic scientific findings. When independent data or estimates are contradictory, the results can reveal data biases or point out underlying conflict dynamics that impede effective measurement. To reach the most accurate understanding of conflict and its consequences, we need to use all available data and methods.

REFERENCES

ABA/CEELI. 2000. *Political Killings in Kosova/Kosovo, March–June 1999: A Cooperative Report by the Central and East European Law Initiative of the American Bar Association and the Science and Human Rights Program of the American Association for the Advancement of Science.* Washington, DC: American Association for the Advancement of Science.

Ball, P. 2000. *Policy or Panic: The Flight of Ethnic Albanians from Kosovo, March–May 1999.* Washington DC: American Association for the Advancement of Science.

Ball, P., W. Betts, F. Scheuren, J. Dudukovich, and J. Asher. 2002. *Killings and Refugee Flow in Kosovo, March–June, 1999.* Washington, DC: American Association for the Advancement of Science and American Bar Association's Central and Eastern European Law Initiative.

Bishop, Y. M., S. Fienberg, and P. H. Holland. 1975. *Discrete Multivariate Analysis: Theory and Practice.* Cambridge, MA: MIT Press.

Boak, M. B., N. M. M'ikanatha, R. S. Day, and L. H. Harrison. 2008. "Internet Death Notices as a Novel Source of Mortality Surveillance Data." *American Journal of Epidemiology* 167(5): 532–539.

Brunborg, H., T. H. Lyngstad, and H. Urdal. 2003. "Accounting for Genocide: How Many Were Killed in Srebrenica?" *European Journal of Population* 19(3): 229–248.

Chao, A. 1987. "Estimating the Population Size for Capture-Recapture Data with Unequal Catchabilty." *Biometrics* 43: 783–791.

Checchi, F., B. Roberts, and O. Morgan. 2009. *A New Method to Estimate Mortality in Crisis-Affected Populations: Validation and Feasibility Study*, version 2. Washington, DC: Food and Nutrition Technical Assistance II Project, Academy for Educational Development.

Checchi, F., and L. Roberts. 2008. "Documenting Mortality in Crises: What Keeps Us from Doing Better?" *PLoS Medicine* 5(7): e146.

Cruz, M., K. Cibelli, and J. Dudukovic. 2003." Preliminary Statistical Analysis of AVCRP and DDS Documents—A Report to Human Rights Watch about Chad under the Government of Hissène Habré." At: http://www.hrdag.org/resources/publications/chad-20031104a.pdf.

Frank, O., and T. Snijders. 1994. "Estimating the Size of Hidden Populations Using Snowball Sampling." *Journal of Official Statistics* 10(1): 53–67.

Hagan, J., H. Schoenfeld, and Alberto Palloni. 2006. "The Science of Human Rights, War Crimes, and Humanitarian Emergencies." *Annual Review of Sociology* 32: 329–349.

Heckathorn, D. D. 1997. "Respondent-Driven Sampling: A New Approach to the Study of Hidden Populations." *Social Problems* 44(2): 174–199.

Howland, T. 2008. "How El Rescate, A Small Nongovernmental Organization, Contributed to the Transformation of the Human Rights Situation in El Salvador." *Human Rights Quarterly* 30(3): 703–757.

Jennings, P. J., and S. Swiss. 2001. Supporting Local Efforts to Document Human Rights Violations in Armed Conflict." *The Lancet* 357(9252): 302–303.

Kaur, J., and S. Dhami. 2007. *Protecting the Killers: A Policy of Impunity in Punjab, India.* New York: Ensaaf and Human Rights Watch.

Khalra, Sardar Jaswant Singh. 1995. Speech given in Toronto, April 1995. Translated by Ensaaf. At: http://www.ensaaf.org/multimedia/?p=219 (accessed November 3, 2010). Video recording available at: http://video.google.com/videoplay?docid=6027286376112784432 (accessed January 27, 2011).

Lavallée, P. 2007. *Indirect Sampling*. Springer Series in Statistics. New York: Springer.

Lum, K., M. Price, T. Guberek, and P. Ball. 2010. "Measuring Elusive Populations with Bayesian Model Averaging for Multiple Systems Estimation: A Case Study on Lethal Violations in Casanare, 1998–2007." *Statistics, Politics, and Policy* 1(1).

Madigan, D., and J. C. York. 1997. "Bayesian Methods for Estimation of the Size of a Closed Population." *Biometrika* 84(1): 19–31.

Martinkus, J. 2001. *A Dirty Little War: An Eyewitness Account of East Timor's Descent into Hell, 1997–2000*. Sydney: Random House Australia.

McKenzie, D. J., and J. Mistiaen. 2009. "Surveying Migrant Households: A Comparison of Census-Based, Snowball and Intercept Point Surveys." *Journal of the Royal Statistical Society, Series A* 172(2): 339–360.

Parrish, G. 2002. *India-Punjab—Who Killed the Sikhs? Dateline*. SBS Australia, Journeyman Pictures Ltd.

Physicians for Human Rights. 1999. *War Crimes in Kosovo: A Population-Based Assessment of Human Rights Violations Against Kosovar Albanians*. Washington DC: Physicians for Human Rights.

Price, M., T. Guberek, D. Guzmán, P. Zador, and G. Shapiro. 2009. "A Statistical Analysis of the Guatemalan National Police Archive: Searching for Documentation of Human Rights Abuses." In *JSM Proceedings, Survey Research Methods Section*. Alexandria, VA: American Statistical Association.

Sekar, C. C., and E. W. Deming. 1949. "On a Method of Estimating Birth and Death Rates and the Extent of Registration." *Journal of the American Statistical Association* 44(245): 101–115.

Silva, R., and P. Ball. 2006. "The Profile of Human Rights Violations in Timor-Leste, 1974–1999." *A Report by the Benetech Human Rights Data Analysis Group to the Commission on Reception, Truth and Reconciliation*. At: http://www.hrdag.org/resources/Benetech-Report-to-CAVR.pdf.

Silva, R., and P. Ball. 2008. "The Demography of Conflict-Related Mortality in Timor-Leste (1974–1999): Empirical Quantitative Measurement of Civilian Killings, Disappearances and Famine-Related Deaths." In *Statistical Methods for Human Rights*, edited by J. Asher, D. Banks, and F. Scheuren. New York: Springer.

Silva, R., J. Klingner, and S. Weikart. 2009. *State Coordinated Violence in Chad under Hissène Habré: A Statistical Analysis of Reported Prison Mortality in Chad's DDS Prisons and Command Responsibility of Hissène Habré, 1982–1990*. Palo Alto, CA: Benetech.

Silva, R., J. Marwaha, and J. Klingner. 2009. "Violent Deaths and Enforced Disappearances During the Counterinsurgency in Punjab, India: A Preliminary Quantitative Analysis." *A Joint Report by Benetech's Human Rights Data Analysis Group and Ensaaf, Inc.* At: http://www.hrdag.org/about/india-punjab.shtml.

Silva, R., J. Klingner, and S. Weikart. 2010. "Measuring Lethal Counterinsurgency Violence in Amritsar District, India Using a Referral-Based Sampling Technique." In *JSM Proceedings, Social Statistics Section*. Alexandria, VA: American Statistical Association.

Spagat, M. 2009. "The Reliability of Cluster Surveys of Conflict Mortality: Violent Deaths and Non-Violent Deaths." Paper presented at the International Conference on Recording and Estimation of Casualties, Carnegie Mellon University, Pittsburgh, October 23–29. At: http://personal.rhul.ac.uk/uhte/014/Pittsburgh%202009.pdf.

Spagat, M., and G. Guerrero Serdán. 2009. "Confidence Intervals in Small Cluster Surveys of Conflict Mortality: How Sure Are We Really? Session 102." In *Proceedings of the 26th IUSSP International Population Conference*, Marrakech.

Spiegel, P. B., and P. Salama. 2000. "War and Mortality in Kosovo, 1998–99: An Epidemiological Testimony." *The Lancet* 355(9222): 2204–2209.

Swiss, S., and P. J. Jennings. 1999. *Violence against Women in Times of War: A Research Study in Liberia*. Washington, DC: International Center for Research on Women and the Center for Development and Population Activities.

Swiss, S., P. J. Jennings, G. V. Aryee, G. H. Brown, R. M. Jappah-Samukai, M. S. Kamara, R. D. H. Schaack, and R. S. Turay-Kanneh. 1998. "Violence Against Women During the Liberian Civil Conflict." *Journal of the American Medical Association* 279(8): 629–629.

Thompson, S. K., and O. Frank. 2000. "Model-Based Estimation with Link-Tracing Sampling Designs. *Survey Methodology* 26(1): 87–98.

UNTAET (United Nations Transitional Administration in East Timor). 2001. "Regulation No. 2001/10: On the Establishment of a Commission for Reception, Truth and Reconciliation in East Timor." UNTAET/REG/2001/10.

# 9 Multiple Systems Estimation Techniques for Estimating Casualties in Armed Conflicts

Daniel Manrique-Vallier, Megan E. Price, and Anita Gohdes

## Introduction

During and after armed conflicts, different groups attempt to gather information on the extent to which violence has claimed human lives. Depending on why the groups or institutions record this information, lists of casualties are compiled with more or less detailed data and coverage. For example, humanitarian organizations collect information on cases known to them, death registries try to keep track of the deceased, and press agencies report on victims fallen in battle. Retrospectively, it is often national truth commissions and human rights nonprofit organizations that document atrocities committed, in order to help recollect the past and provide justice to the victims of conflict.

All these "casualty lists" are prone to incomplete registration, be it for institutional, financial, geographical or political reasons (see chapter 12, by Krüger, Ball, Price, and Hoover Green, in this volume; chapter 5, by Landman and Gohdes, in this volume). Answers to questions about the real magnitude and characteristics of the conflict cannot be obtained from any single "found" data source in a direct way. However, with basic infrastructure and security oftentimes lacking in conflict or post-conflict settings, researchers and practitioners attempting to determine the actual number of casualties that resulted from the conflict commonly find that they must rely on these data sources as the basis of their inquiries. Statistical methods that make it possible to draw conclusions about the entire population, based on these incomplete data sources, are thus desirable.

This chapter offers an introduction to one such statistical tool, multiple systems estimation (MSE) methods for the estimation of casualties in armed conflicts. These methods provide a way to quantify the probability that a death will be missed (i.e., that no enumeration effort will record it), and therefore a way to estimate the undercount. MSE methods comprise a rather broad family of statistical techniques specifically designed to estimate undercounts in situations like the one described here, where multiple intersecting but incomplete lists are available. They offer an opportunity to take advantage of the multiplicity of data sources often found in armed-conflict situations for drawing conclusions about the underlying extent of the conflict they document.

MSE methods date back into the nineteenth century, when they were developed to estimate the size of animal populations.[1] For this reason the language associated with MSE methods frequently refers to "captures," as in "capture probabilities," terminology that has been carried over from studies in which animals are captured, tagged, and released (Petersen 1896). In the twentieth century, MSE methods began to be adapted to deal with human populations, in applications that range from census undercount correction (Sekar and Deming 1949) to problems in epidemiology (Hook and Regal 1999; International Working Group for Disease Monitoring and Forecasting 1995a, 1995b) and casualty estimation (ABA/CEELI 2002, Ball 2003), among others (see chapter 10, by Jewell, Spagat, and Jewell, in this volume for additional references). The use of these methods across different fields has led to the simultaneous development of various terminologies to describe essentially the same class of methods. Names for these methods, in addition to MSE, include multiple recapture estimation, multiple-record systems estimation and, in the particular case of two systems, capture-recapture and dual systems estimation. While we have aimed for consistency by favoring the name MSE (the preferred term for the method applied to human populations), all the terms just listed may be used interchangeably.

We begin with an overview of the statistical intuition that underlies MSE methods, as it has some particularities that set it apart from more traditional and well-known statistical techniques. We deal with the two-list case, develop it into a general multi-list framework, and reflect on two of the classic assumptions of the basic two-list model, as well as the challenge of interpreting and testing these assumptions in the general case. We then address the question of representing unobserved individuals. We occasionally rely on mathematical notation to refer back to concepts that otherwise would require lengthy—and ambiguous—prose to describe. While comfort with mathematical notation and basic probability theory is beneficial, it is not indispensable to understanding this chapter. Finally, we present two case studies, from Kosovo and Peru, to further illustrate applications, challenges, and successes of MSE techniques. The chapter concludes with a discussion of the opportunities and limitations that these methods offer to the field of casualty estimation in armed conflicts.

## Basics of Multiple Systems Estimation

Any effort to enumerate casualties will likely miss some individuals. Certain geographic areas may be too remote to access or still so violent and unstable that researchers cannot safely collect data there. In some areas wide-sweeping violence may not leave behind any witnesses to tell researchers about what happened, or surviving witnesses may choose not to tell their story.

In general, MSE methods attempt to estimate the number of cases that were not included in lists that partially enumerate a closed population. In this context, consider a conflict situation that resulted in the killing of an unknown number, $N$, of individuals. Now, assume that different "counting teams," working independently, have already attempted to enumerate these victims. Each team will have counted a part of the casualty population; some of the individuals will have been counted by more than one team and some will not have been counted at all.

If we had access to all these lists, we could try to pool them into a single comprehensive list. Since some individuals will have been counted more than once and some left out, it is likely that the combined list will also be incomplete. If the teams recorded some identifying information on the individuals, we could remove the duplicates by comparing the datasets and noting which of those individuals and how many of them were included on more than one list. As we will see, this inclusion, or capture pattern (i.e., showing which lists included and which missed an individual) is the crucial piece for the MSE calculations. For now, we can safely state that the identification and removal of duplicate listings of individuals who were included on one or more lists—that is, de-duplication—allows us to compute a lower bound on the total size of the population of interest, assuming that de-duplication efforts were successful. The question that remains is: How many individuals were not counted by any of the teams?

Table 9.1 shows an example of such a de-duplication and matching of different lists into one dataset.[2] Every listed individual now appears in only one row. The last three columns indicate which list recorded the case. This example shows how binary information, indicating "included" (1) or "not included" (0) in list A, B, or C, creates an "inclusion pattern." Figure 9.1 presents the same information in graphical form. Note how each inclusion pattern unequivocally refers to a location in the Venn diagram.[3] Again, each individual appears just once in the diagram. Inclusion patterns represent the link between the concepts of "unique individual" and "records on a list." Also note that since

TABLE 9.1.

Example: "Clipping" of a Matched and De-duplicated List of Casualties

| ID | Sex | Age | Location | Date | List A | List B | List C |
|---|---|---|---|---|---|---|---|
| .. | .. | .. | .. | .. | .. | .. | .. |
| 948 | M | 32 | south-west | 1999 | 0 | 1 | 0 |
| 949 | M | 45 | West | 1995 | 1 | 1 | 0 |
| 950 | F | 30 | south-west | 1990 | 0 | 0 | 1 |
| 951 | M | ? | West | 1991 | 1 | 1 | 0 |
| .. | .. | .. | .. | .. | .. | .. | .. |

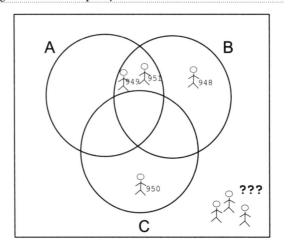

FIGURE 9.1 Schematic Representation of De-duplicated List in Table 9.1

real-life de-duplicated lists can be composed only of individuals who have been observed at least once, no individual with a capture pattern consisting of only 0s can be listed.

MSE techniques attempt to provide an answer to the question of who was *not* included in any of the lists by looking at the inclusion pattern of each individual who *was* included. Intuitively, it is easy to see how inclusion patterns can help us learn the size of the population. Let us assume that one of the teams in our example did a particularly thorough job, and its list is already close to a full enumeration. Then, any additional comparable list by another team is likely to have a considerable number of individual records in common with the first list. Conversely, if the team covered only a very small part of the population, any additional similar list can be expected to share only a few individual records with it, if any at all. Note that if the list were a full enumeration, any additional list could only be a subset of it. Thus, subsequent lists could enumerate only individuals already recorded.

If we formalize the relationships between the probabilities of these inclusion patterns, then we can—with the help of some additional assumptions—estimate the probability distribution of multiple inclusions in lists and, ultimately, estimate the probability that a given individual will not be included in *any* of the lists. The following section illustrates this procedure in the two-list case.

## Classic Two-Systems Estimation

Consider the number of casualties in a conflict to be $N$—more generally, $N$ is the unknown size of a finite population of interest. We assume that we have available two incomplete lists, A and B, that enumerate some of the individuals in the population. If we consider an arbitrary individual, he or she will necessarily fall into one of the following four cases: the individual is included in the first list but not in the second (this case will be represented by $O_{10}$ for the remainder of this chapter), *or*, in the second list, but not in the first ($O_{01}$), *or* in both of the lists ($O_{11}$). Finally, the individual might not be included in either list ($O_{00}$). We call these cases *inclusion patterns*.

It is important to note that although every single individual in the population must fall into one (and only one) of these categories, we can have information only on the individuals that were included in at least one of the lists. We thus observe only individuals that correspond to the first three inclusion patterns, $O_{10}$, $O_{01}$ or $O_{11}$. Pattern $O_{00}$ is unobservable by definition.

Now consider an arbitrary individual, $i$, from the population.[4] We can assign a probability to the event that any one individual ($i$) falls into each of the categories just described. For example, we can consider the probability that individual $i$ is on list A but not on list B. We denote this probability $p^i_{10}=P$(individual $i$ in category $O_{10}$). We then associate each individual with an array (a 4-dimensional probability vector) detailing his or her probability of falling into each of the four inclusion patterns. This vector, ($p^i_{00}, p^i_{01}, p^i_{10}, p^i_{11}$), fully describes the probabilities of individual $i$ being documented (or not) according to each possible inclusion pattern.

As is common when one is using statistical models to describe real-world situations, some assumptions are necessary to estimate the quantities of interest. As the simplest version of this method, the two-list situation requires some strong—and untestable—assumptions. We revisit them in the next section in the context of the existence of multiple lists.

While not the only possibility, the usual assumptions in the two-list case are

1. *Closed system*: The lists refer to a closed system: $N$ must refer to the same population in each dataset.[5]
2. *Homogeneity*: For each list, every individual must have the same probability of being included, or captured.[6]
3. *Independence*: The probability that an individual is (or is not) included on list A is not affected by whether that individual is included (or not) on list B, and vice versa.

Intuitively, the homogeneity assumption is taken to indicate that no individual should be intrinsically "more listable" than the others owing to individual traits. Independence requires lists that have been created without influencing one another (i.e., inclusion on one list does not affect the likelihood of inclusion on another list). Going back to the example, these conditions require that (1) no victim have any distinctive characteristic (e.g., age) that makes her more likely than the others to be in any list, and (2) each team worked without receiving information from any other team. Both the homogeneity and the independence assumptions pose demands to the data that are unlikely to be fulfilled—even approximately—in the casualty estimation context.[7] However, as is the case with other statistical methods, there are means by which we can detect departures from these assumptions and alternatively account for them. We discuss this in more detail in the section entitled "A Closer Look at Homogeneity and Independence."

To estimate the unknown population size, the foregoing assumptions must be mathematically formalized and combined with an *estimator*: that is, a statistical technique that allows the calculation of such numbers. To illustrate this process, the rest of this section shows the derivation of one specific two-list estimator, the Petersen estimator, which is the best known of the two-list estimators (Petersen 1896; Bishop et al. 1975; International Working Group for Disease Monitoring and Forecasting 1995a). Readers without elementary knowledge of probability and statistics can safely skip the rest of this section.

Elementary probability calculations show that the assumptions just stated have two immediate consequences. First, the same set of pattern probabilities applies to every individual—that is, we can drop the index $i$ in the probability vector, making $(p^i_{00}, p^i_{01}, p^i_{10}, p^i_{11}) = (p_{00}, p_{01}, p_{10}, p_{11})$. Second, these probabilities must satisfy the condition $p_{01}p_{10}/p_{11}$ $p_{00} = 1$. These two conditions, together with the fact that the population is finite, define a *model*. Standard statistical techniques can then be used to estimate the parameters of the model, including the population size.

One simple way of obtaining the Petersen estimator is the following. Under the proposed model, the expected values of the number of individuals in each capture category is $m_{ab} = E[n_{ab}] = N \cdot p_{ab}$ $(a=0,1; b=0,1)$,[8] where $n_{ab}$ are the actual (observed and unobserved) counts, N is the true (unknown) population size, and $p_{ab}$ is the general form of the probabilities defined earlier. Then, the preceding condition that $p_{01}p_{10}/p_{11}p_{00} = 1$ can be rewritten as

$$m_{00} = \frac{m_{01}m_{10}}{m_{11}}.$$

We can use the observed counts as estimators for their expected values, $\hat{m}_{01} = n_{01}$, $\hat{m}_{10} = n_{10}$ and $\hat{m}_{11} = n_{11}$ and use them to estimate the undercount:

$$\hat{n}_{00} = \frac{\hat{m}_{01}\hat{m}_{10}}{\hat{m}_{11}} = \frac{n_{01}n_{10}}{n_{11}}.$$

The Petersen estimator, or dual-system estimator, is the best known of the two-system population size estimators and is often used to illustrate the core capture-recapture ideas. It is usually motivated as an extrapolation of capture ratios through a process that implicitly requires the independence and homogeneity assumptions (see, e.g., International Working Group for Disease Monitoring and Forecasting 1995a). It can also be shown to be a conditional maximum likelihood estimate for the two-variable log-linear quasi-independence model under multinomial sampling (Fienberg 1972; Bishop et al. 1975).

## Multiple Systems Estimation (MSE): The General Case

MSE techniques draw inferences about the size of the population of interest from the classification of observed (listed) individuals into multiple inclusion patterns. In the case of 2 lists, there are only 4 possible classifications or "partitions," one of which, $O_{00}$, is unobservable. With only three partitions, the analyst has very limited information on which to base her estimations. This is why strong assumptions like those stated in the preceding section are unavoidable.

Having more than two lists, in contrast, provides a much richer set of information from which to draw inferences. Every additional list has the effect of doubling the number of capture patterns. We therefore gain *observable* information at an exponential rate, while the *unobservable* pattern (individuals not included in any list) remains fixed at one. For instance, 3 lists produce $2^3-1=7$ observable partitions ($O_{001}$, $O_{010}$, $O_{011}$, $O_{100}$, $O_{101}$, $O_{110}$ and $O_{111}$), while 15 lists (see, e.g., Lum et al., 2010) produce $2^{15}-1=32,767$ observable partitions. In both cases, we have only one unobservable pattern ($O_{000}$, and $O_{000000000000000}$, i.e., those that were missed by all 3 and all 15 lists, respectively).

With an increasing number of partitions, we will have more information. This, in turn, enables the use of more sophisticated models, which rely on weaker assumptions than the ones needed for the two-system model. Unfortunately, the modeling of that increasing number of inclusion patterns also requires increasingly sophisticated statistical techniques.

Several families of models have been proposed to deal with the multiple-list situation, each of which makes different sets of assumptions about the population and the list creation processes. For example, log-linear models (Fienberg 1972; Bishop et al. 1975) take advantage of multiple lists to account for the effect of list interdependence by modeling dependence patterns explicitly. Other techniques, making different assumptions, include Bayesian versions of standard approaches (George 1992), discrete mixture models (Basu and Ebrahimi 2001), grade-of-membership models (Manrique-Vallier and Fienberg 2008), and Rasch models (Fienberg et al. 1999), to name just a few.

A generalization of the framework from the two-list case to the multilist case is straightforward: if we have a number, $J$, of lists, then any individual in the population can be classified into one and only one inclusion pattern $O_{X_1 X_2 X_3 X_J}$, where $X_j=1$ indicates presence in list $j$ and $X_j=0$ indicates absence. For each individual, $i$, we can then model the probability distribution over the inclusion patterns. The information about the $2^J-1$ observable patterns is then used to estimate the probability of the single unobserved pattern, $O_{000...000}$. The specific way that this information is used to estimate the probability of the single unobserved pattern varies across the general class of MSE methods.

In addition to allowing weaker—and hopefully, more realistic—assumptions, the use of more than two lists provides the means to *test* the plausibility of some of these assumptions. This feature is crucial because successful estimation of the unobserved pattern depends on accurately modeling the inclusion-exclusion structure present in the population.

Analysts must examine the data to determine appropriate methods and reasonable assumptions. This presents an additional challenge, since this process often results in several plausible models. When a set of inclusion patterns appears to be adequately described by more than one model, a "best" model may often be chosen (an example of this can be found in the Kosovo case study later in this chapter). Another possibility is to produce estimates based on an average of multiple models (see Lum et al. 2010).[9]

It is important to keep in mind that to test the plausibility of any set of assumptions we can only rely on observed data (Fienberg 1972; Bishop et al. 1975; International Working Group for Disease Monitoring and Forecasting 1995a). This means that no matter how well our models describe the observable patterns, the only way of estimating the undercount is through an untestable assumption: the inclusion pattern of unobserved individuals can be described by the same model that describes the inclusion pattern of those we get to observe. This is an inescapable limitation that must be taken seriously. We elaborate on this idea in the section entitled "Representing Unobserved Individuals."

A CLOSER LOOK AT HETEROGENEITY AND DEPENDENCE

Homogeneity and independence are intuitive assumptions that are sometimes reasonable in applications such as very simple animal capture-recapture experiments. However, in more sophisticated settings, such as casualty estimation, we cannot expect them to hold.

In general, victims of violence are likely to be a heterogeneous group. Lists documenting them are unlikely to be independent. People differ in their social visibility as a result of networks, geographic location, and other traits. These characteristics, which often influence the outcome to some extent, are called covariates in statistics.[10] Different documentation projects have different objectives and may have different propensities to record victims with particular characteristics/covariates. Projects will sometimes collaborate or share information with each other, directly inducing dependence between their lists.[11]

When covariate information on the particularities of both victim and context is available, stratification can be used as a means to reduce the effect of heterogeneity. In short, stratification works by partitioning the population into separate and relatively more homogeneous subsets, where the modeling assumptions can be expected to hold better.[12] Estimates are then calculated within each stratum, using the researchers' MSE method of choice. For example, if we think that the place of death can strongly influence capture probabilities (i.e., that this is an important covariate), as is likely to be true in many cases, we can divide the combined sample into geographic subgroups. More precisely, introducing a stratification scheme is equivalent to assuming that, if two individuals, $i$ and $j$, belong to the same stratum (e.g., the same geographic region), then the probability of each pattern of inclusion is the same for both or, more formally, that Pr(individual $i$ in $O_X$)=Pr(individual $j$ in $O_X$).

When relevant covariate information is not available, the only visible effect of heterogeneity is the emergence of dependences between lists. Take, for example, the case of a conflict with two main perpetrators and three available lists documenting casualties. Assume that no list registered the perpetrators of the killings. If two lists were more prone to register people that were victims of a particular perpetrator, while the other one proceeded in a more balanced way, then—assuming for now that no other sources of heterogeneity are as important—the observable effect will be the emergence of (positive) dependence between the first two lists, while the third will remain relatively independent. In cases like these, with no covariate information that could fully explain the observations, the only way we can learn about the heterogeneity structure is through these induced dependencies.

This observable dependence between lists can, however, provide enough information to successfully account for the effects of the heterogeneity. Furthermore, sometimes accounting for the induced dependence amounts to directly controlling for the effects of the heterogeneity. For example, some general patterns of heterogeneity can be successfully represented or approximated by interactions between lists with the aid of log-linear models.[13]

## REPRESENTING UNOBSERVED INDIVIDUALS

The ultimate goal of MSE techniques is to estimate undercounts. This requires estimating probabilities of noninclusion in lists based on information about noninclusion contained in the inclusion patterns of individuals observed at least once. This seems to be a paradox. However, we must note that in a combined *J*-list sample, many individuals are likely to have been missed by one or more lists. This means that the observable inclusion patterns contain a great deal of information about individuals who are not included on a given list. For instance, if we had six lists, we would have $2^6-1=63$ observable inclusion patterns, and 62 of them describe ways of *not being on lists*.[14] Not being in *all* lists simultaneously is just one more way of not being in lists.

The arguably most basic assumption in MSE is that the noninclusion of the fully unobserved individuals (those not included in any list) can be represented by the same model that represents the inclusion (and noninclusion) of those we can observe in at least one list. This is a strong and untestable condition. However, we argue that it is far less demanding than it initially may seem to be.

To better understand this requirement, let us examine its violation. Assuming that nonobserved individuals (those with inclusion pattern $O_{oo}$) differ substantially from observed ones (those with all the other $2^J-1$ patterns), amounts to assuming that the event of *simultaneously* not appearing in all *those particular lists* is somehow an intrinsic attribute of those individuals. In a six-list case, for example, this means that being missed by five lists but not by a sixth is qualitatively different from being missed by those six lists and that, if we added another (seventh) list, being missed by all six original lists but not by the new one is also substantially different from being missed by all seven. Except for a few situations, it appears to us more difficult to reject this requirement than to accept it.

One of these problematic situations is the case of erroneously assumed coverage. Suppose, for example, that our lists were specifically designed to report only events on a particular region—and to ignore any other report—but we assume that we have obtained estimates for a wider region.[15] This situation would lead to the existence of two classes of subjects: those who are, at least in principle, listable and those who are not. In the language of capture probabilities, the first group has a positive probability of inclusion, while for the second, that probability is exactly zero. Any individual who has an intrinsic attribute that *causes* him or her to be unobservable by any list has, by definition, a capture probability of zero. Individuals with capture probabilities of zero cannot be represented by *any* data collection mechanism. In contrast, individuals with nonzero capture probabilities, who just happen to be unobserved by every list (not because of any intrinsic attribute but by chance) are likely to be represented by other, observed individuals (who are also missed by some subset of the lists).

Related to concerns regarding how best to represent unobserved individuals is the belief that MSE techniques can produce valid inferences only when based on lists that are random samples from the target population (see chapter 10, by Jewell, Spagat, and Jewell, in this volume). This point is of particular importance, since arguably most lists of casualties that can be found in practice are unable to meet such a standard. Fortunately, except in some truly problematic cases, this belief is not correct. The key is that the only information that matters for MSE estimation is the relationship between lists, not the lists' composition. It can be shown that the only requirement is that the collection of *inclusion patterns* be representative of the relationships between the lists, not for each list to represent the underlying population. As an extreme example, consider an organization that collected information giving preference to individuals who lived close to their headquarters, and another one that gave preference to older people over younger people. Here, neither partial sample is representative of the characteristics of the target population; moreover, the "homogeneity" assumption, understood as having the same probability of inclusion within each list, is clearly violated. However, if we assume, as seems reasonable, that age is uncorrelated with how close to the organization headquarters the victim lived, we can show that even the simple 2-list Petersen estimator is valid. The example is, of course, artificial,[16] but serves to illustrate the point. As long as we can approximately model the characteristics of the resulting aggregated pattern—independence in our example—the internal characteristics of the lists turn out to be irrelevant.[17]

Real complications may arise, however, if the underlying data structure is such that a "wrong model" can successfully account for the observable part of the inclusion patterns, but not for the full-exclusion one ($O_{o_oo}$), and we are led to choose the "wrong" model over more appropriate ones. In theory, some heterogeneity patterns could lead to such a situation. As an extreme example, consider lists from distinct age groups with little or no overlap. This scenario could plausibly result in most MSE procedures considerably overestimating the actual total counts.[18] This may be an example of a heterogeneity pattern in the population that could plausibly induce a pattern of dependences between lists that would be consistent with an identifiable model for *all* the $(2^J-1)$ observable patterns, but somehow not for the unobserved category $O_{ooo.ooo}$. In this general case, the risk is that we would be led to accept and rely on a model that does not correctly represent the noninclusion of the unobserved individuals and therefore poses a risk for producing biased estimates. However, it is not well understood which plausible patterns of heterogeneity can induce such outcomes; more research is needed on this topic. In the authors' experience, populations in which the same source of heterogeneity strongly affects all lists simultaneously can sometimes generate observable data with the characteristics just described.

However, while acknowledging such extreme situations as real limitations, we should bear in mind that, although plausible, they are unlikely to be completely unknown to researchers. In the example, for instance, a simple tabulation of the counts broken down by age would immediately reveal this special heterogeneity. This would allow researchers to account for it by, for example, stratifying by age group. Moreover, if researchers were able to secure any other list that was less sensitive to that particular source of heterogeneity, even if it were extremely sensitive to another, uncorrelated source, such a list could potentially provide enough information to overcome the problem through direct modeling of the dependence patterns—in theory, even without stratification.

As will be shown in more detail in the case of Peru (here and in chapter 5, by Landman and Gohdes,in this volume,), researchers' knowledge of the situation is crucial. In Peru, two of the lists used for the three-system estimation of killed and disappeared people across the 20-year conflict gravely underreported acts committed by the rebel group Sendero Luminoso. With the help of the third, largest, list provided by the Truth and Reconciliation Commission, the research team was able to use information from all three lists to account for this "perpetrator heterogeneity" and to estimate credible levels of casualties committed by both the state and the insurgent group.

## Case Studies

### KOSOVO

In an investigation of the tragic events that unfolded in Kosovo between March and June 1999, the application of MSE methods significantly improved the knowledge of the extent of violence exercised against Kosovars. The research was conducted by ABA/ CEELI (2002), who used four data sources to conduct MSE analyses of the patterns of refugee flow and killings in Kosovo for those months. The data sources comprised of interviews conducted by the American Bar Association Central and East European Law Initiative (ABA/CEELI), interviews conducted by Human Rights Watch (HRW), interviews conducted by the Organization for Security and Cooperation in Europe (OSCE), and records of exhumations conducted on behalf of the International Criminal Tribunal for the former Yugoslavia (ICTY).

It is important to note that none of these excellent sources of information, which represent exemplary data collection efforts, are uniformly representative of the entire underlying population of individuals killed in Kosovo between March and June 1999. For example, ABA/CEELI conducted interviews in Macedonia (among other locations), relying on referrals from humanitarian organizations, word of mouth, and advertising in local newspapers, as well as information obtained by canvassing refugee camps tent by tent (ABA/CEELI 2002). These were reasonable methods to use in locating individuals with crucial information on killings in Kosovo. Similar methods are employed in a variety of conflict and post-conflict regions and are often necessary to obtain information when there is no hope of a complete census or a sampling frame from which to build a random sample. But it would be unreasonable to assume that these methods result in a representative sample. Therefore we must rely on statistical methods, such as MSE, which are suitable for calculating population-level estimates from available data.

A total of 4,400 individual victims were identified across the four data sources. Many of these were listed in more than one source. Based on the inclusion patterns of these 4,400 identified individuals, an estimated total of 10,356 victims was calculated (95 percent confidence interval: [9,002, 12,122]). This number was surprising, as it implies that more victims went undocumented—namely, 5,956—than were jointly recorded in the four available data sources.

Prior to building and selecting the models necessary to calculate these estimates, exploratory data analysis was conducted to evaluate the plausibility of the classic MSE assumptions outlined earlier. This analysis indicated potential sources of heterogeneity and led researchers to stratify MSE calculations by space (geographic region) and time. Two-systems estimates were also calculated for each pair of sources to identify possible dependences between lists; numerous positive dependences were in fact identified. An extension of this method, using hierarchical log-linear models, was used to examine the relationships between three of the data sources at a time.[19] These results indicated that the pairwise dependencies, identified by the two-systems estimates, were likely well modeled by including two-way interaction terms. Such direct analysis of data patterns (over time and space) and exploratory two- and three-system MSE calculations indicated the need for careful stratification and complex modeling to account for the intricate heterogeneity and dependence structure. This procedure illustrates how, as mentioned earlier in this chapter, assumptions must be checked to ensure that the most appropriate MSE method will be chosen for a given situation.

There were many possible complex models to describe the observed inclusion patterns. Traditional model selection techniques (i.e., best-fit statistics) were used to identify the model used to calculate 10,356 killings with a 95 percent confidence interval of [9,002, 12,122].[20]

It is important to note a few things. First, without MSE calculations, at that time, we would have lacked an estimate of the nearly 6,000 undocumented killings in Kosovo between March and June 1999. Second, if we relied solely on the observable, available data from the four sources, we would have been unable to choose between the contradictory conclusions regarding the pattern of violence over time and space provided by each data source (see chapter 12, by Krüger, Ball, Price, and Hoover Green, in this volume, for an example of comparing geographic regions). And last, thanks to the work of the Humanitarian Law Center,[21] this estimate has recently been largely corroborated. In their attempt to generate an exhaustive list of victims, the center's researchers have documented 9,030 murders and 1,200 persons missing from this time period.[22]

PERU

Between 1980 and 2000, Peru witnessed a bloody armed internal conflict that was primarily carried out between the state forces and the insurgent Communist Party of Peru–Sendero Luminoso (PCP-SLU) movement. This fighting received only limited attention from the international community.

Prior to the establishment of the Truth and Reconciliation Commission (Comisión de la Verdad y Reconciliación, CVR), conventional wisdom had placed the number of victims claimed by the conflict at approximately 25,000. Researchers at the CVR and the American Association for the Advancement of Science (AAAS), however, revealed by means of MSE analyses that the total number of victims was in the vicinity of 70,000 (see Ball et al. 2003). They achieved this result by using three different lists enumerating deaths and disappearances in Peru between 1980 and 2000.

The CVR collected reports documenting deaths and disappearances of approximately 24,000 people, of which 18,397 could be identified sufficiently to be matched with two further lists.[23] Importantly, the addition of the second and third lists resulted in only approximately 6,000 more documented cases, thus exemplifying the fact that the size of the additional lists used for MSE is less important than the pattern of overlap between the lists. Even though almost 75 percent of all reported cases had been recorded by the CVR, the two lists added for MSE delivered the missing information that was required to calculate an estimate.

Because local area experts expected incidences to be reported with varying probability in different regions (i.e., to violate the homogeneity assumption), data were first stratified by geographic location of the death or disappearance. Depending on the amount of information available for each region, the data were stratified by departments, provinces and—where possible—even districts. For example, in the department of Ayacucho, the data could be stratified down to the district level, as all three lists had recorded a disproportionate number of incidences in this department. In addition to the assumption that different regions would produce heterogeneous capture probabilities, it was assumed that the perpetrator who had killed or disappeared a given individual would have an influence on whether the incident was reported. As demonstrated by Landman and Gohdes (chapter 5 in this volume), the three lists offered a very different answer to the question of which perpetrator should be held responsible for the majority of atrocities committed. Of all cases attributed to PCP-SLU, 80 percent were exclusively recorded by the CVR database. For each geographical stratum, the researchers thus attempted to calculate individual estimates for the different perpetrators.

The log-linear models used for the estimation allowed for modeling interactions between the different lists, enabling the researchers to select the best fitting model out of seven possible models for each stratum.[24] The models that were selected with the greatest frequency were those in which there was at least one interaction between the two smaller lists, with the Truth Commission's list being independent. Accordingly, not once was a model selected that assumed an interaction between the Truth Commission's data and *both* of the other lists.

With the help of this method, it was found that the majority of atrocities were actually committed by the PCP-SLU (31,331, 95 percent confidence interval:[24,823; 37,840]) and not by the state (20,458, 95 percent CI:[17,023; 23,893]), as had been assumed by many human rights groups (the data they had collected supported their claim). Moreover, it was found that the conflict had primarily affected the impoverished rural areas of Peru, farthest from the urban agglomeration of Lima. Of the estimated 69,280 (95 percent CI:[61,007; 77,552]), deaths and disappearances, 26,259 could be attributed to the region of Ayacucho alone, which is located in the south-central Andes.

It is important to take into consideration that, despite the horrifying magnitude of these atrocities, the total death toll directly attributable to the conflict represents a minute fraction of the total Peruvian population at the time—approximately 27 million in 1993. This means that other, more traditional, techniques of assessing conflict-related mortality rates, such as survey sampling, might have been unfeasible because of the low prevalence of the effects we would have been trying to detect (see Silva and Ball 2008).

## Conclusion

Multiple systems estimation methods encompass a broad variety of techniques that offer promising solutions to some of the challenges that researchers and practitioners face in casualty estimation in conflict and post-conflict situations. In the demanding circumstances of war-torn regions, obtaining reliable estimates of killed and disappeared persons poses a difficult, sometimes seemingly impossible, task. Documentation of violent events is often rare and often biased, and the lack of infrastructure and resources presents a challenging situation for the conduct of surveys. MSE techniques offer a way to use existing, sometimes unrepresentative, information on casualties to arrive at an estimate of the number of atrocities that is less biased and more complete than would otherwise be possible. While certainly not a "foolproof" class of methods, our case studies of Kosovo and Peru illustrate that in certain situations, the MSE techniques can considerably improve our knowledge of conflict trajectories.

In this chapter, we have attempted to present the general intuition that lies behind MSE methods. Instead of focusing on one particular technique, we introduced a general framework for MSE analysis to allow us to explore more deeply our assumptions about heterogeneity and dependence and the subtle interplay between them. As with any other statistical technique, the most basic forms of MSE rely on strong assumptions that, in real-life applications such as casualty estimation, are almost never met. Fortunately, the availability of more than two lists makes it possible to apply methods that replace those assumptions with more appropriate ones. Furthermore, multiple lists make it possible to test for violations of many of the assumptions implied by different models.

As illustrated in our case studies, researchers must examine the data and choose appropriate methods. This requires both statistical and local area expertise, as contextual knowledge about the data can guide researchers in terms of which assumptions are likely to be violated and which tests to conduct. At the same time, the appropriate method can not only reveal which assumptions are *not* met, it can help to account for these violations.

The Kosovarian and Peruvian cases presented here exemplify the significance of data analysis methods that correct for recording biases in casualty estimation. In both situations, the number of casualties additionally "uncovered" through MSE was larger than the number of killed and disappeared people recorded by truth commissions, NGOs, and international organizations together. The evident political relevance of such results illustrates the importance of understanding the assumptions and possible pitfalls of such estimation techniques.

The many advantages of MSE come at a price of high technical complexity. Considerable statistical expertise is needed to understand the assumptions and limitations of the methods and to apply them correctly. MSE techniques, which differ substantially from other better known statistical techniques, can easily be misunderstood, even by technically sophisticated audiences. A common source of misunderstandings is failure to realize that strict homogeneity and independence assumptions must be in place before any attempt is made to extrapolate assumptions and limitations from the two-list case to the multilist case. Other common misunderstandings, such as believing that MSE requires representative samples from the population, sometimes arise from faulty analogies with more standard statistical techniques.

The complexity of MSE methods constitutes a communication challenge that puts at risk the clear dissemination and discussion of results. Opaque presentations, coupled with the potential misunderstanding of the methods' assumptions and subsequent analysis decisions, entail the risk of undermining the credibility of otherwise sound conclusions. Any such lessening of credibility can be particularly problematic in a politically charged debate, as can almost always be found in the casualty estimation context.

Since their first development for the estimation of wildlife populations over a century ago, recapture methods have significantly progressed. The recent evolution of techniques that address "real-life" problems, such as the estimation of casualties, presents an important step in the continuing development of this class of methods. Although MSE methods do face challenges and limitations, we believe that they are a versatile tool that enables the principled use of data frequently found in practice, and as such should be considered to be part of a standard "casualty estimation toolbox."

REFERENCES

ABA/CEELI. 2002. *Killings and Refugee Flow in Kosova/Kosovo, March–June 1999: A Report to the International Criminal Tribunal for the Former Yugoslavia.* Washington, DC: American Association for the Advancement of Science/American Bar Association Central and East European Law Initiative.

Ball, Patrick, et al. 2003. *How Many Peruvians Have Died? An Estimate of the Total Number of Victims Killed or Disappeared in the Armed Internal Conflict between 1980 and 2000.*" Report to the Peruvian Truth and Reconciliation Commission (CVR). Washington, DC: American Association for the Advancement of Science. Also published as Anexo 2 (Anexo Estadístico) of CVR Report.

Basu, Sanjib, and Nader Ebrahimi. 2001. "Bayesian Capture-Recapture Methods for Error Detection and Estimation of Population Size: Heterogeneity and Dependence." *Biometrika* 88: 269–279.

Bishop, Yvonne M., Stephen E. Fienberg, and Paul W. Holland. 1975. *Discrete Multivariate Analysis: Theory and Practice.* Cambridge, MA: MIT Press, reprinted in 2007 by New York: Springer-Verlag.

Darroch, John N., et al. 1993. "A Three-Sample Multiple-Recapture Approach to Census Population Estimation with Heterogeneous Catchability." *Journal of the American Statistical Association* 88: 1137–1148.

Fienberg, Stephen E. 1972. "The Multiple Recapture Census for Closed Populations and Incomplete $2^k$ Contingency Tables." *Biometrika* 59: 591–603.

Fienberg, Stephen E., Matthew Johnson, and Brian W. Junker. 1999. "Classical Multilevel and Bayesian Approaches to Population Size Estimation Using Multiple Lists." *Journal of the Royal Statistical Society*: Series A *(Statistics in Society).* 162: 383–406.

George, Edward I. 1992. "Capture—Recapture Estimation via Gibbs Sampling." *Biometrika* 79(4): 677–683.

Goudie, Ian B. J., and M. Goudie. 2007. "Who Captures the Marks for the Petersen Estimator?" *Journal of the Royal Statistical Society*: Series A *(Statistics in Society)* 170: 825–839.

Hook, Ernest B., and Ronald R. Regal. 1999. "Recommendations for Presentation and Evaluation of Capture-Recapture Estimates in Epidemiology." *Journal of Clinical Epidemiology* 52(10): 917.

International Working Group for Disease Monitoring and Forecasting 1995a. "Capture-Recapture and Multiple-Record Systems Estimation I: History and Theoretical Development." *American Journal of Epidemiology* 142: 1047–1058.

———. 1995b. "Capture-Recapture and Multiple-Record Systems Estimation II: Applications in Human Diseases." *American Journal of Epidemiology* 142: 1059–1068.

Lum, Kristian, et al. 2010. "Measuring Elusive Populations with Bayesian Model Averaging for Multiple Systems Estimation: A Case Study on Lethal Violations in Casanare, 1998–2007." *Statistics, Politics, and Policy* 1, 2.

Manrique-Vallier, Daniel, and Stephen E. Fienberg. 2008. "Population Size Estimation Using Individual Level Mixture Models." *Biometrical Journal* 50(6): 1051–1063.

Petersen, Johannes C. G. 1896. "The Yearly Immigration of Young Plaice into the Limfjord from the German Sea." *Report of the Danish Biological Station* 6: 1–48.

Sekar, Chandra C., and W. Edwards Deming. 1949. "On a Method of Estimating Birth and Death Rates and the Extent of Registration." *Journal of the American Statistical Association* 44(245): 101–115.

Silva, Romesh, and Patrick Ball. 2008. "The Demography of Conflict-Related Mortality in Timor-Leste (1974–1999): Reflections on Empirical Quantitative Measurement of Civilian Killings, Disappearances, and Famine-Related Deaths." In *Statistical Methods for Human Rights*, edited by Jana Asher at al. New York: Springer, 117–140.

NOTES

1. See Goudie and Goudie (2007) for an account of the origin of these techniques.

2. This is a fictitious table that was created for exemplary purposes. In real-life cases, the information existing for each individual varies profoundly. The covariables included here (age, sex, location) merely describe some of the most frequently encountered victim/incidence characteristics.

3. Since table 9.1 shows only four individuals, not all inclusion patterns are populated in the diagram. A complete list could potentially include individuals captured in all locations of the diagram, except outside all circles.

4. Here $i$ could equal any number between 1 and $N$, indicating the first, second, . . . individual in the population; in mathematical notation we write $i=1,.,N$.

5. For the case discussed here, this assumption is generally met: individuals that were killed in armed conflict add to the number of casualties and cannot "leave" this population.

6. This definition of homogeneity is simple and appropriate in this two-list context. In more complex settings, however, it can be too restrictive to be really useful. A more general definition has to be stated with respect to a model: the recording of each individual can be well described by the same model.

7. A fourth assumption usually made is *perfect matching*: each of the included individuals must be perfectly categorized to be either only included in system A, only included in system B, or included in both systems A and B (see Lum et al. 2010, 3).

8. The subscripts $ab$ are a shortcut to refer to any of the four inclusion patterns: 00, 01, 10, 11.

9. The "model selection" problem is a major subject in statistical methodology, common to a wide range of applications. Although it is a crucial problem in MSE applications, space constraints disallow further elaboration here.

10. Examples of covariates include sex, age, location, and date from table 9.1.

11. Although this may appear to be a pervasive problem, in actual applications, the situation is not as dire. For instance, in the Peruvian study (Ball et al. 2003), shared information was clearly labeled and could be separated readily. As we will see when discussing the applications, thorough knowledge of the data is essential.

12. In other words, stratification will work when the inclusion patterns can be described reasonably well by a particular model.

13. In general, heterogeneity that affects groups of lists, but not every list, can be directly accounted for as interactions between lists in log-linear models. Other, more sophisticated, patterns that simultaneously affect all lists can also have estimable log-linear representations (see, e.g., Darroch et al.,1993, for more details).

14. For instance, the observable pattern O000100 in a 6-list situation not only gives us information about being in list 4, but also about *not being* in lists 1, 2, 3, 5, and 6.

15. This situation is analogous to a survey with a sampling frame that does not cover the totality of the target population.

16. And, depending on the specific situation at hand, it could also be argued that the age distribution could be correlated with geographic location.

17. This is one reason for our belief that understanding homogeneity as equal probability of being in each list can be misleading in this discussion.

18. See also Bishop et al. (1975, ch. 6) for a discussion about essentially the same extreme situation

19. See Bishop et al. (1975) for details on hierarchical log-linear models.

20. See ABA/CEELI (2002) for full analytical methods and results, including model results calculated for space and time strata.

21. www.hlc-rdc.org/index.php?lid=en&;show=kosovo&action=search&str_stanje=1.

22. See Jewell, Spagat, and Jewell, chapter 10 in this volume, for further discussion of this issue.

23. See chapter 5, by Landman and Gohdes, for further details on the other lists.

24. The seven models included one model that assumes independence between the lists, three that assume one interaction (i.e., two lists are dependent), and three that assumed two interactions (i.e., one list interacts with the other two lists, but the other two lists are independent of each other).

# V Estimating Violence

## MIXED METHODS

# 10 MSE and Casualty Counts
## ASSUMPTIONS, INTERPRETATION, AND CHALLENGES
### Nicholas P. Jewell. Michael Spagat, and Britta L. Jewell

## Introduction

Capture-recapture estimation has been used for counting elusive wildlife and human populations since the late nineteenth century. A classical application is to capture fish from a pond, count and tag the fish, and then return them to the pond. Later there is a second capture (the "recapture"). Again the fish are counted but, in addition, a separate tally is made of the number of tagged fish appearing in the recapture. We can then estimate the total number of fish in the pond based on the size of the two catches and the overlap between the two.[1] Intuitively, a large overlap suggests that there are probably few fish in the pond that eluded capture twice, whereas a small overlap suggests that probably most fish were never caught. We can use data from more than two captures to further improve the estimate of the total number of fish in the pond.

Although these methods were originally designed to count wildlife populations, their use has been expanded to count elusive human communities such as the number of crack cocaine users in London (Hope et al. 2005), the autistic population in Lothian, Scotland (Harrison et al. 2006), the lesbian population in Allegheny County, Pennsylvania (Aaron et al. 2003), and the World Trade Center Tower population on September 11, 2001 (Murphy et al. 2007; Murphy 2009), among many other applications. Reviews of the method include a special issue of the *Biometrical Journal* (Böhning 2008), two early introductory papers by the International Working Group for Disease Monitoring and Forecasting (1995a, 1995b), and Chao et al. (2001). Desenclos and Hubert (1994), Hook and Regal (1995, 1997), Papoz et al. (1996), Cormack et al. (2000), and Tilling (2001) all critique the application of capture-recapture methods to human populations.

The specific application of capture-recapture estimation to casualty counting is a more recent development that has now been employed in sufficient examples for the methods to be taken seriously and evaluated. The most prominent applications have been to Guatemala for the period 1960–1996 (Ball 1999; Ball et al. 2003), Kosovo in 1999 (Ball and Asher 2002; ABA/CEELI 2002; Ball 2003), Peru for 1980–2000 (Ball et al. 2003; Manrique-Vallier and Fienberg 2008; chapter 9, by Manrique-Vallier, Price, and Gohdes, in this volume), East Timor (now Timor-Leste) for 1974–1999 (Silva and Ball 2008), Casanare, Colombia, for 1998–2007 (Lum et al. 2010), and Bosnia for 1992–1995 (Brunborg et al. 2006; Zwierzchowsky and Tabeau 2010, and chapter 11 in this volume). In what follows, we raise some general questions to consider in assessing the application of capture-recapture to the casualty estimation field while not dissecting any particular example in detail. Many of the referenced analyses have, in fact, made efforts to address the issues we discuss in this chapter.[2]

There are a variety of nomenclatures for the capture-recapture methodology that are rooted in different contexts and applications. Capture-recapture, or mark-recapture, was originally used by researchers counting animal populations in the wild. These terms suggest two distinct counting exercises, the capture and the recapture, although both the methods and the terminology have been extended to multiple recaptures. In human populations, estimation is based on overlapping incomplete lists that play the role of the different captures: the techniques are sometimes referred to as dual-record estimation when there are two lists and multiple systems estimation when more data sources are available. We believe that the classical capture-recapture terminology is the most evocative and intuitive, and so we will use this term here. Readers should be aware, however, that the literature on casualty estimation generally employs the term "multiple systems estimation" to describe capture-recapture methods.

It is laudable to aspire to produce accurate war-death estimates, bracketed by appropriate confidence intervals to reflect uncertainty. In many conflicts, there is likely to be considerable political pressure to produce such estimates (Andreas and Greenhill 2010), for example, to focus blame on perpetrators of human rights violations or to exert pressure on warring groups. However, it is not always possible to make reasonably accurate capture-recapture estimates, and proceeding in such situations may have the effect of exaggerating the quality of our knowledge. We suggest that in some cases it may be preferable to give credible lower, and perhaps upper, bounds for war deaths based on the lists' data. These bounds can supplement, or even replace, estimates based on uncertain and unverified assumptions; often, they will be sufficient for practical purposes while directly conveying a sense of necessary imprecision. For example, a war crimes prosecution may benefit greatly from a very well documented lower bound on the war deaths attributable to a particular perpetrator, whereas a good estimate of the number of these deaths may arguably add little extra. A poorly founded estimate will only generate confusion.

Another tempting possibility is to try to link variation in counts—over time and geography, for example—to changes in underlying conditions that can be quantified in various ways. Unfortunately, it is sometimes not possible to disaggregate capture-recapture estimates with sufficient reliability to underpin such an analysis. For example, Landman and Gohdes (chapter 5 in this volume) report that available Peru data are simply too sparse for reliable time disaggregation. In such cases, explanatory analyses using raw counts may still be useful even though these counts are known to be incomplete. If, for example, biases within counts are reasonably well known to be relatively consistent, then at least some useful boundaries on the effects of explanatory factors can be derived. We must, however, sometimes accept that available data will not allow any useful inference.

Many basic questions concerning the application of capture-recapture methods to casualty estimation are simple to state but hard to answer fully. The main questions that we at least broach here include the following: When, and under what conditions, can capture-recapture estimation provide accurate and useful counts of the number of conflict casualties? Specifically, how many lists are necessary to appropriately allow for list relationships? How can available data and knowledge of how the various lists were assembled be used to address this question? The last question involves the issue of whether some lists are best aggregated, although such aggregation complicates the understanding of how specific lists were assembled, including their interrelationship.

In the other direction, there may be a need to disaggregate lists according to specific characteristics including chronological time and geography; that is, to stratify the data appropriately to yield lists that better satisfy the assumptions discussed shortly. Necessarily, this raises the question of the type and level of stratification that can be most feasibly used. How are the results and assumptions of a particular capture-recapture analysis best communicated for political actors and the media without undermining the credibility of the approach?

Ultimately, in each conflict situation, the minimum level of data validity that is required for the methods to be applicable must be established. Given that the data meet basic quality standards, which methods are appropriate for choosing among several capture-recapture estimates, hoping to balance the transparency of assumptions with statistical constraints? We cannot tackle all these issues in detail, but we shall touch on some of them, challenging researchers to consider them all when applying these methods to casualty estimation.

## Basic Statistical Assumptions/Requirements

Capture-recapture estimation of conflict deaths requires assumptions that describe how the lists of deaths (captures) are created, including possible links between these multiple, overlapping, and incomplete lists of victims. As in all statistical procedures, the correspondence between reality and assumptions is crucial to the validity of final estimates and their interpretation. In this section, therefore, we examine the assumptions under-lying capture-recapture estimation.

We assume that researchers have more than one distinct list (for convenience, let $k$ stand for the number of lists), with each list providing information and identifiers on casualties in a certain well-defined region for a specified period of time.[3] The basic as-sumptions underlying capture-recapture estimation are loosely summarized as follows.

*Coverage.* We first assume that the population of victims is closed, meaning here that every death has a positive probability of discovery by at least some list. In wildlife appli-cations, this assumption is usually interpreted as meaning no immigration or emigra-tion, in part because it is assumed, for example, that any fish in a pond can be captured unless it exits the pond or dies of natural causes or has not yet arrived before capture at-tempts. However, in conflict situations there may be deaths that will never be observed no matter how many lists are compiled. No statistical cleverness can uncover such deaths. We can only estimate the number of deaths that could have been captured but, *by chance*, were not.

Coverage may be most difficult for real-time counts—due to rapid changes in popula-tions in the midst of conflict and difficulty in immediate casualty ascertainment—but may improve over time for historical estimates. There is, however, a real concern that casualties among families that have become refugees may be lost to discovery by many lists. In this regard, it is particularly important to explicitly define the population of victims that is being considered.

ACCURACY

1. *Perfect matching.* It is generally assumed that matching across different casualty lists is perfect. That is, matched deaths truly are the same deaths, and deaths that are not matched truly are different deaths (this assumption includes the understanding that no two casualties on the *same* list are duplicates).
2. *No false deaths.* Deaths appearing on lists are assumed to be real.

*Homogeneity.* The simplest homogeneity assumption is most easily articulated by re-quiring that each casualty (from the unobserved total list of casualties) have an equal probability of appearing on a specific list, and that this be true for all lists. There is no requirement that these probabilities be equal across lists. So some lists may be more com-prehensive (high probability of capturing a casualty) and some much more sporadic (low probability of capturing a casualty). As discussed in further detail later, an implication of homogeneity is that deaths that do not appear on any list do not possess inherent charac-teristics that make them fundamentally different from deaths that made it onto one or more lists: that is, it is pure chance that some deaths are discovered and others are not. Essentially, it is this projection of the stochastic properties of the discovered deaths onto the undiscovered ones that provides the key leverage for estimation.[4] Unfortunately, it is certainly plausible that undiscovered deaths differ intrinsically from discovered ones. Indeed, this condition reflects a major challenge to the utility of the capture-recapture method. We shall return to the challenge of detecting from observed data whether capture-recapture methods meet the necessary requirements to proceed effectively.

In the next section ("How Strongly Do Casualty Lists Deviate from Capture-Recapture Assumptions?"), we discuss two strategies for addressing nonhomogeneity of detection within lists, namely (1) stratification (which allows for the probabilities of detection to vary across known subgroups defined by, e.g., age or geographic region) and (2) explicit modeling of how the probabilities of detection vary randomly within multiple lists (and thus not according to known subgroups). Each of these situations involves more complicated modeling of the mechanisms that generate the lists (i.e., the processes that determine which casualties are reported on which lists), while still requiring fundamental assumptions regarding list selection properties that allow for valid inference regarding the estimate of the total number of deaths.

*Relationships between the Lists.* The essence of the capture-recapture idea emerges most simply with just two lists ($k = 2$). In this case, it is usually necessary to assume that there is statistical independence between the lists, in the sense that the probability that a particular casualty appears on one list does not depend on whether it appears on the other, and vice versa. Statistical independence is not verifiable from the observed count data from the two lists. Less standard alternative approaches to two lists also require assumptions that cannot be checked using the available lists. Independence of the lists is closely related to homogeneity, as we discuss further in the next section.[5]

If our objective is to provide credible lower and/or upper bounds for the number of war dead, rather than a central estimate, then the weakness of having to assume independence in the two-list case is considerably attenuated because we can accommodate knowledge of intersource dependencies into our bounds. In other words, an independence-based estimate can serve merely as a springboard for a discussion of possible list dependencies and their effects on the range of plausible war-death numbers. Providing clear and precise methods for determining bounds, and their associated uncertainty, would be a valuable topic for future research, particularly when there are many lists with potentially complex relationships, so that pairwise dependencies are not easily described.

One of the major attractions of using more lists ($k > 2$) is that the assumption of list independence can be substantially weakened. However, it is always the case that some unverifiable assumption (typically that, at least, the $k$-order interaction is zero) is required to perform an analysis. (In general terms, the lack of a $k$-order interaction simply means that the intricate dependencies among any set of $k - 1$ lists are not influenced by whether a death is on the remaining $k$th list.) The nature of such an assumption becomes very hard to articulate to interested lay consumers of the information and, indeed, even to people with statistical training; thus the plausibility of the assumption is hard to assess. This is an important problem in the context, for example, of a truth commission, one purpose of which is to provide explanation and closure to the families of victims. Thus, even when more than two lists are available, we recommend initially calculating all possible two-list estimates (or bounds, to be precise)—each assuming independence—and then discussing possible dependencies. This procedure can serve as a basis for understanding more complex estimates should the latter be required.

## How Strongly Do Casualty Lists Deviate from Capture-Recapture Assumptions?

Assumptions will be violated in any application of a statistical model. The interpretation of results requires judgment regarding the impact of these deviations from model requirements rather than merely noting their inevitable existence. This section provides some guidelines for making these assessments in applications of capture-recapture estimation to casualty estimation.

Just as unhappy families are unhappy in their own way (according to Tolstoy), each conflict and data-gathering effort is unique; thus it is understood that every list of war dead will violate the assumptions of capture-recapture analysis in its own distinct manner. Nevertheless, there are some general points we can make about the applications with which we are most familiar. We first address the quality of the available data, turning next more directly to the assumptions themselves.

### DATA QUALITY: PERFECT MATCHING

Unique and reliable identifiers of individuals, such as social security numbers, are available in many epidemiological applications. Individual information on people who have been killed in conflicts will often be much more limited and will have less validity, perhaps using only simple names and addresses at best, perhaps incompletely supplemented by circumstances of death.[6] Each list must be cleansed of any spurious (i.e., false) casualties. One solution might be to attempt to validate all casualty records against population census lists or equivalent official data records, including voter registries. Even when such records exist, however, validation may still be difficult for vulnerable populations and children. Moreover, such validation work may require considerable resources and will be impossible in many situations.

When, information is collected retrospectively, with recall periods greater than a few months, then dates of deaths, or even the fact of whether a death has occurred, will often be recalled with considerable inaccuracy. Other details, such as victims' demographics or the circumstances of their deaths, will often be incorrect. Any inaccuracies complicate the matching of deaths both within and between sources.

Much of the capture-recapture work in the casualty field has relied on the accuracy of extremely distant memories. For example, recall periods reach to nearly 40 years in Ball (1999, 2003), 20 years in Ball et al. (2003) and 25 years in Silva and Ball (2008). Much information supplied in this way must suffer from inaccuracies that are hard to detect, making it difficult to determine when different sources are reporting the same death. Estimates of war deaths are necessarily inflated in capture-recapture estimates to the extent that the same deaths are recorded multiple times but not successfully matched within and across lists.

In addition to systematic errors caused by too little matching of identical deaths, there are random errors in the matching process, an accounting of which must be built into the error bounds for a final count estimator if these are to be realistic. One method to incorporate random matching error is to mark all inconclusive matches with (subjective) matching probabilities as judged by coders. One then can perform a large number of random computer simulations in which records judged to match with probability of $p$ will match in some percentage of the simulations. That is, on each computer run-through, all inconclusive matches are randomly resolved as matching or not matching, based on their assessed matching probabilities; when all these resolutions are complete, an appropriate algorithm calculates a capture-recapture estimate. The final estimate is then the average of these many estimates, each flowing from a particular resolution of all the uncertain matches. The final confidence interval accounts for the variation across these many estimates in addition to other forms of statistical error.

It is important to note the considerable literature on probabilistic record linkage that may usefully be applied here. For example, Fienberg and Manrique-Vallier (2009) discuss links between statistical ideas for record linkage and capture-recapture estimation, with data from casualties in Kosovo used for illustration. In addition, there is research on capture-recapture methods in situations without unique identifiers, a literature that formalizes the suggestion in the last paragraph (Laska et al. 2003; Caldwell et al. 2005). Nevertheless, there are thorny issues associated with matching, and the process is particularly complicated when the data are retrospective. For example, some individuals on some lists may be "anonymous" in that their deaths are recorded accurately but without any identification. Rules must be determined to handle such cases, and to account for additional estimation variability introduced by their presence.

Methods used to implement the matching should ultimately be entirely transparent and reproducible. Consumers of casualty estimates must be convinced of the validity of the matching effort, since small systematic errors or biases may cause large differences in total count estimates.[7]

## COVERAGE AND HOMOGENEITY

The most basic coverage and homogeneity assumptions require that each list employed in capture-recapture estimation behave like a well-designed simple probability sample.[8] However, in practice, lists may reflect substantial "non-random" characteristics. There seems to be a common misperception that capture-recapture estimation can always transform "non-random" convenience data into unbiased statistical estimates complete with quantified sampling errors.[9] Of course, such a claim cannot always be true.

As noted earlier, the assumptions underpinning any statistical model will never be satisfied in any kind of strict sense. However, practitioners must make a case that violations of the assumptions of the models they are applying are not severe enough to call the main results of an analysis into question. We recommend including, as that an important part of the write-up of any capture-recapture estimate, an argument that it is acceptable to treat the lists that are used in estimation as if they were well-behaved probability samples from appropriately modeled data-generating processes. We return shortly to the topic of how to use statistical models to accommodate various list properties and relationships further.

In seeking out multiple lists to understand the extent of casualties, it is of course natural and laudable to try to find new lists that document casualties that are likely to have been missed by other known lists. The acquisition of complementary lists allows a researcher to more fully cover all regions and types of casualties. In this sense, it is desirable that different lists "fish in different ponds." The problem is that when different lists focus on different types of victims, an essential assumption for the most straightforward version of capture-recapture estimation is potentially violated: specifically, it may not be true that all individual deaths have equal chances of being listed on any particular source. The impact of performing capture-recapture estimates based on lists that focus on different types of victims can be very large indeed. Suppose, for example, that separate lists give accurate casualty lists, one for Shiites and one for Sunnis, with minimal overlap between the two. The combined list would provide a full and accurate count, whereas the simplest capture-recapture estimate based on the disaggregated counts would considerably overestimate the actual total count. In such cases, and when there are more than two lists, more complex statistical modeling will be required to accommodate the lack of homogeneity. After a brief digression into a problematic area of capture-recapture estimates. we shall address two strategies for addressing violations of the strictest version of the homogeneity assumption.

There appears to be a misperception that capture-recapture estimates can always uncover deaths—at least, in aggregate—that differ systematically from deaths that appear on lists.[10] The problem is that, when the coverage and homogeneity assumptions are satisfied, deaths estimated as missing in all the sources must necessarily inherit the (possibly complex) sampling characteristics of the known deaths. That is, implicit in the capture-recapture assumptions is that deaths fail to appear on lists only through pure chance. Thus, estimated but unlisted deaths cannot differ fundamentally from listed ones, although it is a challenge to convey in full generality the precise meaning of this fact.[11] The concept is simplest when there are only two independent and perfectly homogeneous lists: in this case if, for example, 10 percent of the victims on a particular list are females then, aside from sampling error, 10 percent of the victims not listed on that source should also be females.[12] The same should be true for any characteristic of the victims, such as ages or the identities of perpetrator groups who killed them. Unfortunately, the situation rapidly becomes more complicated when there are heterogeneous list detection probabilities and/or more than two lists; nevertheless, it is still possible to proceed in some such situations even though demographic characteristics of list members vary substantially across the lists. In more complex scenarios, it is not always clear how to distinguish easily between cases in which appropriate modeling can be effective (in dealing with the complexity of the list properties and their interrelationships) and those in which it cannot.

To produce a convincing capture-recapture analysis, it is important to use the available lists to assess the assumed coverage/homogeneity properties to the greatest extent possible. Each list can be examined for time trends, demographic characteristics of victims and perpetrator groups, and any other major covariate for which there are data. Since, as noted, perfect homogeneity assumes that each list can be viewed as a random sample from the *same* (unknown) master list of total casualties, the sample distributions for each covariate should be similar across lists subject to sampling error. In other words, each source should show similar time trends, a similar geographical distribution of deaths, similar victim demographics, and similarity with respect to other breakdowns for which data are known. Consistency of covariate distributions across sources cannot prove perfect homogeneity, but strong inconsistencies will demonstrate possible heterogeneity and, at the very least, the need for more complex estimation techniques. A systematic approach to this exercise is described in Gohdes (2010), where three data sources paint very different pictures of the conflict in Sierra Leone. (See also chapter 5, by Landman and Gohdes, in this volume.)

Of course, the strictest homogeneity assumption is quite likely to be violated in the context of casualty lists, since it will rarely be true that available lists of deaths really are straightforward homogeneous random samples from the complete list of conflict dead. In the canonical capture-recapture application of estimating the number of animals on some territory, researchers often have the luxury of collecting designed random samples, to make this homogeneity assumption plausible. In the casualty setting, however, the major tools of random sampling are often denied the investigator. The lists tend to arise in a happenstance fashion or to be targeted to collect a specific kind of casualty, such as victims of the government or ones belonging to a particular religious group.

As noted earlier, with multiple lists ($k > 2$), it is possible to proceed with estimation even if homogeneity is not satisfied, by exploiting various statistical modeling approaches.[13] However, stratification remains a plausible first response to the problem of heterogeneous capture probabilities.[14] Effectively, this approach disaggregates the estimation problem into "smaller" problems in fixed covariate subgroups. It will almost always be essential to consider the age of a victim as a potential stratification factor, for example, since it is likely that child deaths will be underreported in some lists owing to the greater social visibility of adults.

In principle, stratification can help because it is possible that within-list capture probabilities are heterogeneous at the aggregate level but can still be usefully treated as homogeneous within strata such as geographical areas or victims of particular perpetrators.[15]

Ball et al. (2003) works with two sources that mainly record victims of the government in the Peruvian conflict, together with a third source that records both victims of the government and the guerrillas (chapter 5, by Landman and Godhes, in this volume). These characteristics of the lists led Ball et al. (2003) to stratify by perpetrator in their analysis, as a means of addressing heterogeneity.

In most cases stratification may not produce sufficient homogeneity to underpin good capture-recapture estimates. Sometimes the necessary grouping variable—upon which a good stratification scheme could be based—may simply be unknown or not measured. In such cases, multiple lists ($k > 2$) can potentially allow the statistician to address the failure of the strictest assumptions through use of more complex modeling and estimation methods that account for heterogeneity (or induced dependencies between the lists).[16] One is however faced with the challenge of using available concomitant (e.g., covariate) data to distinguish between situations in which modeling is adequate to address unknown complex sampling characteristics and ones in which such modeling is not up to this task. We are not currently aware of simple and general direct diagnostic methods that can support the use of statistical models addressing complex data-generating mechanisms with the level of confidence that can be achieved for the simplest situation with perfectly homogeneous/independent lists.

Note that complex modeling within the context of capture-recapture estimation differs essentially from standard statistical approaches to complex sampling techniques that allow for varying selection probabilities. In principle, the degree of complexity of a designed sample should not matter as long as one can access a sufficiently sophisticated statistician who can make valid estimates based on knowledge of the sampling design. If, on the other hand, we have casualty lists that are generated by uncertain or unknown methods, we can still proceed as if the lists were generated by some known random mechanism. However, the problem now is that we will probably have only limited possibilities for understanding and validating this data-generating mechanism. In this case, complex sampling does not translate simply into a challenging puzzle for a statistician—rather, it requires us to make complicated assumptions before we can proceed to capture-recapture estimation. In short, with a designed sample, the complexity of the sampling scheme is a known fact and this complexity is built into the estimation, whereas in capture-recapture estimation the nature of the sampling scheme is an imposed assumption that necessarily influences the results. One hopes that more lists will reduce bias stemming from incorrect assumptions, although it would be good if we could quantify this expectation since, in general, it is not desirable to make complicated assumptions when there is little information.

In summary, we recommend that stratification strategies in capture-recapture estimation include at least four basic components. First, there should be an analysis of how the lists that are being used have been constructed to identify likely sources of heterogeneities in coverage, such as uneven emphasis on certain time periods, geographical areas, or types of victims. Second, there should be an analysis of covariate information at the macro level. This step can further expose major sources of heterogeneity that might be usefully addressed through stratification. Third, based on the first two points, stratification schemes should clearly address the heterogeneity problems that have been identified. In the literature we find some, but not enough, motivation for the rather elaborate stratification schemes that have been used. Finally, extending the foregoing discussion, researchers should assess heterogeneity within each stratum where possible, and make a case that departures from homogeneity within strata are not likely to be pronounced enough to undermine the final estimates or, alternatively, that these heterogeneities can be modeled successfully.

Researchers trying to address heterogeneity through stratification should also bear in mind the tension between increased bias at higher levels of aggregation versus greater variability at lower levels due to smaller strata sample sizes. When different lists focus strongly on different types of victims, it might in some cases make sense to simply combine the lists.[17] Further research on this topic might provide useful practical guidance on how best to proceed.

It would be remiss of us not to note that there are serious efforts in the capture-recapture literature to model heterogeneity by means of approaches other than log-linear models applied to the cross-tabulation of casualty counts by lists (Manrique-Vallier, Price, and Gohdes, in chapter 9 in this volume, also touch on this topic). Many of these approaches involve a form of mixing assumption, namely, that the probability of (a specific) list detection varies across individuals and that this can be described usefully. It is possible that the variation itself will vary across lists, and across time (see, e.g., Coull and Agresti 1999). In many cases, these ideas invoke a notion of what might be called "listability" (a latent class variable), which randomly varies across individuals but is unobserved.[18] In essence, such approaches involve assuming some structure for the population distributions of listability.

INTERDEPENDENCE OF LISTS

Although the assumptions of homogeneity and list dependency appear to be quite distinct, these are, in fact, essentially equivalent concepts expressed differently (Hook and Regal 1995, 255–256), as noted earlier. Formally, the bias of the naïve estimator can be expressed in terms of a contribution completely from dependency, alternatively from unequal capture probabilities completely, or from both sources together. Thus, much of the following discussion returns to issues discussed earlier in terms of homogeneity assumptions.

As with homogeneity, assumptions regarding the independence of lists may be made more plausible with designed samples, as in applications to estimating wildlife populations. This is, again, not generally possible with casualty counts. For example, casualty lists tend to borrow from each other during their creation and updating, a characteristic that violates independence instantly. Comparison of total count estimates based on different pairs of lists can sometimes identify pairwise dependence. More subtle forms of dependence that violate assumptions are harder to detect, as we have discussed.

As noted, the independence assumption, which is essentially required in two-list estimation, can be very much relaxed when multiple lists are available, mirroring our discussion of homogeneity.[19] While it is true that dependency assumptions are less restrictive with more than two lists, one still must make some kind of assumption for ruling out more complicated types of dependency between lists (e.g., the dependency between lists A and B is not influenced by whether a casualty is on list C). In addition, there is the usual statistical price of less precision—implying wider confidence intervals in the ultimate total estimate—to the extent that complicated models are required to allow for more and more complex types of dependency between lists.

An additional problem is that with more than two lists, it becomes challenging to explain the nature of the interdependency assumptions that are being invoked and to assess whether all important dependencies can be suitably captured by a statistical model, making explanations to nontechnical audiences particularly problematic. This again raises the question of how to effectively use concomitant information to support the use of a particular statistical model.

This need for simplicity and transparency suggests the possibility of focusing—initially at least—on two-list estimation by using all different combinations of two lists, accompanied by discussions of heterogeneities and dependencies, which then feed a discussion of likely lower and upper bounds for total war deaths.[20] As a simplistic illustration, we use the three lists of Peru data published in Ball et al. (2003) to obtain three two-list capture-recapture estimates (after stratifying by perpetrator) of 14,000, 56,000, and 99,000. These large differences in pairwise capture-recapture estimates immediately suggest some list dependence. The key issue, of course, is whether they reflect only pairwise dependence, meaning that a three-list estimator will be effective. Since, as noted, it is not clear how this assumption could be meaningfully assessed by means of any available covariate data, we must entertain a healthy skepticism about any three-way estimate derived from the same data. Ball et al. (2003) do use three-list estimation with stratification both by perpetrator and by geography to arrive at an estimate of 69,280 deaths with a 95 percent confidence interval of 61,007–77,552. This estimate, which is considerably higher than the approximately 24,000 deaths plus disappearances recorded by the Peruvian Truth and Reconciliation Commission, must be considered a rather bold one in the first place. It would clearly be helpful here to provide a simple explanation of the strong deviation from the lowest two-list estimate.

## The Analysis and Interpretation of Capture-Recapture Estimates of War Deaths

Even if the assumptions underlying capture-recapture estimation are reasonably well satisfied, there remain a number of thorny issues to address, including (1) an overabundance of possible models to choose from when there are many lists, (2) the need to account for all sources of error in assessing the accuracy of casualty estimates, and (3) the means of conveying the nature of the estimates to an educated public.

## MODEL SELECTION

It is important to understand that, in general, there is not a single capture-recapture model[21] but, rather, a large number of capture-recapture models with the number of available models growing substantially as the number of lists grows.[22] Moreover, different plausible models can yield extremely different estimates, and there is no clearly validated method for choosing among them. This means that the uncertainty affecting capture-recapture estimates based on more than two lists is greater than is generally understood, with most confidence intervals that have been published in the literature likely understating this uncertainty.

With two lists, we must select, in principle, from among only six models although really only one of these is useful in practice (the model that allows the probability of capture to differ between the lists but assumes list independence, as discussed earlier). With more lists, the possible model choices grow rapidly: with four lists there are potentially more than 32,000 log-linear models from which to choose (32,766, to be precise).[23] This large number of models can be reduced substantially by restricting the kinds of model considered plausible[24] and by additional restrictions, such as assuming that all dependencies higher than a certain order do not exist. The point here is not to focus on the exact number of appropriate models to assess, but to emphasize that this number grows quickly as the number of available lists increases. This growth occurs because of the number of possible list dependencies that can be included or not. For example, with only three lists—with three pairwise dependencies possible—there are seven possible ways to include these effects: allow for all three pairwise dependencies, include only two of them (there are three different ways to achieve this, depending on which pair of lists is assumed to be independent), and include only one of them (there are three different ways to do this, depending on which pair of lists is assumed to be dependent). This plethora of possibilities only gets more daunting when we have four or even more lists available.

Several problems may arise from having to select from an abundance of models. First, it is possible that total casualty estimates will vary strongly between models, even among ones that apparently describe the observed data effectively. This is illustrated in Lum et al. (2010), where the two most plausible models in estimating the total number of casualties in Casanare, Colombia, which fit the data almost equally well, differ by a factor of 3. The problem deepens when one realizes that there appear to be few or no systematic, validated techniques for choosing among such models. Averaging over a set of possible models is one way to try to approach uncertainty over what the best model is, reflecting the statistical premise that averaging a set of uncertain estimates is likely to be more reliable than choosing any specific one. York and Madigan (1992) and Madigan and York

(1997) discuss averaging across models in a Bayesian framework, and an application of this type of approach to the Casanare data is given in Lum et al. (2010).

Second, confidence intervals covering the final estimate are usually based on the assumption that the selected model is known with certainty to be correct. This is, of course, a problem in many applications of statistical modeling. The point is that the uncertainty associated with model selection is not accounted for in many reported confidence intervals, with the result that the published margins of uncertainty are too small. We shall return to this in our comments on error estimates. At the very least, it is valuable that investigators report as many potential model estimates as possible so that consumers can see the level of empirical variation associated with various model choices. A good start would be a graph akin to one generated by the Casanare data (Lum et al. 2010, figure 1), which that shows the use of various model estimates, plotted with a measure of how well they fit the data. Such creative approaches may be necessary, since with more than a few lists it is impractical to report all available estimates in a table.

HOW MANY LISTS?

We have noted immediate difficulties with the strict assumptions necessary to allow two lists to provide reasonable estimates. Three lists are better than two, at least in the sense that the independence assumption can be weakened. Does this inevitably mean that 10 lists are better than 3? From an ideal statistical viewpoint, this should still be true, and 20 lists should be even better than 10. But the ideal case assumes that all lists are equally valid and useful, and this is extremely unlikely to be true in conflict situations. What is the "right" number of lists that can support a reliable estimate? Should certain lists be combined? If so, when and under what circumstances? These are all important practical questions that require statistical input and guidance.

A potential first approach with several lists is to focus mostly on multiple two-source estimates using in each case the larger source, where one can predict the likely dependence (positive or negative) across any two sources from external information and information from statistical models. Then it would be clear that the derived estimates likely under- or overestimated the true count. With several such analyses, one might derive a likely lower or upper boundary (and uncertainty estimates on these bounds). At the very least, this kind of analysis may underpin more complex estimates, making them more readily transparent. However, in a detailed but small example, Cormack et al. (2000) found that—paradoxically—discarding the list with the highest coverage was necessary to achieve a satisfactory estimate and inference, in turn confirming that sometimes it may be better to work with a subset of available lists. The statisticians were able to identify this possibility because a gold standard total estimate was available; the challenge, of course, is to determine an appropriate strategy in the absence of any external validation. It may also be better to ignore some sources rather than pooling them, given that the relationship between a pooled constructed list and some other source may be less readily predictable than the relationships between pure sources may be.

It is simplistic to assume that all lists have equal validity. We have already noted that some lists tend to borrow heavily from each other, suggesting that combining such lists might be preferable to trying to disentangle the dependencies. Thus, having a deep understanding of the ways in which the lists are generated may be as important as trying to rely on intricate statistical models to adjust for all forms of association across lists. At some point, the marginal value of an additional list may be small in terms of improving accuracy and, given a list that is poorly constructed or intricately connected with all other sources, might even increase bias. It would be desirable to have a formal statistical procedure to decide when to pool lists and when not to attempt to add a list. A general policy for list selection and combination remains an open question.

ACCOUNTING FOR ERROR (CONFIDENCE INTERVALS)

Casualty estimates should be accompanied by an assessment of possible error, something that would at least take the form of a 95 percent confidence interval in a traditional estimate. Interpreting confidence intervals from capture-recapture estimates on the basis of repeated experimentation (frequentist inference) is somewhat problematic because it is difficult to consider an appropriate (and approximate) stochastic mechanism that truly generates the available lists. At a minimum, proper model-based confidence intervals should account for variation in estimates due to random sources of error in the discovery and de-duplication of deaths, as well as errors in matching deaths across lists and in inappropriately selected models. Currently, capture-recapture confidence intervals in the casualty estimation literature generally account for sampling error only in the discovery of deaths and not other error sources.

An alternative approach to exploring a fuller range of error sources is to simulate the impact of the various error sources on a computer, a procedure informally known as "bootstrapping." In principle, these simulations can be made reasonably transparent through the use of devices such as flowcharts that explain the computer procedures. In practice, however, realistic simulations of errors in capture-recapture estimates raise complicated issues that extend beyond the scope of this chapter.[25]

Bayesian approaches provide an alternative approach to interval estimation and have been widely studied in the context of capture-recapture methods (see e.g. Smith 1988; Madigan and York 1997; Lee et al. 2003; Ghosh and Norris 2005), These methods usually require specification of an assumed prior distribution of the casualty count; subsequently, a posterior distribution of the count is obtained, conditional on the observed data from the lists using Bayes' rule. This approach has now been applied to casualty applications (Lum et al. 2010), where, as we have noted, Bayesian averaging across models is used to combine a large number of estimates. Posterior means can be used as point estimates with credible intervals derived from the full posterior distribution.

In addition to accounting for random variation in the way lists are created, matched, and analyzed, statistical analysts must account for systematic error associated with potential violation of assumptions and model misspecification. While some of these concerns are addressed by averaging estimates across different models and assumptions, sensitivity analyses in one form or another may also be desirable. This largely boils down to sharing with readers a wide range of estimates over a variety of plausible models and assumptions, rather than just presenting one final model or one final estimate that averages over many unseen models. Confidence intervals can thus be extended into plausibility intervals in a form that accounts for both sampling and systematic errors. Achieving consistent analytic and reporting requirements is an important goal.

### TRANSPARENCY OF THE METHOD AND ASSUMPTIONS

We noted earlier that the availability of several lists not only allows more data and therefore improved absolute lower bounds, but also means that the methods make less demanding assumptions on list selection properties. On the other hand, even with as few as three lists, the assumptions underlying a proposed final count estimate are difficult to grasp. Without some level of satisfactory transparency, there is a serious risk of losing credibility. And without credibility, the whole point of an improved count is lost.

Unfortunately, accommodating errors in matching and deviations from implausible model assumptions, such as homogeneity, requires an increasing level of complexity in statistical techniques, which in turn acts against the need to be transparent. Clear description of model, model selection, error assessment, and sensitivity analyses should be reported with every analysis, although it is hard to see how these aspects can be fully assessed by anyone other than statistical experts.

### VALIDATION OF CAPTURE-RECAPTURE TECHNIQUES IN CASUALTY ESTIMATION

Four basic approaches have been developed to provide casualty counts and estimates: (i) survey methods, (ii) capture-recapture estimation, (iii) direct and indirect contemporaneous counts, and (iv) census and other demographic techniques. It is clearly helpful to have more than one method available for a specific conflict assessment, particularly when all the available methods lead to similar results. It can be just as informative, however, to use methods yielding divergent results that highlight the need to examine the assumptions and data on which each method depends, for then it becomes possible to determine and evaluate the conditions that may, with some approaches, produce questionable results. It is crucial, therefore, to look at comparisons of the spectrum of techniques as much as possible.

Currently, the most direct comparisons are available for Kosovo, where there are three principal sources of casualty information: (i) the post-conflict survey of Spiegel and Salama (2000) (i.e., method i in the preceding paragraph), (ii) the capture-recapture estimates from the report by ABA/CEELI (2002) (method ii), and (iii) the more recent and less publicized work of the Humanitarian Law Center called the Kosovo Memory Book (method iii).[26] The latter is an attempt to provide an exhaustive list of all Kosovo victims from the relevant time period, with some basic information provided for each victim.

There is insufficient space here to do justice to a full comparison of the results of each of these methods in Kosovo, an analysis described in our 2011 (unpublished) paper entitled "Cross Validation of Three Methods for Measuring War Deaths" (Spagat et al. 2011). In brief, there is considerable consistency between the three approaches. It is hardest to compare the results of the two other approaches with the estimate of ABA/CEELI (2002), since the latter covers a much shorter time period (albeit the most violent months), and does not provide estimated counts by age. For the time period March–June 1999, ABA/CEELI (2002) estimates 10,356 deaths with a 95 percent confidence interval of 9,002 to 12,122 (based on 4,400 unique named deaths from four lists). For this same period, the Humanitarian Law Center list yields 9,030 "murders" with a further 1,200 "missing." The two methods provide similar quantitative results even if we assume that all missing people are still alive.

The Spiegel and Salama (2000) survey estimates 12,000 deaths due to "war-related trauma" between February 1998 and June 1999 with a 95 percent confidence interval of 5,500 to 18,300. This is comparable to counts by the Humanitarian Law Center list of 11,401 "murders" and 1,567 "missing" for the same time period. These two sources also confirm a general age distribution pattern, with the elderly facing a far higher risk of death than young adults. In addition, the monthly time series for the two methods track each other generally although, of course, there are far larger margin of errors associated with these disaggregated data.

In summary, all three methods emerge with credit and validate the other techniques in turn. Overall, this example appears to be a particularly favorable case for capture-recapture estimation in that the different lists used appear to be quite consistent with one another except in locality, and heterogeneity in the latter survey was also accommodated through geographical stratification. This suggests that the necessary assumptions and selected models are reasonable in this case.

Other opportunities for comparison of the alternative estimation techniques occur in Peru, where Ball et al. (2003) used national census data from 1981 and 1993 to contrast a capture-recapture casualty estimate for the Department of Ayacucho with demographic calculations of the amount of excess mortality (Ayacucho being the region of Peru most affected by armed internal conflict). A description of the comparison (available in appendix 2 of Ball et al. 2003) indicates that the excess deaths estimate exceeds the capture-recapture estimate of violent deaths by 30 percent, taken there as tending to confirm the capture-recapture estimate. However, the general similarity of the estimates is not particularly compelling because the ratio of excess deaths to violent deaths ranges between 1 and 17 in thirteen conflicts assembled in the Geneva Declaration (2008, 40) so that the specific analysis serves principally to illustrate a generally accepted pattern.

Finally, Silva and Ball (2008) discuss similar results obtained from a retrospective mortality survey (16,000 deaths plus or minus 4,400) in East Timor and from a survey that used a two-list capture-recapture estimate (18,600 deaths plus or minus 1,000), providing some mutual validation for the two techniques.

## Challenges for the Future

### ADDITIONAL DATA

Currently capture-recapture estimation for casualty counts has essentially adapted techniques from other applications in wildlife, ecology, and public health. However, casualty lists do not reflect capture-recapture in their creation and are often constructed contemporaneously. While we have noted several issues involving this distinction as it relates to assumptions, attempts to collect and exploit additional information pertaining to the development of casualty lists might prove to be very useful. A key feature of some casualty applications is that being named on a list reflects an event in time separate from the occurrence of the casualty. Although as yet, we have not seen this information widely exploited, we recognize that there will be inevitable errors in reporting dates or substantial levels of missing information.[27] We note that the time between the occurrence of an event and the recording of the associated casualty is likely to be a random variable whose distribution varies from list to list, and even within a specific list. That this distribution is not consistent and is unlikely to be known a priori means that techniques from infectious disease incidence counting—like back-calculation—cannot be implemented here. Nevertheless reporting delays might usefully be recorded when possible and used to characterize lists at the very least.

### SIMULATION AND TEST-BED METHODS

In infectious disease research, both deterministic and stochastic explanatory models based on complex systems of differential equations have played a major role in exploring the properties of epidemics and interventions to change their course. Such models provide the basis for effective simulations that allow an investigator to quantify the sensitivity of estimated incidence patterns to input parameter assumptions, and to compare various approaches to intervention. With casualty reporting and counting, it would be extraordinarily helpful to have analogues of such models to compare estimation techniques in cases in which the true processes and counts are known. In addition, "test-bed" datasets created from such models may provide valuable insights into the sensitivity of estimation methods to particular assumptions or characteristics of how the data have been imperfectly generated from underlying events. In developing such models, perhaps using ideas from agent-based modeling (Bonabeau 2002), it is necessary to simulate the development of a conflict and various sources of casualties and also to simulate the various methods of data collection that reflect the vagaries of discovery/reporting of these casualties. The processes generating casualty events may or may not be linked to those generating the data/lists. Simulations based on these models would permit sensitivity analyses in various forms. The act of creating such explanatory models in itself raises interesting questions in that, in some explanatory models, rapid increases in casualties may tend to be sustained or, on the other hand, may lead to sudden drops in counts (in some cases, the deaths of certain key individuals cause a decline in further deaths). For further provocative reading in this regard, see Epstein (2006) and Williams (2007).

DATA AND SOFTWARE

For statistical methods to be fully developed and validated in the area of casualty counting, two additional factors are important. First, there is need for existing datasets to be made widely available, allowing for redaction and protection of individual identification where necessary. While these changes may no longer allow other investigators to fully recreate the issues involved in matching lists, having the raw data will still provide opportunities to validate various estimation approaches, strategies for model selection, and error estimation and sensitivity analyses. The availability of casualty data from Kosovo, Sierra Leone, Timor-Leste, Liberia, and Casanare from links on the Benetech data page[28] is an important step in this direction. While having summary data is of value, the more detail that can be provided the better, as more detail allows for more nuanced validation of methods.

On a related issue, it is imperative that available open-source software be made available to apply capture-recapture estimation in the casualty setting. Within R, the Rcapture package provides routines for capture-recapture estimation based on the log-linear modeling approach (Baillargeon and Rivest 2007), although to allow for wider use in this setting, it would be helpful to have the methods and documentation more directly related to casualty estimation.

## Recommendations

Finally, we provide a simple list of practical suggestions for future capture-recapture estimates of war deaths.

1. Think about the purpose of estimating war deaths in the first place and whether it might be preferable simply to give a good lower, and perhaps an upper, bound on the number of war deaths. If, for example, the purpose is to support legal prosecutions, then well-documented lower bounds are probably more valuable than count estimates.

2. Presentations of capture-recapture estimates must make a case that it is reasonable to treat lists as amenable to modeling as well-behaved probability samples with appropriate assumptions to address observed or known list heterogeneity and dependence.

3. If stratification is meant to address departures from random selection of deaths onto lists (heterogeneity), then the stratification scheme must be based on the appropriate sources of heterogeneity. Again, the best possible case must be made that, within each stratum, the cross-tabulated list counts can be modeled appropriately.

4. Gather as much information as possible on how each list has been constructed and provide readers with a detailed write-up on the nature of each list.

5. Consider the likely dependencies among lists (i.e., the extent to which the appearance of a death on one list raises or lowers the probability that this death will appear on other lists). Analyze the impact these dependencies are likely to have on estimates.

6. Publish a list of two-list estimates for all pairs of lists (three estimates with three lists, six with four lists, etc.), using appropriate stratification if necessary. These pairings will help identify both dependencies between lists and departures from the simplest homogeneity assumptions; moreover, they may be used to establish initial lower, and possibly upper, bounds. Considerable emphasis should be placed on these two-way estimates because they are much easier to understand and interpret than are estimates based on three or more lists.[29] This analysis will also aid in the interpretation of more complex estimates.

7. Make matching as transparent as possible. At a minimum, provide a large random sample of several categories of matches and non-matches (e.g., matches considered definitive, matches considered likely).

## Discussion

Statistical ideas and estimation methods have provided extraordinary tools for various applications in the social sciences. Having said this, we note as well that not every statistical tool can be implemented immediately for a specific application. The recent past has seen a burgeoning use of capture-recapture estimation as part of the development of a science of casualty counting. The assumptions are certainly open to scrutiny in general and in each specific application. While it is true that the assumptions underpinning any statistical model are never satisfied in a strict sense, it is important in this sensitive area that there be reasonable alignment of theory and reality. Given the intense political and media interest in reported casualty estimates, it is crucial that statisticians agree that any assumptions produce results that are robust to plausible violations. Estimates must be reported with full acknowledgment of the shortcomings or difficulties associated with uncertainty; the preparation of such documents is challenging because of the difficulty of translating the language of statistics into terms usable in the political arena or in standard media reporting. It is important to be aware of the tension between the need for statistical rigor and accuracy and the particular uses that are made of estimates. In many situations, it may be best to never report a single number or point estimate.

Inevitably, the marginal value of a capture-recapture estimate is lessened when other counts or estimates are available to validate the capture-recapture results, since this essentially means that the same information is available from other sources. Even so, the scientific importance of validation should not be underestimated. Capture-recapture estimates alone are potentially valuable, but it is unclear how much weight should be placed on them without validation by other approaches. It is similarly unclear how much we can depend on capture-recapture estimates when these disagree widely with estimates based on other methods. Certainly, capture-recapture estimates that greatly exceed the counts of documented deaths from the combined underlying lists should be scrutinized with particular care. Ironically, estimates that differ strongly from documented counts are precisely the cases for which capture-recapture estimation potentially has the most to offer.

Many casualty lists are created by parties with personal or political views that may influence the way lists are created, manipulated, and analyzed. This matter is of particular concern because independent statistical investigators may not be aware of decisions, taken early in a data-collection process, that have the potential to bias the results. It is a challenge to deal with the role of personal convictions in any statistical analysis, and particularly the estimation and reporting of casualty counts. Fundamental requirements for credibility are wide availability of the data, as well as transparency in all decisions relating to the lists' creation, matching, and statistical analysis. To the greatest extent possible, casualty data should be analyzed by independent statistical investigators.

We reiterate that casualty counting fundamentally differs from many traditional applications of capture-recapture in that the lists are far from being designed probability samples of the total number of casualties. All such estimates, therefore, should be treated with an appropriate level of skepticism. However, it is inevitable that people will keep creating such lists during conflicts for a variety of valid reasons, and that the lists will then be exploited to provide more complete estimates in multiple ways. In addition, other methods for counting casualties face serious statistical challenges, and there is no method that is clearly best for all circumstances. A determination to count casualties pushes us to search for approaches that seek to both minimize assumptions and data problems and maximize validity, rather than attempting to generate perfect numbers.

ACKNOWLEDGMENTS

The authors thank the following individuals for comments on earlier drafts of this chapter: Patrick Ball, David Banks, Josh Dougherty, Baruch Fischhoff, Ernest Hook, Daniel Manrique-Vallier, Megan Price, Nigel Q uinney, and Romesh Silva. Their feedback was enormously helpful and we are deeply appreciative; of course, any errors that remain are our responsibility.

REFERENCES

Aaron, Deborah J., et al. 2003. "Estimating the Lesbian Population: A Capture-Recapture Approach." *Journal of Epidemiological Community Health* 57: 207–209.

ABA/CEELI. 2002. *Killings and Refugee Flow in Kosova/Kosovo, March–June 1999: A Report to the International Criminal Tribunal for the Former Yugoslavia.* Washington, DC: American Association for the Advancement of Science/American Bar Association Central and East European Law Initiative.

Amoros, Emmanuelle, et al. 2008. "Actual Incidences of Road Casualties, and Their Injury Severity, Modeled from Police and Hospital Data, France." *European Journal of Public Health* 18: 360–365.

Andreas, Peter, and Kelly M. Greenhill. 2010. "Introduction: The Politics of Numbers," in *Sex, Drugs, and Body Counts. The Politics of Numbers in Global Crime and Conflict.* Edited by Peter Andreas and Kelly M Greenhill, pp. 1–22. Ithaca, NY: Cornell University Press.

Baillargeon, Sophie, and Louis-Paul Rivest. 2007. "Rcapture: Loglinear Models for Capture-Recapture in R." *Journal of Statistical Software* 19: 1–31.

Ball, Patrick. 1999. "Making the Case: Investigating Large-Scale Human Rights Violations Using Information Systems and Data Analysis." *Report for the Guatemalan Commission for Historical Clarification.* At: http://shr.aaas.org/mtc/chap11.html.

Ball, Patrick. 2003. "Using Multiple System Estimation to Assess Mass Human Rights Violations: The Cases of Political Killings in Guatemala and Kosovo." *Proceedings of the International Statistical Institute*, 54th session, Berlin.

Ball, Patrick, and Jana Asher. 2002. "Statistics and Slobodan: Using Data Analysis and Statistics in the War Crimes Trial of President Milošević." *Chance* 15: 17–24.

Ball, Patrick, et al. 2003. *How Many Peruvians Have Died? An Estimate of the Total Number of Victims Killed or Disappeared in the Armed Internal Conflict between 1980 and 2000.* Report to the Peruvian Truth and Reconciliation Commission (CVR). Washington, DC: American Association for the Advancement of Science. Also published as Anexo 2 (Anexo Estadístico) of CVR Report.

Bishop, Yvonne M., Stephen E. Fienberg, and Paul W. Holland. 1975. *Discrete Multivariate Analysis: Theory and Practice.* Cambridge, MA: MIT Press, reprinted in 2007 by New York: Springer-Verlag.

Böhning, Dankmar. 2008. "Editorial—Recent Developments in Capture-Recapture Methods and Their Applications." *Biometrical Journal* 6: 954–956.

———, and Peter G. M. van der Heijden. 2009. "A Covariate Adjustment for Zero-Truncated Approaches to Estimating the Size of Hidden and Elusive Populations." *Annals of Applied Statistics* 3: 595–610.

Bonabeau, Eric. 2002. "Agent-Based Modeling: Methods and Techniques for Simulating Human Systems." *Proceedings of the National Academy of Sciences* 99: 7280–7287.

Brunborg, Helge, Torkild Hovde Lyngstad, and Henrik Urdal. 2006. "Accounting for Genocide: How Many Were Killed in Srebrenica?" In *The Demography of Armed Conflict*, edited by Helge Brunborg, Torkild Hovde Lyngstad, and Henrik Urdal. Dordrecht, The Netherlands: Springer.

Buckland, Stephen T., and Paul H. Garthwaite. 1991. "Quantifying Precision of Mark-Recapture Estimates Using the Bootstrap and Related Methods." *Biometrics* 47: 255–268.

Caldwell, Betsy L., Phillip J. Smith, and Andrew L. Baughman. 2005. "Methods for Capture-Recapture Analysis When Cases Lack Personal Identifiers." *Statistics in Medicine* 24: 2041–2051.

Chao, Anne, et al. 2001. "The Applications of Capture-Recapture Models to Epidemiological Data." *Statistics in Medicine* 20: 3123–3157.

Cormack, Richard M., Yeu-fang Chang, and Gordon S. Smith. 2000. "Estimating Deaths from Industrial Injury by Capture-Recapture: A Cautionary Tale." *International Journal of Epidemiology* 29: 1053–1059.

Coull, Brent A., and Alan Agresti. 1999. "The Use of Mixed Logit Models to Reflect Heterogeneity in Capture-Recapture Studies." *Biometrics* 55: 294–301.

Da-Silva, Cibele Q. 2009. "Bayesian Analysis to Correct False-Negative Errors in Capture-Recapture Photo-ID Abundance Estimates." *Brazilian Journal of Probability and Statistics* 23: 36–48.

Desenclos, Jean-Claude, and Bruno Hubert. 1994. "Limitations to the Universal Use of Capture-Recapture Methods." *International Journal of Epidemiology* 23: 1322–1323.

Epstein, Joshua M. 2006. *Generative Social Science: Studies in Agent-Based Computational Modeling*, Princeton Studies in Complexity Series. Princeton, NJ: Princeton University Press.

Fienberg, Stephen E., and Daniel Manrique-Vallier. 2009. "Integrated Methodology for Multiple Systems Estimation and Record Linkage Using a Missing Data Formulation." *Advances in Statistical Analysis* 93: 49–60.

Ghosh, Sujit K., and James L. Norris. 2005. "Bayesian Capture-Recapture Analysis and Model Selection Allowing for Heterogeneity and Behavioral Effects." *Journal of Agricultural and Biological Environmental Statistics* 10: 35–49.

Geneva Declaration. 2008. *Global Burden of Armed Violence.*

Gohdes, Anita. 2010. "Different Convenience Samples, Different Stories: The Case of Sierra Leone." The Human Rights Data Analysis Group at Benetech. At: http://www.hrdag.org/resources/publications/Gohdes_Convenience%20Samples.pdf

Harrison, Mark J., et al. 2006. "Prevalence of Autistic Spectrum Disorders in Lothian, Scotland: An Estimate Using the "Capture-Recapture" Technique." *Archives of Disease in Childhood* 91: 16–19.

Hook, Ernest B., and Ronald R. Regal. 1995. "Capture-Recapture Methods in Epidemiology: Methods and Limitations." *Epidemiologic Reviews* 17: 243–264.

——, and Ronald R. Regal. 1997. "Validity of Methods for Model Selection, Weighting for Model Selection, and Small Sample Adjustment in Capture-Recapture Estimation." *American Journal of Epidemiology* 145: 1138–1144.

Hope, Vivian D., Matthew Hickman, and Kate Tilling. 2005. "Capturing Crack Cocaine Use: Estimating the Prevalence of Crack Cocaine Use in London Using Capture-Recapture with Covariates." *Addiction* 100: 1701–1708.

International Working Group for Disease Monitoring and Forecasting. 1995a. "Capture-Recapture and Multiple-Record Systems Estimation I: History and Theoretical Development." *American Journal of Epidemiology* 142: 1047–1058.

——. 1995b. "Capture-Recapture and Multiple-Record Systems Estimation II: Applications in Human Diseases." *American Journal of Epidemiology* 142: 1059–1068.

Landman, Todd. 2006. *Studying Human Rights*. London: Routledge.

Laska, Eugene M., et al. 2003. "Estimating Population Size and Duplication Rates When Records Cannot Be Linked." *Statistics in Medicine* 22: 3403–3417.

Lee, Alan J., et al. 2001. "Capture-Recapture, Epidemiology, and List Mismatches: Several Lists." *Biometrics* 57: 707–713.

Lee, Shen-ming, Wen-han Hwang, and Li-hui Huang. 2003. "Bayes Estimation of Population Size from Capture-Recapture Models with Time Variation and Behavior Response." *Statistica Sinica* 13: 477–494.

Lum, Kristian, et al. 2010. "Measuring Elusive Populations with Bayesian Model Averaging for Multiple Systems Estimation: A Case Study on Lethal Violations in Casanare, 1998–2007." *Statistics, Politics, and Policy* 1, 2.

Madigan, David, and Jeremy C. York. 1997. "Bayesian Methods for Estimation of the Size of a Closed Population." *Biometrika* 84: 19–31.

Manrique-Vallier, Daniel, and Stephen E. Fienberg. 2008. "Population Size Estimation Using Individual Level Mixture Models." *Biometrical Journal* 50(6): 1051–1063.

Murphy, Joe. 2009. "Estimating the World Trade Center Tower Population on September 11, 2001: A Capture-Recapture Approach." *American Journal of Public Health* 99: 65–67.

———, et al. 2007. "Measuring and Maximizing Coverage in the World Trade Center Health Registry." *Statistics in Medicine* 26: 1688–1701.

Papoz, Laure, Beverley Balkau, and Lellouch, Joseph. 1996. "Case Counting in Epidemiology: Limitations of Methods Based on Multiple Data Sources." *International Journal of Epidemiology* 25: 474–478.

Silva, Romesh, and Patrick Ball. 2008. "The Demography of Conflict-Related Mortality in Timor-Leste (1974–1999): Reflections on Empirical Quantitative Measurement of Civilian Killings, Disappearances, and Famine-Related Deaths." edited by Jana Asher et al., *Statistical Methods for Human Rights*, pp. 117–140. New York: Springer.

Smith, Phillip J. 1988. "Bayesian Methods for Multiple Capture-Recapture Surveys," *Biometrics* 44: 1177–1189.

Spagat, Michael, et al. 2011 "Cross Validation of Three Methods for Measuring War Deaths."

Spiegel, Paul B., and Peter Salama. 2000. "War and Mortality in Kosovo, 1998–99: An Epidemiological Testimony." *The Lancet* 355: 2204–2209.

Tancredi, Andrea. 2009. "Bayesian Approaches to Matching and Size Population Problems: A Unified Framework." Paper presented at conference at the Politecnico di Milano. At: www2.mate.polimi.it/convegni/viewpaper.php?id=155&print=1&cf=7.

Tancredi, Andrea. 2010. "Capture-Recapture Models with Matching Uncertainty." Paper presented at the 2010 meeting of the Italian Statistical Society (SIS) in Padua. At: homes.stat.unipd.it/mgri/SIS2010/Program/18-SSXVIII_Luzi/817-1504-1-DR.pdf.

Tilling, Kate. 2001. "Capture-Recapture Methods—Useful or Misleading." *International Journal of Epidemiology* 30: 12–14.

Williams, Mark. 2007. "Artificial Societies and Virtual Violence." *Technology Review* 110(4): 74–76. At: http://www.technologyreview.com/Infotech/18880/.

York, Jeremy. C., and David Madigan. 1992. "Bayesian Methods for Estimating the Size of a Closed Population." Technical Report 234. University of Washington.

Zwierzchowski, Jan, and Ewa Tabeau. M. 2010. "Census-Based Multiple System Estimation as an Unbiased Method of Estimation of Casualties' Undercount." Paper for the European Population Conference. At: http://epc2010.princeton.edu/download.aspx?submissionId=100880.

NOTES

1. The standard estimate is the product of the two catch sizes divided by the number of twice-captured fish.

2. We feel obliged to also point out that none of us have been involved directly in any of the referenced analyses and so are not in a position to comment in detail on any specific case beyond what has been provided in published reports.

3. With only one list, extremely strong and unverifiable assumptions are required to extrapolate meaningfully from who is on a single list to who is not on the list (Böhning and van der Heijden 2009).

4. We note here that this strict homogeneity assumption is a sufficient condition for capture-recapture estimation to be effective. It is not necessary, as even with two lists, for example, it is possible to accommodate heterogeneity in one list if there is perfect homogeneity in the other. In addition, it is possible to have selection heterogeneity in both lists and still produce unbiased capture-recapture estimates if the heterogeneity in one list intersects with that of the other in a mathematically elegant way; however, such advantageous circumstances are unlikely to occur in practice with list creation processes.

5. This is most easily seen by considering a simple example: suppose casualties are equally split between two (unobserved) types, the first of which is always observed in each of two lists, whereas the second type is selected for each list only 50 percent of the time on average. Then, if the two lists are assembled independently by random sampling that reflects these selection properties, the probability of a random casualty being on both lists is 5/8, whereas the probability of being on either list separately is 3/4. Thus, given that type is unobserved, appearance on the two lists is not independent. The dependence between the two lists occurs even though the lists were sampled independently, with the association induced by the heterogeneity of selection probabilities across the two types that is correlated between the two lists. The cross-tabulation of list counts does not provide sufficient information to distinguish between selection heterogeneity and dependence between the list construction processes.

6. Even names might not be useful in matching in, for example, Sikh areas where normally men are named Singh and women are named Kaur.

7. There is a substantial amount of other literature on dealing with matching uncertainty including Lee et al. (2001), Tancredi (2009, 2010), and da-Silva (2009).

8. As noted earlier, and discussed in further detail later in the chapter, these assumptions can be substantially weakened when there are multiple lists ($k > 2$).

9. Landman (2006) writes: "The key difference between the statistical estimation used in public opinion research and MSE [capture-recapture] is that where public opinion research uses random samples of the population, MSE uses multiple non-random samples of the population. Both forms of analysis produce statistical estimates with associated margins of error, . . ." Material posted on the Benetech website (http://hrdag.org/resources/mult_systems_est.shtml) also seems to embody the misperception that capture-recapture necessarily transforms "convenience samples" into good statistical estimates.

10. For example, as Patrick Ball testified before the International Criminal Tribunal for the former Yugoslavia, "the purpose of multiple systems estimation is to determine, given a number of independent sources of information, [comma added for clarity] what might be missing from them. The reason one would do this is that the information that is missing could be in some way systematically different from the . . . data which is known" (ABA/CEELI 2002, 10223).

11. "Capture-recapture methodology has to make an untestable act of faith that in some respect missing individuals resemble listed ones. . . . It may be that the value of multiple lists lies less in the provision of a numerical estimate of population size, more in identifying when substantial undercounting exists, and prompting investigation of possible causes" (Cormack et al. 2000). Bishop et al. also note that the capture-recapture approach can sometimes be misleading "since we are assuming that the model which describes the observed data also describes the count of the unobserved individuals. We have no way to check this assumption" (1975, 254).

12. In fact, approximately 10 percent of the victims both on and off each list used in the estimation should be female if the coverage and simplest homogeneity assumptions of capture-recapture estimation are to be satisfied.

13. Usually, the necessary estimation procedures are couched in terms of log-linear models applied to cross-tabulation of casualties across the available lists (Bishop et al. 1975).

14. See, for example, the work in Guatemala, Peru, and Colombia (Ball 1999; Ball et al. 2003; Lum et al. 2010).

15. In the general case in which statistical modeling can potentially address complex heterogeneity, it may still be easier to support the modeling within strata as preferable to aggregate modeling.

16. Again, this is usually approached through log-linear modeling.

17. We return briefly to this point in the section entitled "Analysis and Interpretation of Capture-Recapture Estimates of War Deaths."

18. In an alternative mixture approach to casualty counts Manrique-Vallier and Fienberg (2008), suggested the use of the method of latent classes, in which individual casualties are allowed to belong partially to all classes. The broader statistical literature uses the term "grade of membership" to describe such models.

19. Usually, the necessary estimation procedures are couched in terms of log-linear models applied to cross-tabulation of casualties across the available lists (Bishop et al. 1975).

20. In doing so, we emphasize that that no single estimate based solely on two lists is likely to be defensible or reliable taken on its own, even if used only to create an upper or lower bound. The combination of all possible two-list estimates must be considered in its entirety, and in light of external knowledge about list construction and estimates based on more complex modeling.

21. For simplicity here, our remarks refer to the use of log-linear models, although the issues are broadly applicable to all modeling strategies.

22. Of course, an advantage of the expanded choice of models is the potential ability to accommodate more complexity in list relationships and heterogeneity in list selection probabilities.

23. Lum et al. (2010) use 15 different casualty lists in Casanare, allowing potential consideration of 2 raised to the $(2^{15} - 1)$th power models (less 2 if we always exclude the log-linear model with only the intercept, and the saturated model. which is overdetermined as noted earlier)— this formula corrects a minor typographical error found there.

24. For example, the number of models can be reduced by considering only hierarchical log-linear models.

25. See, for example, Buckland and Garthwaite (1991), Coull and Agresti (1999), and Amoros et al. (2008).

26. www.hlc-rdc.org/index.php?lid=en&;show=kosovo&action=search&str_stanje=1.

27. The Iraq Body Count records this delay and has used the information to address the incompleteness of their counts in that if a great many casualties were missing from their list, occasionally the media would uncover casualties some time after the deaths occurred; in fact, to give just one example, virtually 100 percent of all recorded car bombings were reported to the media within 24 hours.

28. www.hrdag.org/resources/data_software.shtml.

29. The availability of a third list allows, of course, an empirical assessment of pairwise list dependency that may support external knowledge of list relationships. This is more complicated when four or more lists are available but still worth pursuing insofar as it can add insight into the validity of any specific two-list estimate.

## 11 A Review of Estimation Methods for Victims of the Bosnian War and the Khmer Rouge Regime

Ewa Tabeau and Jan Zwierzchowski

## Introduction

Demography is the scientific, predominantly statistical, study of human populations, including their size, composition, distribution, density, and growth, as well as the causes and socioeconomic consequences of changes in these factors.[1] The demography of war is a recently established subfield that entails research into victimization patterns, causes, and consequences of war (Brunborg 2006). In this chapter we discuss the use of demographic methods to estimate casualties for two past conflicts: the 1992–1995 war in Bosnia-Herzegovina (BH) and the 1975–1979 Khmer Rouge regime (KR) in Cambodia.[2] Differences between the two conflicts make them useful case studies. We also hope our expertise in these conflicts is a basis for a meaningful comparison; we studied the BH war as affiliates of the International Criminal Tribunal for the former Yugoslavia (ICTY) and members of the Demographic Unit (DU), Office of the Prosecutor (OTP). The study of Cambodia was made in 2009 at request of the Khmer Rouge Tribunal in Phnom Penh.[3]

The first episode was a recent conflict in the heart of Europe that ended the socialist era in the former Yugoslavia and led to the disintegration of the country (Becker 1986); the second, more distant in time, was a rapid attempt by the local political faction of Khmer Rouge in Cambodia to introduce an extreme form of agrarian socialism in one of the poorest Southeast Asian societies (Kiernan 1996; Chandler 2008). The duration of the conflict episodes was about four years in each case. The population size in Bosnia-Herzegovina was slightly more than half that in Cambodia at the outbreak of the Khmer Rouge regime, thus not fundamentally different. The numbers of victims estimated for each episode are very different: 100,000 in Bosnia-Herzegovina and about 2 million in Cambodia. Also, the methods of victim estimation were significantly different in these two cases. We offer a brief overview of the methods and sources used for Bosnia-Herzegovina and Cambodia and explain the major reasons for these differences. Among the estimates for the BH war, we present our latest (2010) estimate of the death toll (produced under the auspices of the ICTY and hereafter referred to as "ICTY estimate"). We also suggest the most reliable methods for making such estimates and justify our choices.

## An Overview of the Estimates of Victims of the 1992–1995 War in Bosnia and Herzegovina

At the outbreak of the 1992–1995 war, Bosnia-Herzegovina had a relatively well-developed statistical system for registering vital events and for collecting other information about the population.[4] A census of the population was conducted every 10 years; the last one took place in March 1991, just before the war started; thus there was a good peacetime information system that could be used to supply data about Bosnia-Herzegovina's population size and basic demographic distribution, as well as on Bosnians' socioeconomic status, education, employment characteristics, ethnicity, religion, language, and so on, and about the scale of natural mortality and its causes.[5] Before the war, the BH statistical authority systematically published standard tabulations of data on such categories as population, agriculture, industry, and housing. By every measure, at the outbreak of the 1992–1995 war Bosnia-Herzegovina was a country perfectly familiar with the requirements and standard procedures of data collection, processing, publication, and dissemination.

The war disrupted the usual statistical practices, destroying many documents, including records of vital events; moreover, the belligerents' front lines divided the country into territories inaccessible to parties to the conflict. The war introduced chaos, terror, and combat, which led to massive population movements, high numbers of persons killed or disappeared, and breakdown of the mechanisms that normally make death notifications available to a nation's statistical authority. Therefore, professional statistical sources on war victims cannot be easily found; alternative sources were compiled during and after the war but were often made by nonprofessionals who had clear political biases.

The discussion of the total number of victims of the war in Bosnia-Herzegovina started during the war and has continued until the present. Estimates presented by various authors range from about 25,000 to 329,000 excess deaths (table 11.1). As we will demonstrate, careful analysis shows that most of the estimates produced so far are not scientifically valid and should be viewed with skepticism. This lack of meaningful results is of course due partly to the lack of reliable sources of information; but it is also due to the nontransparent, nonrigorous methodological approaches applied to produce the estimates. To explain these points, we collected several estimates published between 1995 and 2010 and made an overview of their numerical values and methodological foundations. Among the existing estimates, we included our own 2005 ICTY estimate, as well as its update of February 2010.

We initially distinguished between two groups of estimates: those made in Bosnia or Croatia, and those made outside the region of the former Yugoslavia (Tabeau and Bijak 2005). In this chapter, we discuss all estimates jointly, focusing on data and methodology problems rather than political bias.[6] Table 11.1 lists the authors and the values of the estimates of excess deaths in the 1992–1995 war in Bosnia and Herzegovina. Figure 11.1 presents the estimates graphically.

## Initial Estimates of Victims from Bosnia-Herzegovina

The earliest estimated death toll in Bosnia and Herzegovina, 200,000 victims, was presented in 1995 by Cherif Bassiouni, a professor of law at DePaul University and president of the International Human Rights Law Institute. In 1993, he was appointed chairman of the UN Commission of Experts investigating war crimes in the former Yugoslavia, and in particular in Bosnia and Herzegovina. The commission, which operated until the end of April 1994, collected documents and searched for and visited mass graves; its members also visited detention or concentration camps, interviewed witnesses, and collected other information about casualties and various war crimes.[7] Bassiouni (1995) concluded his analysis of the data by mid-1995, when he issued his final report and testified before the U.S. Congress's Commission on Security and Cooperation in Europe. The estimate of 200,000 deaths covered all types of victims in Bosnia-Herzegovina in 1992–1995. The number (clearly high) was in use in the last stage of the war and in the years thereafter. It became an official number of the BH government.

Regarding its methodological and source basis, the approach of the commission was predominantly qualitative, being based on witness statements, reports of international monitors and of local authorities, research reports, visits to the war-affected area, and similar sources. It was thus based on summary statistics on killings and missing persons reported in the many sources the investigators were able to collect, rather than on personal records of victims. It is unlikely that Bassiouni's commission was able to establish individual-level statistical databases and check the individual death records for reliability and uniqueness. The lack of such databases hampers any scientific discussion of the validity of this estimate.

George Kenney, who resigned from the U.S. Department of State in protest over American policy on Bosnia and Herzegovina, also produced an estimate of excess mortality in 1995. In clear contrast to Bassiouni (1995), he believed the 1992–1995 conflict-related death toll in Bosnia-Herzegovina was between 25,000 and 60,000. The sources he used for his estimate included information from the International Committee of the Red Cross (ICRC), the CIA, the State Department Bureau of Intelligence and Research, European military intelligence officers, and relief workers; he believed the sources were reliable. His approach is qualitative, but details on the method and on his sources have not been published.

TABLE 11.1.

Overview of Major Estimates of Death Toll in Bosnia-Herzegovina, 1992–1995

| Victim Categories | Bassiouni (1995) | Kenney (1995) | IPH (1996a) | IPH (1996b) | Prašo (1996) | Bošnjović and Smajkić (1997) | Žerjavić (1998) | Bošnjović (1999) | Tabeau and Bijak (2005) | Tokača (2007) | Obermeyer et al. (2008) | Zwierzchowski and Tabeau (2010) |
|---|---|---|---|---|---|---|---|---|---|---|---|---|
| Killed and disappeared | 200,000 | 42,500 | 156,824 | 278,800 | 329,000 | 258,000 | 220,000 | 252,200 | 102,622 | 97,207 | 176,000 | 104,732 |
| Muslims | NA | NA | NA | 140,800 | 218,000 | 138,800 | 160,000 | 153,000 | 69,874 | 64,036 | NA | 68,101 |
| Croats | NA | NA | NA | 28,400 | 21,000 | 19,600 | 30,000 | 31,000 | 8,554 | 7,788 | NA | 8,858 |
| Serbs | NA | NA | NA | 97,300 | 83,000 | 89,300 | 25,000 | 72,000 | 19,211 | 24,905 | NA | 22,779 |
| Others | NA | NA | NA | 12,300 | 7,000 | 10,300 | 5,000 | 14,000 | 4,983 | 478 | NA | 4,995 |
| Total number of victims | 200,000 | 42,500 | 156,824 | 278,800 | 329,000 | 258,000 | 220,000 | 270,000 | 102,622 | 97,207 | 176,000 | 104,732 |

*Notes:* NA = not available.
(1) All estimates cover the period from April 1992 to December 1995.
(2) All estimates *presumably* include both civilians and soldiers.
(3) IPH stands for the Institute for Public Health in Sarajevo.
(4) Kenney's (1995) figure of 42,500 war deaths is an average of the two ends of his original interval.
(5) Bošnjović (1999) reported another 17,800 other excess deaths (included in his ethnic figures) in addition to those killed and disappeared.
(6) "Other excess deaths" should be interpreted as indirect war victims, that is, people who died *mainly* as a result of diseases and severe living conditions during the war.
(7) Tokača's (2009) reported ethnic structure is as in his 2007 estimate.

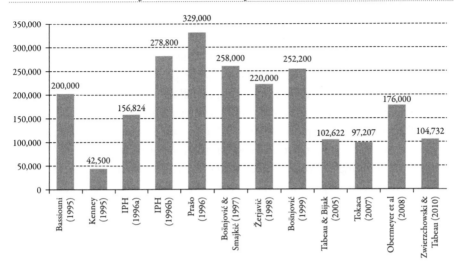

FIGURE 11.1 Overview of Major Estimates of Death Toll in Bosnia-Herzegovina, 1992–1995

Between 1996 and 1999, several organizations and individuals produced a wide range of estimates that lacked scientific validity, most notably because no detailed description of the methods used was ever provided: see the Bosnia-Herzegovina Institute for Public Health (IPH) in Sarajevo (IPH 1996a,1996b; Prašo 1996; Bošnjović and Smajkić 1997; Zerjavić 1998; Bošnjović 1999).[8] Interestingly, all these estimates were based on the same source, namely, wartime weekly reports of the Institute for Public Health in Sarajevo. It is important to note that this BH governmental institute was active throughout the war years, collecting systematic reports from municipalities in Bosnia and Herzegovina controlled by Muslim or Croat forces; the Serb-controlled areas were not covered. Thus, reporting may be biased toward Muslim victims. Furthermore, since personal details were not collected, only aggregate numbers, the IPH statistics are likely to include duplicates.

## Recent Estimates of Victims from Bosnia-Herzegovina

In recent years, several death toll estimates have been produced based on a better foundation than the early estimates. Tabeau and Bijak (2005), Tokača (2007), Obermeyer et al. (2008), and Zwierzchowski and Tabeau (2010) proposed approaches that in terms of sources and methods can be seen as far more reliable and better justified than the earlier attempts.

### EMPIRICAL COUNTING: INTRODUCTION

Tabeau's and Tokača's approaches are sometimes called a "passive surveillance" method (Obermeyer et al 2008), which suggests, somewhat pejoratively, that they are based on existing sources not necessarily compiled for the purpose of casualty estimation. This is not entirely true: several sources used by each group (e.g., missing persons lists, exhumation and identification records) explicitly reported on victims of war. Both these approaches were developed to produce an overall count of excess deaths, or a minimum count if the overall total could not be obtained; a proper count would have to be documented by individual records of the victims, including among other data, a person's name, date of birth, ethnicity, civilian/military status, and date, place, and cause of death. We believe a more appropriate name is "empirical counting," which is a term that normally would be used in statistics to describe this kind of method.

Empirical counting utilizes multiple sources (eyewitness statements, media reports, mortuary records, mass grave information, missing persons lists, etc.), integrated with each other and sometimes reflecting educated guesses in relation to the missing components in order to produce the required count. The main differences between the two empirical counting approaches (Tabeau and Bijak 2005 vs. Tokača 2007) are the sources used for obtaining the counts, the way of dealing with the integration of sources, and the way of validating the candidate records of the deceased. In Tabeau and Bijak's (2005) approach, only the best selected sources are used for estimating excess deaths. Further, individual death records are cross-examined with the pre-war reference source on the BH population (i.e., the 1991 population census), to confirm personal details of the deceased, and to post-war sources on survivors, to eliminate false positives. Finally, the integrated death records in Tabeau's approach are all linked back to their original sources; no editing of records is done. In Tokača's approach, all existing sources on war-related deaths are accepted. Records are not validated by cross-referencing them with the census nor with sources on post-war survivors. Finally, records are edited during the data entry process and evolve to become integrated multiple-source reports, which might be a risky procedure with a weak duplicate search module of the database.

Despite some differences, a high level of correspondence of the death tolls has been produced by these two independent groups. The group that investigated casualties in Bosnia was less rigorous in accepting their sources and making subjective decisions in records editing and duplicate elimination. The ICTY team required a high level of reliability and confidence in their sources and methods. Obviously, the end results are almost the same, which might indicate that commonsense reporting and convenience sources should not be too readily disregarded in this area of research.

## THE BOSNIAN BOOK OF DEAD, 2007

Tokača's database is often called the Bosnian Book of Dead (hereafter: the BBD Database). It is a result of the Population Loss Project of the Research and Documentation Centre in Sarajevo (RDC), headed by Mirsad Tokača.[9] The BBD statistics on victims are obtained from information collected mainly from individual informants, such as eyewitnesses, relatives, friends, and neighbors, who provided their information voluntarily, or from overall sources on war-related victims, such as press reports, grave markers, morgue records, local books, missing persons lists, lists compiled by nongovernmental organizations, and some government sources. No documents were required to prove or document the statements of individual informants. For these reasons, the BBD, as well, may contain inconsistent and less reliable records.

As of mid-2007, the BBD contained about 97,000 cases (or records; precisely, 96,895), each related to one victim (civilian or military) who was killed, died in other war-related circumstances, or disappeared during the war; this number is a minimum count of victims. The 97,000 cases are called "active" and represent those records of the overall total of all collected cases (246,736) that have been approved as final. The nonactive records are basically duplicates. Many active records were reported in several sources, parts of which are now contained in these records. The integration of multiple sources that reported on the same victims (i.e., the editing of records) was done manually and was largely based on individual decisions of data entry teams. The same teams decided which names represented duplications, a number of which are still present in the BBD database.

Between 2007 and 2010, some additional increase was obtained in the BBD-based minimum count, which approached 99,000 (including some indirect victims). Generally, however, including new cases brought only marginal improvement, which indicates that most cases have already been placed in the database.

ICTY DEATH TOLL ESTIMATE, 2010

Details of our new ICTY estimate are discussed in Zwierzchowski and Tabeau (2010). We made this estimate based on an integration of the major micro-level sources on war deaths available at ICTY for Bosnia-Herzegovina. The sources were collected for evidentiary purposes; in particular, for the OTP's proof-of-death projects on victims listed in the ICTY indictments and for expert reports on victims produced by the OTP Demographic Unit, to which the authors belong.

Our ICTY approach to estimating death tolls in Bosnia-Herzegovina is a reconstruction of war-related deaths. Our goal was to collect *all* war-related death records from the territory of Bosnia-Herzegovina in the years 1992–1995. Only individual-level sources were used; our sources included official wartime death notifications obtained from statistical authorities, military records of fallen soldiers and other military personnel, missing persons lists, exhumation and (DNA) identification records, and some "targeted" sources (focused on one group: e.g., on Sarajevo or Srebrenica). Witness statements, press reports, and morgue records of unidentified or preliminarily identified corpses were *not* considered. The names and other details of the deceased allowed for elimination of duplicates within each source and for comparing the sources in order to exclude overlapping records. Searching for duplicates/overlap was largely automated but included extensive visual checks for broad search criteria. Another reason for using individual records was the need to confirm persons' identities and their survival status. The 1991 population census served as the basis for the validation of personal details of the deceased. The 1997–1998 and 2000 registers of voters and internally displaced persons, as well as the refugee records of the BH government, served to verify the reliability of reporting of disappearances or deaths. This was done to exclude *false positives* (i.e., cases of persons reported as dead or missing who might have survived the conflict, as indicated by the appearance of their names on the electoral rolls from the post-war period). Having eliminated the cases of duplication, overlap, and inconsistency, we made a list of individuals whose deaths took place in Bosnia-Herzegovina in the period from April 1992 to December 1995 and were all war related (most of them in a direct way, some indirectly). The list was used for producing statistics on the minimum and overall number of war-related deaths in Bosnia-Herzegovina (i.e., 89,186 victims), and the distribution of victims by sex, age, ethnicity, military status, and other characteristics. Most important, in our 2010 estimate, in addition to the minimum count of war victims, we estimated the undercount of our sources by means of applying the multiple systems estimation (MSE) method to the overlap structure of 12 large sources on victims we had at our disposal (see chapters 9 and 10 in this volume). The undercount of victims was 15,546 (with 95 percent confidence interval of 14,092–17,494), resulting in 104,732 as the total number of BH victims, which is consistent with the previous ICTY estimate (Tabeau and Bijak 2005).

Our 2010 estimate is an improvement over the 2005 estimate in terms of both the sources and the methods used and, most important, because it applied an MSE technique for estimating the undercount on the victims' lists. The 2010 estimate, which was based on more sources than we used in 2005, includes the latest updates of some sources used previously; in addition, the direct approach of integrating the mortality sources was applied instead of the indirect approach used earlier. In 2005, mortality sources were merged together through the population census (thus indirectly). In this procedure the unmatched records were "lost." To compensate, we corrected our 2005 estimate by dividing the minimum numbers of deaths from each mortality source (i.e., the matched records) by the source-specific matching rates. Such corrections were no longer needed in our 2010 approach. By merging all mortality sources directly, and by direct searching and elimination of the overlap of these sources, we were able to ensure that no records were lost.

PROPORTIONAL MORTALITY ESTIMATE, 2008

The most recent estimate of BH victims was that of Obermeyer et al. (2008); it is a survey-based extrapolation, which the authors call a proportional mortality estimate. In brief, for a number of countries they estimated a (sample) proportion of excess deaths (predominantly violent excess deaths) in the overall number of (sample) deaths reported in survey data and applied this proportion to the UN Population Division estimates of total deaths available for all countries of the world, including Bosnia-Herzegovina, from 1955 onward. To estimate the proportions of violent deaths, Obermeyer et al. used the 2002–2003 survey conducted by the World Health Organization, which included a module regarding retrospective sibling death histories. The WHO survey, taken in 70 countries, was designed to measure both population health and the performance of the respective countries' health care systems. For 45 countries, information on adult deaths was collected through specific questions about the survival of siblings of the respondent, a randomly selected household member. Out of 45 surveys with data on siblings' histories, 13 countries reported more than five sibling deaths from war injuries in each given 10-year period. The data from these countries were subjected to a detailed analysis of war deaths. Bosnia-Herzegovina was one of the 13 countries.

For Bosnia and Herzegovina, a sample of 1,028 households was selected; there were 4,095 siblings in the sample. The total of all sibling deaths in this sample was 619 (603 had year of birth reported), of which 111 were war deaths (105 had year of death reported). The sample was representative of the BH population at the time of the survey (2002–2003), but we have serious doubts about its representativeness in terms of the population exposed to the 1992–1995 war. Truly representative samples are impossible to select because of massive out-migration related to the war makes it impossible to identify the subpopulation actually exposed to subsequent war episodes. The second major known problem is that of underrepresentation in any post-war retrospective survey of the households that suffered the heaviest losses during the war.

The authors did correct the survey data for underrepresentation of families with high mortality and for (age) censoring (i.e., the practice of omitting certain age groups). They estimated that based on survey proportions of war deaths and using the UN estimated population size for the years 1995–2002, the unknown overall number of (direct) excess deaths in the 1992–1995 war in Bosnia was 176,000, with a confidence interval of 67,000–305,000 deaths. For the period 1995–2002 alone, the authors estimated 56,000 direct war deaths—obviously an extremely high number, given that the BH war ended in November 1995 and, thus, all 56,000 deaths must be associated with the year 1995. Historians divide the war in Bosnia-Herzegovina into three major episodes in 1995: the fall of Srebrenica in July 1995 (about 8,000 victims), the end of the siege of Sarajevo (about 1,000–1,500 in 1995), and some deaths resulting from the military operations in the area of North-West Bosnia-Herzegovina (bordering Croatia). It seems highly unlikely that the total of these deaths equaled 56,000 in this single year, in comparison to 120,000 violent war deaths between 1992 and 1994.

We find the estimate of Obermeyer et al. (2008) to be unrealistically high, partly because of the survey-based frequencies of war deaths among siblings (which might have included deaths from diseases acquired in wartime) and partly because of the population of Bosnia and Herzegovina during the war years of 1992–1995, as projected by the United Nations. It is unclear, as well, whether the authors controlled for place of death in BH. It is possible that respondents reported deaths from other territories of the former Yugoslavia. Finally, the Obermeyer et al. (2008) report may include deaths of people who migrated to third countries, a category normally excluded from the death toll in Bosnia.

## An Overview of Estimates of Victims of the Khmer Rouge Regime in Cambodia

### THE POPULATION OF CAMBODIA IN THE 1970S

Statistical sources on the population of Cambodia during or around the period from April 1975 to January 1979 are nonexistent. The last population census before April 1975 was taken in 1962 (Siampos 1970; Migozzi 1973); the next one, following January 1979, did not occur until 1998 and was published by the National Institute of Statistics (NIS) four years later (NIS 2002). Thus there is a data gap of 36 years, a gap that must be seen as a dramatic obstacle to the reliable study of demographic developments in Cambodia during this period. Moreover, no statistical system of recording vital events (births, deaths, marriages, etc.) existed in Cambodia in the post–World War II period; nor is the system in place at the present time adequate for our purposes. A rough form of administrative registration of vital events and socioeconomic aspects of the population was (and likely still is) in hands of village chiefs, commune leaders, and district and provincial authorities. Occasionally, these local sources generated approximate, basic figures, which were sent to the central statistical office in Phnom Penh for the purpose of producing indicative country-level statistics about the Cambodian population. The 1980 administrative count is the most widely known example of these Cambodian population figures.

The bad data situation from the 1960s, 1970s, and 1980s has improved in recent years. Ten years after the general population census of 1998, as incorporated into the census of the National Institute of Statistics (NIS 2002), another one was completed (NIS 2008). Both NIS censuses were conducted with subject-matter and financial assistance from the United Nations Population Fund (UNFPA). Both satisfied professional requirements of the latest world standard for the conduct of a national population census.

In addition to the 1998 and 2008 GPCs, several country-wide representative population surveys were conducted more recently in Cambodia, including several demographic and health surveys and socioeconomic surveys of the country. For 1993, a reliable list of registered voters from the United Nations Transitional Authority in Cambodia (UNTAC) is available. Based on the 1998 census and some post-1998 surveys, three sets of population projections became available for Cambodia, of which the second revised projections (1998–2020), based on the 1998 census and the 2004 Cambodia Intercensal Population Survey (CIPS 2004; cf. NIS 2008) are the latest ones. Hence, the existing recent censuses and projections reliably cover the period from 1993 to 2020.

The population size of Cambodia during the 1970s remains a mystery to some extent; yet in the absence of statistical sources on Khmer Rouge and civil war victims, the size of Cambodia's population in this period is essential if indirect demographic methods are to be used to estimate the unknown number of Khmer Rouge victims.

ESTIMATES OF KHMER ROUGE VICTIMS IN CAMBODIA

Despite of the serious shortage of statistical sources for Cambodia in the 1970s, many authors have attempted to produce estimates of civil war and, in particular, of Khmer Rouge victims. We review 12 estimates of the death toll, with publication details of all these studies provided in the chapter references. The studies include estimates made in the period from January 1980 through the estimate of 2007. The 12 studies are by no means the entire universe of available estimates; several others exist and could have been included as well, but doing so would not have fundamentally altered our conclusions. We believe that the following estimates, reviewed here are those most widely known:

- CIA, 1980
- Ea Meng-Try, 1981
- Renakse, 1983
- Kimmo Kiljunen (ed.), 1984
- Michael Vickery, 1984
- Judith Banister and Paige Johnson, 1993
- Marek Sliwinski, 1995
- Ben Kiernan, 1996 and 2003
- Patrick Heuveline, 1998
- Patrick Heuveline and Poch Bunnak, 2007
- Craig Etcheson, 2000 and 2005
- Ricardo Neupert and Virak Prum, 2005

The results obtained by these authors are summarized in table 11.2 and in figures 11.2 and 11.3.[10] To present a clear pattern in the estimates, figures 11.2 and 11.3 show their values graphically. This presentation would not have been possible without taking averages of certain interval estimates originally produced by several authors and without approximating the estimates that were not explicitly presented by certain authors (e.g., CIA 1980). All these averages and approximations are ours.[11]

The initial estimates of excess deaths, from 1980 to 1993 (except for Renakse 1983, whose estimates are excluded from figures 11.2 and 11.3 for reasons described in the next section),[12] all consistently report about one million excess deaths with a relatively small number of violent excess deaths, from 75,000 to 300,000 deaths. Since 1995, however, the prevailing view of the conflict has changed. Most estimates indicate now that excess deaths of Khmer Rouge time in Cambodia were *between 1.4 million and 2.2 million*. Notably, all estimates from this range belong to those obtained by means of the most advanced methodology: sample survey extrapolations, deaths as a residual category between two projections, and mass grave statistics are all covered in this interval.

TABLE 11.2.

Estimated Excess Deaths and Projected April 1975 Population

| Category | Projected Population, April 1975 (millions) | Death Toll (millions) | Average Direct Excess | Reported Direct Excess |
|---|---|---|---|---|
| CIA (1980) | 7.384 | 0.976 | 75,000 | 50,000– 100,000 |
| Ea Meng-Try (1981) | 7.460 | 1.000 | 120,000 | 120,000 |
| Renakse (1983) | 7.098 | 3.314 | 569,000* | Min. 569,000* |
| Vickery (1984) | 7.100 | 0.740 | 300,000 | 300,000 |
| Kiljunen (ed.) (1984) | 7.300 | 1.000 | 112,500 | 75,000–150,000 |
| Banister and Johnson (1995) | 7.300 | 1.050 | 235,000 | 10% men, 3% young to middle- aged women |
| Sliwinski (1995) | 7.566 | 1.879 | 986,000 | Min. 39.3–52.5% of all deaths |
| Kiernan (1996, 2003) | 7.890 | 1.763 | 881,500 | NA: estimated as 50% of the death toll |
| Heuveline (1988) | 7.952 | 2.200 | 1,100,000 | 1.1 million |
| Neupert and Prum (2005) | 7.890 | 1.400 | 700,000 | NA: estimated as 50% of the death toll |
| Etcheson (2005) | 7.952 | 2.200 | 1,100,000 | 1.1 million |
| Heuveline and Poch (2007) | 7.952 | 1.750 | 875,000 | 50% (0.75–1 million) |

*Notes:* The April 1975 population is approximated in this table for: Renakse (as in UN 2008), Etcheson (as in Heuveline 1998), Neupert and Prum (as in Kiernan 1996). For Heuveline and Heuveline and Poch, we used the April 1975 estimate given by Sharp (2005). All these approximations were made as to resemble the most likely figure the authors used.

*Renakse reported about 569,000 deaths in the forest and bodies in pits; this was assumed here as their minimum number of direct excess deaths.

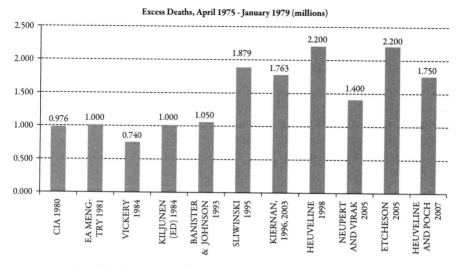

FIGURE 11.2  Excess Deaths Estimates during Khmer Rouge Regime, April 1975 to January 1979 (various authors)

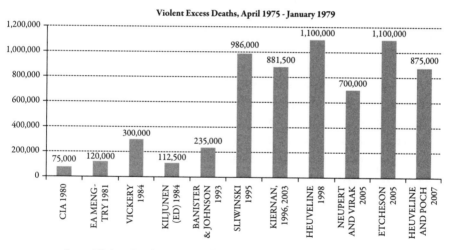

FIGURE 11.3  Excess Violent Deaths Estimates during Khmer Rouge Regime, April 1975 to January 1979 (various authors)

This evolution of the death toll estimates—from low to high—has much to do with a shift from political to scientifically founded estimates. The early estimates all relied largely on the initial number produced by the U.S. Central Intelligence Agency (CIA 1980). The CIA report of 1980 was the first one after the fall of the Khmer Rouge to come up with what then seemed to be highly reliable and detailed figures on the population of Cambodia between 1970 and 1979. The CIA produced, however, a rather low estimate of the population in 1970 (7.06 million), far lower than what earlier leading analysts thought was the figure for that year: Siampos (1970) estimated 7.143 million, and Migozzi (1973) estimated 7.363 million. The CIA also produced a low April 1975 estimate (7.384 million) and a low January 1979 estimate (5.845 million). Notably, the U.S. intelligence agency assumed an unrealistically high level of excess deaths in the civil war of 1970–1975 (i.e., about 600,000–700,000 deaths); the basis for this assumption remains unclear. Interestingly, the CIA did not explicitly report the excess deaths during the Khmer Rouge period of April 1975–January 1979, other than by mentioning about 50,000–100,000 executions by the Pol Pot regime.

The CIA report, coming from an intelligence agency of one of the greatest political powers of the world, which during the 1960s and 1970s had been intensively engaged in the politics and wars in Southeast Asia, became extremely popular among international and national authorities and individual researchers in the 1980s and early 1990s. The CIA (1980) report has had an extraordinary yet unjustified impact on public opinion regarding the size of the population of Cambodia in the 1970s and about the death tolls in the civil war and during the Khmer Rouge regime. We see this report as a source for the magic number of one million deaths attributed to the Khmer Rouge[13] and some serious misunderstandings about the size of Cambodia's population in the 1970s. The authors whose work closely resembles the CIA study include Ea Meng-Try (1981), Kiljunen (1984), Vickery (1984), and Banister and Johnson (1993), all of whom gave 1970s population figures and death tolls under the Khmer Rouge in line with what the CIA had proposed. Unfortunately, the veracity of the CIA estimates is questionable because the report lists no authors, presents the CIA's own expertise in the subject as sufficient validation of the data, and was not subjected to a peer-review process. (The report remained unpublished for many years, but hard copies were widely circulated, and the document is now available on the Internet.)

Unlike the CIA analysts, we believe that the 1970s population size in Cambodia was in agreement with the estimates of Kiernan (1996; 2003), Heuveline (1998), and Neupert and Prum (2005). Kiernan, a renowned historian with much experience in Cambodian matters, worked mainly with a qualitative approach. The quantitative demographers Heuveline and Neupert/Prum have outstanding academic and high-level international credentials. All three authors wrote about Cambodia's tragic decade in the 1990s (Kiernan earlier) and continue to work and publish on these issues. It is remarkable that they came to similar conclusions on the population size and on the death tolls working from two very different methodological approaches, which eventually corroborated one another's results. As we will see in the next section, later estimates of excess deaths have been produced with better baseline data and more reliable methods.

SOURCES AND METHODS USED TO ARRIVE AT ESTIMATES OF THE NUMBER OF
KHMER ROUGE VICTIMS

The following groups of methods can be distinguished in the twelve studies discussed in the subsections that follow.[14]

## Demographic Balancing Equations

Ea Meng-Try (1981) and Michael Vickery (1984) used demographic balancing equations. Regardless of whether this method is applied to population decline or population loss, it offers the most approximate and unreliable means of analysis. There are three components of the equation: births, deaths (natural and excess), and net migration. The level of analysis in this case was the entire population of Cambodia; the data were not even disaggregated by age and sex. Population decline (in absolute terms) was analyzed by comparing population sizes between April 1975 and January 1979. The population at the beginning and end of the analyzed period was decided first, usually on subjective grounds, by means of brief reviews of the estimates of others. In the second step, assumptions were made about the magnitude of births, deaths, and net migration in 1975–1979 in a way that satisfied the equation. In this puzzle, unlike in any real puzzle, there exist several variants of alternatively shaped "pieces" that will always add up to overall decline.

In the absence of reliable data on population size and structure, migration, and fertility and mortality trends, such balancing equations have no value. They express no more than individual authors' subjective views on one of the many possible variants of population development during a given time frame (here, the Khmer Rouge period). The lack of more elaborate justifications in terms of methods and sources makes these methods hard to accept and subjects their results to considerable distrust. However, demographic balancing equations can be also used as a final check on the data resulting from a complex demographic estimation (e.g., a population projection methodology or a scenario). In this case the equation is not the source for its components, or for the excess deaths in particular. The equation is a summary of projection results and as such provides meaningful and important inputs (cf. Banister and Johnson 1993; Kiernan 2003; Neupert and Prum 2005).

## Population Scenarios

Population scenarios, such as those by the CIA (1980) and Banister and Johnson (1993), describe the population change over time and sometimes in space as a result of changes in births, deaths, and migration balance. Thus they are more complex and better justified than those based on demographic balancing equations. These scenarios go deeply into details of population development. The CIA represents a "demographic accounting" approach based on numerous assumptions. Assumptions for the model were generated internally from "intelligence sources" or "CIA analysts' expertise" (CIA 1980).

Banister and Johnson (1993), on the other hand, provide numerous external sources (mostly nonstatistical) on every aspect discussed in their paper (except on Khmer Rouge victims). Their method for obtaining their *plausible scenario* is somewhat unclear, and the reader can elucidate it only by reading between the lines. It is likely a simple population projection. To keep the plausible scenario as real as possible, Banister and Johnson imposed a restriction onto the upper limit of the population change by taking the actual population size and age and sex structure from the year 1980 (i.e., around January 1979) as the one being approximated.

Scenarios are based on a formal model describing population development, a model that has clear assumptions and uses transparently defined initial values of the population size. Once the model has been run, its final outcome is the result of what was put into it. Although scenarios are attractive tools, the lack of reliable population data makes their use in Cambodia of questionable value, although still more convincing than the demographic balancing equations.

Extrapolation of Sample Surveys Results

Several authors, the most important of whom are Sliwinski (1995), Kiernan (1996), and Heuveline and Poch (2007), extrapolated sample survey results over the entire population. Their work was conducted for mainly demographic, anthropological, or historical purposes, and it consisted of retrospective surveys that used either random or non-random sampling. Surveys have as many advantages as shortcomings, however (see chapter 6 by Asher and chapter 7 by Lynch in this volume). The major drawbacks of retrospective and surveillance surveys are the following:

- Researchers who believe that non-random surveys cannot be used for reliable extrapolation of sample statistics have some hesitation in accepting convenience samples.
- Random sample surveys are not suitable when the goal of the research is to provide a representative record of victimization in the entire population of a conflict-affected country, since respondents are selected from survivors, among whom the victims of the most dramatic episodes are underrepresented.
- Sample-drawing mechanisms may produce a significant bias if they do not closely parallel the development of the conflict; for example, refugee camp samples will correctly represent the victim populations from the areas the camp respondents moved from before arriving in the camp, but not necessarily the rest of the country's population.
- Some groups of respondents may see the survey as a form of registration for aid distribution, potentially leading to overreporting of survivors, another bias.
- There is a recall bias in sample surveys: surveys distant in time from a given conflict are known to contain more gaps and misreporting than the early surveys of the same conflict.

Surveys have many advantages, too. Most important, they can be completed within a short period of time and they can provide large quantities of relevant information about the conflict and its victims, including the death rates, which can be estimated without knowing the actual population size. In addition, surveys are easy to implement, require limited resources, and allow for the efficient control of data quality.

Several surveys were reviewed by Kiernan (1996; 2003; see also table 11.3, below) as part of his historical investigation of victimization during the Khmer Rouge period. Kiernan as well used additional materials when he was exploring victimization issues. Examples include his interviews with survivors and witnesses to events under the Khmer Rouge, observations from his frequent visits to Cambodia, relevant statistics from the work of others, and his personal communications with field workers. Kiernan is the only author to have integrated both the results produced in different surveys and survivors' recollections into his own estimate of the death toll under the Khmer Rouge. The strength of his approach is that he divided the population by social and ethnic group. Rather than applying a single percentage obtained in one survey to the entire population of Cambodia in April 1975, he broke down the April 1975 population into subpopulations, such as the NEW and BASE people, and within these groups into rural Khmer, urban Khmer, Chinese, Vietnamese, Lao, Thai, and so on. Each of these subpopulations was assigned a different estimated percentage of excess deaths, which was further used in extrapolation over the entire population. This process increased the validity and reliability of Kiernan's results, as well as the reliability of his approach.

If, however, one would like to base one's views exclusively on the surveys and neglect other sources, several of the surveys would appear to be too small and insignificant to be taken seriously. The samples of 158 (Ebihara 1993), 168 (Honda 1981), or 350 individuals (Honda 1981.) can be considered to be special case studies and no more than that. Only three surveys seem to be large enough to be accepted as serious representations of large groups of the Cambodian population that survived the Pol Pot reign: Heder (1981), Sliwinski (1995), and Heuveline and Poch (2007). Yet these three, too, do not pretend to be representative of the entire population exposed to the risks of death under the Khmer Rouge. It is likely that the victims of the most fatal episodes of that regime are underrepresented in all three surveys. All three studies are consistent in the estimated death toll attributed to the Khmer Rouge; in the three surveyed populations, the death toll is estimated at about 20–25 percent and is consistent with other recent, more reliable estimates.

## Excess Deaths as a Residual Category

In our next method, an estimate of excess deaths attributed to the Khmer Rouge is obtained as a residual category between two population projections that meet at the end of the 1970s, one moving forward from 1970 and one moving backward from the present. Heuveline (1998) and Neupert and Prum (2005) applied this method. A formal model was used with well-justified assumptions. The model represents the most up-to-date demographic standard in population projections (the cohort component model). The level of subjectivity is low compared with other approaches. Both authors build upon the work of others but are critical and selective of those results. Neupert and Prum stop at presenting the overall number of excess deaths in 1970–1979 (and the associated sex and age distribution). Heuveline goes further and separates violent and nonviolent

TABLE 11.3.

Demographic Approaches Used for the Estimation of Death Toll in the 1992–1995 War in Bosnia-Herzegovina and during the 1975–1979 Khmer Rouge Regime in Cambodia

| Country | Approaches to Casualty Estimation | Authors | Sources | Assumptions | Formal Models |
|---|---|---|---|---|---|
| BH | Qualitative assessment and some quantitative sources | Bassiouni (1995), Kenney (1995), IPH (1996a,b), Bošnjović/Smajkić (1997), Zerjavić (1998), Bošnjović (1999) | Survivors, witnesses, research/press/mission reports, books, international observers, mass graves, visits, monitoring statistics, etc. | Not used | Not used |
| BH | Empirical count from ationwide collection project | Tokača (2007) | Victim lists from survivors, research/press/books, international observers, exhumations, burials, etc. | Any source accepted; undercount unknown; duplicate/overlap controls in place | Not used |
| BH | Empirical count: multiple-source, validated and overlap controlled | Tabeau and Bijak (2005), Zwierzchowski and Tabeau (2009) | Statistical sources (military and civilian), missing persons lists (international and national), exhumation/identification records, local surveys, etc. | Meaningful selection of sources; explicit under-count; strict control of duplicates/overlap; explicit overlap of sources | A limited capture-recapture |
| BH | Extrapolation of sample survey results | Obermeyer et al. (2008) | WHO global health survey 2002–2003; population size 1992–1995 as estimated in the UN's World Population Prospects | Sample measures resemble those in the unknown population | Proportional extrapolation of survey estimates over the entire population at the outbreak of war |

| | | | | | |
|---|---|---|---|---|---|
| Cambodia | Demographic balancing equation | Ea Meng-Try (1981), Vickery (1984), Kiljunen (ed.; 1984) | Census 1962; population estimates for Cambodia in 1975 and 1979; assumptions regarding births, deaths, and migration | Assumptions regarding population size, births, deaths, and migration; no sources for justification | Demographic balancing equation |
| Cambodia | Population scenarios | CIA (1980), Banister and Johnson (1993) | Census 1962; population estimates for Cambodia in 1975 and 1979; assumptions regarding births, deaths, and migration | Assumptions regarding population size, births, deaths, and migration; little justification | Simple population projection |
| Cambodia | Extrapolation of sample survey results | Kiernan (1996), Sliwinski (1995), Heuveline and Poch (2007) | Surveys of Heder (1981), Sliwinski (1995), Heuveline and Poch (2007), several others; population estimates for April 1975 | Sample measures resemble those in the unknown population; or those in specific social/ethnic groups | Proportional extrapolation of survey estimates over the entire population at the outbreak of war; also by social/ethnic groups |

*(continued)*

TABLE 11.3. (*continued*)

| Country | Approaches to Casualty Estimation | Authors | Sources | Assumptions | Formal Models |
|---|---|---|---|---|---|
| Cambodia | Excess deaths as a residual category between two projections | Heuveline (1998), Neupert and Prum (2005) | Census of 1962; 1980 administrative count; 1993 voter registration data; assumptions regarding births, deaths, and migration | Assumptions regarding population size, births, deaths, and migration; better justification; lower uncertainty (forward and backward projections) | Cohort component population projection model; forward and backward projections; critically selected assumptions; model life tables |
| Cambodia | Excess deaths as linked to exhumation records | Etcheson (2000, 2005) | Mass grave mapping records of DC-Cam | Assumptions regarding the number of remains in graves; based on witness statements; no exhumations to confirm | Number of remains in mass graves as the basis for the estimation |
| Cambodia | Naïve estimate from nationwide investigation | Renakse (1983) | Testimony from survivors and witnesses; research reports; documents; exhumations; visits to graves, detention centers, etc.; all aggregate | Not used | Not used |

excess deaths from each other and next subtracts civil war deaths from all 1970–1979 excess deaths to obtain his estimate of Khmer Rouge victims. The separation of violent deaths and their distribution into a pre–Khmer Rouge period and a Khmer Rouge period is certainly convincing in Heuveline's work. Heuveline's estimates need, however, to be improved by including births since 1970 and the mortality of persons in that category, and by separation of the victims of starvation in 1979 from the estimated excess violent deaths in 1975–1979.

Neupert and Prum (2005) used the same the population projection methodology as Heuveline (1998). However, they obtained a lower number of excess deaths than did Heuveline (2 million vs. 2.5 million in 1970–1979, and 1.4 million vs. 2.2 million in 1975–1979).[15] Neupert and Prum explain the difference in results by citing the following factors:

- smaller volume of net migration in Heuveline (1998)
- lower normal mortality for the 1970s in Heuveline (1998)
- the 1970 population was larger in Heuveline (1998): 7.662 million in Heuveline (1998) and 7.4 million in Neupert and Prum (2005)
- the 1980 population was smaller in Heuveline (1998)

All in all, it seems that Neupert and Prum produced a relatively low estimate of excess deaths—1.4 million in 1975–1978—whereas Heuveline's estimate of 2.2 million excess deaths in 1975–1978 belongs to the higher range of estimates.[16]

DC-Cam Mass Grave Mapping Project

The Documentation Centre of Cambodia (DC-Cam) was established in January 1995 as part of Yale University's Cambodian Genocide Program (CGP). In 1997, DC-Cam became an independent organization, although funding continued to come from the CGP through 2001. The main focus of DC-Cam activities has been the documentation of the mass killings in Cambodia between April 1975 and January 1979 during the Democratic Kampuchea (DK) regime headed by Pol Pot. As part of its mandate, DC-Cam has "located and mapped 196 prisons, 19,733 mass graves, and 81 genocide memorials" and has cataloged more than 6,000 photographs and roughly 155,000 pages of the 600,000 pages of primary Khmer Rouge documents in its possession.[17]

The DC-Cam mapping project should be seen as a country-wide survey of mass graves in Cambodia prepared and conducted by the DC-Cam staff. Note that DC-Cam has never done any exhumations and thus did not produce direct counts of the victims in the mass graves. Rather, the DC-Cam analysts made estimates of the victims based on witness statements and other related materials collected in the course of the mapping project. The project's surveying approach is reliable enough to permit us to consider the estimates to be very serious, although at the same time they must still be called approximate.

## Excess Deaths as Linked to DC-Cam Records of Mass Grave Mapping

Etcheson (2000; 2005) developed a method of estimating excess deaths that was based on the DC-Cam records of mass grave mapping. In this work, excess deaths caused by the Khmer Rouge during 1975–1978, comprise direct and indirect victims, which remain at the 50:50 proportion. Direct excess deaths are represented by human remains in the mass graves mapped so far in Cambodia: 1.1 million. Indirect excess deaths, which obviously are not part of the set enumerated from the mass graves, must be about the same as the number of individuals in the mass graves (i.e., another 1.1 million victims). The proportional relationship between the two components (i.e., direct and indirect excess deaths) is assumed after Heuveline (1998). Other ratios available from the literature (and based mainly on small sample estimations) are seen as not reliable enough to be used; these other proportions relate to narrower groups of the population.[18]

Although several issues are associated with Etcheson's estimate of 2.2 million excess deaths, this number is fully possible and in line with the most serious attempts to estimate the excess deaths in Cambodia.

## Excess Deaths as a Naïve Estimate from a Nationwide Investigation

Exhumations of mass graves, primarily by nonprofessionals, began in early 1979 and continued in the 1980s.[19] The work was part of a nationwide effort to collect evidence of Pol Pot's crimes.[20] Other types of evidence collected at that time included individual and group survivors' statements called "petitions," witness testimonies, research reports, and documents, as well as lists of victims, torture and detention facilities, intelligence centers, prisons, and so on. All these efforts were coordinated by the Research Committee into the Crimes of the Pol Pot Regime (hereafter: the Research Committee), a creation of the Salvation Front, Renakse, which was called then the Front for National Solidarity, Reconstruction, and Defence of Kampuchea.

The Research Committee had a whole network of local units, including provincial, district, and other committees. The task of all these committees was to collect evidence that could be used in persuading the United Nations to remove the Khmer Rouge representatives from their seat in the UN General Assembly and offer this seat to the legitimate government of the People's Republic of Kampuchea (PRK). On July 25, 1983, the national Research Committee submitted to the PRK government the Renakse Summary Report, which concluded that the death toll under the Khmer Rouge regime was *3,314,768* persons. Of the 3.315 million victims, 568,000 were counted in exhumations and 2.75 million in other settings. An astonishing *1,166,307* persons signed the "petitions."

The Renakse survey entailed no preparations at all in the statistical sense: no territories were distinguished, no standardized questionnaires were developed and used, no trained interviewers took statements, and no professional personnel were involved in the exhumations. The degree of duplication among the death toll of 3.315 million is therefore enormous: at least 50 percent according to Etcheson (2000). Problems in addition to duplication include incompleteness—the Renakse death toll covers only 15 provinces out of 21 (DC-Cam 1991). It is also unclear what fraction of all actual deaths was reported for each province. The problems just cited are related to the unscientific statistical framework of the Renakse survey, which makes it impossible to assess the degree of coverage of the statistics submitted. As such, the Renakse death toll of 3.315 million cannot be considered to be a reliable estimate of the number of Khmer Rouge victims.

## Summing Up the Methods Used

In our assessment, the most valuable studies are those that obtained *excess deaths as a residual category* of two separate projections; the authors of these studies were Heuveline (1998) and Neupert and Prum (2005); *extrapolations based on sample surveys* (Sliwinski 1995; Kiernan 1996; Heuveline and Poch 2007), and *extrapolations based on mass grave data* (Etcheson 2000; 2005). The least valuable studies are those prepared by using demographic balancing equations, scenarios, and the Renakse petitions. The number of excess deaths attributed to the Khmer Rouge by the highest ranking studies ranges from about *1.4 million to 2.2 million*. Violent excess deaths equal approximately *700,000–1.1 million*.

## Discussion

We have presented an overview of approaches used to estimate the number of victims in two distinct conflicts: the 1992–1995 war in Bosnia-Herzegovina and the 1975–1979 Khmer Rouge regime in Cambodia. Most estimation approaches used for each country were demographic; all approaches except for qualitative assessments based on predominantly nonstatistical sources were in fact demographic. In this section we summarize the approaches used (table 11.3). We discuss sources, specific models, and assumptions of these approaches, considering also their political orientation and future research needs. To begin with, we summarize the results on the two conflicts by showing their common and distinct features.

Common features:

- The duration of both conflicts was similar, about four years.
- The population size at the outbreak of conflict was not fundamentally different in the two countries.
- In both conflicts, early post-conflict estimates are the weakest in terms of methods, sources, and transparency.
- In both conflicts, early post-conflict estimates were clearly politicized and were meant for lobbying campaigns.
- In both conflicts, nationwide investigations either were completed spontaneously or were prompted by political processes.
- The results of these investigations have been largely neglected and do not play any role as serious estimates of the respective populations of victims.

- Later estimates were improved by a more careful selection of sources, better methods, and more transparency.
- There is still some degree of disagreement about the estimated death tolls in both conflicts.
- It is hard to pinpoint a single best estimate for either conflict; instead, in each case it is clear that one group of estimates is better than the remaining ones.

Different features:

- The episode in Bosnia-Herzegovina was a civil war that had grown into an international armed conflict, whereas in Cambodia a communist regime had experienced first civil war and then war with Vietnam.
- Despite the similar duration of both conflicts and not dissimilar population sizes in the two countries, the death tolls were not at all the same; this difference must be associated with the specific circumstances of each conflict.
- The range of death tolls in the war in Bosnia-Herzegovina is from 25,000 to 330,000 victims; the range of death tolls from the Khmer Rouge regime in Cambodia is from 740,000 to 3.315 million victims.
- The most likely estimates are approximately 105,000 victims in Bosnia-Herzegovina and 1.6 million to 2.2 million victims in Cambodia.[21]
- The proportion of direct to indirect victims is not exactly known for Bosnia-Herzegovina, but it seems that most people died of direct violent causes. For Cambodia, a 50-50 distribution might be the best approximation.
- With respect to the war in Bosnia-Herzegovina, the early estimates were at the higher end (around 200,000), whereas those more recently published display lower values (100,000).
- For Cambodia, the trend was opposite: from low (early post-conflict: about 1 million) to high death toll estimates (more recent: about 2.2 million).
- Sources used were largely different for each conflict: direct sources on war-related and natural deaths and missing persons were often used in BH estimates, whereas no such sources were used for Cambodia. Sources on pre- and post-war population size, and wartime births, deaths, and migration were used in Cambodia, but not in Bosnia and Herzegovina.
- Methods used in both cases were largely different; only one method was common for both countries, namely, sample survey extrapolation over the entire wartime population. There are two main reasons for this situation:
  - Data availability was not comparable from conflict to conflict: for Bosnia-Herzegovina, many individual-level sources on deaths and disappearances existed and could be used directly in death toll estimation; for Cambodia, such sources were and still are unavailable.

o The scale of victimization was completely different in the two conflicts, and the choice of estimation approaches reflects the specificity of the conflicts.

- One of the best extrapolations of survey results for Cambodia was made by social/ethnic group; no such approach was proposed for Bosnia and Herzegovina.

The foregoing summary confirms that no two countries and no two conflicts are the same, although some post-conflict behavior repeats itself: for example, the "makers" of death toll estimates tend to apply the political approach in early post-conflict settings. In highly politicized post-conflict environments, initial estimates of death tolls are inevitably tools in the struggle for political power, dominance, recognition of suffering, punishment of those responsible for the suffering, justice for the victims and their families, and prosecution of war criminals. In Bosnia-Herzegovina the politically motivated estimates include those by Bassiouni (1995), Kenney (1995), and both IPH estimates (1996a, 1996b). Also, the estimates by Bošnjovic and Smajkić are not completely unbiased, as both these authors are Bosniaks; indeed, Smajkić was the director of the IPH during the war, and the two authors used IPH data exclusively as their source. The IPH was also the main source for Zerjavić, although Zerjavić made an effort to include some qualitative analysis of Serb sources. For Cambodia, the estimate by the CIA (1980) and several others based on the CIA report (i.e., estimated deaths of only one million) must be seen as biased. The estimate by Renakse (1983, unpublished data), in addition to being incompetently prepared, was likely politically motivated, too (see, e.g., Gordon 2007), although obviously not in the same direction as that of CIA.

Estimates of death tolls produced in later stages of post-conflict history are unquestionably improvements in terms of sources, methods, and transparency. Their purpose is scientific; they attempt to produce the most reliable estimates that are possible.

The war in Bosnia-Herzegovina resulted in a relatively low number of victims; some 2.1 percent of the pre-war population was killed or disappeared; the highest death/disappearance ratio observed for Muslims equals 3.1 percent. In the Khmer Rouge regime, about 25 percent of the April 1975 population lost their lives; some groups of the Cambodian population (e.g., the ethnic Chinese) lost as many as 50 percent of their members (cf., e.g., Kiernan 1996), and one group, Khmers of Vietnamese origin, was exterminated altogether (1996).

It is practically impossible to document killings on this scale by producing lists of individual victims, with each death presented in terms of date, exact place, and cause of death (or disappearance). The registration of the (estimated) 1.6 million to 2.2 million Cambodian deaths in a period shorter than four years would pose significant problems even under normal circumstances.

On the other hand, it would not be appropriate to estimate the death toll in a low-victimization conflict, such as that in Bosnia and Herzegovina, by using, for example, the method of war deaths as a residual category between two different population projections. The result would not be reliable, since the estimation error could be extremely high in relation to the estimated death toll.

Also, estimating the death toll of the BH war as directly linked to the exhumation records makes little sense. The number of bodies in mass graves in Bosnia-Herzegovina is relatively small compared with the number of known deaths (both direct and indirect victims). The best approximation of the number of these bodies is the number of missing persons. The latest (2009) ICRC list of missing persons from Bosnia-Herzegovina has about 22,000 cases; another list of BH missing, that of the International Commission on Missing Persons (ICMP) in Sarajevo, contains some 30,000 names, of which 12,621 had been identified as of September 2009.[22] These numbers are rather low compared with the remaining victims whose death details are known (roughly about 22,000 missing vs. some 80,000 known deaths).

In Cambodia, according to the latest statistics from the DC-Cam mapping project, the existence of about 23,745 mass graves has been confirmed and mapped by means of GIS; the estimated number of human remains stands at 1,298,772 persons (Tabeau 2009, own calculation based on Internet data).[23] The identified mass graves contain a sample of all victims; this sample can be said to represent about 60 percent of all victims of the Khmer Rouge regime.[24]

The essential question of this chapter is, Which approaches should be recommended as the best, or just more reliable than others? For low-death-toll conflicts and countries offering good availability of individual-level sources on war deaths, such as in Bosnia and Herzegovina, we argue that empirical counting combined with undercount estimation is reliable. The extrapolation of country-wide random sample surveys is not reliable for several reasons: for example, massive population movements prevent the identification of the right sample.

For high-death-toll conflicts and countries dramatically lacking statistical sources on the population, such as Cambodia, it is far harder to give precise recommendations. The best approach must always be proposed based on realities of the particular conflict studied. The cohort component population projection approach used to estimate the death toll as a residual category between two separately made projections (one forward and one backward) is most certainly worth recommending, although it is not perfect. Another worthwhile alternative is the qualitative historical approach based on multiple sources, cross-referenced and integrated with each other, as in the work of Kiernan (1996).

Finally, the most urgent research needs lie in the field of comparative studies in which different estimation methods are applied to the same conflict. Such studies will help formulate guidelines as to what estimation methods are more reliable than others and what magnitude of error can be expected from each method. Another urgent issue is the registration of war victims, given that, in times of conflict, local statistical systems are nonfunctional. Thus the development of a means of performing this critical task should have very high priority.

REFERENCES

Ball, Patrick, Ewa Tabeau, and Philip Verwimp, 2007. "The Bosnian Book of Dead: Assessment of the Database." Expert report published on the net as Households in Conflict Network Research Design Note 5, June 17. Available at: www.hicn.org.

Banister, Judith, and Paige Johnson. 1993. "After the Nightmare: The Population of Cambodia." In *Genocide and Democracy in Cambodia: The Khmer Rouge, the United Nations and the International Community*, edited by Ben Kiernan, No. 41, 335. New Haven, CT: Yale University, Southeast Asia Studies.

Bassiouni, Cherif. 1995. "Genocide in Bosnia and Herzegovina." Testimony: Hearing before the Commission on Security and Cooperation in Europe. Washington, DC: One Hundred Fourth Congress, Commission on Security and Cooperation in Europe [CSCE 104-X-X], April 4. Transcript of the hearing available at: http:/www/house.gov/csce.

Becker, Elizabeth. 1986. *When the War Was Over.* New York: Simon & Schuster

Bošnjović, Ilija, "Population of Bosnia-Herzegovina in the 2nd Half of the 20th Century." Paper presented at an International Conference in Sarajevo, "Changes in 1990s and the Demographic Future of the Balkans," October 1999.

Bošnjović, Ilija, and Arif Smajkić, 1997. "Health and Social Consequences of the War in Bosnia-Herzegovina—Rehabilitation Proposal." In *Health and Social Consequences of the War in Bosnia and Herzegovina – Rehabilitation Proposal*, 4th ed., edited by A. Smajkić. Sarajevo: Svjetlost and the Institute of Public Health of Bosnia and Herzegovina.

Brunborg, H., E. Tabeau, and H. Urdal (eds.), 2006. *The Demography of Armed Conflict*, Vol. 5 in *International Studies of Population*. New York: Springer.

*Cambodia Inter-Censal Population Survey 2004, General Report.* 2004. Phnom Penh: National Institute of Statistics, Ministry of Planning.

Central Intelligence Agency. 1980. "Kampuchea: A Demographic Catastrophe." Research paper of the U.S. Central Intelligence Agency, January 17. At: http://www.mekong.net/cambodia/demcat.htm.

Chandler, David. 2008. *A History of Cambodia*, 4th ed. [1st ed., 1984]. Boulder, CO: Westview Press.

———. 1981. "Total Statistics of Genocidal Crimes of Pol Pot Regime on the People during 1975–78." The "Renakse Summary Table," signed on July 23, 1983, by the members of the (national) Research Committee into the Crimes of the Pol Pot Regime: Min Khin (chairman), Tith Sunthan (vice chairman), Chea Kean (vice chairman), Kim Ly, Srun Seang Lim, and Tes Heng. Available from DC-Cam archive records on Renakse. Available at: www.dccam.org.

———. 1991. "The Petition: Summary Report." ("Renakse Summary Report"), March 21. DC-Cam document, contents summarized by Vanthan P. Dara, with introduction by Youk Chhang. Available at: www.dccam.org.

———. 2009. Mass Grave Mapping Project. Available at: www.dccam.org.

Ea, Meng-Try. 1981. "Kampuchea: A Country Adrift." *Population and Development Review* 7: No. 2 (June).

Ebihara, May M. 1993. "'Beyond Suffering': The Recent History of a Cambodian Village." In *The Challenge of Reform in Indochina*, edited by Börje Ljunggren. Cambridge, MA: Harvard Institute for International Development, Harvard University Press, pp. 149–166.

Etcheson, Craig. 2000. "The Number: Quantifying Crimes against Humanity in Cambodia." Available at: http://www.dccam.org/Projects/Maps/Mass_Graves_Study.htm.

———. 2005. *After the Killing Fields: Lessons from the Cambodian Genocide.* New York: Praeger Publishers.

Gordon, Amy. 2007. "The Renakse Petitions: Background and Suggestions for Future Use." Research paper. Available at: www.dccam.org.

Heder, Stephen. 1981. "Kampuchea Survives ... But What Now?" *South Asia Chronicle* 77: 1–33.

Heuveline, Patrick. 1998. "Between One and Three Million: Towards the Demographic Reconstruction of a Decade of Cambodian History (1970–79). *Population Studies* No. 52: 49–65.

———, and Poch Bunnak. 2007. "The Phoenix Population: Demographic Crises and Rebound in Cambodia." *Demography* 44 (2): 405–426.

Honda, Katuiti. 1981. *Journey to Cambodia.* Tokyo: Committee of "Journey to Cambodia."

Institute for Public Health. 1996a. Bulletin No. 01.01.1996. [in English] Sarajevo: Institute for Public Health.

———. 1996b, Bulletin No. 25.03.1996. Sarajevo: Institute for Public Health.

Kenney, George. 1995. "The Bosnia Calculation." *New York Times Magazine*, April 23.

Kiernan, Ben. (1996) 2008. *The Pol Pot Regime: Race, Power and Genocide in Cambodia under the Khmer Rouge, 1975–79*, 3rd ed., New Haven, CT, and London: Yale University Press.

———. 2003. "The Demography of Genocide in Southeast Asia: The Death Tolls in Cambodia, 1975–79, and East Timor, 1975–80." Research note, *Critical Asian Studies* 35:4 585–597.

Kiljunen, Kimmo, ed. 1984. *Kampuchea: Decade of Genocide. Report of a Finnish Inquiry Commission.* London: Zed Books Ltd.

Lampe, John R. 1996. *Yugoslavia as History: Twice There Was a Country.* Cambridge: Cambridge University Press.

Malcolm, Noel. 1994. *Kosovo: A Short History.* New York: New York University Press.

Migozzi, Jacques.1973. *Cambodge: Faits et problèmes de population.* Paris: Editions du Centre National de la Recherche Scientifique (CNRS).

Neupert, Ricardo, and Virak Prum. 2005. "Cambodia: Reconstructing the Demographic Stab of the Past and Forecasting the Demographic Scar of the Future." *European Journal of Population* 21: 217–246.

NIS. 2002. *General Population Census of Cambodia 1998: Final Census Results*, 2nd ed. Phnom Penh: National Institute of Statistics, Ministry of Planning.

———. 2008. *General Population Census of Cambodia 2008. Provisional Population Totals.* Phnom Penh: National Institute of Statistics, Ministry of Planning.

Obermeyer, Ziad, Christopher J. L. Murray, and Emmanuela Gakidou. 2008. "Fifty Years of Violent War Deaths from Vietnam to Bosnia: Analysis of Data from the World Health Organization Survey Programme." *British Medical Journal* 336: 1482–1486.

Prašo, Murat. 1996. "Demographic Consequence of the 1992–95 War." *Most*, No. 93, March-April, Mostar, Bosnia and Herzegovina. Reprint, *Bosnia Report, Newsletter of the Alliance to Defend Bosnia and Herzegovina*, No. 16, July–October.

Renakse. 1983. Summary Report of the Research Committee on Pol Pot's Genocidal Regime— The "Renakse Summary" and related materials. (unpublished). See DC-Cam reports and archive records on Renakse. Available at: www.dccam.org.

Republic of Croatia. 1995. "Stanovništvo Bosne i Hercegovine. Narodnosni Sastav po Naseljima." ("The Population of Bosnia-Herzegovina. Ethnic Composition according to Settlements"). Zagreb: National Office for Statistics.

Schulte, William J. [2007?] "The History of Renakse Petitions and Their Value for ECCC Proceedings." Research paper. Available at: www.dccam.org.

Sharp, Bruce, 2005. 'Counting Hell,' Mekong Net. Available at: http://www.mekong.net/cambodia/deaths.htm.

Siampos, George. 1970. "The Population of Cambodia, 1945–1980." *Milbank Memorial Fund Quarterly* 48 (3): 317–360.

Silber, Laura and Allan Little. 1995. *The Death of Yugoslavia.* London: Penguin Books, BBC Books.

Silva, Romesh, and Patrick Ball. 2008. "The Demography of Conflict-Related Mortality in Timor-Leste (1974–1999): Reflections on Empirical Quantitative Measurement of Civilian Killings, Disappearances, and Famine-Related Deaths." In *Statistical Methods for Human Rights.* Edited by Jana Asher, David Banks, and Fritz J. Scheuren, 117–139. New York: Springer.

Sliwinski, Marek. 1995. *Le génocide Khmer Rouge: Une analyse démographique.* Paris: Editions L'Harmattan.

Tabeau, Ewa, and Jakub Bijak. 2005. "War-Related Deaths in the 1992–1995 Armed Conflicts in Bosnia and Herzegovina: A Critique of Previous Estimates and Recent Results." *European Journal of Population* 21(2/3). Reprint, Brunborg et al., eds. (2006).

Tokača, Mirsad. 2007. "The Population Loss Project: Final Results." Paper presented at the Public Promotion of the War Victims Database. Sarajevo, June 21.

UN. 2008.

Vickery, Michael. 1984. *Cambodia 1975–1982.* Chiang Mai, Thailand: Silkworm Books.

Žerjavić, Vladimir. 1998. "Great Serbia: Tragic Outcome." *Globus* [Croatia], January 9.

Zwierzchowski, Jan and Ewa Tabeau. 2010. "The 1992-95 War in Bosnia and Herzegovina: Census-Based Multiple Systems Estimation of Casualties Undercount." Conference paper for the International Research Workshop on 'The Global Costs of Conflict.' The Households in Conflict Network and The German Institute for Economic Research, Berlin.

NOTES

1. For example, http://www.worldbank.org/depweb/english/beyond/global/glossary.html.

2. The war in Bosnia-Herzegovina started in early April 1992 and lasted until late November 1995. The Khmer Rouge regime took power in early April 1975 and lost it in early January 1979.

3. "Khmer Rouge Tribunal" is the common name of the Extraordinary Chambers in the Courts of Cambodia (ECCC).

4. See, for example, Lampe (1996), Malcolm (1994), andSilber and Little (1995).

5. Cf. information on the websites of the statistical authority of the Federation of Muslims and Croats and of Republika Srpska. At: http://www.fzs.ba/Eng/index.htm and http://www.rzs.rs.ba/English.htm.

6. Cf. http://www.fzs.ba/Eng/population.htm. Several publications were issued after each census. For example, the first publication on the 1991 census in BH was entitled "Stanovništvo Bosne i Hercegovine. Narodnosni Sastav po Naseljima" ("The Population of Bosnia-Herzegovina. Ethnic Composition according to Settlements"). It was published by the National Office for Statistics of the Republic of Croatia in April 1995.

7. Some estimates discussed in Tabeau and Bijak (2005) in the *European Journal of Population* article are skipped here owing to their highly questionable character.

8. The Bassiouni Commission not only came up with the overall number of persons killed in Bosnia (200,000), but also with other statistics: 800 prison camps and detention facilities, with a wartime population of about half a million of people; 50,000 persons tortured, 20,000 (estimated) cases of rape, 151 mass graves, some containing up to 3,000 bodies. The materials collected by Bassiouni were rough (sometimes contested) estimates. Nevertheless, they were handed over to the ICTY, which performed further investigation.

9. Details of all these estimates are available from Tabeau and Bijak (2005).

10. Cf. Patrick Ball, Ewa Tabeau, and Philip Verwimp. 2007. *The Bosnian Book of Dead: Assessment of the Database*. Expert report prepared at the request of the ambassadors of Norway and Switzerland, and of Mirsad Tokača, the BBD project leader, for presentation in the final version of the database in Sarajevo, June 21. Published as Households in Conflict Research Design Note 5, June 17, 2007. At: www.hicn.org. The authors' names are listed in alphabetic order; Ewa Tabeau was the project leader. We conducted this project at the invitation of Mirsad Tokača himself and of the embassies of Norway and Switzerland, which were seeking validation of Tokača's work.

11. These and the following figures contain some approximations and averages of original estimates. All approximations were calculated by the authors of this report.

12. For the CIA, we calculated the overall number of deaths in April 1975–January 1979 directly from the population data and death rates produced by CIA for the OLD and NEW people. There were about 1.753 million such deaths. We assumed that this figure includes both natural deaths and the "indirect" deaths of Khmer Rouge victims. We distributed these deaths 50-50, applying thus the uniform distribution into natural deaths and indirect victims (0.876 million–0.876 million). The CIA estimated in their medium variant that in addition there were 100,000 executions under the Khmer Rouge regime. We added the executions to the indirect deaths (0.876 million) and obtained the total of excess deaths being 0.976 million. In our comparisons, we also had to adapt some other original estimates, especially those produced as intervals instead of point estimates; adaptation was necessary, as well, if more than one estimate was produced by the same author in the course of time, or if estimates had been expressed in relative instead of absolute terms (as percentages). For intervals and multiple estimates by the same author, arithmetic averages were taken. We applied estimates expressed as percentages to the appropriate April 1975 population estimated by a given author. We also applied the 50-50 distribution to obtain the number of violent excess deaths if this number was not explicitly reported and the only number available was on the overall death toll.

13. Reasons for treating Renakse as an outlier are explained in the next section. Basically, Renakse does not satisfy any statistical criteria required for a survey or population census.

14. The extremely transparent presentation of the CIA inputs and outputs makes it possible to produce the overall level of all deaths between April 1975 and January 1979, and by distributing it 50-50 into natural and indirect excess deaths, one obtains the overall number of excess deaths under the Khmer Rouge of about 1 million.

15. The discussion of source and methods is based on results of a five-month project Ewa Tabeau completed in 2009 for the Extraordinary Chambers in the Courts of Cambodia in Phnom Penh. The author's report on this project is listed in the chapter references as Tabeau, 2009.

16. We obtained the number of 1.4 million from Neupert and Prum's original estimate of 2 million for 1970–1979. We assumed 300,000 excess deaths for the civil war and another 300,000 for the 1979 famine deaths; in total 600,000 deaths, which we subtracted from 2 million. What

remains from the 2005 estimate of 2 million is the death toll attributable to the Khmer Rouge, April 1975–January 1979.

17. Calculations discussed in this paragraph were all produced by the authors of this report. The 1.4 million estimate includes neither the estimated 300,000 famine deaths in 1979 nor the estimated 300,000 excess deaths in 1970–1975. The 2.2 million estimate already excludes 300,000 deaths during the civil war; the 2.2 million becomes 1.9 million if we additionally exclude about 300,000 famine deaths in 1979.

18. Documentation Center of Cambodia, at: http://www.dccam.org/Abouts/History/ Histories.htm. Statistics as of August 18, 2009.

19. The 50-50 distribution of violent and nonviolent excess deaths, which is likely a good compromise, is strongly supported by Heuveline's solid analysis, by means of model life tables, of excess deaths for Cambodia. In the conflict in Timor-Leste between 1974 and 1999, the distribution was 18 percent of the killed and missing persons to 82 percent of deaths from starvation and diseases (Silva and Ball 2008). Disregarding how similar or dissimilar these two historical episodes are, it is perfectly possible that these two proportions can have extreme values. In such situations, a 50-50 distribution ensures the lowest error.

20. This section was based on DC-Cam materials available at www.dccam.org (e.g., "Renakse Summary Report," "Renakse Summary Table," and commentaries by William Schulte (2007) and Amy Gordon (2007), both of which can be found with the DC-Cam listings in the reference section of this chapter.

21. Pol Pot was the leader of Khmer Rouge. After the regime fell to Vietnamese forces in January 1979, the Khmer Rouge sought refuge in the jungles and mountains on both sides of Cambodia's border with Thailand. Pol Pot was indicted and sentenced (in absentia) to death.

22. The 1.6 million death toll comes from Kiernan (1996); it is the more conservative of his two estimates. The 1.4 million death toll, from Neupert and Prum (2005), is too low because the assumptions the authors used for their projections were not necessarily optimal.

23. ICMP is the International Commission for Missing Persons in Sarajevo, which produces DNA-based identifications of victims exhumed from mass (or surface) graves. For example, see: http://www.ic-mp.org/press-releases/icmp-makes-highest-number-of-dna-assisted-identifications-in-the-world-icmp-putem-dnk-ostvario-najveci-broj-identifikacija-na-svijetu-icmp-realiza-el-mayor-numero-de-identificaciones-por-adn-en-el-mun/#more-1114.

24. See the "List of Mass Graves" available at: http://www.dccam.org/Projects/Maps/ Mapping.htm).

# VI  The Complexity of Casualty Numbers

# 12 It Doesn't Add Up

METHODOLOGICAL AND POLICY IMPLICATIONS
OF CONFLICTING CASUALTY DATA

Jule Krüger, Patrick Ball, Megan E. Price, and Amelia Hoover Green

## Introduction

Scholars of peace and conflict studies, particularly those who seek to end or mitigate violence, are necessarily concerned with understanding violence. And while "understanding violence" is something of a theoretical enterprise, *documenting* violence presents significant challenges, which must be met if theory building is to continue. This is not only a matter of "getting it right" in a scientific sense. Our theories regarding *how* and *why* violence occurs are directly affected by our access to information about *what* violence has occurred. Moreover, both "theories of violence" and information about violence have immediate, consequential policy implications. Practitioners in the human rights and humanitarian communities rely on scientific evidence as they design and implement peacebuilding mechanisms, such as political strategies, peacekeeping operations, developmental policies, aid initiatives, and advocacy campaigns.

In addition to its key role in the process of policy building, data on the dynamics of violence also strongly affect practitioners' *evaluations* of peacebuilding initiatives. For example, considerable debate surrounds the operational standard and appropriateness of particular indicators of peacebuilding success (Diehl and Druckman 2010; Philpott 2010, 7). Any program evaluation requires the measurement of baseline and outcome states; in the context of peace and conflict issues, violence—typically measured as casualties (cf. Diehl and Druckman 2010, 93–132)—is a frequent indicator of program effectiveness. In this chapter, we consider the challenges presented by *incompleteness* and *uncertainty* in databases that collect casualty records. In short, we argue that these databases cannot provide a rigorous evidentiary basis for peacebuilding policy or impact assessment.

Researchers attempting to measure "impact," however defined, must grapple with the fact that commonly used reporting databases cannot provide an accurate account of the scope and nature of violence, either before or after the deployment of a given policy measure. Because the level and type of inaccuracy in any casualty database changes over time *and* with changing policy environments, analysts relying on raw casualty reporting data cannot compare pre- and post-intervention data with confidence.

In this chapter, we consider four examples in which multiple databases, purporting to address the same phenomenon, nevertheless suggest very different statistical patterns and, consequently, imply very different policy choices. A general consideration of database construction supports our conclusion that these databases, composed solely of directly observable information, are incomplete and biased in unpredictable ways. We conclude that it is impossible to produce a statistically valid and reliable measure of violence from a single casualty dataset. Our examples strongly support this contention as well; in each of these widely varying contexts, good-faith data-gathering efforts produced widely varying assessments of the magnitude and pattern of casualties.

In our experience, databases based on observed violence are collected for two primary purposes: case management and statistical description of patterns. Before using a given database to assess the impact of peacebuilding upon the level and pattern of violence, researchers should thus ask how and why the data in question were collected, and which analytical methods are appropriate.

Databases collected for the first purpose are useful in many ways—they document the details of specific cases and provide evidence that specific acts occurred. Such carefully collected information, for instance, can constitute prima facie evidence that an emergency situation requires immediate attention. The simple fact of violence directed against civilians may justify a prompt peacebuilding response in the form of military protection and/or emergency relief.

Responsible reporting from case data must limit itself to qualitative, descriptive analysis of the case material. Such limits do not imply lack of analytical power; for example, Human Rights Watch typically uses information this way. For the sake of clarity, data analysts must state openly that analyses based on casualty reporting data describe only the violence that has been documented in the database under consideration. Similarly, stakeholders in the peacebuilding realm must clarify—to themselves as much as to others—that the true magnitude of civilian suffering is currently unknown to them and that the mere evidence of such suffering entirely justifies their choice to act. In our view, such transparency decouples the potential for short-term action from the unattainable goal of short-term certainty. It invites action without suggesting that "the case is closed" and that further data collection and analysis are unnecessary.

This type of clarity will help analysts avoid the temptation to use data that might seem "good enough" for the short term when in fact analysts have no information about how well the data describe the underlying reality. Any database created from case data—whether from aggregated press accounts, individual testimonies, text messages from witnesses' cell phones, or cases presented at a hospital—will be constrained in the ways we describe here.

Why advocate so strongly for modesty in data analysis? In short, the relationship of reports to reality is complicated. Data collected for case management purposes are related in *unknown* ways to the population from which the data were drawn; that is, there is no necessary reason that case data should be statistically representative of the underlying population. No conclusions can be drawn from such data about more general patterns beyond what has been documented in the observed records themselves. Case data reflect *reporting* patterns—not patterns of violence—which are affected by *reporting bias* (or *selection bias*). "Reporting bias" in this context means that the likelihood that a given event is reported varies with characteristics of the event itself, or with characteristics of the agency collecting the reports. We describe this concept more fully in the next section of this chapter.

The second purpose of data collection, statistical description of true patterns in the population (often called *inference*), requires one of three methods:

1. Statistical projection from several databases using multiple systems estimation (MSE),
2. Complete administrative statistics (e.g., census, voter registration), or
3. Probability-sample surveys.

In many conflict and post-conflict settings, the second and third methods are hard to put into practice (cf. Diehl and Druckman 2010, 98). However, methodological difficulty does not justify invalid interpretations.

The four examples in this chapter draw from conflict situations in Colombia, Sierra Leone, El Salvador, and East Timor (now Timor-Leste). They demonstrate that multiple databases tell multiple, frequently conflicting, stories about the dynamics of conflict violence. These examples, like many others, call into question the reliability of research designs that rely on a single database from one source to test a specific hypothesis regarding conflict dynamics. In addition, these findings raise a difficult question for scholars attempting to draw statistical inferences from multiple databases: Which data source is the most reliable in comparison to the others? In the section entitled "Multiple, Conflicting Statistical Narratives from Multiple Databases," we shall illustrate that, in most cases, there exists no probabilistically based decision rule for choosing among several different, often contradictory narratives; instead, researchers are left to speculate about which might be better.

The remainder of this chapter is organized as follows: we first examine the issue of reporting bias in databases on casualties and human rights violations of other types. Drawing examples from four conflicts, we then illustrate the problematic issues of incompleteness and uncertainty inherent in data on violent events. Subsequently, we present the options available to researchers to address these problems. We conclude with an appeal for increased awareness of reporting bias in the context of quantitative analyses of strategic peacebuilding initiatives. We reiterate the necessity, in the context of the process, over time, of policy building and assessment, of understanding *what* has happened before making claims about *how* or *why*. Again, we do not suggest that scientific rigor should precede emergency action. Rather, we advocate making short-term decisions on the basis of reasoning *other* than "full accounting," specific magnitudes, or falsely precise estimates.

## Reporting Databases Do Not Represent the Full Population of Casualties

Samples are appropriate for statistical inference when they represent the larger, underlying population from which they were collected. Such samples must either contain the entire population (e.g., a census) or accurately represent the whole population by gathering entries according to a *probability sample* (usually called a random sample).

In contrast, *convenience samples*—including all observational casualty databases—are neither complete nor randomly sampled, and so are in general *not* representative of the whole population. Because they are not representative, they lead to biased results when used to describe patterns of violence. For example, such bias can affect testimonies collected by truth and reconciliation commissions, victim and witness statements provided to nongovernmental organizations (NGOs), press reports, government records, and records from UN monitoring missions. These sources represent most data on casualties and other types of conflict violence currently available to researchers.

Data based on convenience samples capture an unknown proportion of the underlying universe of victims or violations. This proportion changes with time, location, and countless other social dimensions. For example, in any given conflict, observers have no *ex ante* knowledge of whether their data record 5 percent or 95 percent of the true number of casualties. This is true regardless of the size of the database: a larger database cannot be assumed to be more representative. Moreover, observers cannot know whether data from two datasets showing equal numbers of casualties reflect one circumstance—that both the projects have entirely covered the true universe of violence—or another, namely, that the two projects simply reflect similar reporting limitations in an area where the true frequency of violations might be very different. There can be no accurate comparison of such areas without specific knowledge of reporting rates (i.e., the proportion of all violations), and these rates become known through some observational mechanism. An estimate of the reporting rate is impossible to obtain by using a single convenience sample (Ball 2005, 192).

A number of factors are likely to determine what we learn about past violent events, and whether we learn about them *at all* (cf. Goldstein 1992; de Vaus 2001; Davenport and Ball 2002; Earl et al. 2004; Kalyvas 2004, 2008; Utas 2005; Guzmán et al. 2007; Daponte 2008; Romeu 2008; Siegler et al. 2008; Silva and Ball 2008; Leiby 2009; Molitor et al. 2009; Diehl and Druckman 2010, Gohdes 2010). The factors that may cause various biases in the reporting of events can be grouped into four main categories:

- *Characteristics specific to the event and nature of violence.* If an event was recent, happened in an urban setting, was severe, produced many victims, or involved killings or disappearances, it is more likely to be reported than an event that happened in the more distant past, occurred in a rural or remote area, was less severe, involved fewer victims, or involved sexual violence (Goldstein 1992, 41; Davenport and Ball 2002, 435–437, 446; Earl et al. 2004, 69; Kalyvas 2004, 164; Silva and Ball 2008, 125; Leiby 2009, 86; Diehl and Druckman 2010, 98).
- *Specific individual characteristics, as well as the capacity and willingness of victims or witnesses to recall and report violent events.* Issues of sex, age, ethnicity, cultural background, memory, trauma, stigma, honesty, access, mobility, or fear determine a person's ability and willingness to testify in a correct, detailed manner (de Vaus 2001, 127; Davenport and Ball 2002, 437, 441; Siegler et al. 2008, 371; Leiby 2009, 80, 86; Gohdes 2010, 8.) Moreover, relationships between the data-gathering institution and the local population may vary over space or population sector; the incentives available to victims (political opportunity, medical assistance, reparations, etc.) may shift (cf. Utas 2005, 409; Guzmán et al. 2007, 7) in ways that affect reporting.
- *Aspects associated with the monitoring and documentation capacity, as well as interests of the data-gathering institution.* A monitoring organization's resources (i.e., local presence, staffing, logistics) change over time (Davenport and Ball 2002, 446; cf. Earl et al. 2004, 69; Gohdes 2010, 2). Each monitoring institution has specific objectives for collecting data on violence which affect how it designs its monitoring system. For example, an organization may focus only on violations of specific types or on certain regions—a focus that will not necessarily match the aim of a particular research or policy question (Davenport and Ball 2002, 446; Molitor et al. 2009, 615).
- *System characteristics.* The overall setting in which violence takes place influences the likelihood of reporting: the more authoritarian a regime, the less power the country's NGOs and independent press are likely to have and the more self-censorship is to be expected. The more intense and violent a conflict, the harder data collection will be (Goldstein 1992, 41; Davenport and Ball 2002, 436–437; Daponte 2008, 57; Kalyvas 2008, 403; Romeu 2008, 68; Blattman and Miguel 2010, 46). Similarly, security situations also change over time, and when violence becomes extreme, reporting may decline.

This list is far from exhaustive. Moreover, analysts cannot expect that factors associated with varying reporting rates will always operate in the same way. For example, very severe violence may cause decreased reporting—but this is not always the case. Increased violence may also be associated with *increased* reporting, as media organizations suddenly deem the crisis newsworthy (cf. Davenport and Ball 2002, 437; Earl et al. 2004, 69). As with all data biases, the analyst can make assumptions, but cannot know *ex ante*, the direction or magnitude of bias in a given situation.

Organizations collecting data in conflict or post-conflict regions face numerous challenges, many of which stem from circumstances beyond their control. Analysts must closely consider the fact that such conditions can produce biased results. However, it is still more important to emphasize that such results cannot and should not be interpreted as an indictment of the data-gathering organization. Biased results do not reflect careless or inadequate data collection; still less do such results reflect malfeasance. Lack of representativeness is an inherent limitation of convenience sampling, not a sign of institutional failure. At the same time, however, users of these data must keep in mind that nonrepresentative samples can lead to results that go beyond distortion to total inversion of the true dynamics of violence. If only one dataset is available, it is impossible to assess the degree of distortion that is present (cf. Ball 2005, 192; Molitor et al. 2009, 616).

## Multiple, Conflicting Statistical Narratives from Multiple Databases

In this section, we produce evidence from four conflict regions to illustrate our claim that each reporting database gathered in a particular conflict presents a distinct narrative of the dynamics of violence. The fact that findings from large datasets frequently disagree underlines the theme of this chapter: for any convenience dataset, no matter how large or carefully collected, another equally large, equally careful effort could produce a very different picture of the conflict. We note particularly that the data sources in question disagree fundamentally over basic questions such as: Where did violence occur? What kind of violence was exercised? When? Against whom?

### CASANARE, COLOMBIA: WHERE DID THE VIOLENCE OCCUR?

A number of studies of security conditions in Colombia have compared violence across specific regions or across specific periods of time, to show that paramilitary disarmament and demobilization programs have succeeded (e.g., Spagat 2006; Dube and Naidu 2009) or that violence against trade union activists is uncorrelated with trade union activities (Mejía and Uribe 2009). To accept these conclusions, one must assume that patterns detected in the available data reflect the true patterns of violence across space and time in Colombia. We shall compare statistical narratives from three data sources, each of which gathers accounts of killings in the Colombian department of Casanare.

The three datasets are denoted as VP, PN, and INMLCF, and all are convenience samples.[1] The Colombian Vice Presidency (VP) maintains a national database of homicides of people who belong to especially "vulnerable groups," such as (former) mayors, councilors, journalists, indigenous representatives, professors, or unionists. Information on killings originates from a variety of sources, which include the Foundation for the Liberty of the Press, indigenous organizations, the Ministry for Social Protection, the National Police, and the Administrative Department of Security (DAS). The VP also monitors press reports. The Colombian National Police (PN) keeps a record of homicides, while the National Institute for Legal Medicine and Forensic Sciences (INMLCF) maintains records of inspected cadavers of victims of violence.

Figure 12.1 illustrates the proportions of killings by municipality for each source.[2] When the municipalities are compared side by side, we can see that the proportion of all killings reported in each one varies across the three datasets for the period of 2000–2007. The three databases are in agreement that a large proportion of killings occurred in the municipality of Yopal, the urban center of Casanare. However, this proportion varies from more than half (according to INMLCF) to just over 30 percent (VP). Similarly, the VP data report that more than 20 percent of homicides occur in Aguazul and more than 10 percent in Villanueva, whereas the INMLCF's records indicate less than 10 percent in Aguazul and essentially zero killings in Villanueva.

Certainty about geographic patterns of violence is crucial to policy decisions regarding strategic responses to that violence. On the most basic level, understanding the true geographic pattern of violence is necessary to ensure the appropriate distribution of resources. In the Casanare case, relying solely on the INMLCF records would support a policy concentrating peacebuilding resources in Yopal. VP and PN archives highlight further important needs, hence increased resource distribution, in Aguazul, Villanueva, and Paz de Ariporo.

Problems with these data go well beyond these broad disagreements over geographic patterns. In theory, INMLCF and PN should report identical patterns of homicides in Casanare, since both organizations play a central role in each and every homicide investigation: The PN's responsibility is to investigate all crime scenes, while INMLCF identifies the cadavers. Yet even these sources conflict considerably over the geographic distribution of violence.

These discrepancies highlight important problems of data completeness in Casanare. More important, they raise questions regarding the process of data generation in each organization. How did INMLCF and PN data come to differ so significantly? INMLCF's Casanare headquarters are based in Yopal; the institute has one other office, in the municipality of Paz de Ariporo. Rural doctors and field visits provide data from the rest of the department. INMLCF staff resources vary considerably across municipalities. By contrast, the National Police maintains a presence in all Casanare municipalities. In addition, police forces have an operational advantage with regard to data collection in areas with active conflict—in the case of Casanare, municipalities such as Aguazul and

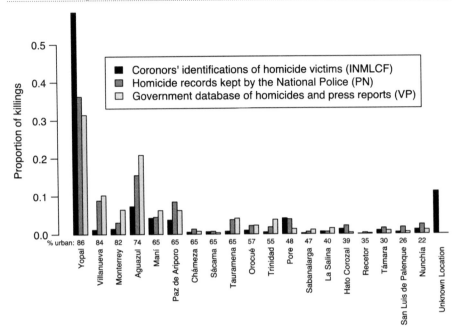

FIGURE 12.1  Reported Killings by Municipality and Source, Casanare 2000–2007

Villanueva. The Vice Presidency, in contrast to the INMLCF and NP, does not maintain a permanent presence in Casanare and relies upon other sources.

All three Colombian databases capture and process information systematically, and all three are trustworthy in the sense that the cases they include are likely to represent killings that actually occurred. Yet the *statistical patterns* derived from these databases *cannot all be true*; indeed, none of them is necessarily accurate. Some of the factors underlying uneven reporting across municipalities can be identified, but most remain unknown. These biases do not "cancel each other out." Nor would combining the sources create a representative sample. If these data are used without adjustment, researchers attempting to analyze the geographic pattern of violence in Casanare can only speculate or use their intuition regarding the relationship of these databases to the true pattern of violence. However, given the richness of the sources, it is possible to create a probability model that narrows assumptions about the data and can thereby make adjustments for selection bias (Guberek et al. 2010; also see note 4).

### SIERRA LEONE: WHAT KIND OF VIOLENCE OCCURRED?

Three reporting databases are available to describe the conflict in Sierra Leone—7,706 statements taken by the Truth (and Reconciliation) Commission (TRC) (Conibere et al. 2004), 2,788 statements collected by the nongovernmental organization Campaign for Good Governance (CGG), and the ABA/Benetech Sierra Leone War Crimes Documentation Survey (SLWCD).[3] Gohdes (2010) finds that these three sources do not

TABLE 12.I.

Overall Ranking of Six Most Frequent Violations in Sierra Leone, 1991–2000

| | | Survey (SLWCD) | NGO Reports (CGG) | Truth Commission (TRC) |
|---|---|---|---|---|
| Ranked Frequency of Violation Type | 1 | Forced displacement | Forced displacement | Forced Displacement |
| | 2 | Assault / Beating | Assault / Beating | Arbitrary detention |
| | 3 | Property destruction | Property destruction | Property destruction |
| | 4 | Killing | Property theft | Property theft |
| | 5 | Arbitrary detention | Arbitrary detention | Assault / Beating |
| | 6 | Property theft | Killing | Killing |

agree on the *ranking* of reported violations, much less on the specific proportions of various violations across space or time. Table 12.1 lists the six most frequently reported violations across all three datasets, ordered by their respective ranks within each dataset.

Although forced displacement is the most frequently reported violation in all three datasets, there is little consistency across sources in terms of the relative frequency of other violations. Assault or beating is the second most frequently reported violation in the SLWCD and CGG datasets, whereas the TRC lists arbitrary detention as the second most frequent violation. Both CGG and the TRC list killing as the least frequently reported violation (among the top six), whereas SLWCD ranks killing fourth and property theft last. It is difficult to know why these studies found such different results. Did the War Crimes Documentation Survey reach more witnesses of killings? Did individuals reporting to the TRC and CGG entertain hopes of being reimbursed for property theft or destruction? Or did the survey and testimony instruments simply word questions differently?

In her analysis, Gohdes (2010) examines the correlation of these relative frequencies among datasets. She finds that each dataset describes a somewhat different narrative of violence according to age, sex, and ethnicity of the victim, time period, and region of the reported violation. As in the case of Casanare, when convenience samples suggest different patterns of violence, it is impossible to determine which, if any, is correct. Thus, decisions about peacebuilding or other interventions made on the basis of quantitative claims from one sample are at risk of being completely wrong. When only one sample is available, we must assume that alternative samples, representing other statistical narratives, exist and remain to be collected. (Landman and Gohdes explore this example from Sierra Leone in more detail in chapter 5 in this volume.)

## EL SALVADOR: WHEN DID THE VIOLENCE OCCUR?

Approximately 25,000 noncombatants were *reported* killed during El Salvador's 1980–1992 civil war (e.g., Hoover Green 2010). Many academic analysts have concluded, often on the basis of Truth Commission data, that violence—including lethal violence—was

concentrated in the early years of war and declined significantly after an American ultimatum in 1983 (e.g., Stanley 1996, Wood 2003). However, other data sources tell a somewhat different story.

The United Nations–sponsored Truth Commission for El Salvador began its work
shortly after the signing of peace accords in 1992. Commission staff collected direct
reports from victims and witnesses of violence, focusing their attention on lethal violence (killings and disappearances). These testimonies yielded reports of approximately
7,000 separate incidents of violence. Torture and other nonlethal physical attacks were
also included, though in much smaller numbers.

Indirect reports to the Truth Commission were gathered from dozens of NGOs that
had collected data throughout the conflict. These secondary sources were compiled in a
second reporting database containing about 14,000 records. Temporal patterns appear
that are generally similar to those found in direct Truth Commission data, although the
two sources occasionally diverge. More important, both are substantially different from
the two datasets considered next.

A third significant source of documentation on civil war violence was the nongovernmental Human Rights Commission of El Salvador (CDHES). CDHES data represent
coded case files, specifically those reported directly to the organization during the course
of the conflict (cf. Ball 2000, 15–24). Although associated with the political Left,
CDHES attempted to document abuses by both government and insurgent forces.
These data include a significantly wider range of violence than do direct or indirect
Truth Commission data. In all, CDHES data contain approximately 22,000 individual
incidents of violence, coded into 16 violation types.

El Rescate, a Los Angeles–based NGO, compiled a fourth dataset. Like CDHES
data, El Rescate data refer to coded case files—in particular, a non-random sample of
case files from the Legal Aid Office of the (Roman Catholic) Archbishopric of San
Salvador. Thus, El Rescate data concern victims and witnesses who were willing and
able to report acts of violence to representatives of the Roman Catholic Church. El
Rescate viewed documentation of state violence as its key mission; incidents of violence
attributed to insurgents were not included in the El Rescate dataset, which contains
approximately 22,000 violations in total and refers to 23 separate violation types
(cf. Howland 2008).

Most academic observers agree that the bulk of the violence in the Salvadoran conflict occurred in the earliest years of the war (1980–1982) and that violence substantially
decreased following a military-aid ultimatum issued by the Reagan administration (e.g.,
Bacevich et al. 1988; Stanley 1996). In December 1983, Vice President George H. W.
Bush delivered a stern message to the Salvadoran military and the country's oligarchic
elite: military aid would cease if embarrassing—and, more important, strategically
disastrous—violence against noncombatants did not decrease significantly.

From a peacebuilding perspective, the accuracy or inaccuracy of the "ultimatum narrative" can be understood as a partial test of competing hypotheses about the causes of

violence (and nonviolence) against noncombatants. Do demands from patron countries to military clients work to reduce violence? To arrive at an answer to this foreign policy question, we must draw conclusions about the pattern of violence over time. More specifically, we must determine whether violence decreased significantly after the ultimatum. From the statistical pictures of several violation types across all four datasets, the evidence for the effectiveness of the Bush ultimatum is unclear.

Figure 12.2 shows the pattern of all reported violence over time. In these plots, direct reports to the Truth Commission datasets (solid lines) largely confirm the "early years" hypothesis just described. Indirect reports to the Truth Commission (not graphed) follow the same pattern. However, NGO data from El Rescate (dashes) and CDHES (dot-dash pattern) provide conflicting accounts. Data from El Rescate suggest that the majority of violence took place in the middle of the war, while CDHES data are concentrated in the conflict's later years. *Ex ante*, there is no useful way to determine which of these narratives is correct. The observed differences may result from any aspect of the

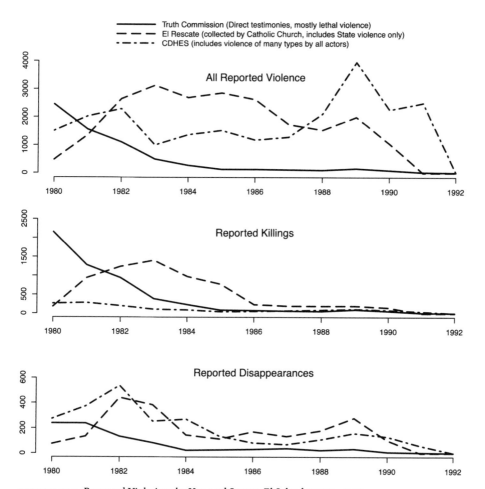

FIGURE 12.2 Reported Violations by Year and Source, El Salvador 1980–1992

widely varying data-gathering processes underlying the three sources. We know, for example, that Truth Commission data were gathered in the post-conflict period and focus on lethal violations, whereas El Rescate and CDHES data were gathered during the conflict. Yet these hints about potential biases offer no statistically defensible way to determine which is more accurate, for all violations or for any particular violation.

One approach to this temporal disagreement is further disaggregation. The picture seems clearer when we eliminate violations other than killing (figure 12.2, center). Data on killings alone suggest that lethal violence, at least, is concentrated in the early years of the war. Here, only CDHES data show no decline after 1983. Still, the data disagree significantly about the size of this decrease and when, relative to the 1983 ultimatum, the decline began. If the decline began well before the ultimatum, we cannot confirm that the ultimatum caused, or even aided, the decline.

The picture is even less clear when we consider disappearances (figure 12.2, bottom), which are as lethal as, but significantly more secretive than, outright killings. While evidence on killings may confirm the "early years" hypothesis, evidence on disappearances, like evidence on all violence, suggests that violence continued throughout the war, albeit in ways that were less embarrassing to the Salvadoran armed forces' American patrons. As in our earlier examples, the Salvadoran data confirm that differing sources offer conflicting statistical narratives; these conflicting narratives imply dramatically different conclusions about American foreign policy and conflict violence more generally. Yet there is no statistical basis on which to prefer one source to another.

## TIMOR-LESTE: DIRECT VIOLENCE, IMPOSED FAMINE, OR BOTH?

The most important quantitative question about the 1975–1999 Indonesian occupation of East Timor (now Timor-Leste) concerns mortality: How many people died as a result of the conflict? During the occupation, advocates estimated total deaths ranging from "over 200,000" people to more than 250,000 (cf. Martinkus 2001, XV). To refute, verify, or fully understand these estimates, we must also ask: How did those people die? In Timor-Leste, the story told in testimonies given to the Commission for Reception, Truth, and Reconciliation (CAVR) differs substantially from the story suggested by estimates from the CAVR's retrospective mortality survey (RMS) (Silva and Ball 2008). As presented in table 12.2, the ratio of killings to deaths due to hunger

TABLE 12.2.

Causes of Deaths by Source in Timor-Leste, 1975–1999

| Dataset | Killings | Hunger/Illness | Ratio |
|---|---|---|---|
| Truth Commission Testimonies (CAVR) | 5,955 | 10,809 | 0.55 |
| Retrospective Mortality Survey (RMS) | 16,090 | 86,539 | 0.19 |

and disease reported in statements given to the CAVR is 0.55, whereas the RMS found the same ratio to be 0.19.[4]

These sources tell markedly different stories about violence in East Timor during the Indonesian occupation, and we can speculate about the causes of this variation. For example, it is likely that in the open-ended, narrative testimonies collected by the CAVR, respondents believed that deliberate acts of killing were more salient than indirect deaths due to hunger and illness. Consequently, respondents were more inclined to come to the CAVR to report deliberate killings than to report indirect deaths (i.e., self-selection bias). Even in the course of a single narrative, CAVR respondents typically recall having witnessed a higher fraction of the deliberate deaths than indirect deaths. During the RMS, by contrast, respondents were specifically asked about whether certain people (their parents, siblings, and children) were alive or had died, and thus all kinds of deaths were captured equally.

In contrast to Casanare, El Salvador, and Sierra Leone, the Timor-Leste case does not represent a comparison of two convenience samples. The RMS drew a random sample of households in all thirteen of Timor-Leste's districts. The statistical findings of the RMS represent the entire country, including people who were not interviewed, and the findings presented from this study can be used to draw inferences about the experience of all people in East Timor during the occupation. In contrast, the collection of reports to the CAVR, which represent only the experiences of those who gave statements to the CAVR, cannot be expected to be representative of the experiences of the general population. Further, because summary information from the CAVR reports contradicts the RMS data, we can conclude that the CAVR testimony data does *not* represent the broader population. To address the original question of causes of death, from the RMS and using the CAVR data in combination with the RMS, it was estimated that there were 18,600 total killings (±1000) and 84,200 (±11,000) deaths due to hunger and illness in excess of what would have been expected by peacetime mortality rates (Silva and Ball 2006).

The CAVR testimonies are nevertheless immensely valuable—they are irreplaceable records of individuals' experiences of violence during the Indonesian occupation. We are not criticizing the data, but highlighting how convenience sources can fail to be representative of the larger population. As in our other examples, it is clear that building policy on the basis of CAVR testimonies alone might lead to overemphasis on interventions designed to remediate violent deaths, rather than (for example) on public health programs aimed at nutrition or food security.

## Methodological Options for the Quantitative Analysis of Violence

The foregoing examples demonstrate that different databases on casualties and other types of violence tell very different stories about the same historical events. Each data source considered is the result of a high-quality, large-scale data collection effort, and only in the cases of Sierra Leone and Timor-Leste is there any basis on which to prefer one story (i.e., one database) over another for any given purpose. The appropriately cautious conclusion is that *no* convenience dataset, no matter its size or quality, can be "chosen" as an accurate representation of reality.

Reporting databases collected as convenience samples, like those described here, are vital tools for human rights advocates, academic researchers, and policy makers. As we outlined in the introduction, these resources may provide sufficient evidence to initiate immediate reactions to human disaster; moreover, they provide an important qualitative description of the violence. However, any interpretation based on these samples must offer a clear accounting of the limitations they embody.

In the long term, effective peacebuilding policies require more rigorous scientific estimates: for example, an estimate of a population total or of patterns of violence by subpopulation. Post-conflict policies for resource allocation, redistricting, or minority protections are just a few examples of such initiatives. If the research goal is to establish facts about the general population, or about patterns and trends over time, space, or any other quantitative comparisons of relative levels of violence, the analysis must rely on multiple systems estimation, complete enumeration, or probability-sample surveys, as described earlier.

Given that complete administrative sources and probability-sample surveys are often (but not always) impossible to obtain in conflict or post-conflict settings, multiple systems estimation (MSE) provides a mechanism for drawing inferences about a population from multiple convenience samples.[5] However, MSE depends on several assumptions and requires complex statistical modeling and model selection. (See chapter 5, by Landman and Gohdes, and chapter 9, by Manrique-Vallier, Price, and Gohdes in this volume for detailed descriptions of MSE.)

We advise against simply aggregating databases in an attempt to reduce reporting bias. Such a strategy *may* ameliorate the worst of the problems identified—but only if the databases have countervailing biases. Whether a collection of convenience samples taken together overcomes all the selection biases is unknowable and leads, ultimately, to the same speculation about bias that attends the use of any single convenience sample. In practice, it is more likely that such aggregate databases share similar biases, reinforcing rather than ameliorating them. Statistical representativeness cannot be achieved by volume alone.

In most contexts, no quantitative inference is possible because MSE cannot be performed and no probability sample exists. In such situations, several analytic strategies are available, many of which do not employ any quantitative techniques. Many policy initiatives depend simply on the observation that something is happening, but not on claims about the magnitude or pattern of the event. A considerable amount of social scientific knowledge can be gleaned from qualitative assessments of the nature or process of violent events. At a highly disaggregated local level, some qualitative data can be used to complement qualitatively tested hypotheses, provided the issues surrounding convenience data are fully explained. In general, when convenience data are used in any capacity, it is best to "stay close to the data," guarding against overly ambitious inferences and quantifying potential biases through sensitivity analyses or other simulation exercises.

## Conclusion: Understanding Violence Requires Understanding Data

This chapter has illustrated how the unavoidable uncertainty inherent in reporting databases precludes inference about patterns of violence. We presented four examples of projects that collected data about past violence. There are many more examples; indeed, the number of examples we presented is limited by the space available for this chapter. For nearly every question in every country for which multiple databases cover the same conflict, those databases provide uncertain or contradictory statistical findings on key hypotheses.

The data challenges to evidence-based peacebuilding initiatives are clear in the context of our examples; we contend that biased data are the rule, rather than the exception. Policy studies based on quantitative evidence must grapple with the issues of bias and representativeness raised in this chapter. Confronted with differing reports of geographical patterns as in Casanare, Colombia, where would a decision maker concentrate security resources? Observing differing accounts of the most frequent violation types in Sierra Leone, what would be the best strategy to assist victims of violence? Presented with a security situation like that of El Salvador in the early 1980s, is the threat of reduced military assistance truly the most effective way to curtail state violence? And assuming that we receive two different narratives of mortality, as offered in Timor-Leste, would we focus our resources on military operations or humanitarian assistance?

In striving to be sustainable and effective, strategic peacebuilding seeks a holistic approach toward the context of particular conflicts, by considering all relevant actors and institutions (Philpott 2010, 4). Casualty data obtained via convenience samples require an equally holistic approach. Researchers must recognize that no convenience sample is representative, that alternative convenience samples will contain alternative statistical narratives, and that all potential narratives are biased in unpredictable ways. On a practical level, such a holistic approach requires, at minimum, careful qualitative investigation of a given dataset's construction. Where, by whom, and under what conditions were the data gathered? What social networks fed data collection efforts, and what social networks avoided enumeration? Even in the absence of a statistically valid estimate, contextual knowledge can, at least, provide stakeholders with a qualitative sense of potential biases and blind spots.

The examples we have considered emphasize the need for rigorous assessment of the many factors affecting data-generating processes. More generally, our analysis refutes the notion that convenience samples provide a "good enough" basis for inference, particularly if the ultimate goal is well-designed, accurately assessed peacebuilding policy. To avoid false conclusions about the scope and pattern of civilian casualties over space and time, analysts must seek a clear understanding of the structure and sources of reporting bias and must use analytical methods appropriate to these data. Policy makers who are concerned with emergent situations must clarify the extent to which their decisions rest on data inadequate for statistical purposes, but potentially useful for qualitative insights.

ACKNOWLEDGEMENTS

The authors wish to thank Anita Gohdes, Tamy Guberek, Daniel Guzmán, Jeff Klingner, Romesh Silva, and the rest of the Benetech Human Rights Program team and partners for their work on the projects from which these examples were collected.

REFERENCES

Bacevich, Andrew, James Hallums, Richard White, and Thomas Young. 1988. *American Military Policy in Small Wars: The Case of El Salvador.* Santa Monica, CA: RAND Corporation.

Ball, Patrick. 2000. "The Salvadoran Human Rights Commission: Data Processing, Data Representation, and Generating Analytical Reports." In *Making the Case: Investigating Large Scale Human Rights Violations Using Information Systems and Data Analysis.* Edited by Patrick Ball, Herbert F. Spirer, and Louise Spirer, 15–24. Washington, D.C.: American Association for the Advancement of Science. At: http://shr.aaas.org/mtc/pdf/chapter%2001.pdf (last accessed October 30, 2010).

Ball, Patrick. 2005. "On the Quantification of Horror: Field Notes on Statistical Analysis of Human Rights Violations." In *Repression and Mobilization.* Edited by Christian Davenport, Hank Johnston, and Carol Mueller, 189–208. Minneapolis: University of Minnesota Press.

Conibere, Richard, et al. 2004. *Statistical Appendix to the Report of the Truth and Reconciliation Commission of Sierra Leone.* A Report by the Benetech Human Rights Data Analysis Group and the American Bar Association Central European and Eurasian Law Initiative to the Truth and Reconciliation Commission. At: http://hrdag.org/resources/publications/SL-TRC-statistics-chapter-final.pdf. Accessed October 17, 2010.

Daponte, Beth. 2008. "Why Estimate Direct and Indirect Casualties from War? The Rule of Proportionality and Casualty Estimates." In *Statistical Methods for Human Rights.* Edited by Jana Asher, David Banks, and Fritz J. Scheuren, 51–63. New York: Springer.

Davenport, Christian, and Patrick Ball. 2002. Views to a Kill: Exploring the Implications of Source Selection in the Case of Guatemalan State Terror, 1977–1995. *Journal of Conflict Resolution* 46(3): 427–450.

Diehl, Paul, and Daniel Druckman. 2010. *Evaluating Peace Operations.* London and Boulder, CO: Lynne Rienner Publishers.

Dube, Oeindrila, and Suresh Naidu. 2009. *Bases, Bullets and Ballots: The Effect of the U.S. Military Aid on Political Conflict in Colombia.* At: http://www.cgdev.org/files/1423498_file_Dube_Naidu_Military_Aid_FINAL.pdf. Accessed October 17, 2010.

Earl, Jennifer, et al. 2004. The Use of Newspaper Data in the Study of Collective Action. *Annual Review of Sociology* 30(1): 65–80.

Gohdes, Anita. 2010. *Different Convenience Samples, Different Stories: The Case of Sierra Leone*. Palo Alto, CA: Benetech. At: http://www.hrdag.org/resources/publications/Gohdes_Convenience%20Samples.pdf. Accessed October 17, 2010.

Goldstein, Robert. 1992. "The Limitations of Using Quantitative Data in Studying Human Rights Abuses." In *Human Rights and Statistics: Getting the Record Straight*. Edited by Thomas B. Jabine and Richard P. Claude, 35–61. Philadelphia: University of Pennsylvania Press.

Guberek, Tamy, et al. 2010. *To Count the Uncounted: An Estimation of Lethal Violence in Casanare*. A Report by the Benetech Human Rights Program. Palo Alto, CA: Benetech. At: http://www.hrdag.org/resources/publications/results-paper.pdf. Accessed October 17, 2010.

Guzmán, Daniel, et al. 2007. Missing People in Casanare. Palo Alto, CA: Benetech. At: http://www.hrdag.org/resources/publications/casanare-missing-report.pdf. Accessed October 17, 2010.

Hicks, Madelyn, and Michael Spagat. 2008. The Dirty War Index: A Public Health and Human Rights Tool for Examining and Monitoring Armed Conflict Outcomes. *PLoS Medicine* 5(12): 1658–1664.

Hoover Green, Amelia. 2010. Repertoires of Violence against Noncombatants: The Role of Armed Group Institutions and Ideologies. Dissertation manuscript, Yale University.

Howland, Todd. 2008. How El Rescate, a Small Nongovernmental Organization, Contributed to the Transformation of the Human Rights Situation in El Salvador. *Human Rights Quarterly* 30(3): 703–757.

Kalyvas, Stathis. 2004. The Urban Bias in Research on Civil Wars. *Security Studies* 13(3): 160–190.

Kalyvas, Stathis. 2008. "Promises and Pitfalls of an Emerging Research Program: The Microdynamics of Civil War." In *Order, Conflict, Violence*. Edited by Stathis N. Kalyvas, Ian Shapiro, and Tarek Masoud, 397–421. Cambridge: Cambridge University Press.

Leiby, Michele. 2009. Digging in the Archives: The Promise and Perils of Primary Documents. *Politics and Society* 37(1): 75–100.

Martinkus, John. 2001. *A Dirty Little War: An Eyewitness Account of East Timor's Descent into Hell, 1997–2000*. Sydney: Random House Australia.

Mejía, Daniel, and Mara José Uribe. 2009. Is Violence Against Union Members in Colombia Systematic and Targeted? At: http://econpapers.repec.org/RePEc:col:000089:006147. Accessed October 17, 2010.

Molitor, Nuoo-Ting, Nicky Best, Chris Jackson, and Sylvia Richardson. 2009. Using Bayesian Graphical Models to Model Biases in Observational Studies and to Combine Multiple Sources of Data: Application to Low Birth Weight and Water Disinfection By-Products. *Journal of the Royal Statistical Society*, Series A (*Statistics in Society*) 172(3): 615–637.

Philpott, Daniel. 2010. "Introduction: Searching for Strategy in an Age of Peacebuilding." In *Strategies of Peace: Transforming Conflict in a Violent World*. Edited by Daniel Philpott and Gerard Powers, 3–18. Oxford and New York: Oxford University Press.

Romeu, Jorge. 2008. "Statistical Thinking and Data Analysis: Enhancing Human Rights Work." In *Statistical Methods for Human Rights*. Edited by Jana Asher, David Banks, and Fritz J. Scheuren, 65–85. New York: Springer.

Siegler, Anne, et al. 2008. Media Coverage of Violent Deaths in Iraq: An Opportunistic Capture-Recapture Assessment. *Prehospital and Disaster Medicine* 23(4): 369–371.

Silva, Romesh, and Patrick Ball. 2006. *The Profile of Human Rights Violations in Timor-Leste, 1974–1999*. A Report by the Benetech Human Rights Data Analysis Group to the Commission on Reception, Truth and Reconciliation. Palo Alto, CA: Benetech. At: http://hrdag.org/resources/Benetech-Report-to-CAVR.pdf. Accessed October 18, 2010.

———. 2008. "The Demography of Conflict-Related Mortality in Timor-Leste (1974–1999): Reflections on Empirical Quantitative Measurement of Civilian Killings, Disappearances, and Famine-Related Deaths." In *Statistical Methods for Human Rights*. Edited by Jana Asher, David Banks, and Fritz J. Scheuren, 117–139. New York: Springer.

Spagat, Michael. 2006. Colombia's Paramilitary DDR: Quiet and Tentative Success. At: http://www.cerac.org.co/pdf/UNDP_DDR_V1.pdf. Accessed October 17, 2010.

Stanley, William. 1996. *The Protection Racket State: Elite Politics, Military Extortion and Civil War in El Salvador*. Philadelphia: Temple University Press.

Utas, Mats. 2005. Victimcy, Girlfriending, Soldiering: Tactic Agency in a Young Woman's Social Navigation of the Liberian War Zone. *Anthropological Quarterly* 78: 403–430.

de Vaus, David. 2001. *Research Design and Social Research*. London and Thousand Oaks, CA, and New Delhi: Sage Publications.

Wood, Elisabeth. 2003. *Insurgent Collective Action in El Salvador*. Cambridge, MA, and New York: Cambridge University Press.

NOTES

1. There exist twelve further datasets that have been used in a full analysis of homicides and disappearances in Casanare (see Guberek et al. 2010). Each of these datasets is also a convenience sample.

2. This figure builds on a graph presented in Guberek et al. (2010, 23).

3. The Sierra Leone War Crimes Documentation Survey (SLWCD) is a probability sample. However, in Gohdes (2010) the results were presented without weighting. Hence, notwithstanding the underlying sampling technique, in this analysis the SLWCD was a convenience sample just like the other two lists analyzed for Sierra Leone.

4. This finding raises questions about the claim that convenience data can be used to construct a "Dirty War Index," as suggested by Hicks and Spagat (2008). Such an index relies on the assumption that different types of violence (including death by different causes) are subject to equal rates of underreporting. This is clearly not the case: datasets collected for human rights purposes will oversample killings relative to deaths due to accident, hunger, or disease because killings are interesting to human rights analysis, while other types of deaths may appear to be irrelevant. There is no reason to expect that the ratio of *reported* killings to other *reported* deaths should be similar to the true ratio of killings to all deaths.

5. It is important to note that MSE does not turn convenience samples into probability samples; rather, it provides a way to model the underlying random components of the convenience samples.

# 13 Challenges to Counting and Classifying Victims of Violence in Conflict, Post-Conflict, and Non-Conflict Settings
## Keith Krause

THE TURN TO "evidence-based" policy and programming in advanced industrial states in a wide variety of issue areas has started to migrate into issues of global public policy. From its origins in public health and social welfare policy debates, the idea that programs, policies, and interventions needed to be based on robust data and analysis has spread to domains as diverse as policing, education, crime prevention, welfare delivery, and development policy.[1] There are a number of reasons for this broad shift in the philosophy of public policy and service delivery. In general, however, the shift is the result of the diffusion of techniques of "new public management" and norms of accountability and transparency in the use of public resources. From a more critical perspective, this could also be regarded as the globalization of what Michel Foucault called "governmentality": the progressive development of forms of state power that are oriented around the "institutions, procedures, analyses and reflections, calculations, and tactics . . . that has the population as its target, political economy as its major form of knowledge and apparatuses of security as its essential technical instrument" Foucault 2007; Neumann and Sending 2010).

How is this relevant to the issue of counting and classifying the victims of violence—in both conflict and non-conflict settings? This chapter will argue that although the general shift toward improving the evidence base on which we analyze armed violence in all its forms is a positive development for research and policy making, critical occlusions and limitations associated with *what is counted* and *how it is counted* pose serious challenges to the goal of developing adequate conflict resolution and violence reduction policies and programs. To make good on this argument, the chapter first summarizes some of the basic justifications for "counting casualties" and then sketches a "state of the art" that reviews how and why casualty counting has developed over the past two decades. This is followed by a discussion of the rationale behind an integrated approach to counting victims of violence that blurs (or effaces) the boundary between "conflict" and "non-conflict" victims of violence, a boundary based on the traditional (and legally oriented) understanding of "armed conflict" as a violent, politically motivated, confrontation between the armed forces of two or more states, or a state and non-state actors (e.g., in a civil war).[2] Some of the more technical and conceptual obstacles that this more integrated approach to casualty counting faces are explained, as well. The last part of the chapter focuses on some of the more philosophical challenges to counting casualties "in the field" and to the development of violence prevention and reduction policies on this basis.

Overall, this chapter draws upon the experience of the team of researchers associated with the Small Arms Survey project in Geneva. Over the past decade, these men and women have conducted field studies and surveys concerned with assessing the negative impacts of armed violence in more than 40 countries around the world, to varying degrees of depth and sophistication. Thus the Small Arms Survey draws upon a number of sources and studies, which include the administration of household surveys in post-conflict environments such as Burundi, Liberia, Côte d'Ivoire, South Lebanon, South Sudan, and Guatemala, as well as the use of local- and national-level data sources (police and hospital/health clinic data), focus groups, key informant interviews, and other tool-kits and data sources on the impacts of conflict and crime on human and community security and well-being.

### From Margins to the Center: The Increased Importance of Conflict Victimology

The idea of counting victims of conflict or violence *within* Western societies is not a new one, but it does have a genealogy. Armies—at least since the late nineteenth or early twentieth century—generally kept track of their dead in battle, as the notion of the citizen soldier required respect for (and sometimes reparation for) the human sacrifices offered to Mars. One need only visit the countless war memorials with names inscribed upon them dotting the landscape in Europe and in North America. Before then, soldiers were (in the seventeenth century) mercenaries in commercial relations with state rulers or part of a permanent professional class (in the eighteenth century), whose professional engagement required no precise accounting. By the Napoleonic era, soldiers were increasingly (and often unwilling) conscripts who also died uncounted. The roughly 400,000 soldiers of Napoleon's *Grand Armée* who are estimated to have died on the way to Moscow, for example, fell to their death by the roadside on the long march or were buried in mass graves, but were never really accounted for in any systematic way (Talty 2009). The reported 618,000 casualties of the Civil War in the United States are similarly estimates based on imperfect demographic, recruitment, and casualty records (Vinovskis 1989). In both these nineteenth-century situations, a huge percentage of deaths were from disease and not battle: more than 50 percent in the case of the Civil War. But the development of more effective military bureaucracies, military pension and care systems, and other administrative structures meant that in the late nineteenth century, and certainly by World War I, counting their own casualties became part of the core business of national armed forces (Gerber 2001).

Counting the *civilian* casualties of war, however, was seldom considered to be an important task of the state, even until the latter part of the twentieth century. When war followed its classical model of battlefield confrontations between opposing forces distinct from the civilian population, this neglect of civilian casualties was of little consequence.[3] But few wars have corresponded to this model, and historically speaking, civilian casualties took one of two forms: *direct* victims of violence, such as in the aerial bombings of cities during the Second World War, or *indirect* victims of violence, residents of war-ravaged areas who died because they had been deprived of access to food, shelter, water, or other basic necessities. Their numbers could be considerable: probably 400,000–600,000 German civilians died in the Allied strategic bombing campaign in the Second World War, in addition to the more than 60,000 British and 67.000 French victims of aerial bombing campaigns.[4] A huge number of civilians died in Central Europe during the Thirty Years' war of the seventeenth century, which claimed up to one-third of the population of the German territories (Parker 1997). Finally, many who qualified to be called casualties of war did not die but were wounded and disabled, thus representing a considerable burden for the families or communities to which they often returned. The costs of war were always much greater than the count of the dead would suggest.

The situation in the latter part of the twentieth century was hardly much better than in earlier decades or centuries. We have today only an imperfect grasp of the number of victims in several large-scale episodes of conflict and violence, such as the Rwandan genocide of 1994 or the mass killings of Pol Pot's Democratic Republic of Kampuchea (1975–1979); even the number of dead from the wars in the former Yugoslavia in the 1990s has been the subject of debate (Heuveline 1998; des Forges 1999; Kiernan 2003). We may have more precise figures for smaller conflicts, such as Malcolm Sutton's *Index of Deaths from the Conflict in Ireland*, which documents 3,536 deaths between 1969 and 2001, or the figure of 8,000–12,000 dead in the conflict in Kosovo in 1999 (Sutton 1994; Wille and Krause 2005). And we have the recent development of some fairly sophisticated measurement and estimation techniques that have been used—as is documented elsewhere in this volume—to arrive at more or less reliable figures on contemporary conflict deaths based on multiple and independent lists and sources.

The basic distinctions just sketched out—between battle deaths of combatants, deaths of combatants outside battle, direct (violent) civilian deaths, indirect civilian deaths, and wounded or disabled victims—are, however, seldom made in the aggregate statistics on the victims of war. And for most purposes, this does not matter. But many of the challenges facing contemporary conflict victimology (defined as the "scientific study of the physical, emotional and financial harm people suffer")—and the related desire to influence global policies—stem from the need to draw these basic distinctions, in addition to the difficulties associated with establishing clear figures for casualties of different sorts.[5] For example, the figure of approximately 30,000 annual conflict deaths in the first decade of the twentieth-first century has been widely cited to demonstrate that the intensity and destructiveness of contemporary conflict has declined dramatically from previous eras (Human Security Centre 2005). Yet this number cannot often be compared to data from previous periods, which sometimes include all of the four potential categories of lethal victims of violence, sometimes only the direct (violent) deaths, and sometimes a complex mix of all of these. It is no surprise that a more refined approach that focuses primarily on battle deaths arrives at lower figures.

A perfect illustration of this is the debate over conflict deaths in the war in Iraq (2003–2010): on the one side, we have the estimate of between 99,711 and 108,846 civilian deaths from violence in the Iraq Body Count (February 15, 2011), or the estimate of 151,000 violent deaths between 2002 and 2006 of the Iraq Family Health Survey Study Group (see also chapters 3 and 4 in this volume) (Iraq Family Health Survey Study Group 2008). On the other side, we have the Uppsala Conflict Data Program database estimates, which document somewhere between 15,000 and 20,000 "battle-related deaths" between 2003 and 2009, most of them resulting from conflicts that pitted various groups against the government of Iraq.[6] Given the difference in counting rules or estimation techniques observed by these various sources, we can conclude little about the evolution of contemporary conflict dynamics from such debates. The potentially instrumental use of different figures for political purposes is also obvious.

Parallel to the development of better data on war deaths has been a growing preoccupation with better documenting the casualties of "non-conflict" violence. From a criminological perspective, the principal category is "homicide"—a legal category to describe deaths of certain kinds and generally "defined as unlawful death inflicted on a person by another person" (Secretariat 2008). Various European states have reasonably good historical statistics: in Sweden and Finland, going back to the 1750s, for example; in Ireland from the 1840s, and in most other countries dating from the nineteenth century. But the situation for the rest of the world is rather different. While reasonably good data exist for the most recent decades throughout Latin America, and a few countries in Southeast Asia, information for much of Africa and Asia is either unavailable or (more often) nonexistent.

Homicide statistics also suffered from shortcomings analogous to those found in conflict data. Different definitions can lead to radically different figures: in Mexico and South Africa, for example, the legal distinction between *intentional* homicide and *manslaughter*—"homicidio doloso" (homicide) vs. "homicidio culposo" (manslaughter) in Spanish—results in a significant difference (between 20 and 30 percent) in counts of violent deaths per year. In addition, different state institutions or administrations have different counting rules for violent deaths: public health data (hospitals, clinics, and morgues) record generally higher levels than are found in police data. Most jurisdictions do not count police killings as criminal deaths, and hence the several hundred people killed in recent years by the Lagos, Rio de Janeiro, or Nairobi police are excluded from the data.[7] In some jurisdictions (Jamaica, Dominican Republic), between 10 and 20 percent of violent deaths are caused by the police and not captured in homicide statistics (Rengifo 2011). And at the international level, although a recently released cross-national dataset on homicide exists, many of the figures are based on estimates or on imperfect levels of national reporting (UNODC n.d.).

In short, counting and classifying casualties from any form of armed violence is a difficult business, virtually wherever one looks. Against this backdrop, why should scholars, analysts, and activists even bother? At least five reasons have been offered in most attempts to collect better data in conflict and non-conflict settings, and they tend to revolve around the idea of influencing public policy debates:

- Better estimates of historical episodes of violence can provide "massive, objective, and undeniable evidence of human rights violations, and giv[e] voice to the thousands of victims and witnesses who have come forward to tell their stories," as well as contributing to the process of "truth and reconciliation" and also transitional justice (Benetech n.d.);
- Better data on battle-related conflict deaths will "ensure that the human consequences of military intervention . . . [are] not neglected," and can potentially lead to more discriminating policies to limit the targeting of civilians (Iraq Body Count);
- Better armed conflict data can be "useful for systematic studies of the origins of conflict, conflict dynamics and conflict resolution" and can allow researchers to "conduct theoretically and empirically based analyses of armed conflict: its causes, escalation, spread, prevention and resolution" (Uppsala Conflict Data Program n.d.);
- Better data on indirect conflict deaths can be used "to improve needs-based preparedness and responses to humanitarian emergencies," as well as Secretariato identify looming (or ongoing) conflict-related humanitarian disasters and to guide relief and humanitarian assistance efforts (CRED n.d.);
- Better data on non-conflict armed violence (homicides, etc.) can be used to improve programs and policies related to crime prevention and the reduction of armed violence.

## An Integrated Approach to Counting Victims of Violence

The preceding section highlighted some of the challenges in counting casualties in both conflict and non-conflict settings, and readers may wonder why the optic has been widened beyond armed conflict–related violence, given that much of the work in this area has dealt exclusively with armed conflicts. Answering this question helps highlight one of the central dilemmas in casualty counting: choosing *what* to count inevitably makes a political (and potential normative) claim about *what not* to count, and can skew public policy debates in potentially unproductive directions. Counting and classifying, as ways of ordering our social world, involve choices that are not politically neutral, as students of communal and ethnic conflicts are well aware (Kertzer and Arel 2002).

So what is the problem with counting casualties of armed conflicts, and why should systematic efforts to count casualties include all victims of violence, and not only those in what are conventionally regarded as conflict zones? The first reason is that the transformation of contemporary warfare has made it almost impossible to draw a clear distinction between conflict and non-conflict violence. Although the claim that we live in an era of "new wars" is somewhat exaggerated, one aspect of the new-wars argument that is significant is the blurring of the lines between conflict and non-conflict violence, and between more purely political versus more purely economic or material motives.[8] Warlords in West Africa, for example, are in many ways indistinguishable from large-scale criminal gangs. Groups such as the Movement for the Emancipation of the Niger Delta (MEND) in Nigeria, while claiming some political motives (e.g., a more equitable distribution of the region's oil wealth), also engage in large-scale rent-seeking behavior and harbor armed groups with a variety of mixed motives. As Judith Asuni argues, the MEND "is a changing mass of groups, some of them criminally motivated, others politically and ideologically driven" with perhaps more than 25,000 members in 48 distinct groups, holding approximately 10,000 weapons (Asuni 2009).[9] Similarly, the Bakassi Boys of Nigeria, who may have started out as a vigilante gang in Aba, soon became a tool of political figures in Abia State (Harnischfeger 2003; Meagher 2007).

On the other side of the ledger, although the Mexican army has deployed up to 35,000 troops to fight against the drug cartels in Northern Mexico, and although more than 27,000 violent deaths have been documented since 2006, this large-scale violence does not figure in datasets that count "armed conflicts" (Stratfor 2010). This circumstance makes sense only after one has recognized that the focus on "armed conflict" presumed that the fighting was a form of political violence that fell within the Clausewitzian paradigm in which war "is the continuation of politics with an admixture of other means." Today, however, the Clausewitzian paradigm is more of a hindrance than a help in arriving at an understanding of contemporary dynamics of political violence. As Martin van Creveld has pointed out, neat distinctions between war and crime break down as states lose their monopoly over organized violence.[10]

A potentially more important dimension of this problem is that conflict and non-conflict (or post-conflict) violent dynamics might be linked, hence ought to be tracked together. Certainly, this assumption is behind the idea of using casualty numbers as a strategic peacebuilding mechanism, or as a metric for assessing successful peacebuilding. Violent conflict, representing as it does a rupture in social, political, and economic relations, can make enduring changes to social relations. In Iraq, for example, the overthrow of Saddam Hussein ended secular authoritarian rule (which was relatively free of interpersonal violence, although highly repressive) and made room for new forms of violent social action, often to advance a particular sectarian or religious agenda. In addition to the intercommunal conflicts that arose from regime change, violence against women (honor killings) appears also to have become more prevalent (Green and Ward 2009). Stopping a casualty count when foreign forces leave (or relinquish an active combat role) seems to miss the point. Similar dynamics concerning violence against women may be at work in the Democratic Republic of Congo, but we have no adequate baseline data on pre-war victimization and death that would allow us to understand what is happening.[11]

A second important reason for integrating conflict and non-conflict violence in casualty counting is that the overwhelming majority of victims of lethal violence are dying in non-conflict settings. As documented by the Geneva Declaration's second *Global Burden of Armed Violence* (Secretariat 2011) report, more than 523,000 people are killed each year as a result of lethal violence: 55,000 in conflicts, and approximately 468,000 in non-conflict settings (intentional homicide, violent "unintentional" homicides, and extrajudicial executions and unlawful killings). This makes the conflict-related violence only about 10 percent of the total global burden of armed violence. (Secretariat 2008) Although the term "homicide" connotes individual interpersonal acts of lethal violence, in many parts of the world, lethal violence is a social and group-related phenomenon associated with gangs (in, e.g., Central America) or intercommunal conflicts (in, e.g., northern Nigeria). Therefore, it can be said that the phenomenon is less "different" from armed conflict than might seem to be the case at first glance. Even when one includes a reasonable estimate of indirect conflict-related deaths (as a multiple of direct conflict deaths), the non-conflict deaths remain vastly more numerous.

Another way of looking at this would be with national comparisons of "violent death rates" normalized to the standard "deaths per 100,000" that are used by epidemiologists. Table 13.1 provides a rough comparison for the 20 countries most affected by lethal violence in 2004–2009. Leaving aside any methodological concerns, what is obvious is that for casualty counters, "armed conflict" is not the only, and perhaps not the most important, concern—only a half-dozen of the top 20 "most violent countries" (Iraq, Colombia, Sri Lanka, Sudan, the Democratic Republic of the Congo, and Somalia) were involved in an armed conflict; if better data were available, Afghanistan, and possibly Yemen, would also appear on this top list. Several other countries (El Salvador, Guatemala, Central African Republic) can be considered to be post-conflict countries; but many more are afflicted with high levels of violence that are not related to an armed

TABLE 13.1.

Death Rates, 2004–2009 (average), for the 20 Countries Most Affected by Lethal Violence

| | |
|---|---|
| El Salvador | 61.86 |
| Iraq | 59.40 |
| Jamaica | 58.10 |
| Honduras | 48.60 |
| Colombia | 45.77 |
| Venezuela | 44.64 |
| Guatemala | 43.20 |
| South Africa | 38.39 |
| Sri Lanka | 37.09 |
| Lesotho | 33.67 |
| Central African Republic | 32.95 |
| Sudan | 32.30 |
| Belize | 31.34 |
| Democratic Republic of the Congo | 31.29 |
| Swaziland | 26.47 |
| People's Republic of the Congo | 26.10 |
| Somalia | 26.03 |
| Brazil | 25.85 |
| Malawi | 25.47 |
| Occupied Palestinian Territory | 23.74 |

Source: Global Burden of Armed Violence II (Secretariat of the Geneva Declaration on Armed Violence and Development 2011).

conflict, as conventionally defined. From a policy perspective, if the goal is reducing levels of global insecurity, arguably as much attention should be paid to El Salvador (in relative terms) as to Somalia; to Venezuela as to Afghanistan. Of course, there is something distinctive about the political and conflict dynamics in each of these countries; as casualty counters, however, we would do best to cast a wide enough net to allow comparisons to be made and distinctions to be drawn based on the evidence, rather than relying on a priori categories that limit our perspective.

Finally, from a practical perspective, if one's goal is promoting human security and reducing violence and insecurity, knowing that wars and armed conflicts are not the most dangerous violent threats that most people face makes it difficult to sustain a restrictive optic on "armed conflict" casualties. The policy consequences of this may also be counterproductive. The Human Security Report 2009/2010, for example, proclaimed that the total number of battle-deaths in 2008 was 27,000, echoing its earlier low estimates

(Human Security Centre 2011). At first glance, 27,000 is a comprehensive estimate, since it includes battle deaths in state-based, one-sided, and non-state armed conflicts—hence appears to be inclusive.[12] Yet the narrow focus on *battle deaths* (of recognized combatants or civilian collateral casualties of battle) and a particular definition of organized group (with political aims) excludes entirely, for example, the violence in Mexico—which claimed more than 74,000 lives between 2004 and 2009 alone! The exclusions of these deaths from the major datasets on armed conflict, while consistent with the particular counting rules and definitions of the Human Security Report Project, is puzzling if one genuinely wishes to adopt a human security perspective. In addition to presenting a misleading picture of the evolution (and mutation) of forms of armed violence worldwide, it can lead to public complacency as the international community welcomes the end of war and the (relative) success of international peacekeeping and post-conflict peacebuilding efforts (Human Security Centre 2005).

## Dilemmas of Victimology: On Accuracy and Responsibility

Although a powerful case can be made both for casualty counting and for casting the net widely enough to include all forms of lethal violence, there are still some serious (and troubling) dilemmas associated with this endeavor, which can be discussed under the labels of "accuracy" and "responsibility." In general terms, those engaged in efforts to improve knowledge as a basis for better policy making must ensure that the degree of accuracy achievable is sufficient for both researchers and policy makers to be reasonably certain that policies can be justified and can be effective. Researchers also have a responsibility to ensure the security of their subjects—and not just in narrow terms of research ethics: researchers must ensure that the knowledge entrusted to them will not, and cannot be, used in harmful ways.

### ACCURACY

The tremendous difficulties in gathering reliable data on different forms of violence and victimization have been well rehearsed in different publications (Obermayer et al. 2008; Secretariat 2008; Spagat et al. 2009; Human Security Centre 2011). Scholars and practitioners are right to be skeptical or outright suspicious about all information, data, figures, and field research results. Although space constraints prevent the inclusion of a detailed overview of the issues, it is important to highlight that at the most general level, researchers and analysts face problems of two sorts. The first is with data collection itself: any particular method or instrument captures only a partial count of a given phenomenon. Even lethal violence goes unreported and unrecorded in many (especially rural) places, and national records of vital statistics, health care systems data, police reports, or journalistic accounts cannot, even under ideal conditions, capture every lethal incident. The question is whether the errors or underreporting are or are not randomly distributed across all the cases—and we have good reasons to think that in most cases they are not. Two noteworthy sources of non-randomness are media access to conflict zones and institutional capacity for data gathering. Regarding the former, evidence from such long-running conflicts as the civil war in Guatemala or the strife in Colombia show that media reports—which are the basis for incident reporting in conflict datasets—undercount by up to 40 percent and, in particular, undercount more as the violence intensifies (Bocquier and Maupeu 2005; Wille and Krause 2005; Restrepo 2011). With regard to the latter, and as Rodrigo Soares (2004) has clearly demonstrated, recorded levels of crime (and possibly to a lesser extent lethal violence) are correlated with overall levels of economic and institutional development. It is *not* the case that as countries grow wealthier they necessarily experience more crime and violence—they are simply better at tracking and recording it as institutional capacity increases.[13] What applies to countries at peace that have relatively low institutional capacity should in principle apply equally to such countries in armed conflict, where all institutions—governmental and nongovernmental (media)—are under extreme stress.

More sophisticated estimation techniques that are used to deal with the weaknesses in incident reporting systems have seldom been independently validated, and whether one uses a demographic survey, a verbal autopsy or victimization survey, or capture-recapture estimation techniques (also called multiple systems estimation by some), there are serious limitations to the results and often very wide confidence intervals.[14] Census and survey data can be and have been manipulated—as appears to have been the case in Rwanda, for example (Kertzer and Arel 2002; Uvin 2002). The lists upon which capture-recapture estimation techniques rely are seldom independent or random—two of the key assumptions of such techniques. And household surveys—as the debate over mortality levels in Iraq and the Democratic Republic of Congo highlight—have a variety of reliability problems (Spagat 2010; Human Security Centre 2011). Nobody should be counted on to tell the truth about life or death matters.

The second major difficulty is the "aggregation problem"—even with relatively clean or good data, it is difficult to combine into a single coherent picture data collected by different sources, and possibly with different counting rules. In the case of casualty counting, incident-based reporting systems assume that similar methods are followed (e.g., equally good media coverage in all contexts, or equally reliable police data). We know this assumption is faulty, but analysts who study the data have no independent means of assessing or comparing the reliability of different sources. It is thus wrong to claim that cross-national quantitative datasets based on incident reports are necessarily superior to more qualitative case studies because "cross-national data on conflict numbers and battle deaths can reveal long-term global and regional trends in the incidence and deadliness of conflicts" (Human Security Centre 2011). All data are *ultimately qualitative* to some degree, in the sense that the data themselves are collected and assessed by individuals, regardless of whether they are consciously participating in the data collection (e.g., as journalists reporting or not on a particular lethal incident).

Therefore, data are subject to tremendous variation, even if the analysis in a certain situation is relatively rigorous.

Given these two issues, one should be extremely wary of attempts to undertake formal and statistical (or perhaps even informal and qualitative) analyses designed to tease out possible underlying or structural causes of lethal violence. Casualty counts are often used in precisely these ways by researchers looking for the structural conditions, such as income inequality, demographic factors (youth bulges), or societal conditions (e.g., ethnolinguistic fractionalization), that may contribute to the onset or duration of conflict or violence, or by criminologists looking at the etiology of homicide. Where good registration systems for births and deaths are in place, as in the United States and Western Europe, perhaps such analyses can contribute to knowledge; in most parts of the world, however, the data are so poor that one can only draw cautious and tentative conclusions. The tradition of work associated with the Uppsala conflict data sources and related datasets highlights the limitations of casualty count data for such approaches: as Raleigh et al. note, "there is evidence to suggest [that information on fatalities] is at best biased and at worst incorrect in the vast majority of event reports" (Bocquier and Maupeu 2005; Wille and Krause 2005; Raleigh et al. 2010; Restrepo 2011).

## RESPONSIBILITY

The question of the responsibility of researchers both to their human subjects and with respect to larger political concerns around the issues that they study is usually interpreted as a question of research ethics, and many studies that count casualties have had to go through ethics review boards in various forms. The general principles are well understood and are elaborations on the Hippocratic oath to do no unnecessary harm through the act of research by observing such procedures as guarantees of respondent anonymity, voluntary participation, and informed consent. The polemical debate around the administration of the household survey in Iraq published in *The Lancet* in 2006 highlights how contentious such issues can be.[15] When one is working with official data or incident-reporting systems based on media or other reports, these concerns do not really arise. But in fieldwork, especially with the administration of survey questionnaires or verbal autopsies, or even archive material, there are some thorny issues beyond the more narrow issues of research ethics (Wood 2006).

The first ethics issue relates to how narrowly or widely to interpret the principle of avoiding harm. While some precautions (such as respondent anonymity or isolating respondents when asking about issues of sexual violence) are clear; less obvious are issues associated with community security and safety, and "retraumatization." There is limited evidence, for example, that participation in truth and reconciliation processes actually improves the psychological well-being of participants, and in some cases it may have negative effects (Thoms et al. 2008; Brounéus 2010). In addition, even data aggregated at the community level can provide sufficient information (say, on attitudes in a particular district toward surrendering weapons or citizens' distrust in state security institutions) to provoke a crack-down or backlash against an entire community, even if individual respondents remain anonymous. The responsibility of the researcher thus should extend to reflection on the broader context in which their information could be used, especially by authoritarian or repressive regimes or institutions. Working to improve the capacity of state institutions to combat violence through improved data gathering and analysis is laudable—as long as one is not facilitating more effective extrajudicial killings and "social cleansing" policies!

Finally, there is the issue of what kind of knowledge is being produced through casu-alty counting, for whom, and with what purpose. Some researchers have clear answers to these questions: informing truth and reconciliation commissions, promoting better humanitarian practice, enhancing post-conflict peacebuilding efforts, and improving programming for the prevention and reduction of armed violence. But the justification is also, in some cases, exclusively to address scholarly puzzles of interest to a Western ac-ademic audience—finishing a thesis, writing a journal article, influencing a particular debate, and so forth. While it would be invidious to point fingers at specific cases, work that is aimed primarily at an academic audience with little attention to its broader polit-ical and practical relevance often instrumentalizes human subjects and treats them as mere "research projects." Academic work reflecting such an attitude toward its subjects does not meet the standard of responsibility promoted by anthropologists and ethnog-raphers, who support the idea of "giving back" research to the community so that it can be used to benefit the people and for their own purposes.

As Sharon Hutchinson, an anthropologist who has worked in South Sudan for more than 20 years, remarked to Daniel Uttech, "we have a huge responsibility to give back to the places we study from" (Uttech 2005). Casualty counters collecting data from the field may recognize this, although one can find few examples of researchers who did undertake to "give something back."[16] Casualty counters working with incident report-ing aggregate datasets do not often meet this personal and professional responsibility.

## Conclusion: On Counting Casualties and Policy Change

Behind the move to evidence-based programming and policy, and the normative push to more effective monitoring of both conflict and non-conflict casualties, is a set of assumptions about the role of data and knowledge in achieving positive change in violent or post-conflict settings. This can take the form of documenting deaths as part of a truth and reconciliation commission (Timor-Leste, Guatemala), improving policing practices (Jamaica), or assessing the effectiveness of conflict resolution or violence prevention programs (Brazil). On the sur-face, it makes eminent sense to use the best available data and evidence to make policy. Yet the assumption that data and evidence can or do directly influence policy is a tenuous one, and researchers whose subject is conflict and violence ought to reflect carefully on how efforts to increase our knowledge may come to be used once they have been injected into a policy process. Two final points for reflection can illustrate this.

The first concerns the way in which criminological data on violent perpetrators and victimization tilt the public policy debate toward an individual (rather than structural) model of intervention. Improved data on perpetrators (who, when, where, with what instruments?) drive policy toward "results orientation" (consistent with theories of new public management) that focuses mainly on policy interventions in accordance with a diagnostics-treatment-results framework. Such an approach may make sense for the development of programs that are directed toward specific target groups, individuals, and instruments of armed violence, which act to manipulate incentives with a view to affecting the behaviors of perpetrators (and to a lesser extent potential victims) of armed violence. In short, it is a rational or cost-benefit approach to social policy that assumes that individuals make (even indirectly or in the aggregate) choices based on an assessment of their expected benefits, the risks involved, and the potential costs (death, injury, or prison time).[17] Such an approach to data collection and analysis leaves aside, however, many interventions that have a deeper "theory of change" for social transformation within communities or institutions, programs that, for example, focus on social and family resilience, building social capital, dignity, access, and rights-based approaches to post-conflict and high-violence situations. This is not just a theoretical issue, since in many contexts, such as intercommunal conflict in Northern Nigeria, gang-related violence in Haiti, or criminal violence in South Africa, broader grievances of particular groups are an important risk factor for large-scale violence (Small Arms Survey 2008). The push to improve data collection on a micro level in conflict settings seems not only to follow this same path but to lead one away from reflection on broader structural factors (poverty, inequality, injustice) that shape the dynamics of conflict and armed violence.

My final observation concerns the implicit "theory of change" that researchers themselves superimpose on their own work and findings. The theory often appears to be based on the idea that the numbers "speak for themselves" and that expert knowledge and scientific credibility are important elements in the attention that is paid to numbers—hence the label "evidence-based policy making." Off-the-cuff estimates, or journalistic accounts, are seen as too fuzzy and imprecise to form a reliable basis for policy. Once good research has been conducted, however, the task of the researcher involves little more than publishing and disseminating results, perhaps briefing officials (and maybe making recommendations), and in general tossing the numbers out there for others to use. Becoming an active part of the policy process as a means to promote change is, however, often seen as a step too far toward advocacy for academics and researchers. This notion of how ideas and expert knowledge influences policy is not one that most political scientists or social scientists would accept as an adequate account of how politics and power work![18]

The effort to improve our understanding of the human consequences of conflict and non-conflict armed violence is an important one, and it deserves greater attention and resources from the scholarly and policy-making communities. Strategies to prevent and resolve conflicts, and to reduce armed violence, do require a fine-grained understanding of the scope and scale of violence, especially against civilians. Important steps toward improving our knowledge base have been taken in the past decade (by many contributors to this volume, as well as others). But much more needs to be done, and the obstacles are not purely methodological or academic—they are often intensely political. Scholars and researchers who engage in counting conflict casualties would thus also do well to reflect on the appropriate application of their own understandings of how power, politics, and knowledge interact to shape their strategies to promote a more secure and less violent future.

REFERENCES

Asuni, Judith Burdin. 2009. "Understanding the Armed Groups of the Niger Delta" (working paper, Council on Foreign Relations, September).

Becker, Gary. 1974. "Crime and Punishment: An Economic Approach." In *Essays in the Economics of Crime and Punishment*, edited by Gary S. Becker and William M. Landes. Cambridge, MA: National Bureau of Economic Research, 1–54.

Benetech. At: http://www.benetech.org/human_rights/hrdag.shtml.

Bocquier, Philippe, and Hervé Maupeu. 2005. "Analysing Low Intensity Conflict in Africa Using Press Reports. *European Journal of Population* 21(2–3): 321–345.

Brounéus, Karen. 2010. "The Trauma of Truth Telling: Effects of Witnessing in the Rwandan Gacaca Courts on Psychological Health," *Journal of Conflict Resolution*, 54(3): 408–437.

Burnham, Gilbert, R. Lafta, D. Shannon, and L. Roberts. 2006. "Mortality after the 2003 Invasion of Iraq: A Cross-Sectional Cluster Sample Survey," *The Lancet*, 368: 1421–1428.

CRED (Centre for Research on the Epidemiology of Disasters). At: http://www.cred.be/.

Dean, Mitchell. 1999. *Governmentality: Power and Rule in Modern Society*. London: Sage.

des Forges, Alison. 1999. *Leave None to Tell the Story: Genocide in Rwanda*. New York: Human Rights Watch.

Flyvbjerg, Bent. 2001. *Making Social Science Matter: Why Social Inquiry Fails and How It Can Succeed Again*. Cambridge: Cambridge University Press.

Foucault, Michel. 2007. *Security, Territory, Population: Lectures at the Collège de France, 1977–78*, trans. Graham Burchell. London: Palgrave Macmillan.

Gerber, David. 2001. "Disabled Veterans and Public Welfare Policy: Comparative and Transnational Perspectives on Western States in the Twentieth Century," *Transnational Law and Contemporary Problems* 11(1): 77–106.

Green, Penny, and Tony Ward. 2009. "The Transformation of Violence in Iraq," *British Journal of Criminology*, 49: 609–627.

Harnischfeger, Johannes. 2003. "The Bakassi Boys: Fighting Crime in Nigeria," *Journal of Modern African Studies*, 41(1): 23–49.

Hazen, Jennifer, with Jonas Horner. 2007. *Small Arms, Armed Violence and Insecurity in Nigeria: The Niger Delta in Perspective*. Geneva: Small Arms Survey, 76–87.

Heuveline, J. H. 1998. "Between One and Three Million: Towards the Demographic Reconstruction of a Decade of Cambodian History (1970–1979)," *Population Studies* 52: 49–65.

Human Rights Council. 2008. *Promotion and Protection of All Human Rights, Civil, Political Economic and Cultural Rights, Including the Right to Development: Report by the Special Rapporteur on Extrajudicial, Summary or Arbitrary Executions: Addendum: Preliminary Note on Mission to Brazil*. A/HRC/8/3/Add. 4 of May 14, 2008. Geneva: United Nations.

Human Security Centre. 2005. *Human Security Report 2005: War and Peace in the 21st Century*. New York: Oxford University Press.

————. 2011. *Human Security Report 2009/2010: The Causes of Peace and the Shrinking Costs of War.* New York: Oxford University Press.

Iraq Body Count. At: http://www.iraqbodycount.org/ (accessed February 16, 2011).

Iraq Family Health Survey Study Group. 2008. "Violence-Related Mortality in Iraq from 2002 to 2006," *New England Journal of Medicine* 358(5): 484–493.

Kaldor, Mary. 2001. *New and Old Wars: Organised Violence in a Global Era.* Stanford, CA: Stanford University Press.

Kalyvas, Stathis. 2001. "'New' and 'Old' Civil Wars: A Valid Distinction?" *World Politics*, 54(4): 99–118.

Karmen, Andrew. 2010. *Crime Victims: An Introduction to Victimology*, 7th ed. Belmont, CA.: Wadsworth Cengage Learning.

Kertzer, David I., and Dominque Arel, eds. 2002. *Census and Identity: The Politics of Race, Ethnicity and Language in National Censuses.* Cambridge: Cambridge University Press.

Kiernan, Ben. 2003. "The Demography of Genocide in Southeast Asia: The Death Tolls in Cambodia, 1975–79, and East Timor, 1975–80," *Critical Asian Studies* 35(4): 585–597.

Lindvall, Johannes. 2009. "The Real but Limited Influence of Expert Ideas," *World Politics*, 61(4): 703–730.

Meagher, Kate. 2007. "Hijacking Civil Society: The Inside Story of the Bakassi Boys Vigilante Group of South-Eastern Nigeria," *Journal of Modern African Studies*, 45(1): 89–115.

Münkler, Herfried. 2005. *The New Wars.* Cambridge: Polity Press.

Neumann, Iver B., and Ole Jacob Sending. 2010. *Governing the Global Polity: Practice, Mentality, Rationality.* Ann Arbor: University of Michigan Press.

Obermeyer, Ziad, Christopher J. L. Murray, and Emmanuela Gakidou. 2008. "Fifty Years of Violent War Deaths from Vietnam to Bosnia: Analysis of Data from the World Health Survey Programme," *British Medical Journal*, 336: 1482–1486.

Office of the High Commissioner for Human Rights. 2009. "UN Special Rapporteur on Extrajudicial, Arbitrary or Summary Executions Mission to Kenya 16–25 February 2009." At: http://www.ohchr.org/EN/NewsEvents/Pages/DisplayNews.aspx?NewsID=8673&LangID=E.

Open Society Institute. 2010. "Open Society Justice Initiative /Network on Police Reform in Nigeria." In *Criminal Force: Torture, Abuse, and Extrajudicial Killings by the Nigeria Police Force.* New York: Open Society Institute. At: http://www.soros.org/initiatives/justice/focus/criminal_justice/articles_publications/publications/nigeria-police-abuse-report-20100519.

Parker, Geoffrey. 1997. *The Thirty Years' War*, 2nd ed. New York: Routledge.

Pettersson, Thérése and Lotta Themnér. 2010. *States in Armed Conflict 2009.* Uppsala: Department of Peace and Conflict Research.

Raleigh, Clionadh, Andrew Linke, Håvard Hegre, and Joakim Karlsen. 2010. "Introducing ACLED: An Armed Conflict Location and Event Dataset: Special Data Feature," *Journal of Peace Research*, 47(5): 651–660.

Rengifo, Andrés. 2011. Personal communication, February 17.

Restrepo, Jorge. 2011. Personal communication, February 17.

Secretariat of the Geneva Declaration on Armed Violence and Development. 2008. *The Global Burden of Armed Violence*, vol. 1, Geneva: Geneva Declaration, 68.

————. 2011. *The Global Burden of Armed Violence*, vol. 2. Cambridge: Cambridge University Press.

Small Arms Survey. 2008. *Small Arms Survey 2008: Risk and Resilience.* Cambridge: Cambridge University Press.

Soares, Rodrigo. 2004. "Crime Reporting as a Measure of Institutional Development," *Economic Development and Cultural Change*, 52(4): 851–871.

Spagat, Michael. "Ethical and Data-Integrity Problems in the Second *Lancet* Survey of Mortality in Iraq" (unpublished paper, 2010).

———, Andrew Mack, Tara Cooper, and Joakim Kreutz 2009. "Estimating War Deaths: An Arena of Contestation," *Journal of Conflict Resolution*, 53(6): 934–950.

Stratfor. "Mexico and the Cartel Wars in 2010." At: www.stratfor.com.

Sutton, Malcolm. 1994. *Bear in Mind These Dead . . . An Index of Deaths from the Conflict in Ireland 1969–1993*. Belfast: Beyond the Pale Publications. Updates at: http://cain.ulst.ac.uk/sutton/book/index.html.

Talty, Stephan. 2009. *The Illustrious Dead: The Terrifying Story of How Typhus Killed Napoleon's Greatest Army*. New York: Crown Publishers.

Thoms, Oskar, James Ron, and Roland Paris. 2008. *The Effects of Transitional Justice Mechanisms: A Summary of Empirical Research Findings and Implications for Analysts and Practitioners*. Ottawa: University of Ottawa, Centre for International Policy Studies.

UNODC (United Nations Office on Drugs and Crime). *International Homicide Statistics*. At: http://www.unodc.org/unodc/en/data-and-analysis/ihs.html.

Uppsala Conflict Data Program. At: http://www.pcr.uu.se/research/ucdp/program_overview/about_ucdp/.

Uttech, Daniel. 2005. "Professor Makes an Impact in Sudan Human Rights," October 20. At: http://www.news.wisc.edu/11721.

Uvin, Peter. 2002. "On Counting, Categorizing, and Violence in Rwanda and Burundi." In *Census and Identity: The Politics of Race, Ethnicity and Language in National Censuses*, edited by David I. Kertzer and Dominique Arel, 148–175. Cambridge: Cambridge University Press.

van Creveld, Martin. 1991. *The Transformation of War*. New York: Free Press.

Vinovskis, Maris. 1989. "Have Social Historians Lost the Civil War? Some Preliminary Demographic Speculations," *The Journal of American History*, 76(1): 34–58.

Wakabi, Wairagala. 2008. "Sexual Violence Increasing in Democratic Republic of Congo," *The Lancet*, 371(9606): 15–16.

White, Matthew. 2012. *Historical Atlas of the Twentieth Century*. At: http://users.erols.com/mwhite28/warstat8.htm.

Wille, Christina, with Keith Krause. 2005. "Behind the Numbers: Small Arms and Conflict Deaths." In *Small Arms Survey 2005: Weapons at War*. Cambridge: Cambridge University Press.

Wood, Elisabeth Jean. 2006. "The Ethical Challenges of Field Research in Conflict Zones," *Qualitative Sociology*, 29: 373–386.

NOTES

1. For an overview, see the website of the Campbell Collaboration, "an international research network that produces systematic reviews of the effects of social interventions." At: http://www.campbellcollaboration.org/about_us/index.php.

2. This discussion draws upon one effort to count casualties in an integrated way associated with the publication of the *Global Burden of Armed Violence* (volumes I and II) and the Geneva Declaration on Armed Violence and Development. See *Global Burden of Armed Violence II* (Cambridge: Cambridge University Press, 2011).

3. This classical idea of warfare of course corresponded imperfectly to reality, and predation and victimization of civilian populations has always been a concomitant of war.

4. See the various sources listed in Matthew White, *Historical Atlas of the Twentieth Century*. At: http://users.erols.com/mwhite28/warstat8.htm.

5. See Andrew Karmen, *Crime Victims: An Introduction to Victimology*, 7th ed. Belmont, CA.: Wadsworth Cengage Learning, 2010, 2. This definition, which focuses on illegal activities, holds for conflict victims as well.

6. As the webpage notes, UCDP includes in its estimates only deaths that are directly related to battle and the use of armed force. At: http://www.pcr.uu.se/research/ucdp/definitions/. See also http://www.ucdp.uu.se/gpdatabase/gpcountry.php?id=77&;regionSelect=10-Middle_East#.

7. In 2007, in Rio de Janeiro, the police recorded 1,330 "resistance killings," which accounted for 18 percent of the total number of killings in the city. (Human Rights Council 2008).

As UN special rapporteur Philip Alston concluded in the case of Kenya, extrajudicial executions by police are "systematic, widespread and carefully planned. They are committed at will and with utter impunity." At: http://www.ohchr.org/EN/NewsEvents/Pages/DisplayNews.aspx?NewsID=8673&LangID=E. On Nigerian police, see "Open Society Justice Initiative / Network on Police Reform in Nigeria," in *Criminal Force: Torture, Abuse, and Extrajudicial Killings by the Nigeria Police Force*. New York: Open Society Institute, May 2010. At: http://www.soros.org/initiatives/justice/focus/criminal_justice/articles_publications/publications/nigeria-police-abuse-report-20100519.

8. See (Münkler 2005), Kaldor (2001), and Kalyvas (2001). The "new wars" argument generally claims that contemporary armed conflicts result in much greater levels of civilian casualties, are driven by economic as much (or more) than political motives, are fought by non-state groups, and take place on shifting, fluid, and de-territorialized battlefields. Few of these phenomena are truly new.

9. Asuni (2009) estimates that there may be up to 60,000 members of different armed groups in the Delta. See also Jennifer Hazen with Jonas Horner (2007).

10. His exact words were: "Often, crime will be disguised as war, whereas in other cases, war itself will be treated as if waging it were a crime" (van Creveld 1991, 204.

11. See, for example, Wairagala Wakabi,(2008, 15–16). Field research by the Small Arms Survey in Liberia and Guatemala also appear to demonstrate higher levels of violence against women and of female homicides, but the evidence is unclear.

12. State-based conflicts are those in which a government is one of the warring parties; non-state conflicts are between organized groups excluding a government; "one-sided violence" describes campaigns of organized violence directed against unarmed civilians.

13. The referenced journal article (Soares 2004) helps, perhaps, explain the suspiciously low rates of lethal violence often reported in sub-Saharan African countries.

14. This point is made by the *Human Security Report 2009/2010*, which also criticized the high totals for "excess" or indirect deaths in the Democratic Republic of Congo in studies by the International Rescue Committee. See *Human Security Report 2009/2010*, chapters 2 and 7.

15. In addition to debates about the results (which claimed 600,000 violent deaths), questions were raised about possible anomalies in the data that could be linked to alleged ethical shortcomings in the study. See Spagat (2010) and Burnham et al. (2006).

16. Rather than pointing at bad practice (which is widespread), it is worth highlighting the rather more positive example of Chris Blattman, whose work is both scholarly and "policy oriented," being grounded in local needs and issues. See http://chrisblattman.com/.

17. This can be traced to the influence framework advanced more than 30 years ago by Gary Becker, "Crime and Punishment: An Economic Approach," in Gary S. Becker and William M. Landes, eds. (1974).

18. See, for two different approaches to the same problem, Lindvall (2009) and Flyvbjerg (2001).

# VII Conclusion

# 14 Moving toward More Accurate Casualty Counts
## Jay D. Aronson, Baruch Fischhoff, and Taylor B. Seybolt

## Introduction

Accurate civilian casualty data can enhance peacebuilding processes in many ways. Civilian casualty data provide policy makers with more than just the numbers of people who are suffering, directly or indirectly, from violence. They reveal patterns of violence that indicate social and institutional determinants of conflict, which peacebuilders may be able to use in designing strategies to reform societies and their institutions.[1] They offer a measure of dignity to families and communities that have experienced loss of life, and they serve to validate the trauma. They give formerly warring parties and the communities from which they come a factual basis for peace negotiations, legal actions against war criminals, and reconciliation efforts.

The science of casualty counting, however, is not readily accessible to the peacebuilding practitioners who need it. Even academic researchers who lack the requisite training may not be able to penetrate the technical literature. This volume has been specifically designed to make the field more accessible. It brings together the expertise of professionals who are not usually part of the peacebuilding community, including statisticians, epidemiologists, and demographers. The cross-disciplinary perspectives in this volume demonstrate how the science of civilian casualty counting and estimation can aid societies working to build peaceful political, social, and economic institutions and relationships.

The chapters provide both hopeful and cautionary assessments of the possibilities for accomplishing these missions. The most optimistic of the contributors to this volume see ways to achieve reasonably accurate, or at least useful, estimates, as long as those who count casualties possess the needed methodological rigor, can draw on sufficient human and material resources, and have access to data (see especially the chapters by Sloboda, Dardagan, Spagat, and Hicks; Asher; Klingner and Silva; Manrique-Vallier, Price, and Gohdes; and Tabeau and Zwierzchowski). However, even these guardedly hopeful authors acknowledge the limits both to the science itself and to the opportunities for its application.

Other authors are more pessimistic, citing the problems posed by politically motivated or incomplete records and estimates (Lynch; Jewell, Spagat, and Jewell; Krüger, Ball, Price, and Hoover Green). Keith Krause goes even further, arguing that quantification itself can be part of the problem by unduly focusing attention on the perpetrators and victims of violence while neglecting the social and economic conditions that foster and legitimate the violence itself. From the perspective that casualty counts, however accurate, have limited value per se, Krause challenges researchers to take an active role in seeing that their work promotes policies that address the toll violence takes.

Throughout this volume, one important but deceptively straightforward question is raised, explicitly or otherwise: When are records accurate enough to be used? Some contributors see value in even rough estimates, if properly qualified. Others insist on highly reliable information, fearing that imprecise estimates will discredit their producers, thereby ceding the field to politically motivated claims. Citing limits to even the best intentioned, most committed casualty recording and estimation, these critics raise cautions about the enterprise overall.

The first half of this chapter assesses the state of the science and practice for the three main approaches to casualty recording and estimation: incident-based data analyses, surveys, and multiple systems analysis. For each approach, we note both advances in the science and some challenges that remain. The second half proposes two strategic responses to these challenges. One is to create a set of guidelines to help nonspecialists evaluate casualty estimates. The second is to establish an international convention on recording civilian casualty that obligates signatories to create records that will both demonstrate respect for victims and provide inputs to scientifically sound estimates.

## Incident-Based Data Analysis

The chapters in part II of this volume consider how to use data collected about violent incidents. They show how those data can be biased, either reflecting deliberate attempts to highlight some casualties (and hide others) or as an indirect result of normal social processes. For example, media reports may be biased both by political pressure to suppress some reports and by commercial pressure to gain audience market share. Hospitals reports may be biased by intimidation of victims who fear to seek medical help and by economic constraints on treatment. Religious organizations naturally focus on members of their faiths and may be hostile or indifferent to others. NGOs may focus on one type of violence, such as rape or child abuse, while neglecting others. When a diffuse network of observers collects the data, it is hard to ensure consistency and completeness. As Landman and Gohdes note (in chapter 5), event reports may have different foci: the event, the people involved in it, or the violence itself. To ensure complete, comparable records, Ball (1996) has advocated using a "Who did what to whom?" approach.

Well-implemented, incident-based methods can provide sound lower estimates for the number of civilian deaths, even though they will miss deaths that no one has recorded authoritatively. These methods often link records of civilian deaths to other information about the victims (e.g., location of death, demographic information, place of residence, profession), allowing analyses of a conflict's dynamics: for example, calling attention to groups for which casualties seem to be underreported might reveal that such groups have not been receiving needed attention. However, these methods engender debates over victims who may be invisible because of their standing within society or their inaccessibility to the people or agencies filing casualty reports.

To gain the benefits of incident-based recording methods and avoid the risk of allowing contentious debates about casualty counts to undermine strategic peacebuilding efforts, these methods must be accompanied by clear statements of what they can do (establish a reasonably accurate minimum number of casualties) and what they cannot (provide a completely accurate picture of casualties). Strong lower estimates may suffice to establish some patterns, such as the effects of the policies of the U.S.-led coalition in Iraq, NATO forces in Afghanistan, or Middle Eastern governments that repress prodemocracy movements. Indeed, a strong lower estimate may suffice to establish guilt in a war crimes tribunal—and to avoid distracting controversies over weaker records.

Moreover, the extent of the undercount in incident-based records can be estimated with statistical and data methods described in this volume. For example, analyses suggest that the *Bosnian Book of the Dead* has relatively complete records of casualties from the fighting in Bosnia from 1991 to 1995. Tabeau and Zwierzchowski describe how analysts used demographic data collected for other purposes (e.g., censuses before and after the war) to validate information collected by the Bosnian Research and Documentation Centre. Ball, Tabeau, and Verwimp (2007) report similar results.

The release by WikiLeaks of the U.S. military's incident reports on casualties in Iraq since the invasion of 2003 confirmed many of the 100,000-plus civilian casualties recorded by Iraq Body Count, while revealing 15,000 deaths not reported by the media and official sources upon which the IBC has relied. Yet other sources are needed to assess the completeness and accuracy of the WikiLeaks incident reports. Without such additional sources, the exact count of civilian casualties may never be known—a fact that does not diminish the value of having created a record for each individual who has been recognized. Aronson's analysis (chapter 3) finds that the IBC count lies within the range of the best survey-based estimate, but not the second much higher (and more controversial) estimate published by *The Lancet* (see the discussion of Burnham et al. 2006 in the section that follows).

## Surveys

When consistent, comprehensive records are absent or inaccessible, surveys can provide a useful but also imperfect method for assessing casualties and their causes, as illustrated in the chapters by Asher and Lynch in part III of this volume. A survey's value depends on the representativeness of its sample, the completeness of the record for each victim, and the quality of its questions and the responses that they elicit. One common threat to the representativeness of the populations surveyed in casualty studies is that people move because of the very conflict being studied, as seen in controversies over casualty numbers in Iraq (see Aronson, chapter 3). Other threats to the validity of survey data include the physical risks and cultural norms faced by survey respondents and researchers—both of which can also threaten the candor of the responses (Lynch, chapter 7).

Asher proposes practical methods for overcoming these limits. For example, she shows how to identify the ways that infrastructure damage, threats of violence, and resource limits can make representative sampling strategies difficult or even impossible to use. She also provides guidance on conducting pre-tests that improve the quality of survey responses.

Lynch criticizes the fundamental assumption that structured casualty surveys, however well designed, can elicit valid accounts. Based on general ethnographic considerations and illustrated by her own research experience, she argues that people affected by violence often do not respond honestly during their initial encounters with survey personnel. She advocates having researchers establish trusting, empathetic relationships with interviewees, letting people tell their stories in their own words within their own narrative structure, and then interpreting these rich accounts in terms of researchers' questions (rather than forcing respondents to answer specific questions directly).

The best-known casualty survey in recent times is undoubtedly the *Lancet* study in Iraq, which concluded that approximately 600,000 civilians had been killed in 2003–2006 during the U.S-led invasion and occupation (Burnham et al. 2006). The other major survey of these civilian casualties, the Iraq Family Health Study, produced a much lower estimate of 151,000. Although this disparity suggests the need for caution when one is relying on any single survey, that wariness need not lead to paralysis. As noted, a strong lower estimate will suffice for some purposes. The Iraq Family Health Survey, like the Iraq Body Count, shows a terrible civilian toll. For other purposes (e.g., calculating reparations), more accurate estimates are needed.

While acknowledging concerns like Lynch's, Klingner and Silva suggest that it is possible to get a sense of the reliability of survey data by comparison with "found data" produced for other purposes (e.g., census returns, voter registration records, obituaries, gravestones, and media reports). They show how even small datasets from representative samples can clarify the strengths and weakness of surveys with unknown sampling biases (as Asher cautions), if the datasets draw on some of the same populations.

Using estimates wisely (whatever their source) requires understanding their limits. Such understanding requires not only a professional commitment to candid disclosure, but also the kind of methodological research reported by the authors in this volume, which allows assessing the strengths and weaknesses of specific studies. Sometimes surveys can complement other data. Sometimes surveys are all that policy makers have— and must be used as wisely as possible.

## Multiple Systems Estimation

Multiple systems estimation is a statistical procedure for integrating multiple, incomplete databases with overlapping information to produce better estimates of the total number of victims. Since the mid-1990s, researchers have used MSE to improve civilian casualty estimates drawn from partial records maintained by different institutions. Landman and Gohdes (chapter 5) show how MSE changed our understanding of the dynamics of civilian casualties in Peru and Sierra Leone. They note that different sources of data often give very different pictures, complicating the peacebuilding process by supporting competing views of events. One of Landman and Gohdes's major conclusions is that it is never safe to rely on a single data source for estimating casualties.

In chapter 9, Manrique-Vallier, Price, and Gohdes discuss critical technical issues that arise in connection with the application of MSE, paying particular attention to its key assumptions, namely: that all victim lists emerge from the same population; that each casualty from that population has the same probability of being recorded on each list; and that each victim's chance of appearing in one database is independent of its chance being included in another. Both these authors and Jewell, Spagat, and Jewell (chapter 10) note that these assumptions are almost always violated in some way in conflicts. Manrique-Vallier, Price, and Gohdes argue that the magnitude of these violations typically still leaves MSE able to provide information useful to peacebuilding; for example, the results of this technique can illuminate the shortcomings of other counts and estimates.

Jewell, Spagat, and Jewell are more circumspect. They worry that the complexity of MSE makes it difficult for policy makers to assess the validity of applications and that even experts can struggle to understand how much a group of datasets deviates from the core assumptions of MSE. They argue that MSE-based casualty estimates should always be validated with other methods. An additional limitation of MSE, noted both by Jewell, Spagat, and Jewell and by Landman and Gohdes, is that it typically cannot estimate the number of casualties at specific places or times (both critical to understanding casualty dynamics), because that information is lacking. In other words, MSE can highlight the faults in casualty data that it cannot overcome.

## Asking the Right Questions

Drawing on the analyses in this volume, we offer the following questions for critical consumers of conflict casualty data.

- **How well do the data represent the relevant population?** With surveys, one would ask (a) how complete was the researchers' sampling frame (i.e., list of people) and (b) how randomly were individuals chosen from it? With casualty lists, one would ask (a) how completely did researchers cover the population and (b) how unbiased were they in their selections? With incident-based recording methods, one would ask how (a) how thorough was the coverage of the primary sources (e.g., media, military reports) and (b) how effectively did researchers locate eyewitness accounts of less visible events (e.g., execution-style murders, killings in isolated areas, killings of marginalized or persecuted minority groups)?
- **Which casualties are likely to be underreported?** Assessing representativeness requires substantive knowledge of reporting biases. One source of underreporting arises when the lives, hence deaths, of individuals are hidden from view, as is true of women in male-dominated societies, illegal immigrants, members of nomadic groups, and those engaged in criminal activity. A second source is discrimination, which results when a society does not even care to record some groups (e.g., the poor, the aged, or migrants). A third source of bias lies in the nature of media reporting, which tends, for example, to emphasize graphic stories of individuals' fates over the deaths of a multitude of people. Some biases are common knowledge; others require good familiarity with research methods or local conditions.
- **What political biases could affect the data?** Both those providing data and those analyzing them may affect the conclusions, whether through deliberate distortion or by being insufficiently critical of results that affirm their expectations (e.g., Rosenthal 1978). As discussed by Aronson (chapter 3), results that were produced by people with political motives are not automatically invalidated. In the Bosnian case, for example, the Research and Documentation Centre was politically motivated (by the desire to scrutinize seemingly inflated casualty counts being used by the Muslim-dominated Bosnian government for political gain). Nonetheless, its tally of civilian deaths seems to have been reasonably accurate.
- **What quality assurance and control mechanisms were used to ensure data quality?** Has the research team's protocol documented the steps taken to ensure that information about events and people is recorded accurately, consistently, and completely, with suitable quality checks? The answers to some of these quality assurance questions are straightforward (e.g., whether data entries have been double-checked); others require technical expertise (e.g., evaluating sample

selection and estimating error rates and their implications) and consultation with research experts.

- **How did field conditions limit the recording process?** With surveys, one could ask which of the participants selected for a sample could not be reached owing to bad weather, poor security, or poor infrastructure—and how the absence of their data was accommodated. If designated participants who had not been interviewed were replaced by more easily reached people and the appropriate statistical adjustments were not made, findings may be biased (e.g., with respect to demographics, exposure to violence, or access to medical care for treating injuries). With case records, one could ask whether some places were inaccessible to reporters, whether some casualties never reached a hospital or morgue (where they would have been recorded) and whether cultural, economic, or political factors made certain respondents reluctant to discuss or even acknowledge deaths.

- **How consistent are the study's conclusions with those of related studies?** Consistency is a virtue when achieved through converging methods offering independent perspectives. It is a problem if the studies share common biases. Evaluating consistency requires a "forensic" analysis reflecting issues like those raised in this volume. Were there, for example, differences in how the target populations and the perpetrators were specified? Were there different threats to the sampling procedures (e.g., in researchers' ability to reach rural locations)? Given the inevitable flaws in any empirical study, policy making and peacebuilding should be guided by the weight of the evidence as a whole, not by any single study.

Researchers bear a professional responsibility to answer such questions for users of their work. Those users might encourage disclosure by asking questions like those just suggested, demonstrating their desire for candid answers, as well as their ability to use the answers. The dialogue around such issues will encourage greater transparency and shared understanding of casualty reporting and estimation procedures.

## A Call for Guidelines

We hope that the chapters in this volume offer individuals without technical expertise a place to start in evaluating studies of casualty recording and estimation. The more insistently they ask these questions, the greater will be the incentives for researchers to follow and report standard, accepted procedures for their work, accompanied by guidance on the strengths and weaknesses of different approaches and the implications of different imperfections. A model for such guidance might be found in the Cochrane Collaboration (www.cochrane.org), a cooperative international body that has established quality standards for improving the design, reporting, and aggregation of medical clinical trials. (See also the website of the Campbell Collaboration, which provides systematic reviews of interventions in education, social welfare, and justice: www.campbellcollaboration.org).

The quality, credibility, and acceptance of such guidelines will be enhanced to the extent that they arise from a deliberative process involving representatives of all disciplines relevant to casualty reporting and estimation. Those disciplines might include demography, statistics, sociology, political science, epidemiology, journalism, medicine, psychology, and post-conflict justice and reconstruction. A group consisting of representatives of these fields could create not only a shared understanding of the issues but also a collaborative community committed to producing and disseminating the desired studies, especially if the guidelines are created, maintained, and disseminated by a standing group of experts who enjoy the trust of their professional colleagues.

The guidelines would recognize that the consumers of casualty-related studies have different goals: for example, setting the historical record straight, memorializing individuals, preparing for war crimes trials, informing reconciliation processes, and estimating survivors' needs. Although each goal is part of the broader enterprise of strategic peacebuilding, requirements may differ in, say, the completeness of samples and records. For example, war crimes tribunals may not need to cover all cases but must strongly document either a set of individual cases or a lower estimate of the number of dead. In contrast, memorialization requires complete records on individuals and their fate.

Guidelines might address such issues as

- how to choose sampling procedures for different conditions;
- how to elicit accurate survey responses in the midst of conflicts;
- how to use demographic data to estimate civilian casualties;
- how to create reliable casualty records; and
- how to avoid pitfalls in performing MSE on casualty data.

Greenhill (2012) provides a related list of questions to consider in evaluating analyses.

The group that produces these guidelines would need to be independent of institutions and governments with a vested interest in the results of specific casualty estimates. Checchi and Roberts (2008, 1060) propose achieving sustained independence by (1) providing non-earmarked, long-term funding from diverse donors; (2) letting projects be selected without consulting donors; (3) selecting experts based on technical competence; and (4) requiring independent review by professional peers and representatives of civil society who have been provided with needed technical support.

Following such guidelines could protect researchers from individuals or entities that try to discredit studies by raising minor or specious methodological problems. With casualty counting and estimation, as with other scientific research having political implications, vested interests have seized on legitimate scientific disagreements and exaggerated them in hopes of persuading the public that the uncertainties are so great that no solid conclusions can be reached. Differences of scientific opinion have also been manipulated to launch ad hominem attacks against scientists producing inconvenient results (Oreskes and Conway 2010; Pidgeon and Fischhoff 2011).

Scientists are, of course, not above political debates. Professionalism, however, dictates that their values determine their choice of research topics, but not the conduct of that research, which must follow scientific procedures. Those procedures include ensuring that their work undergoes independent peer review; being candid about assumptions, methods, and data manipulation; and participating in collegial debate. Political partisans do not always follow these norms of scientific discourse and may seize on an issue that can open the way to attacks on unwelcome results or inconvenient scientists. A respected panel might help create the conditions needed for the vigorous debates essential to scientific work, while providing needed perspective on the policy implications of the disagreements (e.g., at times when all plausible estimates would lead to the same practical conclusions).

Several notable efforts have been made to adopt variants of this strategy, all involving both practitioners and specialists, and all seeking to produce methods that are sound, useful, and trusted. Here we shall mention three.

The Working Group for Mortality Estimation in Emergencies, an ad hoc group of medical and public health specialists from crisis response organizations located in Europe and North America, has produced recommendations for using survey methods to estimate casualties in humanitarian crises (Working Group 2007; Mills et al. 2008).

The Oxford Research Group (ORG), the host institution of the Iraq Body Count, has convened a network of nongovernmental organizations under the name "Every Casualty" (www.everycasualty.org), aiming to "build the technical and institutional capacity, as well as the political will, to record details of every single victim of violent conflict worldwide." ORG argues that creating these records will produce "a memorial for posterity and a recognition of our common humanity across the world. Most importantly, it will ensure that the full cost of conflict is known and can be understood to the greatest extent achievable. In turn, such understanding may become an immediately applicable component, and resource for, conflict prevention and post-conflict recovery and reconciliation."[2]

The Standardized Monitoring and Assessment of Relief and Transition (SMART) initiative is an international, multiagency, multidisciplinary effort to improve data collection for efficient resource allocation in humanitarian interventions (http://smartindicators.org and http://smartmethodology.org). Its standards are now used by relief agencies around the world to assess mortality, nutritional status, and other measures quickly, in ways that facilitate data integration and comparability across humanitarian emergences—along with fostering the building of needed capacity in both developed and developing countries. SMART's developers face problems similar to those of casualty recording and estimation (e.g., balancing the desires to achieve complete coverage and to protect researchers; determining the level of accuracy needed to guide specific actions).

## A Call for an International Convention on Casualty Recording

The UN Security Council and Secretary-General Ban Ki-moon, following the initiative of his predecessor, Kofi Annan, have shown considerable interest in the protection of civilians. Relevant mandates have been written into more than ten Security Council resolutions authorizing peace operations. The protection of civilians has been designated a crosscutting theme within the UN system. A May 2011 "Update Report" on civilian protection called for "ensuring an accountable approach by developing indicators for systematic monitoring and reporting on the protection of civilians" (UN Security Council Report 2011).

The Every Casualty initiative points to a problem facing all those interested in casualty recording and estimation: the lack of reliable records. ORG proposes remedying this situation by legally requiring the parties to a conflict to report civilian casualties. ORG notes that international humanitarian and human rights law already requires governments to record all casualties of official combatants. The Oxford Research Group argues for extending this requirement to all civilians, and for obliging governments to start counting systematically from the outset of hostilities, not just "as soon as military conditions allow," using vaguely defined "effective measures."[3] ORG contends that protecting the human rights of the missing and the dead requires a clearly worded legal obligation to employ such practices as "organized pauses in hostilities to collect the wounded and dead."[4] The language of its charter appears in the accompanying box.

We wholeheartedly support this proposal and advocate extending it to create an International Convention on Casualty Recording that would establish a legal obligation, binding on state and non-state actors, to record all civilian and military casualties. Once ratified and deposited with the United Nations, the convention would give the weight of treaty law to an obligation that some legal scholars argue is implied in existing international legal conventions and protocols on human rights.[5] As with all such agreements, the International Convention on Casualty Recording would be binding only on signatory states. However, its very existence would assert a moral obligation of *all* belligerent parties, including non-signatory states and non-state actors, to record casualties.[6] Such a convention would achieve two ends that are essential to peacebuilding: memorializing those who have died and facilitating systematic analyses of conflicts.

Implementation of a convention like the one just proposed would call for the development of standard protocols for creating those records. The protocols would require broad political support and would necessarily reflect strong technical expertise. A standard set of features to include in every record would have to be determined by a panel of scientific experts, in consultation with policy makers and leaders of civil society. That panel could incorporate the best available recording procedures, updating them as methods improved, avoiding the many problems described in the chapters in this volume. The panel would have to confront the controversy latent in the process for determining what features to include (gender? nationality?) and how to define such socially constructed

## A CHARTER FOR THE RECOGNITION OF EVERY CASUALTY OF ARMED VIOLENCE

This Charter is founded on the principle that no person should die unrecorded, and calls on states to uphold this principle for the victims of armed violence.

It is a universal Charter which applies equally to every person, and encompasses every party to armed violence. Its terms are few, but far-reaching.

Armed violence causes many kinds of harm to people and communities, including some that are indirect, non-lethal or delayed. This Charter is for those most immediate and direct victims whose violent deaths, and identities, are all too often forever lost to the public record. It therefore applies equally to all forms and conditions of armed violence where victims are commonly unrecorded, be it due to armed conflict, extensive lethal criminality, or any other breakdown in civil security.

We, the civil society organisations and concerned parties who endorse this Charter, call for resolute action by states to ensure that every direct casualty of armed violence is:

- Promptly recorded;
- Correctly identified; and
- Publicly acknowledged.

States bear particular responsibility for populations under their control or jurisdiction, or who are endangered by their actions. Information on deaths and the identity of the dead must be made public, after first informing bereaved families, where possible. Only when there is a genuine risk of harm to the living should the implementation of these measures be delayed, but never indefinitely.

While accepting that we cannot erase the harm already done to the dead, their families and friends, we are convinced that much good will flow from these measures, as they will:

- Fulfill the rights of victims of armed violence;
- Reduce the additional agony of not knowing the fate of loved ones who are missing, presumed dead;
- Provide a human face to the many nameless, hidden, often distant victims of armed violence;
- Enable more timely, transparent, reliable and comprehensive monitoring of armed violence than has been achieved before;
- Bring states and parties to armed violence into better compliance with the spirit as well as the letter of international law; and
- Support post-conflict recovery and reconciliation, which must always be grounded in truth.

*(continued)*

A CHARTER FOR THE RECOGNITION OF EVERY CASUALTY OF
ARMED VIOLENCE

From the moment they begin to be implemented these measures will assert and strengthen the recognition of our common humanity across the globe. In doing so, they may move us closer to a world where armed violence is no longer the scourge it is today.

*Source:* http://www.everycasualty.org/charter.

terms as "civilian," "adult," or "cause of death" (Krause, chapter 13). Where possible, it might choose the most literal measure possible, allowing users to impose their own definitions (e.g., giving age and not categories, giving geographical coordinates and not place names). No standard or convention will avoid controversies, especially when people are deeply invested in different accounts of conflicts. However, having widely accepted and formally adopted procedures can shift at least some of the burden of proof from those who in fact follow the procedures to those who would attack their work. Ideally, the process would become as routine as completing the U.S. Standard Certificate of Death (Fischhoff et al. 2007). Although we recognize the challenges of getting combatants to record casualties in the midst of battle, the "rules of war" followed by almost all nations show the power of conventions, even conventions that are not followed fully.

Institutional support for implementing the convention would require an independent, politically impartial organization, like that proposed here for casualty estimation. It might be located within the UN system, perhaps as a designated secretariat in the Office of the Secretary-General, like the one that oversees compliance with the 1997 Convention on the Prohibition of the Use, Stockpiling, Production and Transfer or Anti-Personnel Mines and on Their Destruction. That secretariat has regular contact with the states party to the convention and can convene fact-finding missions (United Nations Office in Geneva 1997). Alternatively, the convention might be situated in an existing independent organization, like the War Crimes Documentation project run by the Rule of Law initiative of the American Bar Association. Or, it might require a new organization, one that, like the International Bureau of Weights and Measures, is independent of existing intergovernmental and nongovernmental institutions. The international consultative process needed to resolve these issues would itself draw attention to the importance and complexity of creating respectful, useful records of civilian casualties in conflicts.

## Conclusion

The chapters in this volume show the progress made by insightful researchers determined to produce accurate records and estimates of civilian casualties in conflict despite the intellectual difficulties and, for some, physical and political dangers. The authors also show the problems that remain if these records are to fulfill their essential role in strategic peacebuilding. High on that list of challenges is systematically comparing casualty records and estimates produced by different methods while identifying the gaps that they share. Knowing the respective strengths and weaknesses of different methods in different contexts helps researchers select the most appropriate methods, employ them most effectively, and integrate their results. It helps decision makers make best use of the science that they have—and could have—in the service of peacebuilding.

The keys to creating useful information about the victims of violent conflict are more data and better science. Producing them is part of the commitment needed to demonstrate a civilized society's duties to respect the victims of war and to provide an essential foundation to building peace. To that end, we call for an international convention on recording civilian casualties in times of war, supported by the scientific and material resources needed to conduct the work with the quality and the dignity that it deserves. Honoring that commitment should, over time, reduce state and non-state actors' ability to kill civilians with impunity and, no less important, promote respect for the human rights of the dead, their families, and their communities.

REFERENCES

Ball, Patrick. 1996. *Who Did What to Whom? Planning and Implementing a Large-Scale Human Rights Data Project.* Washington, DC: American Association for the Advancement of Science.

Ball, Patrick, Ewa Tabeau, and Philip Verwimp. 2007. *The Bosnian Book of the Dead: Assessment of the Database.* Sussex, U.K.: Households in Conflict Network.

Burnham, G., R. Lafta, S. Doocy, and L. Roberts. 2006. "Mortality after the 2003 Invasion of Iraq: A Cross-Sectional Cluster Sample Survey." *The Lancet* 368: 1421–28.

Checci, Francesco, and Les Roberts. 2008. "Documenting Mortality in Crisis: What Keeps Us from Doing Better?" *PLoS Medicine* 5(7): 1025–1032.

Fischhoff, Baruch, Atran Scott, and Noam Fischhoff. 2007. "Counting Casualties: A Framework for Respectful, Useful Records." *Journal of Risk and Uncertainty* 34: 1–19.

Greenhill, Kelly. 2012. "Dead Reckoning: Challenges in Measuring the Human Costs of Conflict." At: http://sites.tufts.edu/reinventingpeace/2012/02/10/dead-reckoning-challenges-in-measuring-the-human-costs-of-conflict/ (accessed March 18, 2012).

International Criminal Court. 2005. "Warrant of Arrest for Joseph Kony issued on 8th July 2005 as amended on 27th September 2005." ICC-02/04–01/05-53; ICC-02/04-01/05. At: http://www.icc-cpi.int/Menus/ICC/Situations+and+Cases/Situations/Situation+ICC +0204/Related+Cases/ICC+0204+0105/Court+Records/Chambers/Pre+Trial+Chamber+II/Warrant+of+Arrest+for +Joseph+Kony+issued+on+8th+July+2005+as+amended+on+27th+September+2005.htm (accessed March 19, 2012).

Mills, E. J., F. Checchi, J. J. Orbinski, M. J. Schull, F. M. Burkle, C. Beyrer, C. Cooper, C. Hardy, S. Singh, R. Garfield, B. A. Woodruff, and G. H. Guyatt. 2008. "Users' Guides to the Medical Literature: How to Use an Article about Mortality in a Humanitarian Emergency." *Conflict and Health* 2: 9–17.

Oreskes, Naomi, and Eric M. Conway. 2010. *Merchants of Doubt.* New York: Bloomsbury Press.

Pidgeon, Nick, and Baruch Fischhoff. 2011. "The Role of Social and Decision Sciences in Communicating Uncertain Climate Risks." *Nature: Climate Change* 1:35–41.

Rosenthal, R. 1978. "How Often Are Our Numbers Wrong?" *American Psychologist* 11: 1005–1008.

UN Security Council Report. 2011. "Update Report: Protection of Civilians." May 3, no. 1. New York: United Nations.

United Nations Office in Geneva. 1997. "Anti-Personnel Landmines Convention."

Working Group for Mortality Estimation in Emergencies. 2007. "Wanted: Studies on Mortality Estimation Methods for Humanitarian Emergencies, Suggestions for Future Research." *Emerging Themes in Epidemiology* 4: 9–18.

NOTES

1. Practitioners of recording methods and inferential methods disagree strongly over the validity of drawing conclusions about patterns from databases of recorded events. See chapter 5 by Sloboda, Dardagan, Spagat, and Hicks, and chapter 12 by Krüger, Ball, Price, and Hoover Green for the arguments on each side.

2. http://everycasualty.org/about

3. See http://www.oxfordresearchgroup.org.uk/publications/briefing_papers_and_reports/discussion_paper_legal_obligation_record_civilian_casualtie

4. Ibid.

5. The Oxford Research Group lists the following relevant multilateral treaties: the Universal Declaration of Human Rights (1948), the European Convention for the Protection of Human Rights and Fundamental Freedoms (1950), the International Covenant of Civil and Political Rights (1966), the International Covenant on Economic, Social and Cultural Rights (1966), and the UN Convention Against Torture and Other Cruel, Inhuman or Degrading Treatment or Punishment (1984). http://www.oxfordresearchgroup.org.uk/publications/briefing_papers/forthcoming_article_obligations_record_civilian_casualties_rcac_legal_t.

6. An analogue can be found in the expectation that commanders of rebel groups are to be held responsible for war crimes and crimes against humanity even though they are not signatories to the Geneva Conventions and Additional Protocols. Joseph Kony, leader of the Lord's Resistance Army, has been indicted by the International Criminal Court for crimes against humanity (International Criminal Court 2005).

# Index